D0918249

8/17

Understanding Angry Groups

Understanding Angry Groups

Multidisciplinary Perspectives on Their Motivations and Effects on Society

Susan C. Cloninger and Steven A. Leibo, Editors

With the assistance of Mohammad Amjad

 PRAEGER™

An Imprint of ABC-CLIO, LLC

Santa Barbara, California • Denver, Colorado

Library of Congress Cataloging-in-Publication Data

Names: Cloninger, Susan C., 1945- editor. | Leibo, Steven A., 1950- editor.
Title: Understanding angry groups : multidisciplinary perspectives on their motivations and effects on society / Susan C. Cloninger and Steven A. Leibo, editors ; with the assistance of Mohammad Amjad.
Description: Santa Barbara, California : Praeger, [2017] | Includes bibliographical references and index.
Identifiers: LCCN 2016034547 (print) | LCCN 2016047788 (ebook) | ISBN 9781440833502 (hard copy : alk. paper) | ISBN 9781440833519 (ebook)
Subjects: LCSH: Intergroup relations. | Anger—Political aspects. | Political participation—Psychological aspects. | Social action—Psychological aspects. | Political sociology.
Classification: LCC HM716 .U53 2017 (print) | LCC HM716 (ebook) | DDC 306.2—dc23
LC record available at https://lccn.loc.gov/2016034547

ISBN: 978-1-4408-3350-2
EISBN: 978-1-4408-3351-9

21 20 19 18 17   1 2 3 4 5

This book is also available as an eBook.

Praeger
An Imprint of ABC-CLIO, LLC

ABC-CLIO, LLC
130 Cremona Drive, P.O. Box 1911
Santa Barbara, California 93116-1911
www.abc-clio.com

This book is printed on acid-free paper ∞

Manufactured in the United States of America

Contents

Introduction

Susan C. Cloninger and Steven A. Leibo

The phenomena of angry groups can best be understood by combining insights from a variety of disciplines, ranging from neuroscience to sociology, from history to political science. At the biological level, the legacy of evolutionary selection has produced a species with emotions that can fuel angry attacks, but also higher mental processes that can channel and sometimes check such expressions, as well as a social nature that predisposes individuals to group influence and leadership. Sociology details such group processes and the ways that leaders influence group behavior. The track record of such processes is written in the pages of history, across time and throughout the world, and political scientists describe the various forms that government and popular uprisings take.

Brain studies reveal that different brain circuitry is involved when a person experiences anger, in contrast to fear. Anger activates active, aggressive behavioral circuitry; with fear the person is more likely to avoid the situation or run away. Fear and anger may co-exist. Social influences—norms (of courage and justice, for example) and the rhetoric of leaders—can cause people to accentuate their "angry" aggressive potential and not follow their fear-motivated flight response. In addition, higher-level brain processes such as values and thought, can either over-ride or encourage the biological predilection to express anger in aggressive behavior.

Evolutionary theory describes the broad behavioral (as well as physical) tendencies that modern humans possess, as a legacy from the pressures of natural selection that our ancestors, in their time, faced. These pressures have shaped a social species in which leaders can coordinate the aggressive and defensive behaviors of group members to increase the chances of survival and reproduction. The coordinated behavior of groups brings a shared advantage to the group as a whole, against other human groups and the threats from the nonhuman environment that our ancestors faced. Humanity evolved largely within small bands of between 20 and 30 individuals, whose successful communal interaction made survival more likely. Everyone beyond that small group was seen as an outsider, the other. Indeed, there is considerable research to suggest that humans do not comfortably operate in groups much larger than 150 individuals whom they can know personally and perceive as one of their own. Humans, as a species, seem to be hard-wired to belong to groups that compete with other groups.

Social neuroscience is a field that studies the biological basis within individuals of what appear to be more complex social behaviors, finding that such phenomena are not simply learned but have a biological basis. Looking closer, *empathy* is a near-universal emotion that supports prosocial cooperative behaviors and so mitigates some of the potential negative impact of individual and group anger, and no doubt helped facilitate the small band environments within which humanity evolved. Some individuals, with more empathy, are inclined to sacrifice individual advantage for others in their group. In contrast, individuals with less empathy are likely free-loaders, profiting from the empathic tendencies of others without taking the attendant risks themselves. Various lines of research suggest that people who are labeled *psychopaths* are deficient in empathy, and show lower brain activity in the areas of the prefrontal cortex associated with moral-emotional processing and fear conditioning. This lack of empathy could provide them with an alternative adaptive advantage, enabling them to exploit others without the encumbrances of empathic hesitations, a particularly advantageous survival strategy under hostile social environmental conditions. The presence of selfish, psychopathic individuals in their midst might even enhance group survival, explaining the re-emergence of such psychopaths, even in leadership roles, throughout history. We may speculate that other members of the group can be served by the presence of such low-empathic, psychopathic individuals when their violent behavior is directed outside the group, as in warfare against enemies. Add charismatic leadership to the equation and their ability to harness other group members to their aggressive actions is multiplied. Indeed, we may speculate that threat from outside the group incentivizes the selection of such individuals to leadership positions in modern societies.

Besides stable individual differences such as psychopathy, neuroscience describes brain circuits present in everyone that may be activated at some times but not others. A "hot" emotional circuit leads more directly from angry feelings to violent behavior. A "cool" thinking circuit takes time to reflect, delaying or even preventing the aggression. Studies of social perception show quicker recognition of angry, threatening faces than happy ones, further short-circuiting the path from anger to action.

Fear, though, is also an immediate response to situations, and it has the opposite effects from anger: flee rather than fight. Social norms that hold fear in check further tip the balance toward aggression. To become aggressive, we must stay in the situation ("fear not" so you don't flee). Shame, too, can be activated by social pressures to keep people from running away. Norms of courage shame those who are afraid, greasing the machinery of aggressive acts of war and mob violence.

The human capacity for thinking and reasoning, from our most developed brain areas, has been a major focus of social science research. Although people surely do not always carefully think through their choices before acting, thoughts do nonetheless matter. One important element of that process is the concept of *efficacy*, the belief that one is capable of effective action (such as giving up tobacco, or organizing an environmental movement). People who are physically capable of effective action will not attempt to do it unless they have a sense of efficacy; hopelessness becomes a self-defeating prophecy. Efficacy can be enhanced by working together with others in groups: *collective efficacy*. To combat drunk driving, the organization Mothers Against Drunk Driving, for example, works within the political system. Its acronym, MADD, cogently conveys the emotional underpinning of this coordinated group effort.

People not only reason about how to achieve their goals, but they are also usually committed to some basic principles, including their own self-worth, fairness, and ideas about right and wrong, which can attenuate the impulse to act destructively. From a social psychological perspective, anger is often produced when people think they are worse off than others with whom they compare themselves, according to relative deprivation theory. Shared public understandings about the equitable distribution of wealth are thus important, and these are embedded in political systems to which people share allegiance.

Principles of right and wrong are not always active, however. Individuals can use a variety of strategies of "moral disengagement" to permit them, despite moral principles, to engage in terrorism, war, and other atrocities, as social psychologist Albert Bandura suggests. They may label their actions in more acceptable euphemistic terms, for example, or blame others for their actions, or dehumanize the victims of their violent acts. Robert J. Lifton, the well-known psychiatrist who has spent a lifetime studying genocidal behavior, has reminded us that given a sense of "virtue," human beings are capable of the most reprehensible acts. Because of the possibility of moral disengagement, we suggest that situational influences that activate or de-activate moral principles also play a role in understanding angry behavior.

Turning to a social-historical perspective, easily one of the most important causes of "anger" in the modern world is the phenomenon of "nationalism" and "nationalist identity." With the dawn of settlement some 10,000 years ago and the emergence of significantly larger communities from North Africa to Southwest Asia, humanity was usually forced to survive in far larger societies than our more distant ancestors, a situation that most certainly challenged their very strong need for a sense of belonging and familiar group membership. For millennia, that sense of belonging was filled by associations with a series of communities, from religious- and ethnic-based clans, to feudal relationships or geographical association, to be an Athenian, if you will. But modern society since at least the 18th century began to develop a new identity, a nationalist identity that has exploded the possibilities of geo-political anger as different communities, be they Greek or Turkish, British or Irish, into a force that has enormously expanded the platform for geopolitical anger. Complicating matters is the common phenomenon of conflating religious sentiment with nationalism, creating a nationalism within which the language of religion is used to provide legitimacy to what are largely nationalist territorial claims. The examples, of course, are widespread, but particularly obvious among more recent groups such as the Islamic State that evokes a pre-modern religious image of their supposed Caliphate, provoking an angry outburst against all that are perceived as enemies. Even more confusing are groups such as Irish Catholics and Protestants or Israeli Jews and Muslim Palestinians, whose differences are even less theologically expressed than that of the Islamic state, despite the identity differences their respective religious communities provide them. In other words, inter-group anger may masquerade as religious conflict but is not, fundamentally, that.

Although pre-modern governments often based their legitimacy on more other-worldly governing principals, from China's famous Mandate of Heaven to the idea of a Divine Right of Kings in early modern Europe, the 18th century's so-called Era of Democratic Revolution eventually spawned the idea that sovereignty ultimately resided in the masses, thus creating the idea of popular sovereignty. That increasingly accepted idea, that all governments ultimately drew their legitimacy from the "consent" of the masses, produced the French Revolutionary ideas of universal suffrage in the early years of the revolution and the autocratic Napoleon's window dressing plebiscites of early 19th century. Many governments came to believe they needed to provide the appearance of popular consent. The support of the masses, they found, could be facilitated by calling upon the common human emotion of anger, as political leaders in both democratic and authoritarian societies have enthusiastically done. Indeed, directing popular anger against a political class or group has often proven to be one of the most effective tools of building a governing consensus regardless of the nature of a particular government.

By the early 20th century, the use of anger as a tool was especially exploited by those referred to often as the New Right of Fascism, which initially in Italy rallied its supporters by arousing anger against Italy's perceived ill treatment at the Paris Peace talks and also the threat of socialism, which had just recently emerged in the form of communism during the Russian Revolution. A decade later, in Germany, the Nazis came to power largely on the votes of angry German voters, whose anger against the World War I peace treaties, the political left, and of course the Jews, whom they blamed for much of Germany's problems.

With the rise of more democratic societies in the last 30 years, the role of anger has taken on an even more influential role in global politics as genuine democratic leaders, and pseudo-democratic and even authoritarian governments have felt the need to use anger as a tool simply because it is often more effective at arousing public enthusiasm than dry and usually "wonkiest" policy statements focused on societal policies. In short, it is often simply easier to blame someone or something rather than analyze reams of data.

The Internet has provided a particularly rich environment for provoking and inspiring anger. The very nature of social media, an offshoot of an increasingly global means of communication, allows people who would normally never encounter each other to do so inexpensively and quite easily. Although that can lead to a more globalizing world view, it is also capable of provoking an angry backlash when individuals of distinctively different perspectives are encountered, especially given the anonymous nature of the 21st century's digital universe, within which expressions of anger can become increasingly inflammatory.

Preview of Chapters in This Volume

With the above in mind, we turn to an overview of the extraordinarily diverse series of articles that our contributors have prepared for this volume.

In Section One, several chapters offer diverse perspectives from the social sciences and the humanities. **Donald Saucier, Russell Webster, Conor O'Dea, and Stuart Miller,** based on empirical research from a variety of countries, describe dimensions of differences among individuals with respect to anger: political orientation (liberal or conservative), prejudice and related attitudes (authoritarianism and social dominance orientation), and social vigilantism. Certain constellations of extreme attitudes predispose individuals to anger and its behavioral consequences.

Stuart Miller, Amanda Martens, and Donald Saucier analyze the cognitive processes that contribute to angry inter-group behavior from the perspective of attribution theory. A variety of attributions about prejudice (including race, gender, and sexual orientation) are possible, depending on such factors as social identity, ideology, and perceived injustice, with different behavioral outcomes.

Jarryd Willis describes how controlled laboratory experiments on group polarization help us understand how groups move toward extremism. It is an advantage of laboratory studies, though they may seem artificial on the face, that they permit investigation of pre-determined parameters to advance our understanding, and perhaps contribute in the long run to wisdom about how to influence such processes in the real world.

Kate Dahlstedt and **Edward Tick** describe work with veterans through their Soldiers' Heart Center. Kate Dahlstedt's chapter focuses on women, both veterans and their families, who are often overlooked in our tendency understand anger, aggression, and war as predominantly male concerns. She joins with her husband Ed Tick in another chapter that describes their use of narratives from the humanities and ancient mythology to help understand and heal the suffering of those returning from war. They suggest that the American cultural response to veterans and to those who served in the Vietnam War in particular, unnecessarily brought additional pain instead of a heroic welcome and re-integration.

The next three chapters draw on the humanities. **David Salomon** describes and criticizes biblical stories of anger, including divine anger, treating, of course, the bible as a work of literature, rather than as a literal historical work. **Rob Edelman** focuses on the film genre, ranging from romance to drama, and on gender and racial issues as they are reflected in modern cinema. Edelman's analysis attests that a variety of narratives of anger are possible. He comments on many recent films' denial of anger in children, whose portrayal of children in anger-provoking situations is inadequate. The novels by J. K. Rowling about Harry Potter and his fictional adventures are described by **Sybillyn Jennings** as a variety of developmental trajectories or sequences that youth may follow during the development years to deal with anger.

In Section Two, we turn to a broader historical and geo-political focus. **Frank Jacob**'s chapter on angry exile groups in the aftermath of the French and Russian Revolutions offers insights into one of the most common phenomena of modern history. These lessons have implications for yet another enormous surge in emigration from conflict zones in the aftermath of the Arab Spring and the Syrian/Iraqi civil wars now in the early 21st century.

Turning to more recent developments in the United States, the next two chapters explore the increasingly angry American right wing communities that have become so much more vocal in recent decades. **Ryan Shaffer**'s contribution on the extreme right and American Neo-Nazism brings our discussion of anger to bear on the post-war perception of a "zero-sum" competition over rights that, having been long dominated by Anglo-Americans, are now perceived as threatened by a diversifying America society. **Carmen Celestini** focuses on the sources and inspirations that drive the American radical right's world view, analyzing the infamous fictional *Turner Diaries* that has since the 1970s captured the imagination of an enormous range of activists on the fringes of the American right, including White Supremacists and the militia movement.

Moving beyond the American fringe, **Terry Weiner** offers a case study of the Affordable Health Care Act, describing the use of anger as an inflammatory political tool within mainstream American politics. In this case, of course, the vitriolic campaign against the Affordable Care Act was not provoked by an obscure novel like the *Turner Diaries* but a concerted effort by right wing AM radio hosts and their conservative backers to arouse the public, in the midst of what became known as the Great Recession, against the principal legislative goal of the nation's first Black president.

Moving toward a broader more international focus, **Trevor Rubenzer** offers an overview of the way anger has played out in Florida with respect to Cuban issues, both among the Cuban American community and against the Castro Regime in Havana and Washington for various policy decisions that the refugee community found wanting. Staying within the Western Hemisphere, we then turn to the American role in Latin America. The United States, a community that has long thought of itself as a benevolent nation associated with global leadership, human rights, and progress, is presented, by **Jeffry Cox**, in a very different light, as a nation that in the years after World War II, provoked an extraordinary level of explosive anger among its Latin American neighbors.

David Elliott describes anger that has risen over economic issues, from the extraordinarily complicated relationship between the relatively less sophisticated economy of Greece and the larger, wealthier northern European nations of the Larger European Union. **Olakunle Folami** and **Taiwo Olaiya** describe anger over economic and environmental issues in Nigeria, specifically the exploitative relationship between local communities in the Niger Delta and international oil corporations bent on gaining access to the region's fossil fuel resources regardless of the impact on local communities. **Mohammad Amjad** turns our attention to Iran, analyzing recent politics within the context of the Iranian Islamic Republic and focusing on the role of such forces as frustration, deprivation, and anger in the political process within Iran since the early 1950s. He describes not only external factors such as Iran's exploitation by outsiders for the purpose of exploiting the nation's oil resources, but also the struggle against the Shah and in more recent years politics within Iranian theocracy.

Although anger as an emotion is not often associated with the popular image of a peaceful Buddhism, **Jeannine Chandler**'s contribution opens us up how anger has influenced the Tibetan community through the experience of exile and the formation of the Tibetan Independence Movement. Lastly, **Cory Davenport**'s work takes us into one of the most dramatic and frightening elements of contemporary society: the growth of terrorism, which has so profoundly impacted contemporary life on a global scale. Especially important is his specific focus on the role of anger as part of the radicalization process so common to the analysis of terrorism.

From the Social Sciences and the Humanities

CHAPTER ONE

The Role of Individual Differences in Inciting Anger and Social Action

*Donald A. Saucier, Russell J. Webster,
Conor J. O'Dea, and Stuart S. Miller*

Anger is a social emotion. Individuals and, consequently, groups get angry. Their anger is often instigated by political or social issues and events that they find objectionable or threatening. This, in turn, may prompt social actions ranging from peaceful acts such as voting, campaigning, and boycotting to more violent acts such as rioting and revolution. However, individuals might experience different levels of anger based on the same instigating events, as well as have different reasons for being angry. The purpose of our chapter is to examine several individual difference variables that might help to explain why some individuals become angry in response to political or social issues and events and, consequently, are moved to collective action. These will include individual difference factors connected directly to specific worldviews and beliefs (i.e., political orientation, right-wing authoritarianism [RWA], and social dominance orientation [SDO]) as well as individual difference factors more generally related to the strength and perceived superiority of individuals' beliefs and attitudes (i.e., attitude strength and social vigilantism). Our overall objective is to discuss how individual difference factors are associated with the arousal of anger and the inspiration for action when individuals' social and political beliefs are challenged.

Political Orientation

People get angry over political issues. The political divide between liberal and conservative individuals (especially in the United States) appears to be real and growing (Voteview, 2015; for a historical retrospective, see Webster, Saucier, & Parks, 2011).[1] This is likely due to Republicans becoming more conservative since the early 1980s, and Democrats becoming more liberal since the 1940s (Haidt & Abrams, 2015). Political affiliations (Democrat, Republican, Independent, etc.) correlate highly (but not perfectly) with political orientations (liberal vs. conservative), with Republicans being generally more conservative, and Democrats being more liberal (Jost, 2006). This increasing division between Republicans and Democrats functions to increase conflict, anger, and antagonism between them. Indeed, there has been more gridlock in the U.S. Congress during President Obama's tenure than in any other time in history, per the number of cloture votes to break Republican filibusters (U.S. Senate, 2015).

Several researchers have attempted to identify the variables that underlie the differences between liberals and conservatives. Jost and colleagues (Jost, 2006; Jost, Federico, & Napier, 2009) have argued that support for social equality and openness to social change explain the differences between liberals and conservatives, with liberals being more likely to support and conservatives being more likely to oppose social equality and change. Empirical support exists for their model. Generally, liberals do tend to support social action that increases social equality (e.g., affirmative action) and tend to report less prejudice toward disadvantaged groups (e.g., Blacks, gay men, and lesbian women) than do conservatives. Additionally, various proxies for general attitudes toward social equality (e.g., SDO; see the next section, "Dual Process Model of Ideology and Prejudice," for more information) and social change (e.g., RWA; see the next section, "Dual Process Model of Ideology and Prejudice") help explain the differential support for these more specific policy positions and intergroup attitudes by liberals and conservatives (e.g., Webster, Burns, Pickering, & Saucier, 2014; Wetherell, Brandt, & Reyna, 2013).

Although emotion plays only a small part in Jost and colleagues' (2009) theoretical model (see p. 319), it is important to note that there is a strong link among emotion, social prejudices, and social actions (Cottrell & Neuberg, 2005; Whitley & Kite, 2010). Of particular importance in this chapter, our goal is to illustrate the functional role that emotions play in maintaining individuals' core belief systems about their social world. Individuals may develop particularly negative emotions and attitudes toward social groups (e.g., gay men, Blacks) because the groups are perceived to threaten or violate the individuals' worldviews (e.g., eliminating or violating traditional gender norms, violating meritocratic principles through affirmative action). To help alleviate the perceived threat, individuals may endorse sociopolitical actions that directly impede the threatening group (e.g., greater opposition to same-sex marriage; Saucier & Cawman, 2004; Smith, Zanotti, Axelton, & Saucier, 2011; Webster & Saucier, 2010). According to this perspective, perceived violations of individuals' core social belief systems or worldviews may produce the differences in anger experienced by liberals versus conservatives, leading to their opposition to, or support for, sociopolitical actions that either create or restrict opportunities for other social groups.

In an effort to explain why emotional reactions to perceived worldview transgressions differ between liberals and conservatives, Graham, Haidt and their colleagues offered the moral foundations theory (MFT; Graham et al., 2013), which complements Jost and colleagues' theoretical model of political attitudes. MFT states that there are five universal moral foundations: *care/harm* (the ability to feel and dislike the pain of others), *fairness/cheating* (supporting justice, rights, and autonomy), *loyalty/betrayal* (adhering to your ingroups, from your family to your nation), *authority/subversion* (obeying tradition and legitimate authority), and *sanctity/degradation* (the belief that the body is a temple and should not be contaminated by impure things). Liberals and conservatives differentially support these moral foundations. Given that liberals focus on increasing social equality and social progress, they endorse the moral foundations of care and fairness more so than do conservatives; concurrently, conservatives endorse loyalty, authority, and sanctity more so than do liberals (Graham, Haidt, & Nosek, 2009). Haidt and colleagues are clear in explaining that these results do not mean that conservatives, for example, do not regard care or fairness as good; it is just that liberals tend to emphasize these foundations more. MFT predicts that violations of each moral foundation result in negative emotions (while, unsurprisingly, affirmations of these moral foundations result in positive emotions). These emotions then function to influence moral reasoning, judgment, and action (for similar models, see Cottrell & Neuberg, 2005; Haidt, 2001). Accordingly, the strength of an individual's emotional reactions to violations of his or her moral foundations and subsequent social action will be dependent on the individual's political orientation and the type of moral foundation that is violated.

For example, disgust seems to be most closely related to violations of sanctity.[2] However, disgust and anger (as well as contempt) are very closely related. Self-report measures and physiological measures both show that disgust and anger are moderately correlated, yet are distinct constructs (e.g., Hutcherson & Gross, 2011; Vrana, 1993). Anger occurs more frequently when individuals perceive themselves as victims, whereas disgust occurs more frequently when individuals evaluate others' behaviors (Hutcherson & Gross, 2011). Further showing support for these differential emotions, after prompting individuals to think about circumstances that may affect their perceptions of the severity of moral violations, their levels of anger decreased, but levels of disgust were unchanged. Unfortunately, these studies did not assess differences as a function of political orientation. Nonetheless, much research does show that conservatism is positively related to disgust sensitivity (especially about sex; Jarudi, 2009), and that disgust sensitivity correlates with intergroup hostility and support for more restrictive social legislation on sanctity issues, such as gay marriage and abortion (Inbar, Pizzaro, & Bloom, 2009, 2011; Inbar, Pizzaro, Iyer, & Haidt, 2012).

Research has also examined whether individuals' perceptions of violations to their care and fairness moral foundations produce anger and social action. Three studies showed that among non–Aboriginal Australians, those who perceived the existence of unfair ingroup advantages (over their minority counterparts) felt greater anger and guilt about their advantages. Their levels of anger and, to a lesser extent, their levels of guilt positively predicted their willingness to engage in political action to minimize marginalized groups' disadvantages (Small & Lerner, 2008). Additionally, Small and Lerner (2008) showed that experimental inductions of sadness increased financial allocations for individuals in need, but inductions of anger decreased such allocations.

However, although this research does show that perceived violations of care and fairness foundations are related to anger and social action, there is little empirical support linking liberalism, violations of the care and fairness foundations, and social action (although research has shown that liberals express more prejudice toward right-wing groups because liberals perceived these groups as generally threatening people's *rights*, relating to the moral foundation of fairness; Crawford, 2014). Although we expect that political orientation may moderate these effects (e.g., with liberals being more likely than conservatives to feel guilty or angry about marginalized groups' disadvantages and therefore be more prone to political action), more research is needed to confirm our expectations. Research by Napier and Jost (2008), who showed that conservatives are generally happier than liberals, suggests that liberals will be angrier about, for instance, increasing income inequality than conservatives will be. Furthermore, from their data they argue that differences between liberals' and conservatives' levels of happiness are at least partially explained by the tendency of liberals to not endorse system-justifying beliefs that rationalize social injustices and perceived violations of fairness (Jost & Banaji, 1994).

Research linking lower endorsement of system-justifying beliefs to higher levels of moral outrage and increased willingness to help the disadvantaged (Wakslak, Jost, Tyler, & Chen, 2007) suggests that liberals' moral concerns about fairness may lead to increased anger about social and economic inequalities. This may lead to intentions to engage in political action to address these issues. Other speculations from the system justification perspective suggest that justifying the system can reduce the negative emotional responses related to perceiving harm caused to others, such as in the aftermath of Hurricane Katrina (Napier, Mandisodza, Andersen, & Jost, 2006; Saucier, McManus, & Smith, 2010). Thus, in this situation, because liberals (compared to conservatives) may have been less likely to rationalize the (then Republican-led) government's inadequate helping response to those in need following the hurricane, they may have experienced greater levels of anger as they perceived their stronger moral concerns about care to have been violated by government's inadequate helping response. This process likely replicates continually, with liberals and conservatives championing different causes in response to different violations of their moral foundations that have instigated their anger and compelled their social action.

It is important to understand that the effects of political orientation on anger and on social action may not be entirely linear, especially considering that individuals on the political extremes (i.e., those who are very conservative *or* very liberal) may exacerbate the perceived differences between their groups. Politically extreme individuals show greater differences for specific sociopolitical issues (e.g., health care reform; van Boven, Judd, & Sherman, 2012) as well as for the five moral foundations (Graham, Nosek, & Haidt, 2012), and how these processes work for politically moderate individuals is less well-documented. In addition, other individual difference variables that are unrelated to specific sociopolitical or moral values may interact with political orientation (see the "Attitude Strength" and "Social Vigilantism" sections) to predict anger and social action.

We face many global problems today that are unlikely to be solved by political conflict and further polarization (e.g., climate change). So what can be done to decrease the levels of anger and conflict between liberals and conservatives? Perhaps small changes can be made to the way that we portray the political divide. Referring to individuals as "liberal" and "conservative" suggests a polarized dichotomy, and although we use this same convention in this chapter in order to better illustrate the ideological and emotional processes associated with political orientation, emphasizing this dichotomy may function to further polarize political attitudes and emotional reactions. A recent study illustrates this point. Rutchick and colleagues (Rutchick, Smyth, & Konrath, 2009) demonstrated that viewing pictures of electoral maps that clearly indicate whether electoral votes went to the Democratic (blue states) or Republican (red states) candidate increased perceived differences between liberals and conservatives when compared to viewing a proportional "purple" map that weights the ratio of "blue" to "red." Perhaps by making small changes, such as the media showing proportional voting maps, we may actually lessen the divide between liberals and conservatives (i.e., break down intergroup "boundaries" and create more of a feeling of "oneness"; Cialdini, Brown, Lewis, Luce, & Neuberg, 1997; Gaertner, Dovidio, Anastasio, Bachman, & Rust, 1993), lessen negative morally charged feelings, and foster compromise among those on the political extremes.

However, small changes may not be enough. Perhaps the best way to break down group boundaries and encourage more collaborative social action is to foster positive intergroup contact between liberals and conservatives (Pettigrew & Tropp, 2006). This may be a difficult task. Haidt and Abrams (2015) suggest that changes to Congressional work habits by Newt Gingrich and the Republican Congress in 1995 contributed to the current political divide. Gingrich encouraged new members of Congress not to move to Washington because they would perhaps become too moderate after socializing with members of Congress (and their families) across party lines. Gingrich and the Republican Congress also eliminated the seniority system for committee chairs and positions. Instead, such positions were filled based on one's perceived loyalty to the party, which decreased individuals' willingness to reach across the aisle (in fear of not appearing loyal to the party). Haidt and Abrams (2015) noted that the divide between Congressional Democrats and Republicans has seemingly permeated the American public over time, which is highlighted in stark regional differences, with rural areas becoming increasingly more conservative, and urban areas becoming increasingly more liberal, since the late 1980s. People who have the privilege to choose where they live may increasingly choose to live in areas that are more politically homogeneous. This could reduce the potential for intergroup contact across party lines, and further contribute to the polarization of political attitudes and adversarial tendencies.

In sum, MFT (Graham et al., 2013) provides a useful framework for examining the relationship among political orientation, collective anger, and social action. Accordingly, violations of conservatives' most deeply held moral foundations (loyalty, authority, and sanctity) may provoke negative emotional reactions in conservatives that compel their collective action. Similarly, violations of liberals' most deeply held moral foundations of care or fairness may provoke their negative emotional reactions in liberals that compel their collective action. Unfortunately, the differences in the moral emphases of conservatives and liberals may create collective anger and action in these groups that puts them in constant, and potentially unavoidable, conflict.

Dual Process Model of Ideology and Prejudice

Related to theories of political orientation, theories of intergroup attitudes and prejudice also attempt to explain the individual differences associated with anger-related emotional reactions to sociopolitical issues. In addition to political orientation, individual differences in ideologies, especially those that are intimately related to individuals' perceptions of their social world, may be instrumental in understanding when individuals may experience anger and be moved to collective action in the political and social domain. Two broad, ideologically based individual difference factors are entwined in the fabric of social hierarchy, impacting both political/social attitudes and intergroup attitudes, such as prejudice. Duckitt and colleagues' (Duckitt, 2006; Duckitt & Sibley, 2010) dual process model of ideology uses one model to integrate two of the best individual difference predictors of prejudice and discrimination: RWA (Altemeyer, 1981) and SDO (Pratto, Sidanius, Stallworth, & Malle, 1994).

RWA is a constellation of three broad worldviews (Funke, 2005): opposition to social progress (i.e., adherence to more traditional or conventional norms), submission to authority (especially that of parents and religion), and sanctioned aggression against those who violate conventional norms or such authorities. Duckitt (2006) posits that an upbringing that fosters the perception of the world as a dangerous place results in greater RWA, which in turn fosters negative attitudes and social action against "socially deviant" groups who are perceived to threaten conventional norms or relevant authorities. Thus, for individuals who more strongly endorse RWA ideology, anger and hate may be experienced in response to groups who are perceived to present "symbolic" threats to one's way of life (Stephan, Ybarra, & Morrison, 2009).

SDO, on the other hand, is a constellation of two broad worldviews (Jost & Thompson, 2000): opposition to social equality and justified aggression by ingroup members to protect resources that are either material (e.g., money) or abstract (e.g., power). Individuals who have had an upbringing that fosters the perception of the world as a "competitive jungle" often have higher levels of SDO, which in turn fosters prejudice and social action against "socially subordinate" groups who are perceived to threaten the "natural" ingroup-outgroup hierarchy. Thus, for individuals who more strongly endorse SDO ideology, anger and hate may be experienced in response to groups who are perceived to present "realistic" threats to their resources (Stephan, Ybarra, & Morrison, 2009). Accordingly, individuals who have greater perceived social status (e.g., men, Whites, CEOs) typically score higher in SDO (Sidanius & Pratto, 1999).

Duckitt and colleagues have amassed an impressive body of research to support the dual process model (see Duckitt & Sibley, 2010). As with emotion and political orientation, MFT can combine with the dual process model to theoretically ground the links between RWA/SDO, emotion, and social action. SDO and RWA are best thought of as attitudinal constructs that exhibit relative stability over time, but experimental manipulations can increase or decrease the levels of RWA and SDO that participants report. Experimentally inducing the perception of a dangerous world can increase individuals' reported levels of RWA (Duckitt & Fisher, 2003), while experimentally inducing the perception of the world as a competitive jungle, or increasing one's group status, can increase individuals' reported levels of SDO (e.g., Guimond, Dambrun, Michinov, & Duarte, 2003; Schmitt, Branscombe, & Kappen, 2003). However, to our knowledge, no research has examined the effects of these experimental manipulations of dangerous-world and competitive-jungle threats on emotion and social action as a function of RWA or SDO, which likely is a fruitful direction for future research.

Based on RWA's emphasis on opposition to social progress and obedience to authority, RWA should—and does—most closely and positively relate to endorsing the moral foundations of loyalty, authority, and sanctity (i.e., the "binding" or "communal" foundations). Thus, violations of loyalty, authority, or sanctity should make individuals higher in RWA angrier (or more disgusted), and more greatly support social action to remedy the violation. There is some preliminary support for this hypothesis. By using a Polish sample, Kossowska, Bukowski, and Van Hiel (2008; see also Van Hiel & Kossowska, 2006) found that individuals higher in RWA reported feeling angrier in general across a one-month period. Moreover, as people scored higher on RWA, the link between dispositional anger and intergroup prejudice/discrimination toward the Roma (a socially subordinate group in Europe that is also perceived to be socially deviant) also increased. Experimentally inducing anger also exacerbated the link between RWA and prejudice toward the Roma. Kossowska, Bukowski, and Van Hiel (2008) further investigated the link between SDO and emotion. Individuals higher in SDO adhere less to the moral foundations of care and fairness (Federico, Weber, Ergun, & Hunt, 2013). As certain sectors of society push for greater social equality, individuals higher in SDO will more likely fear the collapse of the social hierarchy and their consequent loss of access to resources. Thus, Kossowska et al. (2008) found that as individuals scored higher in SDO, the link between fear and prejudice toward the Roma strengthened.

Previous research has examined the effects of RWA and SDO on emotional reactions and responses to the 9/11 terrorist attacks and found that RWA and SDO significantly predicted support for military aggression in Iraq as well as negative attitudes toward Middle Eastern individuals (Crowson, 2009; Crowson, DeBacker, & Thoma, 2005; Heaven, Organ, Supavadeeprasit, & Leeson, 2006; Henderson-King, Henderson-King, Bolea, Koches, & Kauffman, 2004; McFarland, 2005; Skitka, Bauman, Aramovich, & Morgan, 2006). These effects are grounded in social dominance theory (Sidanius & Pratto, 1999). Providing empirical support for this, Henry, Sidanius, Levin, and Pratto (2005) examined a sample of individuals from Lebanon and the United States, comparing support for violence toward one another. Similar to the previously discussed findings, the findings showed support for their hypothesis that the effects of SDO on support for violence would be domain-specific; they found that individuals high in SDO from high status groups (i.e., from the United States) supported greater violence in response to terrorism. These results suggest that individuals who have both higher status and higher levels of SDO get angrier in response to threat, and consequently support even very extreme collective actions to repel the threat.

Further, Hodson and Costello (2007) examined the link between disgust sensitivity, RWA, SDO, and intergroup attitudes toward immigrants. As predicted, RWA strongly and positively correlated with disgust sensitivity, but SDO also moderately and positively correlated with disgust sensitivity. Although Hodson and Costello (2007) did not examine anger, they tested and confirmed that SDO and RWA helped explain the link between disgust sensitivity and negative attitudes toward immigrants. In a more recent study in which anger was measured, SDO more strongly predicted Palestinians' anger toward Americans through perceptions of economic threats, while RWA more strongly predicted disgust toward Americans through perceptions of values threat (Levin, Pratto, Matthews, Sidanius, &

Kteily, 2013). In sum, it appears that the negative emotional reactions of anger, fear, and disgust are related to individual differences in RWA and SDO. These two sociopolitical ideologies may be especially important for eliciting action-oriented emotions, such as anger, and aggressive responses related to approach-oriented tendencies (Corr, Hargreaves-Heap, Tsutsui, Russell, & Seger, 2013). Given the positive correlations between such negative emotions, future research should pursue more systematic study of each emotion in relation to RWA, SDO, and social action.

Individual differences in political orientation and ideological worldview beliefs, such as RWA and SDO, help to explain why some individuals perceive threat, experience anger, and are moved to collective action in social and political domains. Individuals differ in how they perceive threats in these domains on the basis of these individual difference factors in predictable ways. However, it may be that other individual differences that are less related to specific ideological positions may also contribute to understanding the foundations for collective anger and action. We will now consider two of these, attitude strength and social vigilantism, as potential inspirations for collective anger and action.

Attitude Strength

Beyond organized belief systems, such as those represented by liberal and conservative political orientations, individuals might, simply, have strong beliefs toward a particular issue. The strength of their position on that one issue may create the opportunity to form social connections to others who share that position. These groups may then rally around that position, experiencing anger when their position is challenged or threatened, and engaging in collective action to defend or advance their position. In this way, the strength of individuals' attitudes toward specific political or social issues is a factor likely to influence the ways in which individuals respond in situations related to those issues.

Attitude strength (Krosnick, Boninger, Chuang, Berent, & Carnot, 1993; Visser, Krosnick, & Simmons, 2003) generally refers to the extent to which an attitude demonstrates "durability or impactfulness or both" (Krosnick & Petty, 1995, p. 3). Unsurprisingly, strong attitudes are resistant to change (Eagly & Chaiken, 1993; Jacks & Devine, 2000; Krosnick & Petty, 1995; Zuwerink & Devine, 1996). Krosnick and Petty (1995) identified 10 intercorrelated dimensions of attitude strength: extremity, intensity, certainty, importance, interest, knowledge, accessibility, direct experience, latitudes of rejection and noncommitment, and affective-cognitive consistency. Each of these dimensions may independently and/or collectively predict anger in response to challenges or threats to strongly held attitudes or beliefs.

Attitudes about all topics or "objects" may vary in strength. Thus, it is the strength of the attitude, and not the attitude itself, that is important when considering how challenges or threats to strong attitudes may provoke collective anger and action. Consistent with our discussion of moral foundations above, research on attitudes confirms that moral convictions are particularly strong attitudes that are related to intergroup behavior (Skitka, Bauman, & Sargis, 2005) and emotions (Mackie, Devos, & Smith, 2000). As such, moral attitudes, and by extension political attitudes, may be particularly strong, and thus particularly prone to producing collective anger and action when threatened. And strong attitudes are hard to change (Jacks & Devine, 2000; Saucier & Webster, 2010; Zuwerink & Devine, 1996).

In response to being challenged or threatened, attitudes manifest their strength in several ways. Indeed, as individuals' levels of attitude strength increase, so do their tendencies to engage in resistance strategies to protect the attitude in the face of challenge (Jacks & Cameron, 2003). There are several different resistance strategies that individuals may employ in protecting their attitudes. Research that assessed how individuals reported that they would respond to a challenge to their opinions identified seven such strategies (Jacks & Cameron, 2003). These included *assertions of confidence* (stating one's position cannot be changed), *attitude bolstering* (supporting one's own position without refuting the opposing position), *counterarguing* (directly refuting the opposing position), *negative affect* (getting angry or upset), *selective exposure* (withdrawing from the challenge), *social validation* (thinking about others who share one's position), and *source derogation* (insulting and/or dismissing the opposing position and the opponent). These strategies are unsurprisingly correlated (Saucier, Webster, Hoffman, & Strain, 2014), given that each strategy is motivated by individuals' overall levels of attitude strength. However, these strategies are also arguably distinct. These strategies are commonly used to resist persuasion (Cameron, Jacks, & O'Brien, 2002; Jacks & Cameron, 2003; Wellins & McGinnies, 1977). Strategies such as counterarguing and attitude bolstering are most commonly used (Jacks & Cameron, 2003). However, their value for successfully resisting persuasion varies, with the strategy of counterarguing being particularly effective (Abelson, 1959; Cameron, Jacks, & O'Brien, 2002; Festinger & Maccoby, 1964; Jacks & Cameron, 2003; Jacks & Devine, 2000; Wellins & McGinnies, 1977). Further, the use of these resistance strategies in the face of challenges to individuals' attitudes, beliefs, and opinions generally increases as the individuals' challenged attitudes, beliefs, or opinions are stronger (Jacks & Cameron, 2003; Saucier, Webster, Hoffman, & Strain, 2014).

Because many attitudes are goal-directed, and resistance strategies have the goal of protecting challenges to personally held attitudes, the frustration-aggression hypothesis (Berkowitz, 1989; Dollard, Doob, Miller, Mowrer, & Sears, 1939) may help explain how threats to attitudes result in anger and hostility. According to this hypothesis, perceived barriers to goal attainment arouse frustration and anger. The resistance strategy of negative affect is most obviously connected to the elicitation of anger following a challenge to individuals' attitudes, beliefs, and opinions. The arousal of negative affect in response to this challenge serves the dual purpose of resisting the challenge and inspiring subsequent action in response the challenge. Additionally, because anger is an approach-related emotion associated with appetitive behaviors (Carver & Harmon-Jones, 2009), the approach-related resistance strategies may be particularly more likely to be used when anger is aroused. These would include resistance strategies such as source derogation (by which angry individuals would attack the source of the challenge or threat) and counterarguing (by which angry individuals would counterattack the position taken by the challenge or threat). Other resistance strategies that relate to actions that may be motivated by angry responses to threats to one's attitudes include the strategies of assertions of confidence, attitude bolstering, and social validation, with each of these strategies manifesting as behaviors intended to resist the challenge through direct action. Of the seven resistance strategies offered by Jacks and Cameron (2003), only selective exposure fails to be obviously related to the arousal of anger that leads to action in defense of the challenged attitudes, beliefs, or opinions. Although withdrawing from the challenge is an action, the action of selective exposure does not directly resist the challenge in the ways that the other strategies do. This leaves a wide variety of strategies that arise in response to attitude challenges that may combine to be the direct foundations for collective anger and action. Further, it is possible that individuals may do more than simply attempt to resist persuasion, but because anger may be experienced in response to persuasion attempts, individuals may engage in approach-related behaviors by attempting to turn the tables on an opponent.

Beyond the seven resistance strategies identified by Jacks and Cameron (2003), Saucier, Webster, Hoffman, and Strain (2014) hypothesized that another strategy individuals could enact when faced with challenges to their attitudes would be to attempt to impress their own positions onto the challengers. Beyond just refuting the position of the challengers, such as would be the case with counterarguing, this sort of counter-persuasion would be motivated to perpetuate their own positions onto others, such that the attitude challenge would present an opportunity not only to maintain one's own positions, but to spread them to others. Indeed, they found that the extent to which individuals reported that they would attempt to impress their positions onto others when faced with a challenge to their attitudes was predicted by each of the nine dimensions of attitude strength that they assessed across two studies and three different political topics for which they assessed their participants' attitudes (i.e., abortion, the war in Iraq, the constitutional rights of pornographers). This resistance strategy directly relates to the concept of collective action; the attempt to impress one's views onto others is a common purpose for collective action in political and social discourse, and that the engagement in this attempt is related to attitude strength through the previously discussed mechanisms, in the way that moral outrage demonstrates the importance of attitude strength in understanding the etiology of collective anger and social action.

Research suggests that individuals' feelings of anger in response to challenges to their attitudes, and their actions motivated to protect and advance those attitudes, may be more extreme when the attitudes being challenged are stronger or are associated with moral convictions. The implications here are that when individuals have stronger attitudes, they will be more moved to anger and action, but will be less moved to anger and action when they have weaker attitudes. Although we believe this to be true, we also believe that some individuals will be more predisposed to become angry and be moved to action, regardless of the strength of their attitudes. That is, we believe an individual difference factor accounts for the predisposition toward defending one's own attitudes against challenges and impressing one's own attitudes onto others, above and beyond the strength of those attitudes. We have labeled this individual difference "social vigilantism."

Social Vigilantism

Social vigilantism is an individual difference in one's tendencies to resist persuasion and assert one's own "superior" beliefs onto others. We recently designed a scale to assess social vigilantism as an individual difference factor, and established the scale's internal consistency and test-retest stability, as well as its convergent, discriminant, predictive, incremental, and construct validity (Saucier & Webster, 2010). Our research to date suggests and confirms that social vigilantism is an important individual difference factor to consider in understanding the inspirations for collective anger and action.

To begin, social vigilantism as a measured construct is composed of three interrelated subfactors (Saucier & Webster, 2010). The first of these subfactors refers to individuals' tendencies to believe that their own attitudes, beliefs, and opinions are superior to those of others, and that it is their responsibility to spread these attitudes, beliefs, and opinions to others. The second of these subfactors refers to individuals' tendencies to perceive others and, in particular, those who disagree with them as ignorant or stupid. The third of these subfactors refers to individuals' tendencies to believe that others do not base their attitudes, beliefs, and opinions "on good evidence." Thus, at its core, the individual difference of social vigilantism taps into a predisposition that one's own positions are superior to those of others, whose positions are categorically inferior. Thus, individuals with high levels of social vigilantism, logically, would be expected to experience challenge or threat if someone were to oppose their positions, would be expected to experience negative affect and anger in response, and would be expected to defend and advance their positions relentlessly.

Our empirical work on the construct of social vigilantism supports these predictions. In one study, we asked participants to read and respond to an individual's set of opinions. We constructed these opinions so that they reflected either an extremely liberal (e.g., *I am grateful for political correctness; I hate the rich and I pity the poor*) or an extremely conservative political position (e.g., *I am sick of political correctness; I don't hate the rich and I don't pity the poor*), such that even participants who considered themselves to be politically affiliated in the same direction as the individual would be unlikely to fully agree with the stated opinions. Participants wrote a response to the individual. Our results showed that participants' levels of social vigilantism were positively related to both their reported and actual levels of counterarguing in response to the individual's opinions, and that this effect was mediated by the participants' perceptions of their own beliefs as superior (Study 2; Saucier & Webster, 2010). We replicated this effect in a subsequent study (Study 3; Saucier & Webster, 2010). These results demonstrate that social vigilantism is an important individual difference factor in predicting individuals' tendency to engage in actions to repel opposing attitudes through behaviors such as counterarguing, which, as noted above, is one of the most effective strategies for resisting persuasion (Abelson, 1959; Cameron, Jacks, & O'Brien, 2002; Festinger & Maccoby, 1964; Jacks & Cameron, 2003; Jacks & Devine, 2000; O'Dea, Zhu, & Saucier, in progress; Wellins & McGinnies, 1977).

We then examined how social vigilantism would predict actual resistance to persuasion. We discussed a study above that examined how attitude strength was related to levels of attitude change after a challenge to participants' attitudes about teaching sex education in public schools. In that study, we also measured the participants' levels of social vigilantism. We found that participants' levels of social vigilantism were associated with both their reported use of counterarguing as a resistance strategy and their resistance to persuasion as indicated by their lower levels of attitude change following the challenge. Moreover, these effects held even after controlling for the effects of attitude strength (Study 4; Saucier & Webster, 2010). These results further confirmed our hypotheses that individual differences in social vigilantism are important for understanding how individuals respond to attitude challenges.

Having established that individuals' levels of social vigilantism predict their successful defense of their attitudes in response to challenges, such as by engaging in counterargument, we sought to more closely examine social vigilantism's relationships with the various attitude strength dimensions and as a predictor of a variety of strategies to resist persuasion. In this work, we examined how social vigilantism predicted resistance strategies, including, but also extending beyond, counterarguing (Saucier, Webster, Hoffman, & Strain, 2014). We asked participants to report their attitudes toward political issues (i.e., abortion, the war in Iraq, or the Constitutional rights of pornographers) along with the strength of those attitudes along nine attitude strength dimensions (i.e., extremity, certainty, importance, knowledge, intensity, interest, direct experience, accessibility through talking, and accessibility through thinking). We then used these to predict the participants' use of the eight resistance strategies discussed above (i.e., *assertions of confidence, attitude bolstering, counterarguing, negative affect, selective exposure, social validation, source derogation,* and *impression of beliefs*). We also assessed the participants' levels of social vigilantism, which allowed us to assess how social vigilantism levels were associated with both their levels of the various dimensions of attitude strength and their levels of reported use of the various resistance strategies. Across two studies, we found that participants' levels of social vigilantism were generally unrelated to their levels of attitude strength. But, consistent with our hypotheses, we found that participants' levels of social vigilantism were correlated with their reported use of several of the resistance strategies, including negative affect, source derogation, counterarguing, and impression of views, and that these effects emerged even after controlling for the participants' levels of argumentativeness and attitude strength. Importantly, these findings suggest that while those who have higher levels of social vigilantism may not necessarily have stronger attitudes, they do tend to attempt to defend and advance them more, providing further evidence that social vigilantism is a key individual difference factor that relates to the arousal of anger and the inspiration for action in political discourse and debate.

Further, some of our work in progress suggests that social vigilantism may be associated with extreme political ideologies on both the liberal and conservative ends of the political spectrum, and may predict extreme attitudes toward specific political policies above and beyond individuals' general political ideologies (Till, Miller, & Saucier, 2015). In that study, participants completed the Social Vigilantism Scale (Saucier & Webster, 2010), a measure of political orientation, and reported their attitudes toward several contemporary political issues (e.g., Affordable Care Act, same-sex marriage laws, welfare programs). The results showed that participants' levels of social vigilantism were positively correlated with the extremity of their political orientations, but not the direction of their political orientations (i.e., as liberal vs. conservative). Similarly, participants' levels of social vigilantism were positively correlated with the extremities, but not the directions, of their attitudes toward the political issues. This latter relationship held even after controlling for the extremity of the participants' political orientations. These results suggest that social vigilantism may be an individual difference factor that contributes to ideological conflict by its association with extreme positions, both on the political spectrum and in relation to specific political policies. That social vigilantism would correlate with the extremity, but not the direction, of these positions indicates that those with extreme political beliefs and attitudes, be they extremely liberal or extremely conservative, would be equally likely to consider their own beliefs and attitudes to be superior to the attitudes of others, and that their own beliefs and attitudes should be defended and advanced in response to challenge. Accordingly, social vigilantism may be a key factor in understanding the anger and action that arise during political debate in members of both ends of the political spectrum.

Other recent studies that we have conducted more directly illustrate how social vigilantism may result in individuals acting in ways that impede the sharing and consideration of others' points of view and consequently sabotage productive conversations and resolutions about political and social issues. In a correlational study, we showed that individuals' levels of social vigilantism are associated with the strategies they employ when handling conflict, such that higher levels of social vigilantism were associated with greater use of strategies to force their position onto an opponent in a conflict (e.g., doing anything to win). Further, higher levels of social vigilantism were marginally associated with lesser use of strategies to avoid conflict (e.g., such as not trying to avoid a confrontation about their differences; Saucier, O'Dea, & Zhu, in progress). These results combine with our previously reported research on social vigilantism's associations with strategies to resist persuasion, to suggest that social vigilantism may be a driving force in individuals' persistence in discussions of political and social issues. Holding their own beliefs and attitudes to be superior, individuals with high levels of social vigilantism may be predisposed to advancing their own beliefs and attitudes over those of others, and be motivated, in a sense, to "win" the discussion. This further suggests that individuals higher in social vigilantism, who become angry, resist persuasion, and attempt to force their own positions onto others, will be less willing to engage (and perhaps less capable of engaging) in productive discussions or in reaching compromises between opposing positions.

We further examined how individuals' levels of social vigilantism were associated with their actual conflict management strategies, particularly their resistance to compromise, in a behavioral study of negotiation about political issues. We asked participants to engage in a task in which they, with a partner, divided a sum of money to be donated to two nonprofit organizations. The study began with the participants' choosing the organization to which they would donate their portion of the sum from a list provided. Their partners, who were actually confederates in the study posing as participants, then chose an organization from the list that had a mission that conflicted with the mission of the organization chosen by the participants. For example, if a participant chose to make his or her donation to Planned Parenthood, a liberal organization that supports women's reproductive rights, then the confederate chose to make his or her donation to the National Right to Life Committee, a conservative organization that is anti-abortion. The participants and confederate then engaged in a series of offers and counteroffers in which they negotiated the division of the money between the two organizations. Our results showed that participants' higher levels of social vigilantism were associated with their taking more rounds of negotiation to accept the division of the money between the two organizations. Further, participants' higher levels of social vigilantism were associated with their reported motivations to devote as much money as possible to their chosen organization, but were even more highly associated with their reported motivations to prevent money from being donated to the other organization (Webster, Cooper, & Saucier, 2015).

Social vigilantism is an individual difference factor that is associated with individuals' use of strategies to defend their positions when they are challenged or threatened. Beyond ideological factors, such as political conservatism, and even attitude strength, individuals higher in social vigilantism appear to have a predisposition to experiencing approach-oriented emotions (such as anger) and engaging in approach-oriented behaviors (such as source derogation, counterarguing, and impression of views) when their attitudes and beliefs are challenged. Thus, our research on social vigilantism suggests that some individuals are primed for collective anger and action, and these responses just need to be triggered by challenge or threat in political or social discourse. Of further note, it may be that these same individuals who are primed for collective anger and action would be the ones who naturally gravitate toward groups who engage in collective action. Additionally, such individuals may have the loudest, most ardent voices in those groups, potentially making them attractive candidates for leadership roles where their anger, activism, and self-righteousness may become contagious. We expect that research on social vigilantism in the near future will further confirm the importance of this individual difference factor in understanding the processes underlying collective anger and action.

Implications for Individual Differences Related to Collective Anger and Action

Our exploration of how various individual differences may relate to collective anger and action leads to a number of potentially troubling conclusions. One such conclusion is that the possession of more extreme levels of political orientation, and higher levels of RWA, SDO, social vigilantism, and attitude strength, may predispose individuals to experience and display collective anger and action. Although these individual differences are likely not as stable as pure personality traits (e.g., the Big Five, Costa & McCrae, 2011; the HEXACO model, Ashton & Lee, 2007) in that their levels may more dynamically develop and change over time, they are likely to exhibit some degree of temporal stability. What this means is that these individual differences likely motivate greater degrees of collective anger and action in response to challenge or threat to the individuals' political and social positions, and that this reaction will be relatively stable. If individuals have, at the center of their being, some tendency toward collective anger and action, then thwarting these reactions becomes a more difficult endeavor.

A second troubling conclusion is that these individual differences are associated with tendencies to see one's attitudes and beliefs as superior, and to see opposing attitudes and beliefs as threatening. It is possible that these tendencies may drive individuals toward careers and social activities that engage them in discussions of these attitudes and beliefs. Consequently, political and social leaders engaging in these conversations and navigating potential compromises may be those among us who are most suited to championing their own positions but least suited to finding the common ground between competing positions. Anyone who has observed the bipartisan conflicts in American government has witnessed evidence of this possibility. Ironically, it may be that Republicans and Democrats are too different in their specific attitudes and beliefs, and too similar in their underlying tendencies (i.e., both of them being high in political extremity, attitude strength, and social vigilantism), to even allow for the possibility that anger and social conflict be avoided in their interactions.

Conclusion

Several individual difference factors contribute to how individuals experience and demonstrate collective anger and action. Some of these individual difference factors, such as political orientation, RWA, and SDO, are directly connected to a specific constellation of beliefs, attitudes, and moral foundations, such that individuals on different sides of an issue may experience and demonstrate collective anger and action differently. Other individual difference factors, such as attitude strength and social vigilantism, are independent of individuals' specific beliefs, attitudes, and moral foundations. As such, individuals on different sides of an issue who are higher on attitude strength and social vigilantism may experience and demonstrate collective anger and action similarly, resulting in conflict. As long as disagreement occurs in the nature of social and political discourse, these individual difference factors may contribute to perceptions that the attitudes and beliefs individuals hold dear are threatened, and this provokes anger. As we stated at the beginning of this chapter, anger is a social emotion. As individuals find others who share their anger, and build social power and momentum toward collective action, they will seek to better their societies by promoting the beliefs that they know to be exclusively right. Optimistically, we hope that the honest and true exchange of ideas will result in communication that leads to more critical consideration of alternative perspectives and better collective understanding, rather than to collective anger and action.

Notes

1. Political orientation can be measured both categorically as discrete groups (liberal, moderate, conservative, etc.) or continuously (e.g., on a Likert-type numerical scale). Generally, we find similar results regardless of how we measure political orientation (e.g., Webster, Burns, Pickering, & Saucier, 2014). Thus, for simplicity, we will refer to political orientations categorically in this chapter.

2. Although Jost and colleagues' (2009) model of ideology is limited by its lack of inclusion of disgust, they do argue that conservatives are more concerned with managing *existential* fears related to death, uncertainty, and ambiguity. However, we are unsure as to whether such existential fears can be operationally included under the construct of "emotion." Nonetheless, given that the focus of this chapter is on anger, we will not discuss this further.

References

Abelson, R. P. (1959). Modes of resolution of belief dilemmas. *Journal of Conflict Resolution, 3*(4), 343–352.

Altemeyer, B. (1981). *Right-wing authoritarianism*. Winnepeg, Canada: University of Manitoba Press.

Ashton, M. C., & Lee, K. (2007). Empirical, theoretical, and practical advantages of the HEXACO model of personality structure. *Personality and Social Psychology Review, 11*(2), 150–166.

Berkowitz, L. (1989). Frustration-aggression hypothesis: Examination and reformulation. *Psychological Bulletin, 106*(1), 59–73.

Cameron, K. A., Jacks, J. Z., & O'Brien, M. E. (2002). An experimental examination of strategies for resisting persuasion. *Current Research in Social Psychology, 7*(12), 205–224.

Carver, C. S., & Harmon-Jones, E. (2009). Anger is an approach-related affect: Evidence and implications. *Psychological Bulletin, 135*(2), 183–204.

Cialdini, R. B., Brown, S. L., Lewis, B. P., Luce, C., & Neuberg, S. L. (1997). Reinterpreting the empathy–altruism relationship: When one into one equals oneness. *Journal of Personality and Social Psychology, 73*(3), 481–494.

Corr, P. J., Hargreaves-Heap, S., Tsutsui, K., Russell, A., & Seger, C. (2013). Personality and social attitudes: Evidence for positive-approach motivation. *Personality and Individual Differences, 55*(7), 846–851.

Costa, P. T., Jr., & McCrae, R. R. (2011). The five-factor model, five-factor theory, and interpersonal psychology. In L. M. Horowitz & S. Strach (Eds.), *Handbook of interpersonal psychology: Theory, research, assessment, and therapeutic interventions* (pp. 91–104). Hoboken, NJ: John Wiley & Sons.

Cottrell, C. A., & Neuberg, S. L. (2005). Different emotional reactions to different groups: A sociofunctional threat-based approach to "prejudice." *Journal of Personality and Social Psychology, 88*(5), 770–789.

Crawford, J. (2014). Ideological symmetries and asymmetries in political intolerance and prejudice toward political activist groups. *Journal of Experimental Social Psychology, 55*, 284–298.

Crowson, H. M. (2009). Nationalism, internationalism, and perceived, UN irrelevance: Mediators of relationship between authoritarianism and support for military aggression as part of the war on terror. *Journal of Applied Social Psychology, 39*(5), 1137–1162.

Crowson, H. M., DeBacker, T. K., & Thoma, S. J. (2005). Does authoritarianism predict post-9/11 attitudes? *Personality and Individual Differences, 39*(7), 1273–1283.

Dollard, J., Doob, L., Miller, N., Mowrer, O., & Sears, R. (1939). *Frustration and aggression*. New Haven, CT: Yale University Press.

Duckitt, J. (2006). Differential effects of right wing authoritarianism and social dominance orientation on outgroup attitudes and their mediation by threat from competitiveness to outgroups. *Personality and Social Psychology Bulletin, 32*(5), 684–696.

Duckitt, J., & Fisher, K. (2003). The impact of social threat on worldview and ideological attitudes. *Political Psychology, 24*(1), 199–222.

Duckitt, J., & Sibley, C. G. (2010). Personality, ideology, prejudice, and politics: A dual-process motivational model. *Journal of Personality, 78*(6), 1861–1894.

Eagly, A. H., & Chaiken, S. (1993). *The psychology of attitudes*. Orlando, FL: Harcourt Brace Jovanovich.

Federico, C. M., Weber, C. R., Ergun, D., & Hunt, C. (2013). Mapping the connections between politics and morality: The multiple sociopolitical orientations involved in moral intuition. *Political Psychology, 34*(4), 589–610.

Festinger, L., & Maccoby, N. (1964). On resistance to persuasive communications. *Journal of Abnormal and Social Psychology, 68*(4), 359–366.

Funke, F. (2005). The dimensionality of right-wing authoritarianism: Lessons from the dilemma between theory and measurement. *Political Psychology, 26*(2), 195–218.

Gaertner, S. L., Dovidio, J. F., Anastasio, P. A., Bachman, B. A., & Rust, M. C. (1993). The common ingroup identity model: Recategorization and the reduction of intergroup bias. *European Review of Social Psychology, 4*(1), 1–26.

Graham, J., Haidt, J., Koleva, S., Motyl, M., Iyer, R., Wojcik, S. P., & Ditto, P. H. (2013). Moral foundations theory: The pragmatic validity of moral pluralism. *Advances in Experimental Social Psychology, 47*, 55–130.

Graham, J., Haidt, J., & Nosek, B. (2009). Liberals and conservatives rely on different sets of moral foundations. *Journal of Personality and Social Psychology, 96*(5), 1029–1046.

Graham, J., Nosek, B. A., & Haidt, J. (2012). The moral stereotypes of liberals and conservatives: Exaggeration of differences across the political spectrum. *PLoS One, 7*(12), 1–13.

Guimond, S., Dambrun, M., Michinov, N., & Duarte, S. (2003). Does social dominance generate prejudice? Integrating individual and contextual determinants of intergroup cognitions. *Journal of Personality and Social Psychology, 84*(4), 697–721.

Haidt, J. (2001). The emotional dog and its rational tail: A social intuitionist approach to moral judgment. *Psychological Review, 108*(4), 814–834.

Haidt, J., & Abrams, S. (2015, January 7). The top 10 reasons American politics are so broken [Web log post]. Retrieved from http://www.washingtonpost

.com/news/wonkblog/wp/2015/01/07/the-top-10-reasons-american
-politics-are-worse-than-ever

Heaven, P. C. L., Organ, L., Supavadeeprasit, S., & Leeson, P. (2006). War and prejudice: A study of social values, right-wing authoritarianism, and social dominance orientation. *Personality and Individual Differences, 40*(3), 599–608.

Henderson-King, D., Henderson-King, E., Bolea, B., Koches, K., & Kauffman, A. (2004). Seeking understanding or sending bombs: Beliefs as predictors of responses to terrorism. *Peace and Conflict: Journal of Peace Psychology, 10*(1), 67–84.

Henry, P. J., Sidanius, J., Levin, S., & Pratto, F. (2005). Social dominance orientation, authoritarianism, and support for intergroup violence between the Middle East and America. *Political Psychology, 26*(4), 569–583.

Hodson, G., & Costello, K. (2007). Interpersonal disgust, ideological orientations, and dehumanization as predictors of intergroup attitudes. *Psychological Science, 18*(8), 691–698.

Hutcherson, C. A., & Gross, J. J. (2011). The moral emotions: A social–functionalist account of anger, disgust, and contempt. *Journal of Personality and Social Psychology, 100*(4), 719–737.

Inbar, Y., Pizarro, D. A., & Bloom, P. (2009). Conservatives are more easily disgusted than liberals. *Cognition and Emotion, 23*(4), 714–725.

Inbar, Y., Pizarro, D. A., & Bloom, P. (2011). Disgusting smells cause decreased liking of gay men. *Emotion, 12*(1), 23–27.

Inbar, Y., Pizzaro, D. A., Iyer, R., & Haidt, J. (2012). Disgust sensitivity, political conservatism, and voting. *Social Psychological and Personality Science, 3*(5), 537–544.

Jacks, J. Z., & Cameron, K. A. (2003). Strategies for resisting persuasion. *Basic and Applied Social Psychology, 25*(2), 145–161.

Jacks, J. Z., & Devine, P. G. (2000). Attitude importance, forewarning of message content, and resistance to persuasion. *Basic and Applied Social Psychology, 22*(1), 19–29.

Jarudi, I. N. (2009). *Everyday morality and the status quo: Conservative concerns about moral purity, moral evaluations of everyday objects, and moral objections to performance enhancement* (Doctoral dissertation). Retrieved from Proquest database. (Accession No. 3362199).

Jost, J. T. (2006). The end of the end of ideology. *American Psychologist, 61*(7), 651–670.

Jost, J. T., & Banaji, M. R. (1994). The role of stereotyping in system-justification and the production of false consciousness. *British Journal of Social Psychology, 33*(1), 1–27.

Jost, J. T., Federico, C. M., & Napier, J. L. (2009). Political ideology: Its structure, functions, and elective affinities. *Annual Review of Psychology, 60*, 307–333.

Jost, J. T., & Thompson, E. P. (2000). Group-based dominance and opposition to equality as independent predictors of self-esteem, ethnocentrism, and social policy attitudes among African Americans and European Americans. *Journal of Experimental Social Psychology, 36*(3), 209–232.

Kossowska, M., Bukowski, M., & Van Hiel, A. (2008). The impact of submissive versus dominant authoritarianism and negative emotions on prejudice. *Personality and Individual Differences, 45*(8), 744–749.

Krosnick, J. A., Boninger, D. S., Chuang, Y. C., Berent, M. K., & Carnot, C. G. (1993). Attitude strength: One construct or many related constructs? *Journal of Personality and Social Psychology, 65*(6), 1132–1151.

Krosnick, J. A., & Petty, R. E. (1995). Attitude strength: An overview. In R. E. Petty & J. A. Krosnick (Eds.), *Attitude strength: Antecedents and consequences* (pp. 1–24). Hillsdale, NJ: Lawrence Erlbaum Associates.

Levin, S., Pratto, F., Matthews, M., Sidanius, J., & Kteily, N. (2013). A dual process approach to understanding prejudice toward Americans in Lebanon: An extension to intergroup threat perceptions and emotions. *Group Processes and Intergroup Relations, 16*(2), 139–158.

Mackie, D. M., Devos, T., & Smith, E. R. (2000). Intergroup emotions: Explaining offensive action tendencies in an intergroup context. *Journal of Personality and Social Psychology, 79*(4), 602–616.

McFarland, S. (2005). On the eve of war: Authoritarianism, social dominance, and American students' attitudes toward attacking Iraq. *Personality and Social Psychology Bulletin, 31*(3), 360–367.

Napier, J. L., & Jost, J. T. (2008). Why are conservatives happier than liberals? *Psychological Science, 19*(6), 565–572.

Napier, J. L., Mandisodza, A. N., Andersen, S. M., & Jost, J. T. (2006). System justification in responding to the poor and displaced in the aftermath of Hurricane Katrina. *Analyses of Social Issues and Public Policy, 6*(1), 57–73.

O'Dea, C. J., Zhu, Q., & Saucier, D. A. (in progress). Fight fire with fire: Social vigilantism, negative affect, and social challenge. *Manuscript in preparation.*

Pettigrew, T., & Tropp, L. (2006). A meta-analytic test of intergroup contact theory. *Journal of Personality and Social Psychology, 90*(5), 751–783.

Pratto, F., Sidanius, J., Stallworth, L. M., & Malle, B. F. (1994). Social dominance orientation: A personality variable predicting social and political attitudes. *Journal of Personality and Social Psychology, 67*, 741–763.

Rutchick, A. M., Smyth, J. M., & Konrath, S. (2009). Seeing red (and blue): Effects of electoral college depictions on political group perception. *Analyses of Social Issues and Public Policy, 9*(1), 269–282.

Saucier, D. A., & Cawman, A. J. (2004). Civil unions in Vermont: Political attitudes, religious fundamentalism, and sexual prejudice. *Journal of Homosexuality, 48*(1), 1–18.

Saucier, D. A., McManus, J. L., & Smith, S. J. (2010). Discrimination against outgroup members in helping situations. In S. Sturmer & M. Snyder (Eds.), *The psychology of prosocial behavior: Group processes, intergroup relations, and helping* (pp. 103–120). Oxford, UK: Wiley-Blackwell.

Saucier, D. A., O'Dea, C. J., & Zhu, Q. (in progress). Social vigilantism and strategies for handling conflict. *Manuscript in preparation*.

Saucier, D. A., & Webster, R. J. (2010). Social vigilantism: Measuring individual differences in belief superiority and resistance to persuasion. *Personality and Social Psychology Bulletin, 36* (1), 19–32.

Saucier, D. A., Webster, R. J., Hoffman, B. H., & Strain, M. L. (2014). Social vigilantism and reported use of strategies to resist persuasion. *Personality and Individual Differences, 70,* 120–125.

Schmitt, M. T., Branscombe, N. R., & Kappen, D. M. (2003). Attitudes toward group-based inequality: Social dominance or social identity? *British Journal of Social Psychology, 42*(2), 161–186.

Sidanius, J., & Pratto, F. (1999). *Social dominance: An intergroup theory of social hierarchy and oppression*. New York, NY: Cambridge University Press.

Skitka, L. J., Bauman, C. W., Aramovich, N. P., & Morgan, G. S. (2006). Confrontational and preventative policy responses to terrorism: Anger wants a fight and fear wants "them" to go away. *Basic and Applied Social Psychology, 28*(4), 375–384.

Skitka, L. J., Bauman, C. W., & Sargis, E. G. (2005). Moral conviction: Another contributor to attitude strength or something more? *Journal of Personality and Social Psychology, 88*(6), 895–917.

Small, D. A., & Lerner, J. S. (2008). Emotional policy: Personal sadness and anger shape judgments about a welfare case. *Political Psychology, 29*(2), 149–168.

Smith, S. J., Zanotti, D. C., Axelton, A. M., & Saucier, D. A. (2011). Individuals' beliefs about the etiology of same-sex sexual orientation. *Journal of Homosexuality, 58*(8), 1110–1131.

Stephan, W. G., Ybarra, O., & Morrison, K. R. (2009). Intergroup threat theory. In T. D. Nelson (Ed.), *Handbook of prejudice, stereotyping, and discrimination* (pp. 43–59). New York, NY: Psychology Press.

Till, D. F., Miller, S. S., & Saucier, D. A. (2015). Personality or politics? Social vigilantism contributes to political extremism. *Poster presented at the annual meeting of the Southwestern Psychological Association,* Wichita, KS.

U.S. Senate. (2015). *Senate action on cloture motions*. Retrieved from http://www .senate.gov/pagelayout/reference/cloture_motions/clotureCounts.htm

van Boven, L., Judd, C. M., & Sherman, D. K. (2012). Political polarization projection: Social projection of partisan attitude extremity and attitudinal processes. *Journal of Personality and Social Psychology, 103*(1), 84–100.

Van Hiel, A., & Kossowska, M. (2006). Having few positive emotions, or too many negative feelings? Emotions as moderating variables of authoritarianism effects on racism. *Personality and Individual Differences, 40*(5), 919–930.

Visser, P. S., Krosnick, J. A., & Simmons, J. P. (2003). Distinguishing the cognitive and behavioral consequences of attitude and certainty: A new approach to testing the common-factor hypothesis. *Journal of Experimental Social Psychology, 39*(2), 118–141.

Voteview. (2015). *The polarization of congressional parties*. Retrieved from http://voteview.com/political_polarization_2014.htm

Vrana, S. R. (1993). The psychophysiology of disgust: Differentiating negative emotional contexts with facial EMG. *Psychophysiology, 30*(3), 279–286.

Wakslak, C. J., Jost, J. T., Tyler, T. R., & Chen, E. S. (2007). Moral outrage mediates the dampening effect of system justification on support for redistributive social policies. *Psychological Science, 18*(3), 267–274.

Webster, R. J., Burns, M. D., Pickering, M., & Saucier, D. A. (2014). The suppression and justification of prejudice as a function of political orientation. *European Journal of Personality, 28*(1), 44–59.

Webster, R. J., Cooper, J., & Saucier, D. A. (2015). The effects of social vigilantism on political persuasion and negotiation. *Poster presented at the annual meeting of the Society for Personality and Social Psychology,* Long Beach, CA.

Webster, R. J., & Saucier, D. A. (2010). The effects of death reminders on sex differences in prejudice toward gay men and lesbians. *Journal of Homosexuality, 58*(3), 402–426.

Webster, R. J., Saucier, D. A., & Parks, G. S. (2011). New bottle, same old wine: The GOP and race in the age of Obama. In G. S. Parks & M. Hughey (Eds.), *The Obamas and a (post) racial America* (pp. 266–284). New York, NY: Oxford University Press.

Wellins, R., & McGinnies, E. (1977). Counterarguing and selective exposure to persuasion. *Journal of Social Psychology, 103*(1), 115–127.

Wetherell, G. A., Brandt, M. J., & Reyna, C. (2013). Discrimination across the ideological divide: The role of value violations and abstract values in discrimination by liberals and conservatives. *Social Psychological and Personality Science, 4*(6), 658–667.

Whitley, B. E., & Kite, M. E. (2010). *The psychology of prejudice and discrimination* (2nd ed.). Belmont, CA: Wadsworth.

Zuwerink, J. R., & Devine, P. G. (1996). Attitude importance and resistance to persuasion: It's not just the thought that counts. *Journal of Personality and Social Psychology, 70*(5), 931–944.

CHAPTER TWO

Attributions to Prejudice: Collective Anger and Action

Stuart S. Miller, Amanda L. Martens, and Donald A. Saucier

Throughout human history, groups have been oppressed, marginalized, stigmatized, and forced to bear the chains of lower status. Societies have allowed, and continue to allow, status hierarchies to deem some groups less worthy than others, and to treat them accordingly. It is only when the members of society recognize the discrimination that faces lower-status groups that their collective anger and action may work to combat the status hierarchies that oppress those groups. In the United States, the recognition of the oppression that has faced racial minority groups has prompted members of both racial majority and minority groups to reform society over the last two hundred years, such as by abolishing slavery and establishing civil rights that had been previously withheld. Humanity has made great strides in terms of social justice when the recognition of prejudice has inspired collective anger and action. But the work is not over.

Through the years, several incidents involving the commission of violence by White police officers against Black men (e.g., Amadou Diallo, Michael Brown, Rodney King, and Walter Scott) have aroused controversy. For instance, in 2014, Michael Brown was unarmed when he was shot and killed by police officer Darren Wilson, leading many to blame the killing on racism. Many individuals attributed events such as these to factors having nothing to do with race, or even attributed the violence to the targets' inappropriate behavior (e.g., Darren Wilson claimed that his life was threatened by Michael Brown's behavior). Others have attributed these events to racism, and their consequent anger has produced a variety of collective actions (e.g., Black Lives Matter). The shooting of Philando Castile, in the St. Paul suburb of Falcon Heights, Minnesota, in 2016 more recently demonstrates the collective anger and action that such events inspire when police violence is attributed to racism. The different attributions people make in reaction to these events may be explained by a combination of factors associated with perceiving group-based injustices. These factors include individuals' general beliefs about the prevalence of racial prejudice that relate to their propensities to make attributions to prejudice, their social identities, and their politically motivated views about the legitimacy of existing social hierarchies. We assert that these individual difference variables help explain both the perceptions of events involving interracial aggression as well as the collective anger and action these events inspire.

Because people derive a sense of identity from the social groups to which they belong (Tajfel & Turner, 1986), feelings of anger are likely to result when individuals believe that they have been mistreated because of their group membership, or when they believe that others in their social group have been mistreated. Discrimination and other acts that violate principles of justice and fairness based on prejudicial attitudes and stereotypical beliefs are a chronic source of mistreatment, especially for lower-power, lower-status social groups, such as women and racial minorities. In this chapter, we discuss the psychological factors that increase or decrease individuals' tendencies to attribute prejudice as the cause of others' transgressions against one's social group, how perceptions of injustice attributed to racism and sexism create a sense of collective anger, and how collective anger may translate into collective action aimed at addressing these injustices. Because perceiving injustice toward one's social group is considered to be the initial factor for eliciting the feelings of anger and indignation that lead to collective action, we begin this chapter with a discussion of the factors that influence individuals' attributions to prejudice.

Factors Influencing Attributions to Prejudice

Whether or not a perceived transgression is indeed racist or sexist depends on the internal motivations of the transgressor. But because current social norms condemn expressions of prejudice against many different oppressed social groups (Crandall, Eshleman, & O'Brien, 2002), the motivation behind the behavior is likely to be masked or otherwise justified in terms of non-prejudicial motivations (Dovidio, 2001). This masking of one's true intentions creates *attributional ambiguity*, leaving room for subjective interpretation. Thus, individuals' judgments about whether prejudice has been expressed are influenced by a variety of psychological factors related to the characteristics of the individual perceivers. Accordingly, individuals often differ in terms of whether or not they believe that racism is a factor in events such as the shooting of Michael Brown or believe that sexism is a legitimate explanation for why women typically earn less money than men do for equal work. Consequently, individuals are likely to experience varying levels of anger about the poor treatment and lower status of social groups at the bottom of the social hierarchy.

Theories of attribution, motivated cognition, and racial prejudice help explain why individuals arrive at different conclusions about the causes of these perceived injustices. In this section, we describe how individuals' tendencies to make attributions to prejudice (i.e., tendencies to see prejudice as the cause of other's behaviors), and contrary tendencies to discount prejudice as an explanation, are influenced by psychological factors such as collective identities (and their related motivations) and general beliefs about expressions of prejudice. Researchers have examined the attributional processes and eliciting circumstances from the point of view of individuals belonging to groups that are chronically targeted by prejudice and discrimination (e.g., Blacks), as well as the point of view of individuals belonging to groups that are the prototypical perpetrators of prejudice (e.g., Whites). Much of the focus of this work has been on how individual differences in beliefs and expectations related to expressions of prejudice, individuals' social identities, and their ideological belief systems or worldviews function to inhibit or reinforce attributions to prejudice and discrimination.

Expectations

Perhaps the most proximal factor influencing targets' judgments of prejudice is their expectations to be mistreated because of their membership in a stigmatized social group. This is a concept Pinel (1999) termed *stigma consciousness*. Much of the work on stigma consciousness has focused on women as a stigmatized, lower-power social group (e.g., Pinel, 2002; Pinel & Paulin, 2005; Pinel, Warner, & Chua, 2005; Wang, Stroebe, & Dovidio, 2012). Women's expectations to be treated stereotypically have been shown to predict quicker reaction times in perceiving facial expressions of male contempt (Inzlicht, Kaiser, & Major, 2008) and attentional vigilance toward subliminal cues related to sexism (i.e., sexist words presented at preconscious speed) (Kaiser, Vick, & Major, 2006). These findings demonstrate that, for women, the expectation to be treated prejudicially is related to heightened sensitivity to indicators of prejudice.

Attributing one's negative outcomes (e.g., social rejection, being passed over for a promotion) to the prejudice of others may be self-protective. In cases where the achievement of some desired goal (e.g., obtaining employment or a promotion) depends on the judgment of another individual (e.g., an employer), making an external attribution for the failure to reach that goal may reduce self-blame, reduce negative self-directed emotions, and protect self-esteem. Several studies have found that when individuals who identify with a group that is chronically targeted by prejudice and discrimination (e.g., women, Blacks) attribute a negative evaluation to the prejudice of the evaluator, their self-evaluations are more positive than those of individuals who do not attribute their outcomes to prejudice (e.g., Major, Kaiser, & McCoy, 2003; Major, Kaiser, O'Brien, & McCoy, 2007; Major, Quinton, & Schmader, 2003). Presumably, when one makes an attribution to prejudice in these situations, the negative emotions that might otherwise be directed inward are experienced as anger and resentment toward a perceived transgressor. Thus, a general tendency to make attributions to prejudice is thought to be an adaptive response that protects a positive self-image for individuals belonging to stigmatized groups (Wang et al., 2012).

The cognitive process by which tendencies to make attributions are thought to operate can be illuminated by applying foundational theories of perception. Signal detection theory (SDT) describes a process by which perceiving the presence or absence of a signal is a function of individuals' thresholds for detecting the signal under conditions of uncertainty. These thresholds are theorized to represent decisional or judgmental criteria, such that the presence of a stimulus or attribute is perceived once the signal is stronger than the threshold and not perceived when the signal is weaker than the threshold. According to SDT, the extent to which individuals directly experience being targeted by prejudice and discrimination, and/or their beliefs about the extent to which their social group is targeted by prejudice, affects their thresholds for perceiving prejudice toward oneself or one's group. Different thresholds for detecting prejudice may express themselves in individuals' accuracy for detecting the presence or absence of prejudice, or in their response bias toward or away from tendencies to make attributions to prejudice (Barrett & Swim, 1998).

According to the SDT perspective, more frequent experiences of prejudice, or knowledge of the extent of historical expressions of prejudice (Nelson, Adams, & Salter, 2013), are hypothesized to affect individuals' thresholds for detecting prejudice given the presence or absence of various cues for prejudice (e.g., the actors' intent to racially discriminate, or perceived harm done to the target) (Swim, Scott, Sechrist, Campbell, & Stangor, 2003) that may or may not be present in a given situation. For example, individuals who expect others to act according to their prejudices, and individuals who are more vigilant in attending to potential signals of prejudice, may have lower thresholds for detecting prejudice. They may consequently be more likely to interpret others' behaviors as expressions of prejudice. Alternatively, individuals who think that prejudice is uncommon and who rarely think about it or look for it may have a higher threshold for detecting prejudice, and thus be less likely to see prejudice when it is expressed. In other words, differences in individuals' beliefs and expectations related to expressions of prejudice may work to set different thresholds for detecting prejudice.

To test the hypothesis that individuals' prior beliefs and expectations related to expressions of prejudice would predict their actual attributions to prejudice, Miller and Saucier (in press) designed a measure of individual differences in observers' tendencies to make attributions to prejudice: the Propensity to Make Attributions to Prejudice Scale (PMAPS). As an extension of the measure of stigma consciousness that measures targets' expectations to be treated stereotypically (Pinel, 1999), the PMAPS items are worded to measure third-party observers' attitudes. This allows researchers to measure the attitudes of members of social groups who are chronically targeted by prejudice (e.g., racial minorities, women), as well as the attitudes of members of social groups who are prototypically the perpetrators of discrimination (e.g., Whites, males). The PMAPS expands upon existing measures of expectations for prejudicial treatment by measuring additional, theoretically related constructs. Specifically, the PMAPS was designed to measure four related dimensions of general tendencies to make attributions to prejudice. These were conceptualized as: (a) *expectation*, or perceptions of the pervasiveness of prejudice (i.e., beliefs about the base-rates for prejudice); (b) *vigilance* in spotting instances of prejudice; (c) *trivialization* of targets' claims and concerns about being treated prejudicially (which would be inversely related to greater tendencies to make attribution to prejudice); and (d) *self-efficacy*, or self-confidence in recognizing instances of prejudice. In combination, these constructs were hypothesized to underlie individuals' tendencies to make attributions to prejudice.

Initial research on propensities to make attributions to prejudice (Miller & Saucier, in press) demonstrated that these tendencies predict perceptions of racism even when it is blatantly expressed. That is, even when instances of racism are obvious (e.g., voicing a racial slur), there is variability in recognizing it as such. These results suggest that tendencies to not make attributions to prejudice may be a factor in whether or not prejudice is perceived, even when the prejudice is blatant and presumably difficult to ignore. In one study, the authors manipulated the level of ambiguity such that participants read one of three sets of scenarios that differed in terms of the ambiguity in which prejudice was expressed. The low-ambiguity, non-prejudice scenarios all contained a race-neutral explanation for the actors' behaviors (e.g., *A White driver flips off a Black driver for driving dangerously in traffic*). In other words, the scenarios in the non-prejudice condition described the actor's behavior as being motivated by situational factors that had nothing to do with the target's race (e.g., in the example above, the White driver may be responding to the Black driver's behavior, not race). In the ambiguous prejudice condition, no explanations were given for the actor's behavior (e.g., *A White sales associate keeps a close eye on a Black customer*). In the blatant prejudice condition, the scenarios described a more obvious expression of prejudice (e.g., *A White individual shouts, "Go back to Mexico," at a group of Hispanics at a civil rights protest*). Observers' tendencies to make attributions to prejudice predicted perceptions of prejudice across all three levels of ambiguity. These findings are consistent with theories of perception that emphasize how attributional ambiguity leaves room for top-down processing of information in ways that are consistent with existing beliefs and expectations. These findings suggest that tendencies to make attributions to prejudice may be related to the discounting of alternative, non-prejudice explanations when prejudice is ambiguously expressed. Furthermore, these data support the conclusion that tendencies to *not* make attributions to prejudice or to deny prejudice as an explanation may influence perceptions even when prejudice is more overtly and obviously expressed. Thus, even when prejudice and discrimination are clearly present, some individuals may be less willing to recognize or admit to this fact.

In summary, existing research supports the conclusion that general expectations and beliefs about expressions of prejudice are related to different thresholds for making attributions to prejudice. One social psychological factor that may help explain why individuals differ in their tendencies to make or not make attributions to prejudice, and the level of anger and indignation they experience from attributing prejudice to personal or group mistreatment, is the extent to which individuals derive a sense of identity from belonging to a particular social group.

Social Identities

According to social identity theory (Tajfel & Turner, 1986), individuals may vary in terms of how much personal meaning they derive from their social group memberships, and to what degree their group-level identities shape their cognitive interpretations of the social world. One interesting prediction made by this theory is that the increased importance of individuals' social groups to their self-concept increases the likelihood that social interactions with outgroup members will be interpreted through the lens of their group identities. Stronger group identification is thought to increase the tendencies for stigmatized individuals to attribute others' ambiguously prejudiced behaviors to group-level causes (e.g., being a member of a stigmatized social group), rather than to individual-level causes (e.g., their own idiosyncratic behaviors). Consistent with this reasoning, research shows that members of oppressed groups report higher tendencies to make attributions to prejudice than do members of higher-status groups (Miller & Saucier, in press). Additionally, individuals who more strongly identify with a stigmatized group are more likely to perceive that they have been the target of group-based discrimination. Major and colleagues (2003) found that, after receiving negative feedback, women who more strongly identified with their gender group (i.e., for whom being a woman was a more important element of their social identity) were more likely to attribute the negative feedback to sexism. Similar studies have found that racial minorities who more highly identify with their racial group are more likely to interpret subtle, or ambiguous, prejudice cues (e.g., avoiding eye contact) as expressions of prejudice (Operario & Fiske, 2001), as well as being more likely to believe that they have been the target of prejudice and discrimination in the past (Eccleston & Major, 2006; Sellers & Shelton, 2003).

Despite the notion that members of lower-status groups who claim discrimination are motivated to protect favorable group identities and self-concepts, and that members of higher-status groups are similarly motivated to deny responsibility for discrimination, basic human needs for social acceptance and belongingness (e.g., Baumeister & Leary, 1995) may heighten or minimize attributions to prejudice depending on the group membership of the perceiver and the social group from which one seeks social approval. Self-concerns may sometimes lead individuals of chronically oppressed groups to not perceive prejudice when it is expressed, and members of powerful groups may denounce expressions of prejudice for selfish reasons. For example, racial minorities who either explicitly or implicitly believe that acceptance by the higher-status racial majority is an important part of achieving upward social mobility may be less likely to experience and express anger and outrage over highly publicized sources of racial tension related to discrimination. Because confronting prejudice is typically an act of moral condemnation toward transgressors and their social groups, and as is likely to be perceived as antagonistic (Czopp,

Monteith, & Mark, 2006), members of lower-status groups may fear social reprisal from members of higher-status groups (Kaiser & Miller, 2001). Thus, this desire for acceptance along with the social fears of confronting prejudice may function to minimize perceptions that they have been the target of prejudice and discrimination (Carvallo & Pelham, 2006).

Conversely, whereas members of lower-status groups may discount prejudice as an explanation for potentially prejudicial behaviors in order to gain acceptance from, and entrance into, higher-status groups, members of higher-status groups may be motivated by impression management concerns to denounce prejudice and discrimination against oppressed groups. Research on interracial interactions demonstrates that members of groups who are perceived to be the primary perpetrators of group-based discrimination (e.g., Whites, men) may attempt to overcome the stereotypes of prejudice attributed to their group (e.g., as the "White racist" or the "male sexist"; Goff, Steele, & Davies, 2008). In voicing statements condemning prejudice toward oppressed groups, such as by denouncing sexist statements or historical representations of racism such as slavery, individuals who harbor prejudices may believe that they are distancing themselves from being perceived as sexist or racist (e.g., Monin & Miller, 2001). Furthermore, individuals who are more deeply and intrinsically concerned about ridding themselves of their own racist thoughts and behaviors because it is important to their self-concept (e.g., Plant & Devine, 1998) may be more likely to make attributions of prejudice to others in order to condemn such behavior. Prior research has found that general tendencies to make attributions to prejudice are related to such internal motivations to suppress prejudice (Miller & Saucier, in press).

Impression management concerns may also function to increase tendencies to label other social groups, or individuals belonging to these groups, as prejudiced. For example, people may use attributions to prejudice as a form of moral condemnation that serves to convey the impression that oneself or one's social group is morally superior to other individuals or social groups (e.g., liberals who claim that conservatives are more likely to be racist). Although this hypothesis that claiming other groups are more prejudiced than one's own has not been directly tested, such self-serving expressions of moral condemnation may be motivated by a desire to build coalitions with other social groups (see Webster, Saucier, & Parks, 2011). For example, Democrats who attempt to win over the "Black vote" or who paint Republicans as sexist may be motivated by desires to build the party base. In a political climate where social groups compete for legitimacy, support, and power, understanding the motivations behind labeling one's adversaries as racist or sexist may be ripe for further empirical research.

Collectively, research and theory on how identity and self-presentational concerns are related to judgments about prejudice demonstrate that individuals may be motivated to make attributions to prejudice, or alternatively, to make attributions to non-prejudiced causes, depending on the social concerns of the perceiver to identify or affiliate with a particular social group or to portray a positive self-image to oneself or others. In addition to general expectations and beliefs associated with propensities to make attributions to prejudice discussed in the previous section and the motivations related to social identities discussed in this section, an understanding of perceptions of prejudice can be further illuminated by the examination of how a variety of different ideological beliefs work to increase or decrease tendencies to make attributions to prejudice.

Ideological Beliefs

People tend to hold strong beliefs that play an integral role in how they interpret and understand their social world. Individuals' ideological and foundational beliefs about how individuals attain high social status and about reasons for why socially constructed groups are hierarchically organized in terms of their social statuses, resources, and power may be particularly strong sources of influence on beliefs about the extent to which prejudice is a prevalent social issue that needs to be addressed. Social psychologists have given particular attention to how individuals' endorsements of meritocratic worldviews affect their general beliefs about prejudice and their attributions to prejudice in different contexts. Meritocratic worldviews involve beliefs that people are individually responsible for their own successes or failures and that people are rewarded or punished by others based on decisions that are just and fair. According to meritocratic worldviews, social status is primarily attributed to the merit of individuals' self-determined choices and at the same time, external or environmental explanations are often underappreciated or unrecognized (e.g., Jost, Banaji, & Nosek, 2004; Lerner, 1980). Thus, when confronted with the existence of race- or gender-based social and economic inequalities, individuals who more strongly endorse meritocratic worldviews are thought to justify existing social hierarchies by attributing blame and negative stereotypes to lower-status groups, rather than by acknowledging the problems of prejudice and discrimination.

From the perspective of an individual belonging to a lower-status, stigmatized social group, more strongly endorsing meritocratic worldviews may function to make individuals less likely to believe that they have been targets of discrimination and prejudice. Believing that one has been treated unfairly is discordant with beliefs that the world is meritocratic, just, and fair, and may additionally make individuals pessimistic about their chances for upward social mobility. To avoid the discomfort associated with this dissonance, individuals who believe that the attainment of social status is meritocratically determined may minimize the extent to which they perceive discrimination and prejudice directed at themselves or their social group. Indeed, multiple studies have found that more strongly endorsing meritocratic worldviews may lead chronic targets of discrimination to fail to perceive instances of discrimination because it threatens their belief in meritocracy (Kaiser, 2006; Kaiser et al., 2006; Kaiser & Major, 2006; Major, Quinton, & McCoy, 2002) and lowers their self-esteem (Major et al., 2007). At the group level, we speculate that aggregated levels of the extent to which different groups believe that social status is awarded meritocratically may at least partially explain group-level differences in perceptions of injustice related to prejudice and discrimination as well as in experienced levels of anger that they feel in response to these injustices.

From the perspective of higher-status groups, research by Miller and Saucier (in press) suggests that beliefs related to higher levels of racial prejudice, and ideologies that function to justify existing social hierarchies, are associated with higher-status group members' tendencies to not make attributions to prejudice. For example, lower tendencies to make attributions to prejudice as measured by the Propensity to Make Attributions to Prejudice Scale (PMAPS, described previously) were related to higher levels of modern racism (i.e., harboring beliefs that racial prejudice and discrimination are no longer a problem, and expressing antipathy toward Blacks because of their social activism; McConahay, 1986). Additionally, lower tendencies to make attributions to prejudice were found to be associated with higher levels of social dominance orientation (i.e., preference for social hierarchy; Pratto, Sidanius, Stallworth, & Malle, 1994), and right-wing authoritarianism (i.e., preference for cultural homogeneity and fear of stereotypically threatening groups; Altemeyer, 1988)—two worldviews that function to justify prejudice toward lower-status groups and that function to justify existing power structures that favor Whites (Crandall & Eshleman, 2003; Duckitt & Sibley, 2007; McFarland, 2010). Consistent with findings that targets' system-justifying ideologies are associated with whether or not they make attributions to prejudice and discrimination, observers' lower tendencies to make attributions to prejudice appear to also be related to system-justifying beliefs and the denial that racial prejudice is a social justice problem. Thus, individuals who tend not to make attributions to prejudice are presumably much less likely to become angry about prejudice because they fail to recognize it; in fact, because of their motivations to protect the existing social hierarchy, they may be more likely to become angry when lower-status groups claim discrimination (see Saucier, Webster, O'Dea, & Miller, this volume).

In contrast to third-party observers who tend not to make attributions to prejudice, observers who have greater tendencies to make attributions to prejudice when considering the reasons behind the poor treatment of lower-status groups may be more likely to experience anger. Research by Miller and Saucier (in press) reports evidence that tendencies to make attributions to prejudice are associated with dispositional empathy and perspective taking, suggesting that greater tendencies to make attributions to prejudice may be related to higher levels of empathy for the targets of racial prejudice and discrimination. Higher levels of dispositional empathic concern, combined with greater tendencies to make attributions to prejudice, might additionally create feelings of anger in individuals as they witness the anger expressed by groups who claim to be the targets of prejudice and discrimination. Additionally, findings by Miller and Saucier (in press) suggests that observers' greater tendencies to make attributions to prejudice are associated with stronger support for humanitarian and egalitarian beliefs, and personal commitments to be free of one's racial biases. This is compelling evidence that tendencies to make attributions to prejudice are positively related to a constellation of dispositions related to beliefs that prejudice is wrong and that discrimination based on socially constructed categories is unjust. How and when these psychological patterns of beliefs and attributions in higher-status groups translate into the experience and expression of anger is ripe for further empirical investigation.

Discrimination and oppressive practices still permeate society, and often manifest in forms that are less blatantly obvious. Individual tendencies to perceive prejudice in society, having experiences as the target of that discrimination and oppression, and other individual difference factors influence whether or not people will recognize the plight of lower-status groups. This recognition is necessary for collective anger and action to follow with the goal of ending that discrimination and oppression. But while the discrimination and oppression may not always be recognized, it is important to consider what happens when individuals do recognize the events in the world around them as discriminatory, oppressive, and motivated by more global group-based injustice.

Collective Action against Prejudice and Discrimination

Is the future simply bleak for the members of chronically disadvantaged lower-status groups, or is there a way for groups to alter the discriminatory status quo? What researchers and scholars have found is that recognizing unfair disadvantage promotes "action emotions" such as anger (Mackie, Devos, & Smith, 2000; Smith, 1993). *Collective anger,* defined as anger on behalf of the groups, in turn drives groups to collective action (e.g., Leonard, Moons, Mackie, & Smith, 2011; van Zomeren, Spears, Fischer, & Leach, 2004; van Zomeren, Postmes, & Spears, 2008). *Collective action* occurs when an individual or a group works toward social change and justice to improve the entire group's status (Tajfel & Turner, 1979; van Zomeren et al., 2008; Wright, Taylor, & Moghaddam, 1990). Collective action by an individual may seem counterintuitive; however, collective action is defined by the intention of the action to improve the group's status, not the number of individuals engaging in the action to improve the group's status (Brady, 1994; Klandermans, 1997). As long as an individual is participating in action for the betterment of a specific group (e.g., by voting, contributing money, signing an online petition, changing his or her Facebook profile picture to an equality sign), one is participating in collective action. Thus, at its core, collective action is the behavioral actualization of individuals' motivations and abilities to create change for themselves and others.

Researchers and scholars have noted that collective action is a very effective way of establishing social justice (e.g., Klandermans, 1997; Wright et al., 1990) and promoting the values of the disadvantaged group (e.g., the marriage equality message that "love is love" that is promoted by efforts to support same-sex marriage rights). Indeed, this mechanism of social change has historically played a large role in challenging the status quo and furthering efforts toward equality. For example, voting rights for women were hard won by the collective action of activists in the Women's Suffrage Movement (1848–1920). These activists engaged in collective action to further women's rights by writing essays depicting women's points of view, marching in the streets in solidarity, and participating in group protests (Baker, 2002). Thirty years later, collective action also played a major role in reducing racial segregation and discrimination in the United States. Individuals in the American Civil Rights Movement (1954–1968) used acts of nonviolent protests and civil disobedience to promote their message and drive social change.

Contemporary forms of collective action may also include nonviolent protests that take advantage of ever-evolving technological advances and online social networks. For example, many forms of the movements for Black Lives Matter (#blacklivesmatter) and Marriage Equality (#loveislove) mirror those of their predecessors (e.g., nonviolent protests). Individuals were able participate in these movements by signing online petitions, posting on blogs and writing articles online, sharing information on social media, or changing their Facebook profile pictures to show support for the movement. With the advances in online communications and social media, it appears that the sharing of collective anger and opportunities for collective action are on the rise.

Because collective action has the potential for major social change, scholars and researchers are particularly interested in the social and psychological factors that drive or inhibit individual participation in collective action. Within this framework, researchers have identified three key factors related to participation (or lack thereof) in collective action. First, members of the disadvantaged group must perceive their relatively lower social status as unlikely to be improved by attempts to gain entry into the higher-status group (Ellemers, Wilke, & Van Knippenber, 1993). Second, the social structure that creates the low and high status groups must be perceived as unstable, such that there is at least some perceived probability that the status quo can be changed (e.g., Wright et al., 1990). Third, the disadvantaged group's relatively lower social status must be perceived as unfair and illegitimate (e.g., Mummendey, Kessler, Klink & Mielke, 1999).

The recognition of unfair disadvantage and injustice, for example, by attributing the lower status of one's social group to prejudice and discrimination, promotes collective action by arousing action-oriented emotions such as anger (Mackie et al., 2000; Smith, 1993). Feelings of anger and resentment are well-established antecedents of collective action (e.g. Leonard et al., 2011; Stürmer & Simon, 2009; van Zomeren et al., 2004; van Zomeren et al., 2008). Relative deprivation theory describes a social comparison process in which lower-status group members' perceptions of deprivation relative to members of higher-status groups result in perceptions of injustice and feelings of anger (for a review, see Walker & Smith, 2002). According to relative deprivation theory, collective anger resulting from perceived injustices against the group drives individuals to take collective action in an attempt to rectify these perceived inequalities (e.g., van Zomeren et al., 2004). It is important to note that these feelings of deprivation and anger must be on behalf of the group in order to inspire collective action. When individuals do not attribute their own disadvantage or deprivation to their group status, they may use other means that are less psychologically taxing (e.g., venting to a friend) to reduce their negative emotions (see Smith & Ortiz, 2002). Thus, only when anger is experienced as an intergroup emotion does it facilitate collective action (Smith & Ortiz, 2002; Stürmer & Simon, 2009; van Zomeren et al., 2004; Walker & Smith, 2002).

The initial psychological factor associated with collective action is perceived group-based injustice and, therefore, psychological accounts of collective action share similarities to psychological accounts of attributions to prejudice and discrimination already discussed in this chapter. For example, social identity theory (Tajfel & Turner, 1986), introduced earlier in this chapter as a factor that helps explain tendencies to make attributions to prejudice, has also been applied to the explanation of the psychological factors that lead to collective action (e.g., Stürmer & Simon, 2004). Researchers have repeatedly found that the more individuals identify with their disadvantaged group, the more likely they are to participate in collective action to elevate the status of their group (van Zomeren et al., 2008). Additionally, evidence also suggests that the perception that one's social group has been targeted by discrimination reinforces a sense of collective identity and affiliation with other social groups who also experience discrimination (Craig & Richeson, 2012).

As previously mentioned, perceived injustices are associated with the experience of group-based anger (Mummendey et al., 1999; Wright et al., 1990). However, although anger and perceived injustice are related, when these factors are tested against each other, researchers have found that affective reactions (i.e., anger) are stronger predictors of collective action than are cognitive reactions (e.g., perceived injustice; for a review, see van Zomeren et al., 2008). Further, the importance of affective antecedents to collective action is demonstrated by evidence that suggests that for perceived injustice to motivate individuals to participate in collective action, members of the disadvantaged group often must harbor extremely negative feelings toward the higher-status group, frequently going as far as to vilify members of higher-status groups (Cohen-Chen, Halperin, Saguy, & van Zomeren, 2014). In turn, these negative attitudes toward the higher-status group may help foster a sense of group identity that further increases participation in collective action (Simon & Klandermans, 2001).

Thus, the experience of anger plays an integral role in determining whether individuals engage in collective action. However, it may not be enough to simply experience collective anger about the prejudicial treatment or the status of one's social group to motivate collective action. While individuals may want to challenge an oppressive status hierarchy that has aroused their collective anger through engaging in collective action, they may feel powerless to do so. Accordingly, perceived group efficacy also plays a major role in individuals' willingness to participate in collective action (for a review, see van Zomeren, Leach, & Spears, 2012). *Group efficacy* reflects the extent to which the members of the group feel that the goals of the group can be accomplished. A sense of group efficacy can be fostered by perceptions that the unfair social structure is unstable or malleable (Cohen-Chen et al., 2014). Further, beliefs that the out-group's prejudices are malleable, as opposed to fixed, result in stronger collective action tendencies through increased group efficacy.

In summary, the main factors that influence collective action are perceptions and emotions of group-based injustice, social identity, and group efficacy. Meta-analytical findings have confirmed that these factors are theoretically and practically instrumental in inciting collective action (van Zomeren et al., 2008). Of specific importance to the collective action process is the recognition of unfair or illegitimate group-based disadvantage; without this recognition, and the subsequent anger-related emotions, the motivations for collective action would not arise (van Zomeren et al., 2008). However, modern expressions of prejudice tend to be subtle, indirect, and ambiguous, or otherwise justified in terms of non-prejudiced principles that are often motivated by the desire to maintain existing social hierarchies (Dovidio, 2001; Jost et al., 2004). This masking of prejudicial intentions often makes it difficult for the perceiver to determine whether prejudice or discrimination has occurred. In other words, the very nature of modern prejudice undermines the "key catalyst" (i.e., the recognition of injustice) of participation in collective action (Ellemers & Barreto, 2009).

Furthermore, some forms of prejudice may actually be perceived positively by the disadvantaged group. For example, benevolent sexism, a form of sexism in which the gender status hierarchy is maintained by perceiving and treating women as individuals who must be protected and cherished (Glick & Fiske, 1996), has the potential to be perceived as flattering (Jackman, 1994). Therefore, instead of perceiving behaviors of benevolent sexism as patronizing, women may instead feel favorably toward those who engage in benevolent sexism. This not only undermines the key catalysts to collective action (i.e., perceptions of unfair treatment and the subsequent anger), but it also serves to undermine women's identification with their disadvantaged group (Becker & Wright, 2011; Wright & Lubensky, 2009). This highlights the instability of the foundation of collective action. Status hierarchies must be recognized as discriminatory in order for collective anger and collective action to arise. But status hierarchies are self-maintaining, with higher-status groups wielding greater levels of political, social, and economic power. Thus, collective action is most effective when members of higher-status groups join in the efforts to demolish the inequalities within those hierarchies.

The Role of Higher-Status Groups in Collective Action

Research on collective action is extremely heterogeneous; many different approaches and methods (e.g., observation, survey, experimental) have been employed by researchers and scholars in their study of this phenomenon. One commonality is that researchers and scholars have primarily focused on collective action among the disadvantaged or lower-status groups, and on the psychological processes and emotions these group members experience (e.g., van Zomeren & Iyer, 2009; see also Crosby, 1976; Runciman, 1966; Tajfel & Turner, 1979; Smith & Ortiz, 2002; Walker & Smith, 2002). However, researchers have recently widened their attention to groups in power (e.g., Iyer, Schmader, & Lickel, 2007; Leach, Iyer, & Pedersen, 2006; Leach, Snider, & Leach 2002; Simon & Klandermans, 2001).

On June 26, 2015, the Supreme Court in the United States ruled in favor of legalizing same-sex marriage nationwide. Millions of Americans' fight for marriage equality was finally won. Notably, both members of the LGBT community and heterosexual individuals (i.e., allies) participated in behaviors that qualified as collective action (e.g., protests, demonstrations) in support of legalizing same-sex marriage. In this case, members of the higher-status group (i.e., those who could already legally marry) supported members of the lower-status group (i.e., those who could not legally marry) in their fight for marriage equality. Facebook and Twitter were flooded by individuals sharing equality signs and the #marriagequality hashtag as means of support. Accordingly, these higher-status members, in their support for marriage equality efforts, apparently worked against their own positions of privilege to extend to others the rights that they themselves enjoyed. However, not all heterosexual individuals supported this movement. In fact, some of these higher-status group members did engage in action, but did so instead to thwart the marriage equality efforts, attempting to protect the discriminatory status hierarchy by joining together to protest marriage rights for anyone other than heterosexuals. The cause of these disparate choices of higher-status individuals of whether to support or oppose marriage equality may be explained by the same initiating emotion that causes lower-status individuals to engage in collective action. Researchers have established that anger not only drives collective action by lower-status group members, but also drives collective action by members of higher-status groups; the anger, though, may inspire collective action that is intended either to raise up (Iyer, Schmader, & Lickel, 2007) or keep down (e.g., Simon & Klandermans, 2001) those in the lower-status group. Therefore, it is likely that perceived injustice and anger inspired the collective action of higher-status group members in both cases. Those who supported marriage equality likely experienced perceived injustice and anger in reaction to same-sex couples not having the right to marry (and were moved to collective action to challenge the existing status hierarchy), whereas those who opposed marriage equality likely experienced perceived injustice and anger in reaction to same-sex couples pursuing the right to marry (and were moved to collective action to preserve the existing status hierarchy).

The marriage equality struggle demonstrates that members of higher-status groups can help lower-status groups to challenge and defeat an oppressive status quo by joining in collective action behaviors. However, we would like to offer one caveat. Unfortunately, experiences that may reduce intergroup prejudice (e.g., positive contact with members of the higher-status group) may ironically work to undermine the psychological processes (e.g., group-based identities, anger, mistrust) that lead to collective anger and action to address inequalities and injustices (Dixon, Durrheim, & Tredoux, 2007; Dixon, Tropp, Durrheim, & Tredoux, 2010; Saguy, Tausch, Dovidio, & Pratto, 2009; Wright & Lubensky, 2009). For example, having contact with the higher-status group may result in members of the lower-status group perceiving the higher-status group more favorably (e.g., perhaps from seeing members of the higher-status group supporting their group). Thus, this contact may weaken the perceived distinction between the lower-status and the higher-status group, and potentially undermine lower-status group members' identification of their own group as one that is disadvantaged (Wright & Lubensky, 2009). Therefore, trying to help the lower-status group by showing support may actually hinder individuals' motivation to participate in collective action. Interestingly, a counterpoint to this is that higher-status group members can help spread awareness, knowledge, and values through their collective actions to those it might have otherwise never reached. Subsequently, this may lead to more individuals joining the movement and acknowledging their support for the disadvantaged group. Thus, we in no way recommend that individuals refrain from participating in collective action because of the potential for hindering the movement. We instead recommend that they acknowledge their support for the disadvantaged group and help by spreading information and values of equality, but also continue to recognize the existence of inequality inherent in a social status hierarchy.

Higher-status members have great power to help or hinder the station of lower-status groups through their own collective action efforts, and with great power comes great responsibility. Higher-status members may choose to wield this power to help the lower-status group members in their pursuits of equality, or they can oppress and hinder these pursuits. Anger, a key component of collective action, not only drives members of the lower-status group to collective action, but it drives the members of the higher-status group to use their power to assist or thwart the goals of the lower-status group. And as we demonstrated earlier, the choice to help or hinder lower-status groups through collective action is likely dependent on their willingness and ability to recognize the existence of social injustice around them.

Conclusion

Collective anger and collective action are solutions to remedy the continued existence of social inequality, discrimination, and oppression in contemporary society. The foundations of collective anger and action lie in individuals' willingness and ability to perceive the discrimination that serves to advance the political, social, and economic power of higher-status groups at the expense of lower-status groups. Thus, individual differences, including propensities to make attributions to prejudice, social identification with higher-status and lower-status groups, and politically motivated ideologies about status hierarchies, become important as necessary, but insufficient, factors in motivating collective anger and action. Even when social injustice is perceived, effective collective action to combat it requires that lower-status group members believe that they have the ability to win that battle. It may be that the surest path by which collective anger and action successfully bring about social change that increases fairness and justice within society is through collective efforts in which higher-status group members ally themselves with the cause. This will likely require higher-status group members to experience collective anger and engage in prosocial collective actions themselves. Until the collective anger and collective action by all members of society unite to correct the inequality of the existing social hierarchy, the work is not over.

References

Altemeyer, B. (1988). *Enemies of freedom: Understanding right-wing authoritarianism.* San Francisco, CA: Jossey-Bass.

Baker, J. H. (2002). *Votes for women: The struggle for suffrage revisited (viewpoints on American culture).* New York, NY: Oxford University Press.

Barrett, L. F., & Swim, J. K. (1998). Appraisals of prejudice and discrimination. In J. K. Swim & C. Stangor (Eds.), *Prejudice: The target's perspective* (pp. 11–36). San Diego, CA: Academic Press.

Baumeister, R. F., & Leary, M. R. (1995). The need to belong: Desire for interpersonal attachments as a fundamental human motivation. *Psychological Bulletin, 117,* 497–529.

Becker, J. C., & Wright, S. C. (2011). Yet another dark side of chivalry: Benevolent sexism undermines and hostile sexism motivates collective action for social change. *Journal of Personality and Social Psychology, 101,* 62–77.

Brady, H. E. (1994). Political participation. In J. P. Robinson, P. R. Shaver, & L. S. Wrightsman (Eds.), *Measures of political attitudes* (pp. 737–801). San Diego, CA: Academic Press.

Carvallo, M., & Pelham, B. W. (2006). When fiends become friends: The need to belong and perceptions of personal and group discrimination. *Journal of Personality and Social Psychology, 90*, 94–108.

Cohen-Chen, S., Halperin, E., Saguy, T., & van Zomeren, M. (2014). Beliefs about the malleability of immoral groups facilitate collective action. *Social Psychological and Personality Science, 5*, 203–210.

Craig, M. A., & Richeson, J. A. (2012). Coalition or derogation? How perceived discrimination influences intraminority intergroup relations. *Journal of Personality and Social Psychology, 102*, 759–777.

Crandall, C. S., & Eshleman, A. (2003). A justification-suppression model of the expression and experience of prejudice. *Psychological Bulletin, 129*, 414–446.

Crandall, C. S., Eshleman, A., & O'Brien, L. (2002). Social norms and the expression and suppression of prejudice: The struggle for internalization. *Journal of Personality and Social Psychology, 82*, 359–378.

Crosby, F. J. (1976). A model of egotistical relative deprivation. *Psychological Review, 83*, 85–113.

Czopp, A. M., Monteith, M. J., & Mark, A. Y. (2006). Standing up for a change: Reducing bias through interpersonal confrontation. *Journal of Personality and Social Psychology, 90*, 784–803.

Dixon, J., Durrheim, K., & Tredoux, C. (2007). Intergroup contact and attitudes toward the principle and practice of racial equality. *Psychological Science, 18*, 867–872.

Dixon, J., Tropp, L. R., Durrheim, K., & Tredoux, C. (2010). "Let them eat harmony": Prejudice-reduction strategies and attitudes of historically disadvantaged groups. *Current Directions in Psychological Science, 19*, 76–80.

Dovidio, J. F. (2001). On the nature of contemporary prejudice: The third wave. *Journal of Social Issues, 57*, 829–849.

Duckitt, J., & Sibley, C. G. (2007). Right wing authoritarianism, social dominance orientation and the dimensions of generalized prejudice. *European Journal of Personality, 21*, 113–130.

Eccleston, C. P., & Major, B. N. (2006). Attributions to discrimination and self-esteem: The role of group identification and appraisals. *Group Processes and Intergroup Relations, 9*, 147–162.

Ellemers, N., & Barreto, M. (2009). Collective action in modern times: How modern expressions of prejudice prevent collective action. *Journal of Social Issues, 65*, 749–768.

Ellemers, N., Wilke, H., & Van Knippenber, A. (1993). Effects of the legitimacy of low group or individual status on individual and collective status-enhanced strategies. *Journal of Personality and Social Psychology, 64*(5), 766–778.

Glick, P., & Fiske, S. T. (1996). The Ambivalent Sexism Inventory: Differentiating hostile and benevolent sexism. *Journal of Personality and Social Psychology, 70*, 491–512.

Goff, P. A., Steele, C. M., & Davies, P. G. (2008). The space between us: Stereotype threat and distance in interracial contexts. *Journal of Personality and Social Psychology, 94,* 91–107.

Inzlicht, M., Kaiser, C. R., & Major, B. (2008). The face of chauvinism: How prejudice expectations shape perceptions of facial affect. *Journal of Experimental Social Psychology, 44,* 758–766.

Iyer, A., Schmader, T., & Lickel, B. (2007). Why individuals protest the perceived transgressions of their country: The role of anger, shame, and guilt. *Personality and Social Psychology Bulletin, 33,* 572–587.

Jackman, M. R. (1994). *The velvet glove: Paternalism and conflict in gender, class, and race relations.* Berkeley, CA: University of California Press.

Jost, J. T., Banaji, M. R., & Nosek, B. A. (2004). A decade of system justification theory: Accumulated evidence of conscious and unconscious bolstering of the status quo. *Political Psychology, 25,* 881–919.

Kaiser, C. R. (2006). Dominant ideology threat and the interpersonal consequences of attributions to discrimination. In C. van Laar & S. Levin (Eds.), *Stigma and group inequality: Social psychological approaches* (pp. 45–64). Mahwah, NJ: Lawrence Erlbaum.

Kaiser, C. R., & Major, B. (2006). A social psychological perspective on perceiving and reporting discrimination. *Law and Social Inquiry, 31,* 801–830.

Kaiser, C. R., & Miller, C. T. (2001). Stop complaining! The social costs of making attributions to discrimination. *Personality and Social Psychology Bulletin, 27,* 254–263.

Kaiser, C. R., Vick, S. B., & Major, B. (2006). Prejudice expectations moderate preconscious attention to cues that are threatening to social identity. *Psychological Science, 17,* 332–338.

Klandermans, B. (1997). *The social psychology of protest.* Oxford, UK: Basic Blackwell.

Leach, C. W., Iyer, A., & Pedersen, A. (2006). Anger and guilt about ingroup advantage explain the willingness for political action. *Personality and Social Psychology Bulletin, 32,* 1232–1245.

Leach, C. W., Snider, N., & Leach, C. W. (2002). "Poisoning the consciences of the fortunate": The experience of relative advantage and support for social equality. In I. Walker & H. J. Smith (Eds.), *Relative deprivation: Specification, development, integration* (pp. 136–163). New York, NY: Cambridge University Press.

Leonard, D. J., Moons, W. G., Mackie, D. M., & Smith, E. R. (2011). "We're mad as hell and we're not going to take it anymore": Anger self-stereotyping and collective action. *Group Processes and Intergroup Relations, 14,* 99–111.

Lerner, M. J. (1980). *The belief in a just world: A fundamental delusion.* New York, NY: Plenum.

Mackie, D. M., Devos, T., & Smith, E. R. (2000). *From prejudice to inter-group emotions; Differentiated reactions to social groups.* New York, NY: Psychology Press.

Major, B., Kaiser, C. R., & McCoy, S. K. (2003). It's not my fault: When and why attributions to prejudice protect self-esteem. *Personality and Social Psychology Bulletin, 29,* 772–781.

Major, B., Kaiser, C. R., O'Brien, L. T., & McCoy, S. K. (2007). Perceived discrimination as worldview threat or worldview confirmation: Implications for self-esteem. *Journal of Personality and Social Psychology, 92,* 1068–1086.

Major, B., Quinton, W., & McCoy, S. (2002). Antecedents and consequences of attributions to discrimination: Theoretical and empirical advances. *Advances in Experimental Social Psychology, 34,* 251–329.

Major, B., Quinton, W. J., & Shmader, T. (2003). Attributions to discrimination and self-esteem: Impact of group identification and situational ambiguity. *Journal of Experimental Social Psychology, 39,* 220–230.

McConahay, J. B. (1986). Modern racism, ambivalence, and the Modern Racism Scale. In J. F. Dovidio & S. L. Gaertner (Eds.), *Prejudice, discrimination, and racism* (pp. 91–125). New York, NY: Academic Press.

McFarland, S. (2010). Authoritarianism, social dominance, and other roots of generalized prejudice. *Political Psychology, 31,* 453–477.

Miller, S. S., & Saucier, D. A. (in press). Individual differences in the propensity to make attributions to prejudice. *Group Processes and Intergroup Relations.*

Monin, B., & Miller, D. T. (2001). Moral credentials and the expression of prejudice. *Journal of Personality and Social Psychology, 81,* 33–43.

Mummendey, A., Kessler, T., Klink, A., & Mielke, R. (1999). Strategies to cope with negative social identity: Predictions by social identity theory and relative deprivation theory. *Journal of Personality and Social Psychology, 76,* 229–245.

Nelson, J. C., Adams, G., & Salter, P. S. (2013). The Marley hypothesis: Denial of racism reflects ignorance of history. *Psychological Science, 24,* 213–218.

Operario, D., & Fiske, S. T. (2001). Ethnic identity moderates perceptions of prejudice: Judgments of personal versus group discrimination and subtle versus blatant bias. *Personality and Social Psychology Bulletin, 27,* 550–561.

Pinel, E. C. (1999). Stigma consciousness: The psychological legacy of social stereotypes. *Journal of Personality and Social Psychology, 76,* 114–128.

Pinel, E. C. (2002). Stigma consciousness in intergroup contexts: The power of conviction. *Journal of Experimental Social Psychology, 38,* 178–185.

Pinel, E. C., & Paulin, N. (2005). Stigma consciousness at work. *Basic and Applied Social Psychology, 27,* 345–352.

Pinel, E. C., Warner, L. R., & Chua, P. P. (2005). Getting there is only half the battle: Stigma consciousness and maintaining diversity in higher education. *Journal of Social Issues, 61,* 481–506.

Plant, E. A., & Devine, P. G. (1998). Internal and external motivation to respond without prejudice. *Journal of Personality and Social Psychology, 75,* 811–832.

Pratto, F., Sidanius, J., Stallworth, L. M., & Malle, B. F. (1994). Social dominance orientation: A personality variable predicting social and political attitudes. *Journal of Personality and Social Psychology, 67,* 741–763.

Runciman, W. G. (1966). *Relative deprivation and social justice: A study of attitudes to social inequality in twentieth-century England.* Berkeley, CA: University of California Press.

Saguy, T., Tausch, N., Dovidio, J. F., & Pratto, F. (2009). The irony of harmony: Intergroup contact can produce false expectations for equality. *Psychological Science, 20,* 114–121.

Sellers, R. M., & Shelton, J. N. (2003). The role of racial identity in perceived racial discrimination. *Journal of Personality and Social Psychology, 84,* 1079–1092.

Simon, B., & Klandermans, B. (2001). Politicized collective identity: A social psychological analysis. *American Psychologist, 56,* 319–331.

Smith E. R., (1993). Social identity and social emotion: Toward new conceptualizations of prejudice. In D. M. Mackie & D. L. Hamilton (Eds.), *Affect, cognition, and stereotyping: Interactive processes in group perception* (pp. 297–315). San Diego, CA: Academic Press.

Smith, H. J., & Ortiz, D. J. (2002). Is it just me? The different consequences of personal and group relative deprivation. In I. Walker & H. J. Smith (Eds.), *Relative deprivation: Specification, development, and integration* (pp. 91–115). Cambridge, UK: Cambridge University Press.

Stürmer, S., & Simon, B. (2004). Collective action: Towards a dual-pathway model. *European Review of Social Psychology, 15,* 59–99.

Stürmer, S., & Simon, B. (2009). Pathways to collective protest: Calculation, identification or emotion? A critical analysis of the role of group-based anger in social movement participation. *Journal of Social Issues, 65,* 681–705.

Swim, J. K., Scott, E. D., Sechrist, G. B., Campbell, B., & Stangor, C. (2003). The role of intent and harm in judgments of prejudice and discrimination. *Journal of Personality and Social Psychology, 84,* 944–959.

Tajfel, H., & Turner, J. C. (1979). An integrative theory of inter-group conflict. In W. G. Austin & S. Worchel (Eds.), *The social psychology of inter-group relations* (pp. 33–47). Monterey, CA: Brooks/Cole.

Tajfel, H., & Turner, J. C. (1986). The social identity theory of intergroup behaviour. In S. G. Worchel, & W. G. Austin (Eds.), *Psychology of intergroup relations* (2nd ed., pp. 7–24). Chicago, IL: Nelson-Hall.

van Zomeren, M., & Iyer, A. (2009). Introduction to the social and psychological dynamics of collective action. *Journal of Social Issues, 64,* 645–660.

van Zomeren, M., Leach, C. W., & Spears, R. (2012). Protestors as "passionate economists": A dynamic dual pathway model of approach coping with collective disadvantage. *Personality and Social Psychology Review, 16,* 180–199.

van Zomeren, M., Postmes, T., & Spears, R. (2008). Toward an integrative social identity model of collective action: A quantitative research synthesis of three socio-psychological perspectives. *Psychological Bulletin, 134,* 504–535.

van Zomeren, M., Spears, R., Fischer, A. H., & Leach, C. W. (2004). Put your money where your mouth is!: Explaining collective action tendencies through group-based anger and group efficacy. *Journal of Personality and Social Psychology, 87,* 649–664.

Walker, I., & Smith, H. J. (2002). *Relative deprivation: Specification, development, and integration*. Cambridge, UK: Cambridge University Press.

Wang, K., Stroebe, K., & Dovidio, J. F. (2012). Stigma consciousness and prejudice ambiguity: Can it be adaptive to perceive the world as biased? *Personality and Individual Differences, 53*, 241–245.

Webster, R. J., Saucier, D. A., & Parks, G. S. (2011). New bottle, same old wine: The GOP and race in the age of Obama. In G. S. Parks & M. W. Hughey (Eds.), *The Obamas and a (post) racial America* (pp. 266–284). New York, NY: Oxford University Press.

Wright, S. C., & Lubensky, M. E. (2009). The struggle for social equality: Collective action vs. prejudice reduction. In S. Demoulin, J. P. Leyens, & J. F. Dovidio (Eds.), *Intergroup misunderstandings: Impact of divergent social realities* (pp. 291–310). New York, NY: Psychology Press.

Wright, S. C., Taylor, D. M., & Moghaddam, F. M. (1990). Responding to membership in a disadvantaged group: From acceptance to collective protest. *Journal of Personality and Social Psychology, 58*, 994–1003.

CHAPTER THREE

Moving toward Extremism: Group Polarization in the Laboratory and the World

Jarryd Willis

The debt ceiling crisis of 2011, the government shutdown of 2013, and the extension of partisanship past the water's edge into the Israeli election and the Iranian Nuclear Deal are all recent examples of how polarized American politics has become. Longitudinal congressional data and findings from the American National Election Survey (ANES, 2014) complement geographic and laboratory research in illustrating the increase in partisan animus in the last half a century. Despite the growing desire and necessity for more compromise in American politics, "the systematic study of compromise remains surprisingly under-developed" (Bellamy, Kornprobst, & Reh, 2012, p. 276). This chapter describes laboratory research testing a core premise of American Democracy: that citizens create Congress and that citizens who value compromise could incentivize more integrative negotiations than those who wish to reinforce intergroup animus.

The Absence of Compromise: Divided and Divisive Government

". . . when politics goes well, we can know a good in common that we cannot know alone."

—Sandel, 1998 (p. 183)

Compromise is essential for reaching goals in America's political arena, particularly in times of divided government. Divided government refers to times when the Democratic and Republican parties share control of America's bicameral legislative branch (with one party controlling the Senate and the other the House of Representatives), or when the party occupying the White House differs from the party in control of the legislative branch. It is noteworthy that a divided government has been the norm for nearly half a century, as the Democratic and Republican parties have shared control of every legislative body since the end of Lyndon Johnson's Presidency, except for President Jimmy Carter's first two years in office (1977–1978) and a few months of President Barack Obama's first year (2009) in office. Despite the norm of divided government, politicians' willingness to compromise has grown increasingly rare.

Having a divided government is not inherently a cause of partisanship. Indeed, the divided Congresses over which President Dwight Eisenhower presided were no more polarized than the one-party rule that Presidents John F. Kennedy and Lyndon B. Johnson presided over (Poole, 2008). Over the past 30 to 40 years, however, there has been an ideological realignment in Congress to the point that there is virtually no ideological overlap between the two parties (Abramowitz & Saunders, 2008; Carroll et al., 2013). In other words, there are no longer any Republicans who are more liberal than the most conservative Democrat, and no Democrats who are more conservative than the most liberal Republican (Barber & McCarty, 2013). The result has been an increasingly polarized Congress, increased use of the filibuster (a procedural mechanism to prevent invoking cloture on a piece of legislation), fewer laws passed, and less overall compromise between the two parties (Binder, 2014; Marziani & Liss, 2010).

Ironically, the very people who are most affected by Congress's failures are the citizens who elect the members of Congress and then re-elect them to serve the country. Therefore, it is important that social scientists attempt to understand the factors that influence voters' choice among candidates, the degree to which the voting electorate desires compromise, and the extent to which compromise can be branded as a desirable quality in congressional candidates. The study of intergroup compromise is more than an academic interest, because increasing the proportion of politicians who value compromise (whether intrinsically or because it is desired by voters) can further the interests of the entire country.

Partisan Negotiators: Citizens Create Congress

In this chapter, I seek to answer the following question: *Can voters incentivize compromise?* Given that politicians are dependent on their constituents to win elections, it is expected that they would approach political negotiations with the interests of their voters in mind, and that constituent accountability pressures would incentivize policymakers to compromise. It is important to begin by identifying what the negotiation literature tells us about the psychological factors underlying individuals' amenability to and resistance toward inter-group compromise. Unfortunately, "the systematic study of compromise remains surprisingly under-developed" (Bellamy et al., 2012, p. 276). However, an abundance of research has catalogued the effect of group polarization on negotiation outcomes, and understanding the seeds of partisanship may help us identify factors that inhibit brinksmanship and promote compromise. Below I review research on inter-group negotiation and political polarization, and I also discuss conditions that lead individuals to employ a cooperative approach to inter-group negotiations.

Hawks Fly Higher Than Doves

Compromise, by definition, requires both parties to mutually and voluntarily "let go of something dear, but not invaluable," to reach an outcome neither can obtain unilaterally (Bellamy et al., 2012, p. 286). Compromise entails the belief that bipartisan accommodation will produce a deal that meets the goals of both parties better than what either individually proposed. Partisanship reduces the desire or willingness to accept something undesirable (e.g., a path to citizenship for undocumented immigrants) even if offered something desirable (e.g., tougher border security), or to forgo something desirable (e.g., funding for Planned Parenthood) to achieve something even more desirable (e.g., avoid going over the nation's debt limit).

To date, no experiment has investigated if the degree to which voters value compromise influences the degree to which elected officials engage in integrative negotiations, and no research has investigated if branding compromise as *valuable* influences voters' choice among political candidates. However, a recent study by Aaldering and De Dreu (2012) provides a useful methodological approach for conducting experiments on this understudied issue.

In Aaldering and De Dreu's (2012) experiment, participants were randomly assigned into dyads to represent dovish (desiring cooperation with the outgroup representative) or hawkish constituencies (desiring competition with the outgroup representative). The dyads were then instructed to negotiate a collective employment contract with the outgroup representative. They received points based on the nature of their negotiation, and no points if they failed to reach an agreement in the 15 minutes they were given. Aaldering and De Dreu (2012) found that representatives' joint outcomes were higher with dovish majorities. Such findings are consistent with those of other negotiation experiments, which found representatives to be more lenient toward the out-group when they had a constituency that desired cooperation, and more aggressive toward the out-group when their constituency desired competition (Enzle, Harvey, & Wright, 1992; Haccoun & Klimoski, 1975; Van Kleef, Steinel, Knippensberg, Hogg, & Svensson, 2007).

Factors That Influence Negotiations

". . . constituencies that favor cooperation influence their representative to take a more cooperative approach. The bad news is that small factions favoring a competitive approach counteract the good intentions of a cooperative majority."
—Steinel, De Dreu, Ouwehand, and Ramirez-Marín, 2009 (p. 11)

The patterns illustrated by Aaldering and De Dreu (2012) are consistent with real-world politics and underscore the importance of citizens' orientation toward compromise when considering legislators' willingness to negotiate across party lines. Political candidates are elected by citizens and tend to act on behalf on their constituents' interest. Thus, if voters in particular districts or states prefer a candidate who is less likely to compromise, then joint outcomes and 50-50 compromises are less likely to occur. Making matters worse is the finding that the most partisan voters are the most likely to vote in both midterm and general elections in U.S. politics (Abramowitz & Saunders, 2008). It comes as no surprise then that hawks tend to carry more weight than doves when representatives have both sets of voters in their constituency (Steinel et al., 2009). In such a scenario, failure to reach an agreement will become the norm, which was the case with the 113th U.S. Congress, which was quantitatively the most partisan and least productive Congress in American history (Carroll et al., 2013).

What, then, can be done to increase compromise and remedy the partisan gridlock that has engulfed U.S. politics? Foster, Mansbridge, and Martin (2013) argue that negotiators should find the zone of possible agreement (ZOPA), or bargaining range, within which to reach a joint outcome. Decreasing the bargaining range increases the possibility of reaching an agreement. Doing so also requires that negotiators communicate which items are taboo tradeoffs that they are not willing to discuss (Tetlock, 2003). Unfortunately, establishing such an open dialogue is no small feat, as many individuals enter into intergroup negotiations with fixed-pie assumptions and feel that any benefit to the other party will be at their expense (Baron, Shonk, & Bazerman, 2002). Such a defensive predisposition reduces the likelihood that negotiators will exchange information relevant to establishing their ZOPA (Thompson & Hastie, 1990). For example, Thompson, Peterson, and Brodt (1996) found that less than a quarter of individuals in a negotiation shared information about their own interests or sought to learn the interests of the other party. However, for negotiators who did share their own and ask about their opponent's priorities, information exchange was moderately positively correlated with higher joint gains. Thus, it is important to encourage negotiators to have an open dialogue and an open debate to the extent practically possible.

Increasing open dialogue and information exchange between political parties seems easy enough to manipulate in experimental settings with college undergraduates debating value-free (i.e., amoral, non-political) issues, but the odds of successfully using this approach have dwindled in recent years in the U.S. Congress. Thus, the second factor to address in intergroup negotiations is partisan intransigence: a preference for gridlock as an alternative to an agreement that is objectively within the zone of possible agreement (Foster et al., 2013). As the degree of polarization has increased between Democrats and Republicans, so has legislative obstructionism. Consider the increase in the use of the Senate filibuster in the past 20 years—a development that has created a 60-vote threshold for anything to pass (Marziani & Liss, 2010). The Hastert Rule has had similar effects in the House of Representatives, which states that a majority of the majority must support a bill for it to pass the lower chamber (Fechner, 2014). What this means is that even if the former Speaker of the House, John Boehner, knew that a desired piece of legislation would pass with a majority of votes from the other party and a minority of votes from their own party, the bill would not be allowed to come up for a vote out of concern that the desired legislation would pass with support from the *wrong* party. To quote former senator Olympia Snowe (R-Maine) in 2012, "Congress is becoming more like a parliamentary system where everyone simply votes with their party and those in charge employ every possible tactic to block the other side."

Organic Political Negotiations

The aforementioned negotiation research sheds light on the dynamics that affect negotiation outcomes, but the generalization of the findings is limited because political negotiations are not context-free social events in which individuals enter with minimal intergroup histories and exit assuming that the other participants' attitudes have little real-world consequentiality

(Barley, 1991). Democrats and Republicans have a preexisting history of distrust that is substantively reinforced through the media and is structurally reflected in the demographic makeup of the two parties (Abramowitz & Saunders, 2008; Brownstein, 2013; Harwood & Murray, 2002). Moreover, political issues are not interchangeable or equidistant in value across parties (or demographic groups), because some issues are characterized by protracted conflict in a way that others are not. In the following section, I will discuss the consequences of partisan media, demographic differences, and culture wars for interparty negotiations.

Partisan Programs

The 24-hour news cycle increases the pressure legislators feel to remain consistent on issues, even when they may be open to negotiation in closed-door settings (Gutmann & Thompson, 2012; Levendusky, 2013; Warren & Mansbridge, 2013). News outlets such as MSNBC (a progressive station) and FOX (a conservative station) serve as echo chambers where partisans are reinforced in their beliefs and their antipathy for the opposing party (Goren, Federico, & Kittilson, 2009; Lee, 2009; Stroud, 2010). The resulting increase in polarization has measurable electoral and policy consequences, because candidates feel pressure to accommodate the increasingly partisan positions of their constituents (Brady, Han, & Pope, 2007; Layman, Carsey, Green, Herrera, & Cooperman, 2010).

These effects are most pernicious in non-competitive (e.g., 80–20 party divide) districts where an incumbent fears a primary election challenge. In non-competitive districts, the incumbent has no incentive to even pretend to be moderate because a majority of the registered voters are already supporters. However, as was well-documented after FOX News's influence in the 2010 Tea Party wave, partisan media can encourage primary election voters to support the ideologically purest candidates (Williamson, Skocpol, & Coggin, 2011). There are generally only two possible outcomes in such a scenario: either the incumbent abandons any previous departures from the party platform, or the more extreme candidate wins.

One consideration to combat electoral incentives that increase polarization is to increase the electoral influence of citizens who value compromise. Although branding compromise as a desirable attribute may be a challenge in itself (particularly among those who see compromise as a dirty word), the media can play an instrumental role by highlighting responsible lawmakers who assist in shepherding through compromises that benefit America rather than a particular political party. To quote Chambers (2009), media should "promote dialogue, not monologue" (p. 330).

Disparity in Demographic Diversity

Race is arguably the greatest fault-line in American politics (more so than same-sex marriage or abortion; Harwood & Murray, 2002), and it is not surprising that strong social norms exist that make any discussion of race almost taboo (McVeigh, Cunningham, & Farrell, 2014; McWhorter, 2004; Milligan, 2012; Saad, 2010, 2013). To paraphrase Harwood and Murray (2002), "Race is the social issue burned most deeply in the American psyche . . . with many leading Democrats consistently advancing many causes embraced by Blacks, and many leading Republicans consistently opposing them" (p. 1).

Political bias, however, is not arrested by any social norms, and partisans are often encouraged to express hostility toward the other party (and at times even being rewarded for it) (Iyengar & Westwood, 2015). Rather than explicit political bias decreasing with age (as in the case of explicit racial bias), explicit political animus appears to increase with age as adults incorporate a political identity into their overall social identity (Baron & Banaji, 2006; Iyengar, Sood, & Lelkes, 2012). Their political identity is reinforced by the aforementioned partisan television channels; it predicts selective exposure to content on social media (Rainie & Smith, 2012); and it is related to an increase of morally homogeneous neighborhoods (Howard, Gibson, & Stolle, 2005), a sharp decrease in people exchanging vows with a spouse from the opposing party (Alford, Hatemi, Hibbing, Martin, & Eaves, 2011), and less parental acceptance of children who marry outside the family party (Iyengar et al., 2012). To quote Iyengar and Westwood (2015), "partisan animus in the American public exceeds racial hostility" (p. 2).

There is an abundance of political science, psychological, and observable congressional data illustrating the influence of differential racial/ethnic (and sexual orientation) perceptions between the Democratic and Republican parties (Bartels, 2000; Brewer & Pierce, 2005; Campbell & Herman, 2010; Crawford & Bhatia, 2012; Cunningham, Nezlek, & Banaji, 2004; Daniel, 2012; Mangum, 2013; Miller, Brewer, & Arbuckle, 2009; Nosek, Banaji, & Jost, 2009; Tritt, 2009; Xu & Lee, 2013). There exists an asymmetry in social group perceptions between Democrats and Republicans that is inseparable from their interactions with and treatment of (both perceived and actual) various social groups. The clearest consequence of this asymmetry is the growing disparity in demographic diversity between the Democratic Party and Republican Party, particularly since the 1960s. The Republican Party has not won more than 22% of the overall non-White vote since 1972 (Brownstein, 2013). The Democratic

Party has become increasingly diverse in both its voting base and its elected officials, with over a third of Democratic legislators being minority group members. In contrast, the Republican Party was no more diverse in 2014 than it was in the late 1980s, with minorities representing fewer than 2.2% of Republican lawmakers. As I stated earlier, citizens create Congress, and the values of the citizens from the Democratic and Republican parties have resulted in one polyglot party and one racially homogeneous party, respectively.

The etiology of this demographic disparity brings me to my final point, which is that the outcomes of negotiations have consequences that may permeate the public's mind long after Congress has adjourned (e.g., Blacks will likely remember which party supported voter ID laws and which party supported strengthening Section 4 of the Voting Rights Act). In short, constituents do not observe the negotiating context as a "blank slate" in which artificial inputs and outputs, equal in their comparative inconsequentiality, are computed, free from any residue from previous arguments or anticipated confrontations once the current negotiation concludes (Kramer, 2004). Instead, citizens (especially active voters) act as political auditors: They have taken account of Democrats' and Republicans' historical stances on various issues and, thus, the manner in which they approach present-day policy debates is contextually dependent on the legislation being debated.

It is clear that the preexisting history of distrust between Democrats and Republicans affects political negotiations in a way that is not easily captured in laboratory experiments with minimal groups that have no preexisting history of interpersonal experiences, norms, or expectations. The way partisan negotiators approach interparty interactions depends on their appraisal of political history, which is shaped and reinforced by partisan media and is nested in a social identity in which their political, racial, religious, gender, and sexual identities are inextricably linked.

Culture Wars

In political negotiations, the participants tend to debate issues in which there are established moral divisions and varying degrees of consequentiality, and more often than not the issues are embedded in individuals' social identity (or the identity of their constituents). Thus, one of the first steps to achieving a successful negotiation is deciding on and accepting the ideological limits, or "scope conditions," for each party. For example, Democrats are unlikely to enter any negotiation if restrictions to abortion access are among the demands, and Republicans are unlikely to enter any negotiation if gun control measures are among the demands (Allen, 2013; Bash,

Desjardins, Silverleib, Steinhauser, & Walsh, 2009). One example of such limits can be found in the 2013 budget deal between Representative Paul Ryan and Senator Patty Murray, in which they agreed from the outset on which issues were not up for consideration.

Partisan negotiators' willingness to compromise differs based on the relevance to "core values" of the issue under consideration. Understood in this way, individuals' disposition to compromise and the emotional valence of the issue under consideration interact to determine the likelihood of reaching an integrative agreement. Thus, the most judicious investigation of the degree to which compromise can be incentivized would be an investigation using issues where a compromise is realistically plausible, as opposed to issues that breach the ideological limits of the other negotiating party.

Therefore, a key procedural consideration in the research described below was choosing issues in which the discrete stances of Democrats and Republicans would be nonetheless discernible (even for Introduction to Psychology students), but where there existed the possibility for amicably resolved, if not well-articulated, integrative agreements. It is for that reason that the following four issues were selected for this experiment: Immigration Reform, Gun Control, Voter ID Laws, and ObamaCare.

This Laboratory Study

Based on the literature discussed above, a laboratory study was devised and conducted to provide an empirical test of the following question: *Can voters incentivize compromise?* I emulated the design used in the study by Aaldering and De Dreu (2012) and adapted it for an explicitly political context. Participants engaged in a semi-structured dyadic negotiation task in which they played the role of a legislator in the House of Representatives seeking re-election from their hypothetical voters. The distributive (non-equidistant) allocation of points in the negotiations were based on both the Democrat and the Republican agreeing to one policy idea from the opposing party—effectively making each agreement a compromise. The key variable was the different incentives I gave participants (based on the desires of their hypothetical constituents) to change how they approached the negotiation. Half of the dyads were informed that they represented districts in which their voters wanted them to compromise, whereas the other half were informed that they represented districts in which their voters wanted them to adhere to their values (i.e., to behave in a partisan manner).

The key outcome measure was the discrepancy between Democrats' and Republicans' scores. Each party had four options to choose from for each of the four issues, and each option awarded points to one party while subtracting points from the other. For example, agreeing to repeal the individual mandate in ObamaCare would lead to increased points for Republicans and a loss of points for Democrats, whereas agreeing to amnesty for undocumented immigrants would lead to increased points for Democrats and a loss of points for Republicans. The point system was designed with mutually beneficial agreements across all four issues so that joint outcomes (combined score for Democrats and Republicans) would be higher for dyads who negotiated in good faith.

Two of the key components in the design were the use of individuals who identify with the Democratic or Republican parties as research participants (placed in dyads of one Democrat and one Republican), and the task of negotiating joint outcomes on four policy issues in which the parties are known to disagree (but are not considered taboo tradeoffs). The implicit advantage in having partisan identifiers is that participants already understand the consequentiality of the issues, and many may have an emotional investment in any one of them.

In summary, this experiment is, to my knowledge, the first experimental investigation of intergroup compromise between representatives of the Democratic and Republican parties, and the degree to which political partisans can be incentivized to compromise.

Hypothesis 1

I hypothesized that participants whose voters desired compromise (compromise-condition dyads) in exchange for re-election would negotiate higher joint outcomes than participants whose voters wanted them to adhere to their values (value adherence-condition dyads). If compromise is consequential for victory, then individuals should be inclined to reach agreements that are worth more points interdependently than they could reach with an independent, partisan strategy.

Hypothesis 2

I hypothesized that the discrepancy between Democrats' and Republicans' scores would be higher for value adherence-condition dyads than for compromise-condition dyads. The rationale for this prediction is that value-adherence dyads will be motivated to maximize their individual scores, and they will be inclined to compromise only to the extent necessary to ensure that the other participant does not leave the negotiation altogether (leaving both players with zero points).

At a university in the southern United States, 195 undergraduate students ages 18–57 years old ($M_{age}=21.85$, $SD=6.43$), participated in this experiment. Participants in psychology courses enrolled in either the

Democratic ($n = 111$) or Republican ($n = 84$) version of this experiment based on their response to a political affiliation item included in the psychology department's Sona prescreening survey (Sona Systems; Fidler, 1997). Participants who met the eligibility requirements for a particular political party received email invitations through Sona indicating when timeslots were available. Psychology participants were compensated with 1.5 research credits.

Democratic participants were 47 male and 64 female students, and Republicans were 40 males and 43 females. One participant declined to specify their gender. The ethnic composition for Republicans was as follows: 40 White, 13 Asian, 12 Black, 11 Hispanic, and 8 mixed. The ethnic composition for Democrats was as follows: 35 Black, 26 Asian, 21 Hispanic, 20 White, and 7 mixed (two Democratic participants did not indicate their race/ethnic identity). The fact that the disparity in diversity between the parties resembles national trends suggests that the procedure to sort participants by political affiliation was successful. Additional evidence stems from my participants' responses to the demographic survey questions: Republicans in my sample were 79.2% Pro-Life and 65.5% anti-Gay Marriage advocates, whereas Democrats in my sample were 71.6% Pro-Choice and 70.9% Marriage Equality advocates.

One hundred and twelve participants took part in the negotiation (a total of 56 dyads), with 28 Democratic-Republican dyads randomly assigned into the Compromise condition and 28 Democratic-Republican dyads randomly assigned into the Value Adherence condition.

The experiment was conducted in a laboratory room containing two long conference tables and chairs so that participants could sit across from one another during the political negotiation. When scheduled participants arrived, the experimenter greeted them, asked that they sit directly across from one another at the negotiating table, and asked their names. Asking their names ensured that the materials for the Democratic and Republican participant would be given to the person registered under the heading for that political party. Each participant was then given a consent form to complete with one of the two pens placed on the table. Upon completing the consent forms, participants were asked to complete a questionnaire packet. The questionnaire packet asked participants demographic items (e.g., age, sex, sexuality, race/ethnicity, socioeconomic status [SES], religion), items intended to discern their political orientation, and two measures meant to assess their ideology and amenability to compromise (respectively).

The scale that assessed their ideology was a modified 20-item measure of Political (Liberal-Conservative) Ideology used by Shook and Clay (2011) and Clay (2012). Participants were asked to respond by using a 1 (strongly disagree) to 6 (strongly agree) Likert-type scale, with higher scores indicating liberal attitudes. Overall, this was a highly reliable measure for both Republican and Democratic respondents.

The measure that assessed their amenability to compromise was the Intergroup Compromise Inventory (ICI), a 26-item measure developed in previous research by Willis and DeNobrega (2013). A secondary goal of this research was to determine the construct validity of the Compromise (8 items), Animus (8 items), and Distrust (10 items) scales of this measure. A univariate analysis of variance found higher Compromise scores for Independents than for Democrats or Republicans. A subsequent univariate analysis of variance (ANOVA) found lower Animus scores for Independents than for Democrats or Republicans. No differences were found for the Distrust scale.

Once both participants completed and returned the questionnaire packet to the experimenter, they were given a blue (Democratic) or red (Republican) negotiation folder (based on their political party). The experimenter then read instructions from page one of the negotiation materials. The experimenter then asked participants to turn to the next page (the manipulation page) and informed participants either that their constituents wanted them to compromise with the other political party and get things done (Compromise condition), or stay true to their values while negotiating with the opposing political party (Value Adherence condition). The experimenter then explained how the compromise scorecard point system worked, with particular emphasis on selecting "no action" and avoiding multiple selections from a single participant.

On each issue, participants would have to choose exactly one of the four Democratic options (A, B, C, or D) from the left side of the page, one of the four Republican options (E, F, G, or H) from the right side of the page, and place the agreed upon letters in the box below the corresponding column. If they were unable to agree on one letter from each column then they could choose "no action" and move on to the next issue. In addition, all four issues had distributive point systems, with immigration and gun control favoring Democrats in points available, and voter ID and Obama-Care favoring Republicans in points available. There was no integrative negotiation issue in this experiment, and participants were advised not to share their points with one another during the negotiation. Once participants appeared to grasp the point system, the experimenter collected their practice materials (except for the example of the scorecard practice topic), informed them that they would have 20 minutes to complete the four negotiation topics, and left the room so that the participants could negotiate without the experimenter being present. Participants were told to come see the experimenter if they had any questions or finished in less than 20 minutes.

Once 20 minutes expired (or participants indicated that they were done), the experimenter returned to the room to hand participants a post-negotiation questionnaire and a debriefing form. After completing the post-negotiation questionnaire, participants were asked not to share the nature of the experiment with other students and were dismissed.

The dyad was the unit of analysis for negotiation outcomes. The data were structured in the Statistical Package for the Social Sciences (SPSS) such that the joint outcomes (one score per dyad) and the party-specific outcomes (separate scores for the actor and partner) could be assessed by using univariate and mixed-model ANOVAs, respectively.

There were four main dependent variables. The first was joint outcomes (the combined score for the Democratic and Republican participants), which I predicted would be higher in the compromise condition because dyads incentivized to work together should produce greater results than dyads incentivized to prioritize partisan gains. The second dependent variable was discrepancy (the difference between the Republican minus Democratic participants' outcomes), which I predicted would be higher in the value adherence condition because dyads incentivized to prioritize partisan gains will be more polarized (by definition), talk past each other, and end up farther apart in their negotiations. The final two dependent variables were simply the individual scores for the Democratic and Republican participants, which I predicted would be higher in the compromise condition.

Hypothesis 1, which predicted that compromise-condition dyads would negotiate higher joint outcomes than value adherence-condition dyads, was not supported. Hypothesis 2, however, was supported. The discrepancy between Democrats' and Republicans' scores was higher for value adherence-condition dyads than for compromise-condition dyads. This finding suggests that dyads incentivized to compromise worked harder to reach mutual agreements rather than partisan gains. However, the finding that joint gains did not differ between conditions suggests that either those in the compromise condition simply agreed to the *low hanging fruit* in order to reach a compromise or that those in the value-adherence condition (particularly Republicans) had great partisan success. These possibilities will be explored in the discussion.

Finally, a mixed-model analysis of variance was conducted to delineate party-specific differences in outcomes for the two negotiation conditions, and thus shed some light on the discrepancy between conditions. The analysis revealed a significant interaction between political party and negotiation condition. Republicans' negotiation outcomes were higher in the value adherence condition than in the compromise condition, whereas Democrats' negotiation outcomes did not differ between the compromise and value-adherence condition. Moreover, in the value adherence condition, Republicans' outcomes were significantly higher than Democrats', but the scores for the two did not differ in the compromise condition.

Democratic participants' general willingness to acquiesce to a more competitive Republican negotiation partner (even though both were given the partisanship incentive) may reflect their general belief in government to address national issues. If their political disposition is to make government work, then matching Republicans in competitiveness would have been counterproductive. Thus, any sense of dejection from achieving fewer individual outcomes may be tempered by the success of reaching an agreement. On the other hand, Republicans in the compromise condition may have acquiesced more to Democrats because the manipulation explicitly conveyed that they would be rewarded only for working together. Thus, any sense of dejection from conceding greater ground to Democrats may be tempered by the expected electoral rewards of doing so. The degree to which philosophical differences between parties may have been a factor will be explored further in the discussion.

A subsequent analysis assessed dyadic composition; specifically, whether or not the dyad had a self-identified independent (i.e., participants who identified themselves as leaning left, leaning right, or moderate) from either party, an independent from both parties, or was a pure-party dyad (i.e., no independents). Univariate analyses indicated that whether or not the Republican was independent made the most difference. Dyads in which the Republican was an independent showed no differences between the compromise or value adherence conditions for any outcome measure, including Democrats' negotiation outcomes. However, if the Republican was a self-identified conservative or member of the Tea Party, then the outcomes of both Democrats and Republicans varied significantly between conditions, such that the discrepancy between Democrats' and Republicans' scores was more pronounced for these dyads, both for those in the compromise and value adherence conditions. Democrats' negotiation outcomes were significantly higher than Republicans' in the compromise condition but lower in the value adherence condition, and Democrats had higher scores in the compromise condition whereas Republicans had higher scores in the value-adherence condition.

Although finding that the manipulation was influential only on dyads with a partisan Republican (those most reflective of our current Congress) was unexpected, it suggests that such an incentive may help reduce the toxicity in the current political atmosphere.

I proceeded to assess the degree to which the Intergroup Compromise Inventory (ICI) scales predicted negotiation outcomes. For dyads in the compromise condition, a pair of regression analyses found that Republicans' animus scores predicted higher discrepancies in negotiation outcomes (with Democrats' outcomes being higher, albeit not significantly) between parties, and Democrats' animus scores predicted lower joint outcomes. For dyads in the partisanship condition, Republicans' animus scores predicted lower negotiation outcomes for their Democratic opponents. The other two scales were not significant predictors of negotiation outcomes.

In short, both parties negotiated in good faith when incentivized to compromise. Even though their joint outcomes were not higher, their individual negotiation outcomes more mutual and less competitive. In contrast, Republicans in the value-adherence condition were more competitive, an approach that yielded greater individual gains but less mutual gain.

Discussion

This experiment was an attempt to determine whether or not constituents' desire for compromise makes it enough of an electorally consequential incentive that it influences the outcomes of interparty negotiations. I will begin with a discussion of the dyadic negotiation findings and their implications for the political process, and conclude with a discussion of limitations and directions for future research.

If the results of hypotheses 1 and 2 are taken together, they suggest that dyads reached the same overall joint outcomes regardless of whether they were incentivized to compromise or obstruct by their hypothetical constituents, but Republicans in the value adherence condition were more combative and achieved better personal outcomes by acting that way. Findings in the political science literature have demonstrated that the increase in polarization in the U.S. Congress since the realignment of the South has been asymmetric and largely driven by increased Republican partisanship (Barber & McCarty, 2013; Hare, McCarty, Poole, & Rosenthal, 2012; Mann & Ornstein, 2013). Thus, consistent with real-world findings, Republicans in the current study were more competitive overall than Democrats, most likely because they were personally rewarded for it.

There is one clear yet profound truth about the United States' current political climate that underlies the focus of this chapter: partisanship is our current default. The finding in this experiment that political partisans can be incentivized to compromise, while hopeful, must be considered in a real-world context. Legislators weigh political animus and electoral considerations more heavily than upholding legitimacy and public trust in the legislative process. A compromise scorecard that was consequential for re-election may help mitigate some of the factors, but certainly not all. A key concern that remains unaddressed is the degree to which the public cares. This experiment assumed that a compromise scorecard already exists, that it was deemed legitimate by voters, and that lawmakers saw it as consequential to winning their election. However, a clearer understanding of the voters who turn out in different elections (midterm versus general) is important in determining the electoral scenario in which the scorecard would be most influential.

Voter Efficacy

Voter efficacy posits that the more eligible voters feel their vote can make a difference, the more likely they are to vote (Pinkleton, Austin, & Fortman, 1998). For any scorecard to be effective, whether it is for the National Rifle Association, VotoLatino Immigration scores, or a compromise scorecard, the voting-eligible constituents reviewing the scorecard information for their elected official must believe that their vote is consequential. Moreover, the lawmaker must believe that their constituents' votes are consequential to their re-election, as political science has found that legislators tend to fit their ideology to the voters they expect will turn out (McCarty, Rodden, Shor, Tausanovitch, & Warshaw, 2014).

The distinction between midterm and general elections is critical given the demographic differences between the two electorates (Oakford, 2015). Unfortunately, it is difficult to make a strong argument for the remedial value of a compromise scorecard in midterm elections, as voter efficacy among moderates and independents is likely to decrease with the overall turnout. This is because the most partisan voters are the ones most likely to vote in midterm elections (Abramowitz & Saunders, 2008). Given that turnout is higher in general (presidential) elections than in midterm elections, and significantly higher in swing states than in partisan states, a compromise scorecard may be particularly effective in competitive races during general elections (McDonald, 2015).

> Voters in competitive states are more interested in politics, more aware of the policy positions their U.S. senators have taken, and more likely to hold them accountable for those positions at election time. (Jones, 2013, p. 3)

The overwhelming majority (379 of 435) of elected House officials represent non-competitive districts—a trend that only worsened following the 2014 midterm elections (Kondik, 2014). What this means is that most legislators are incentivized to behave with as much position-extremity as possible to avoid a primary challenge within their own party (usually from a challenger who is even more acrimonious than the incumbent). Moreover, being in a non-competitive district means the candidate who is partisan enough to win the primary election will not have to move back toward the moderate-center in the general election. In short, a compromise scorecard would have no consequentiality in most congressional districts; in fact, it may backfire such that incumbents do their best to get a low score to prove how much they hate the word "compromise."

Limitations and Future Research

Although this research has obtained some interesting findings, several caveats should be kept in mind when generalizing the results.

Perhaps the most obvious limitation of all is the youth and limited political IQ of the sample. Screening potential participants with items that assess political knowledge (not just ideology) would help ensure that only those with at least basic political knowledge (e.g., knowing who the vice president is) would be allowed to participate in the study. In addition, a sample of political activists would serve as an effective remedy in future research, because their knowledge of the issues would make them more reliable sources from which to discern the influence of the compromise manipulation.

There are also ecological limitations to the generalizability of this experiment. The semi-structured dyadic interactions used for the negotiations took place in an explicitly political context and, therefore, the results should not be applied to or used to predict the outcomes of negotiations concerning non-political issues. More importantly, it was embedded in a political context but was removed from other relevant factors that contribute to an overall political atmosphere.

First, participants were not provided with demographic information about hypothetical constituents (e.g., race, sex, age, gun ownership, income, education), a factor that is known to influence how legislators position themselves on key issues (Damore, 2015; Walter, 2013). Given the demographic shifts in the United States, including information about the racial/ethnic composition of hypothetical constituents, would provide insight into the influence of demographic incentives.

Second, there was no experimental condition in which hypothetical lobbying groups offered participants monetary or endorsement incentives based on their selection of particular options, which is known to influence party positions on issues ranging from reducing CO_2 emissions to pledging never to raise taxes on high-income earners (Grasse & Heidbreder, 2011). Research by Gilens (2012) indicates that lawmakers tend to sponsor legislation that favors the interests of a few wealthy donors rather than their less wealthy campaign contributors. Moreover, out-of-district contributors tend to be more partisan and such contributions have increased following the Supreme Court's ruling in *Citizens United* (Bonica, 2013; Gimpel, Lee, & Pearson-Merkowitz, 2008). Given the degree to which campaign contributions incentivize legislation, future research could include conditions with different monetary incentives to determine the degree to which negotiators balance value-driven incentives with financial incentives.

Third, there was not a group of confederates who played the role of the media, or artificial news reports that cheered or condemned the participants' actions. The growth of the 24-hour news cycle since the 1990s is regarded as a key factor in the growth of hyper-polarization (Goren et al., 2009). Finally, even though the structure of this experiment was partially inspired by the successful negotiation between Paul Ryan and Patty Murray, most political negotiations take place in groups where conformity, obedience to party leadership, coercion (e.g., "vote against this bill or you will lose your chairmanship"), groupthink, and affectively charged group-level biases operate in concert to recalibrate the parameters of each negotiation (Bazerman, Tenbrunsel, & Wade-Benzoni, 2008; De Dreu & Beersma, 2001; De Dreu, Koole, & Oldersma, 1999; Maoz, Ward, Katz, & Ross, 2002).

Personality traits (e.g., openness, conscientiousness, extraversion, agreeableness, and neuroticism) are also related to one's political identity and may predict individuals' disposition toward partisanship and compromise (Gerber, Huber, Doherty, & Dowling, 2012). Openness to experience is a predictor of liberal attitudes and conscientiousness is a predictor of conservatism. Additional research will be needed to determine the degree to which traits predict political negotiation outcomes.

Finally, and in relation to the ecological concerns noted above, the structure of the compromise scorecard point system was such that points for one issue were detached from the others. What this means is that participants could not have agreed to an item on ObamaCare in exchange for an agreement on gun control. Even for the few participants who may have attempted such a strategy, those tradeoffs were not captured in the scoring system. Future research could change the instructions so that participants have the option to complete negotiations by making agreements across topics rather than being restricted to completing topics one at a time.

Concluding Remarks

At the 2013 Association for Psychological Science convention in Washington, D.C., Dr. Diane Halpern (2013) suggested that the media and political organizations should encourage (and perhaps create) the use of a cooperation point system. Organizations such as the National Rifle Association score lawmakers on their support for guns, and VotoLatino scores lawmakers on their support for immigration. These scorecards are intended to serve as incentives to influence the nature of legislators' negotiations, and their influence is proportional to the degree to which an individual legislator's constituents support the specific issue at hand.

The results of the experiment discussed in this chapter provide support for the view that negotiators will adjust the position they take in political negotiations to satisfy the disposition of their voters. These findings indicate that implementing a compromise scorecard system during general (not primary) elections, particularly in swing states with competitive seats, could help reduce the increasing animosity across party lines. In a sense, the results reinforce the most promising, appealing, and reassuring aspect of our democracy: Citizens create Congress.

References

Aaldering, H., & De Dreu, C. K. (2012). Why hawks fly higher than doves: Intragroup conflict in representative negotiation. *Group Processes and Intergroup Relations, 15*(6), 713–724.

Abramowitz, A. I., & Saunders, K. L. (2008). Is polarization a myth? *Journal of Politics, 70*(2), 542–555.

Alford, J., Hatemi, P., Hibbing, J., Martin, N., & Eaves, L. (2011). The politics of mate choice. *The Journal of Politics, 73*(2), 362–379.

Allen, J. (2013, April 6). 12 GOP senators back Paul on guns. *Politico.* Retrieved from http://www.politico.com

ANES. (2014). *User's guide and codebook for the ANES 2012 time series study.* Ann Arbor, MI and Palo Alto, CA: The University of Michigan and Stanford University.

Barber, M., & McCarty, N. (2013). Causes and consequences of polarization. *Task Force on Negotiating Agreement in Politics.* Washington, DC: American Political Science Association.

Barley, S. R. (1991). Contextualizing conflict: Notes on the anthropology of disputes and negotiations. In M. H. Bazerman, R. J. Lewicki, & B. H. Sheppard (Eds.), *Research on negotiations in organizations* (Vol. 3, pp. 165–199). Greenwich, CT: JAI Press.

Baron, A. S., & Banaji, M. R. (2006). The development of implicit attitudes: Evidence of race evaluations from ages 6 and 10 and adulthood. *Psychological Science, 17*(1), 53–58.

Baron, J., Shonk, K., & Bazerman, M. H. (2002). Enlarging the societal pie—A cognitive perspective. *SSRN Working Paper Series.*

Bartels, L. M. (2000). Partisanship and voting behavior, 1952–1996. *American Journal of Political Science, 44*(1), 35–50.

Bash, D., Desjardins, L., Silverleib, A., Steinhauser, P., & Walsh, D. (2009, November 6). Abortion threatens House health care bill. *CNN*. Retrieved from http://www.cnn.com

Bazerman, M. H., Tenbrunsel, A., & Wade-Benzoni, K. (2008). When "sacred" issues are at stake. *Negotiation Journal, 24*(1), 113–117.

Bellamy, R., Kornprobst, M., & Reh, C. (2012). Introduction: Meeting in the middle. *Government and Opposition, 47*(3), 275–295.

Binder, S. (2014, January 13). How political polarization creates stalemate and undermines lawmaking. *The Washington Post*. Retrieved from http://www.washingtonpost.com

Bonica, A. (2013). Ideology and interests in the political marketplace. *American Journal of Political Science, 57*(2), 294–311.

Brady, D. W., Han, H., & Pope, J. C. (2007). Primary elections and candidate ideology: Out of step with the primary electorate? *Legislative Studies Quarterly, 32*(1), 79–105.

Brewer, M. B., & Pierce, K. P. (2005). Social identity complexity and outgroup tolerance. *Personality and Social Psychology Bulletin, 31*(3), 428–437.

Brownstein, R. (2013, September 5). Bad bet: Why Republicans can't win with Whites alone. *National Journal*. Retrieved from http://www.nationaljournal.com

Campbell, M. E., & Herman, M. R. (2010). Politics and policies: Attitudes toward multiracial Americans. *Ethnic and Racial Studies, 33*(9), 1511–1536.

Carroll, R., Lewis, J., Lo, J., McCarty, N., Poole, K., & Rosenthal, H. (2013). DW-NOMINATE scores with bootstrapped standard errors. Retrieved from http://voteview.com/dwnomin.htm

Chambers, S. (2009). Rhetoric and the public sphere: Has deliberative democracy abandoned mass democracy? *Political Theory, 37*(3), 323–350.

Clay, R. (2012). *The evolution of conservative attitudes as a complement to cognitive threat detection mechanisms* (Doctoral dissertation, Virginia Commonwealth University). Retrieved from http://scholarscompass.vcu.edu

Crawford, J. T., & Bhatia, A. (2012). Birther nation: Political conservatism is associated with explicit and implicit beliefs that President Barack Obama is foreign. *Analyses of Social Issues and Public Policy, 12*(1), 364–376.

Cunningham, W., Nezlek, J., & Banaji, M. (2004). Implicit and explicit ethnocentrism: Revisiting the ideologies of prejudice. *Personality and Social Psychology Bulletin, 30*(10), 1332–1346.

Damore, D. F. (2015). An overview of Latino influence in the 2014 elections. *Latino Decisions*. Retrieved from http://www.latinodecisions.com

Daniel, D. (2012). *How Blacks became blue: The 1936 African American voting shift from the party of Lincoln to the New Deal coalition* (Pell Scholars and Senior Theses). Retrieved from http://digitalcommons.salve.edu (Paper 77)

De Dreu, C. K. W., & Beersma, B. (2001). Minority influence in organizations: Its origins and implications for learning and group performance. In C. K. W. De Dreu & N. K. De Vries (Eds.), *Group consensus and minority influence: Implications for innovation* (pp. 258–283). Oxford, UK: Blackwell.

De Dreu, C. K. W., Koole, S. L., & Oldersma, F. L. (1999). On the seizing and freezing of negotiator inferences: Need for cognitive closure moderates the use of heuristics in negotiation. *Personality and Social Psychology Bulletin, 25*(3), 348–362. doi: 10.1177/0146167299025003007

Enzle, M. E., Harvey, M. D., & Wright, E. F. (1992). Implicit role obligations versus social responsibility in constituency representation. *Journal of Personality and Social Psychology, 62*(2), 238–245.

Fechner, H. (2014). Managing political polarization in Congress: A case study on the use of the Hastert rule. *Utah Law Review, 2014*(4), 757–771.

Fidler, J. (1997). *The experiment management system.* Washington, DC: Sona Systems.

Foster, C., Mansbridge, J., & Martin, C. J. (2013). Negotiation myopia. In C. J. Martin & J. Mansbridge (Eds.), *Negotiating agreements in politics* (pp. 73–85). Washington, DC: American Political Science Association.

Gerber, A. S., Huber, G. A., Doherty, D., & Dowling, C. M. (2012). Personality and the strength and direction of partisan identification. *Political Behavior, 34*(4), 653–688.

Gilens, M. (2012). *Affluence and influence: Economic inequality and political power in America.* Princeton, NJ: Princeton University Press.

Gimpel, J., Lee, F., & Pearson-Merkowitz, S. (2008). The check is in the mail: Interdistrict funding flows in congressional elections. *American Journal of Political Science, 52*(2), 373–394.

Goren, P., Federico, C. M., & Kittilson, M. C. (2009). Source cues, partisan identities, and political value expression. *American Journal of Political Science, 53*(4), 805–820.

Grasse, N., & Heidbreder, B. (2011). The influence of lobbying activity in state legislatures: Evidence from Wisconsin. *Legislative Studies Quarterly, 36*(4), 567–589.

Gutmann, A., & Thompson, D. (2012). *The spirit of compromise: Why governing demands it and campaigning undermines it.* Princeton, NJ: Princeton University Press.

Haccoun, R. R., & Klimoski, R. J. (1975). Negotiator status and accountability source: A study of negotiator behavior. *Organizational Behavior and Human Performance, 14*(3), 342–359.

Halpern, D. (2013). The psychological science behind hyperpartisanship and what to do about it. Speech presented at APS Award Address at the 25th Annual Convention for the Association for Psychological Science. Retrieved from https://vimeo.com/70656685

Hare, C., McCarty, N., Poole, K. T., & Rosenthal, H. (2012). Polarization is real (and asymmetric) [Web log post]. Retrieved from http://themonkeycage .org/2012/05/polarization-is-real-and-asymmetric

Harwood, J. & Murray, S. (2002, December 19). Year after year, race remains Washington's greatest divider. *The Wall Street Journal*. Retrieved from http://www.wsj.com

Howard, M., Gibson, J., & Stolle, D. (2005). *The U.S. Citizenship, Involvement, Democracy Survey*. Washington, DC: Georgetown University Center for Democracy and Civil Society. Retrieved from http://www.icpsr.umich.edu /icpsrweb/ICPSR/studies/4607

Iyengar, S., Sood, G., & Lelkes, Y. (2012). Affect, not ideology: A social identity perspective on polarization. *Public Opinion Quarterly, 76*(3), 405–431.

Iyengar, S., & Westwood, S. J. (2015). Fear and loathing across party lines: New evidence on group polarization. *American Journal of Political Science, 59*(3), 690–707.

Jones, P. E. (2013). The effect of political competition on democratic accountability. *Political Behavior, 35*(3), 481–515.

Kondik, K. (2014). House 2016: Republicans start with a commanding edge. *Sabato's Crystal Ball* at the University of Virginia Center for Politics. Retrieved from http://www.centerforpolitics.org

Kramer, R. M. (2004). The "dark side" of social context: The role of intergroup paranoia in intergroup negotiations. In M. J. Gelfand & J. M. Brett (Eds.), *The handbook of negotiation and culture* (pp. 219–237). Stanford, CA: Stanford University Press.

Layman, G. C., Carsey, T. M., Green, J. C., Herrera, R., & Cooperman, R. (2010). Activists and conflict extension in American party politics. *American Political Science Review, 104*(2), 324–346.

Lee, F. (2009). *Beyond ideology: Politics, principles, and partisanship in the U.S. Senate*. Chicago, IL: University of Chicago Press.

Levendusky, M. S. (2013). Why do partisan media polarize viewers? *American Journal of Political Science, 57*(3), 611–623.

Mangum, M. (2013). The racial underpinnings of party identification and political ideology. *Social Science Quarterly, 94*(5), 1222–1244.

Mann, T. E., & Ornstein, N. J. (2013). *It's even worse than it looks: How the American constitutional system collided with the new politics of extremism*. Philadelphia, PA: Basic Books.

Maoz, I., Ward, A., Katz, M., & Ross, L. (2002). Reactive devaluation of an "Israeli" vs. "Palestinian" peace proposal. *Journal of Conflict Resolution, 46*(4), 515–546.

Marziani, M., & Liss, S. (2010). *Filibuster abuse*. Brennan Center for Justice at New York University School of Law. Retrieved from http://www.brennancenter .org

McCarty, N., Rodden, J., Shor, B., Tausanovitch, C. N., & Warshaw, C. (2014). *Geography, uncertainty, and polarization*. Retrieved from http://home.gwu .edu/~dwh/shor_workshop.pdf

McDonald, M. P. (2015). Presidential voter turnout rates, 2000–2014. *United States Elections Project.* Accessed February, 2015. Retrieved from http://www .electproject.org/home/voter-turnout/voter-turnout-data

McVeigh, R., Cunningham, D., & Farrell, J. (2014). Political polarization as a social movement outcome: 1960s Klan activism and its enduring impact on political realignment in Southern counties, 1960 to 2000. *American Sociological Review, 79*(6), 1144–1171.

McWhorter, D. (2004). Why Americans hate Democrats—A dialogue: Morality is the new "race." *Slate.com.* Retrieved from http://www.slate.com

Miller, K. P., Brewer, M. B., & Arbuckle, N. L. (2009). Social identity complexity: Its correlates and antecedents. *Group Processes and Intergroup Relations, 12*(1), 79–94.

Milligan, S. (2012). Why race is still an issue. *USNews.com.* Retrieved from http://www.usnews.com/opinion/blogs/susan-milligan/2012/10/26/john -sununu-barack-obama-and-why-race-is-still-an-issue

Nosek, B. A., Banaji, M. R., & Jost, J. T. (2009). The politics of intergroup attitudes. In J. T. Jost, A. C. Kay, & H. Thorisdottir (Eds.), *The social and psychological bases of ideology and system justification* (pp. 480–506). Oxford, UK: Oxford University Press.

Oakford, P. (2015). The changing face of America's electorate: Political implications of demographic shifts. *Center for American Progress.* Retrieved from https://www.americanprogress.org/issues/immigration/report/2015/01 /06/101605/the-changing-face-of-americas-electorate

Pinkleton, B. E., Austin, E. W., & Fortman, K. K. (1998). Relationships of media use and political disaffection to political efficacy and voting behavior. *Journal of Broadcasting and Electronic Media, 42*(1), 34–49.

Poole, K. T. (2008). The roots of the polarization of modern U.S. politics. *Revista deficiencia política,* 1–53. Retrieved from http://www.cerium.ca/IMG/pdf /2012_07_10_SEANCE_1-2.pdf

Rainie, L., & Smith, A. (2012). Politics on social networking sites. *Pew Research Center's Internet and American Life Project.* Retrieved from http://www .pewinternet.org/2012/09/04/politics-on-social-networking-sites

Saad, L. (2010). Four moral issues sharply divide Americans. *Gallup.com.* Retrieved from http://www.gallup.com

Saad, L. (2013). In U.S., 52% back law to legalize gay marriage in 50 states. *Gallup.com.* Retrieved from http://www.gallup.com

Sandel, M. J. (1998). *Liberalism and the limits of justice.* Cambridge, MA: Cambridge University Press.

Shook, N. J., & Clay, R. (2011). Valence asymmetry in attitude formation: A correlate of political ideology. *Social Psychological and Personality Science, 2*(6), 650–655. doi: 10.1177/1948550611405219

Snowe, O. (2012, March 1). Olympia Snowe: Why I'm leaving the Senate. *The Washington Post.* Retrieved from https://www.washingtonpost.com

Steinel, W., De Dreu, C. K., Ouwehand, E., & Ramírez-Marín, J. Y. (2009). When constituencies speak in multiple tongues: The relative persuasiveness of hawkish minorities in representative negotiation. *Organizational Behavior and Human Decision Processes, 109*(1), 67–78.

Stroud, N. J. (2010). Polarization and partisan selective exposure. *Journal of Communication, 60*(3), 556–576.

Tetlock, P. E. (2003). Thinking the unthinkable: Sacred values and taboo cognitions. *Trends in Cognitive Sciences, 7*(7), 320–324.

Thompson, L., & Hastie, R. (1990). Social perception in negotiation. *Organizational Behavior and Human Decision Processes 47*(1), 98–123.

Thompson, L., Peterson, E., & Brodt, S. E. (1996). Team negotiation: An examination of integrative and distributive bargaining. *Journal of Personality and Social Psychology, 70*(1), 66–78.

Tritt, S. M. (2009). Stereotyping and society: A barrier to achieving social equality. *Opticon1826* (6), 1–11. Retrieved from http://www.ucl.ac.uk

Van Kleef, G. A., Steinel, W., Knippenberg, D., Hogg, M. A., & Svensson, A. (2007). Group member prototypicality and intergroup negotiation: How one's standing in the group affects negotiation behaviour. *British Journal of Social Psychology, 46*(1), 129–152.

Walter, B. F. (2013). Civil wars, conflict resolution, and bargaining theory. In W. Carlsnaes, T. Risse, & B. A. Simmons (Eds.), *Handbook of international relations* (pp. 656–672). London, UK: Sage Publications.

Warren, M. E., & Mansbridge, J. (2013). Deliberative negotiation. In J. Mansbridge & C. J. Martin (Eds.), *Negotiating agreement in politics* (pp. 86–120). Washington, DC: American Political Science Association.

Williamson, V., Skocpol, T., & Coggin, J. (2011). The Tea Party and the remaking of Republican conservatism. *Perspectives on Politics, 9*(01), 25–43.

Willis, J., & DeNobrega, A. (2013, May 25). *The moral foundations of social cognition.* Poster presented at 25th Association for Psychological Science Convention, Washington, DC.

Xu, J., & Lee, J. C. (2013). The marginalized "model" minority: An empirical examination of the racial triangulation of Asian Americans. *Social Forces, 91*(4), 1363–1397.

CHAPTER FOUR

The Anger of Women Warriors

Kate Dahlstedt

One of the blessings of my life has been the opportunity to meet and sit with veterans, active duty troops, and their family members. I never would have imagined creating an organization to do such things when I was a young woman protesting the war in Vietnam back in the 1960s. But, when the opportunity became apparent in 2006, I found myself passionate and excited.

My husband, Ed Tick, had just published the book, *War and the Soul*, which, based on our work with veterans, is a groundbreaking look at the true impact of the military on one's heart and soul. Both psychotherapists in private practice, we were flooded with email and phone calls for help from veterans of all wars, people serving in Afghanistan and Iraq as well as stateside, parents, spouses, siblings, adult children, and other loved ones. It was then that we founded our non-profit organization, Soldier's Heart, the name used during the Civil War for what is now called post-traumatic stress disorder (PTSD).

Our first war healing retreat in 2007 included mostly veterans from the Vietnam War, and only a few from our recent wars in Iraq and Afghanistan. There were also a few wives who came with their husbands and some interested community members. But there were no female veterans. I was curious about why, but had little ability to be in contact with them. It wasn't until a few years later, when they began trickling into our war healing retreats and sharing their experiences, that I understood their disillusionment, mistrust and anger. I determined, then, to create my Women and War project.

Having specialized in college in the study of female psychology, I naturally focused on servicewomen as well as female family members, who seem to carry the brunt of the post-military care of loved ones. Not surprisingly, it is often military family members and loved ones who first reach out for help. Thus, I began offering specialized retreats for female family members.

Despite having studied the issues military family members face, I was walking in uncharted territory. There are no models or templates for the healing process for family members of those who are serving or have served in the military. This makes the process especially difficult, as there are many stages families must go through when one of its members joins the military. Each stage (enlistment/draft, boot camp, advanced training, deployment—before, during—and return home/reintegration) brings forth a variety of issues that are often handled differently by each family member. There are also a myriad of circumstances that can influence how family members feel and react.

Many military family organizations tend to "do" things to support the troops, such as sending care packages and meeting returning troops at the airport. Rarely, if ever, do they discuss their personal fears, concerns, or anguish with one another. I began to focus on the person of the caregiver. What is it like in their hearts, what hurts the most, what was most angering, what has helped the most? I started a weekly teleconference support group for female family members from around the country and eventually started to run weekend retreats for them as well. What I found was that wives, mothers, girlfriends, daughters, and sisters were most profoundly helped by sharing their stories with one another and providing each other heartfelt support for self-care.

Shortly after my first military family members retreat, female troops and veterans began coming to our war healing retreats more frequently. After spending personal time with each of them, I had enough rudimentary understanding of the complex nature of being a woman in the military to decide to conduct separate retreats for military women and veterans. Again, I knew I was on uncharted ground. Although we have records of how cultures around the world and throughout time have brought their male warriors home and helped them reintegrate, there are few examples that refer to the unique needs of women.

Again, I found that having the chance to talk with a room full of interested women with similar experiences and concerns has been a major step for the women at my women veteran healing retreats. Because of the competition among military women in the field, they do not usually bond with each other the way male troops create "a brotherhood." Any sign of weakness would likely be detrimental to one's career. Consequently, the natural feminine urge to bond and be social and supportive is undermined. After military service, many women isolate and do not have ongoing relationships with former comrades. By coming together in the unthreatening atmosphere of a retreat with other women, they can open up in new ways.

I am extremely grateful for the events that have made it possible for me to meet and know the veterans and their family members and be privy to their stories. I have a particularly soft spot for the wonderful women, some of whom are in these pages, who have taught me so very much about the military, about being female, about speaking the truth, and ultimately about grace. In the following pages I will share a few of their stories to illustrate some of what I have learned. To preserve confidentiality, all names have been changed and some of the ancillary facts have been altered. However, I have consciously kept the integrity of the illustrations intact.

Women Warriors

During the Revolutionary War, a woman named Mary Ludwig Hays joined her husband on the battlefield to provide food and water to the troops. During the battle of Monmouth, New Jersey, Mary was given the nickname of Molly Pitcher for the endless buckets of water she carried. When her husband then fell to exhaustion from his cannon post, Mary put down her bucket and took his place at the cannon, where she remained the rest of the day until the battle was over. The name Molly Pitcher quickly became the term given to all of the women who, like Mary Hays, provided food, water, medical care, and solace to the Continental army.

Women have always participated in war, as family members tending from the sidelines, or taking up arms as Mary Ludwig Hays did, and yet it is only very recently that they have done so officially as members of the armed forces. In 1942, the Women's Army Auxiliary Corps (WAAC) was established as the women's branch of the U.S. Army, but it was still considered auxiliary. The Women Accepted for Voluntary Emergency Service (WAVES), also established in 1942, was a division of the U.S. Naval Reserve. Both provided a variety of supportive duties in roles such as secretaries, switchboard operators, mechanics, cooks, and drivers. However, it wasn't until 1948 that women became a permanent part of the military and, by 1950, they represented only 2% of the military population.

Today, women in all branches of the military comprise about 15% of the total female armed forces population in the United States. Out of high heels, nurses' caps, and secretarial pools, they are now on the ground, in combat boots, and trained to kill with their bare hands. They serve in war zones side by side with male troops where there is no clearly delineated "front line." Improvised explosive devices (IEDs) are everywhere and mortar attacks take place regularly on military bases. All of our troops are at risk. The Department of Defense claims that two-thirds of today's military women are exposed to combat. And yet, despite these realities, women were not officially allowed by government policy to be in military combat units until 2016.

On the home front, women veterans are four times as likely to be homeless as their civilian peers. Their suicide rates are higher than their male counterparts, as are their rates of depression, substance abuse, chronic health problems, post-traumatic stress disorder (PTSD) and military sexual trauma (MST). And their sense of betrayal cannot be overstated (Boyd, Bradshaw, & Robinson, 2013).

Donna is a tall, slightly overweight woman who served in Iraq during the Gulf War. As part of the engineer corps, she and another woman were assigned to a job a few miles from her base. They each set out in construction vehicles to the vast emptiness of the hot desert.

Once they were at their coordinates, they began working, each operating a different machine. Donna glanced at her companion's bulldozer and suddenly saw an Iraqi man who had "appeared out of nowhere" heading toward it with a machine gun. She saw him leap up on the bulldozer, about to kill her comrade. Out of instinct, Donna grabbed her own gun and shot the man dead.

Shocked and in horror of what she had just done, Donna could barely speak. She and the other soldier held each other in stunned silence. Aside from the pain of taking another life, Donna knew that, as a woman, she was not allowed by military regulations to fire her weapon without an order to do so. She could be court-martialed even for saving the life of a fellow soldier. Both women knew what it would mean if they told command what had happened. After much consideration, they decided that the only option was for them to bury the Iraqi man and tell no one.

The pain of that moment has stayed with Donna ever since. She agonized for many years about who the man was and who he may have left behind. She knew that his family would never know what happened to him or where he was buried. Maybe he had a wife and children who suffered because of his death. Maybe they had hopes and dreams as a family that would never be realized.

Donna also agonized because military regulations had prevented her from acknowledging her part in his death. If she had been allowed to fire her weapon, as her male counterparts were, she would not have had to bury him. At least his friends and family would have a corpse to bury in their own religious tradition. She may have even been awarded a medal. But the double standard of the military at that time caused her to violate her own heart. Although she has come to peace with herself for her actions, she is still angry that the military put her and her partner in such danger without legal means to protect themselves. Her sense of being disposable, marginal, and unworthy in the eyes of the military has never left her. Neither has her outrage.

The 2008 documentary, *Lioness*, which traces some of the first American women to be sent into direct ground combat, is a moving portrayal of the deep divide between military policy and practice. Faced with the potential for Islamic women to be combatants, the military needs our female troops to do the "pat down" to detect weapons. They must accompany male troops in house-to-house searches, which often result in fierce firefights (McLagan & Sommers, 2006).

The women in the film went on several such raids. Yet none of them were eligible for awards or promotions or combat pay for their actions. One of the missions, in which they were instrumental in the successful outcome, was reported on national television, but they were not even mentioned. Such invisibility under such horrendous conditions is demoralizing at best. Most of the women in the film seem resigned to their plight, but the anger and betrayal they feel is palpable (McLagan & Sommers, 2006).

In my work with female veterans I have heard other stories about not being believed when they tell civilians about the combat experiences they have had. Because of military regulations excluding women from combat, many people have a hard time accepting that, in practice, the current policies are not upheld. Whether this is attributed to a reluctance to believe that women can be effective fighters or to the wish that they are not put in danger is hard to say. In any event, the truth is denied and the women who have served in combat are often alone in their suffering.

Feeling alone is common for female veterans in today's military. Unlike the WAVESs and the WAACs, who lived and worked together, military women today serve on bases where they may be one of a handful of women with several thousand male troops. Often, on large bases, they are separated from each other and rarely come in contact. One would think they would seek each other out for support and camaraderie. But there is another factor at play that keeps them apart.

Servicewomen and female veterans tell me repeatedly that to be successful in the military, they have to work twice as hard as their male counterparts. They are generally more likely to be overlooked for promotions and special awards. Although these are issues that are prevalent in the civilian workplace as well, the rigors and dangers of the war zone make them ever more distressing. The desire to fit in, to be accepted as a full member of the team, creates an extremely competitive environment for women.

Instead of bonding, as often happens in the civilian workplace, servicewomen often become competitive with one another. In the military, women have to put aside their more feminine instincts—compassion, relationship, emotional vulnerability. They need to adapt to the "man's world" they have entered. Their success is measured by how well they can conform to the masculine norms around them. Being "one of the guys" becomes all-important and being "the girl" is anathema. Seeking out other women for support or friendship could undermine their efforts.

Trust is also a huge issue for women in the military. Telling a female confidant about vulnerable feelings may not be wise if she is competing for the same promotion or task. Any sign of vulnerability or "weakness" is shunned. Betrayal of confidences is not at all uncommon in such an environment, especially for those in the underdog position that many women in the military face.

To further complicate a woman's identity, their male compatriots often refer to them only as whores, dykes, or bitches. I have heard this complaint from several of the women I have worked with over the years, especially those who have served in Iraq and Afghanistan. Apparently, if you agree to a sexual encounter, that makes you a whore and if you refuse, that makes you a dyke or a bitch. The catch-22 here is that you can never be seen for who you are. Your identity is defined solely by your sexual behavior, and for no other reason than that you are a woman. Your ability as a soldier and as a person is not a consideration as it is with male troops.

Male veterans commonly talk about the importance of the brotherhood that forms between troops who are facing challenges together. This kind of brotherhood is so strong that troops will give their lives for one another. It has been written about since Homer's time (see Shay, 2002; Tick, 2014). Many veterans state that the brotherhood among troops, which is often stronger than family ties, is what kept them going in the hardest times. Knowing that someone has your back at all times is a crucial reassurance that those on the battlefield rely on. And pledging the same to another is experienced as a sacred oath.

Many servicewomen do not have that kind of bond with those with whom they are working with side-by-side in life-and-death situations. The lack of such bonding leaves them much more emotionally vulnerable than their male peers. It cannot be overstated that the lack of trusted comrades in the war zone leaves troops, male or female, psychologically isolated, putting them at greater risk for breakdown. Feeling marginalized as well, women troops also sometimes fear for their own lives.

Allie was an officer in the infantry in Kandahar, Afghanistan. Because of her proven leadership skills, she was made team leader. Out on a mission, she gave an order to one of the men under her. In an act of insubordination, he refused. With no time to waste because of the danger involved, Allie did the task herself, asking only to be "covered" in the event that she was fired upon. It turned out to be a treacherous undertaking. When she returned, she discovered that her team member had fallen asleep, and would not have been able to help her had she taken fire.

That incident left Allie feeling totally alone, with no one in her platoon to watch her back. It reinforced her sense of being "disposable" in the minds of her fellow troops, for no other reason than that she was a woman. She reports being on guard at all times for fear of her fellow troops.

Despite such feelings, Allie held on to the knowledge that she was a very good soldier. She did her job as ordered and did it well. She knew she could have been a good Ranger, but women were not allowed to be Rangers. When she received a promotion, others accused her of having "slept with the right people." Although she was angry for some time, she states that she eventually became desensitized to such slights.

Already suffering from the toll of the war zone, with no showers for days on end, often not able to eat for days at a time, extreme heat and humidity, constant vigilance, being responsible for the lives of others, going out on dangerous missions, using her weapon when needed, Allie was also raped by one of her officers. Afraid that her commander would dismiss her claims, and possibly blame, demote, or transfer her, she chose not to report it.

When she returned home and shared her combat experiences with others, she was shocked to find that she was not believed. Although she suffers from PTSD, MST, and traumatic brain injury (TBI), she is not seen by others as having a disability. When she goes to the Veterans Administration (VA) for medical services, she is assumed to be the wife of a veteran, not a veteran in her own right. She had risked her own life and had saved the lives of other troops, but her own community does not acknowledge her role.

When Allie was serving, she felt she had a purpose. She knew she was good at what she did and felt proud and important, even if unrecognized. Once home, she no longer felt that confidence. She tried college, but found that her TBI prevented her from keeping up with the work, and the college offered no accommodation for that. Feeling betrayed by the military and by her community, she has difficulty trusting anyone. The anger she felt in the military is still with her and she finds it harder to "just deal." She states that her most rewarding relationship now is with her dog.

Allie's experiences in the military are not uncommon. She experienced what many other women have shared with me as well. Sarah, a tall, attractive woman, served on the Korean border between north and south in the late 1970s. She was young and alone, but confident and prepared. She was an obedient soldier who looked forward to using her military benefits to go to college when she was discharged.

One evening, after her watch duty, Sarah's team leader invited her for a drink. Being young and relatively innocent, she had little experience with alcohol. However, she was flattered and wanted to get to know him better. Later in the evening when he began making sexual advances, Sarah told him that she was a virgin and asked him to stop. However, he continued to insist, and eventually he overpowered her.

Shaken and disoriented, Sarah didn't sleep for the rest of the night. She didn't know where to turn or who to go to in order to report the incident. When she finally worked up the courage to tell her commanding officer, she was told to "suck it up."

Later that day, there was a skirmish. Sarah's team leader, who was also her rapist, ordered her to a dangerous spot below their position. Although she had a weapon, because she was a woman she was not allowed by military regulations to have any ammunition. Her team leader knew this but ordered her anyway. Alone in a very dangerous situation and with no useable weapon to defend herself, Sarah felt as if she were being sent to her own execution. She managed to take some protection lying flat behind a few rocks long enough for the shooting to stop.

That incident was formative for Sarah. She felt totally helpless to prevent her own death. She believed that if she continued to pursue justice for being raped, she would likely be "accidentally" killed. She got a clear message, as Allie did, that no one there had her back. She was alone and the enemy was everywhere! Her rage was so intense that she was afraid she would do or say something that would get her in trouble. She responded by clamming up and going inward, avoiding eye contact and only speaking when spoken to.

When Sarah was discharged, she began drinking heavily as a way of trying to control her anger. She managed to hold down a few menial jobs, but college proved too much for her. Like Allie, she too felt invisible to her community. No one believed that she had been in combat, especially in Korea. The VA had no special provisions for female veterans. Support groups there, as well as at the Vet's Center, were all-male, and she did not feel safe or comfortable sharing her story.

Sexual assault is a rampant problem in the military. Current statistics from the 2014 Department of Defense (DoD) Annual Report and the RAND Military Workplace Study indicate that there were 20,300 reported cases of sexual assault that year. Although slightly more than half of these were male victims, because women represent only 15% of the overall military, their rates are obviously statistically much higher.

Further, 76% of women who did report were assaulted at least twice, making the number of incidents much higher. Of those who did report, 62% faced retaliation and the majority of them faced reprisals from superiors and commanders. The report indicates that the vast majority of victims (86%) did not report the assaults, and it is easy to understand why. The report further states that 1 in 4 women (compared to 1 in 14 men) experienced persistent, severe sexual harassment or gender discrimination, much of which lasted several months (Rand Report, 2014).

The very informative documentary film, *The Invisible War,* gives a vivid picture of what military women who are sexually assaulted are up against (Ziering, Barklow, & Kirby, 2012). Unlike the civilian world, the military has its own "military justice" system. Consequently, any infractions have to go "up the chain of command." However, commanders are reluctant to report cases of sexual assault to those higher up, because it reflects badly on their unit and, consequently, on them. If the perpetrator happens to be the commander, which is not uncommon, reporting is not even an option. It is most common for commanders to dismiss reports of sexual misconduct, or worse, to blame victims and tell them to "suck it up," as in Sarah's case.

To "suck it up" means to go back to your work and act like it didn't happen, to go out on missions as a "team" alongside the perpetrator, to possibly have to follow the perpetrator's orders, and to possibly ride in the same vehicle, eat meals, and sleep next door to the perpetrator. Under such conditions, how could anyone ever feel safe? How could anyone feel protected by fellow troops? How could anyone not feel terrified and betrayed?

As is documented in *The Invisible War,* it is also common for women who report sexual assault to be transferred to a different unit, where they don't know their peers and have to start a new job and new relationships after such a traumatic event. Or they are referred to Military Behavior Health, where they receive a mental health diagnosis, which can sometimes lead to being discharged with no benefits (Ziering, Barklow, & Kirby, 2012).

In one of the worst cases of apparent assault, 19-year-old LaVena Johnson was found dead on her base. Her face had been battered, her genitals doused with acid, and she had been shot in the head and burned. The army labeled it a suicide (Democracy Now, 2008).

Women veterans who survive military sexual assault often take years or a lifetime to recover. They often feel depressed, anxious, and ashamed. They find it difficult to trust anyone when they return home. They can have nightmares and flashbacks and often feel helpless and numb. It is not unusual for them to develop chronic medical problems and eating disorders as a result.

Once home, when friends and family don't believe their stories, when they are not recognized as veterans by the VA, when they have no military comrades to turn to, many women deal with their anger and despair by turning to drugs and alcohol, which, in turn, can unravel their lives. Or, worse, they turn to suicide. They report feeling isolated, mistrustful, despairing, and alone. And they feel betrayed by the military, betrayed by their comrades, and betrayed by the country that they served.

My retreats for women troops and veterans always include community witnesses. Interested and compassionate women represent the larger community as they embrace the lives and experiences of our military women. In the circle of women, half of whom are veterans or currently serving in the military, and the other half of whom are civilians, the discussion quickly gets personal. The issues of discrimination for being women, the cultural assumptions about who we are and what we are capable of, and the expectations of how we should behave, come pouring out. So does our outrage. But such feelings are compounded by the military environment with all of its constraints.

Civilian women gain an insight into the gruesome conditions in which our military sisters are often put. Although the issues may be the same, civilian women have many more options and protections. Employers must conform to labor laws. Corporations are sued for equal pay. Sexual harassment and assault are taken seriously, treated as a crime, and legal assistance is available. Civilian women usually have the freedom to get away from a perpetrator, to get to safety. But military women are trapped and have no recourse. For many, our retreat is the first place they feel safe enough to share their stories and their rage.

Civilian women are frequently moved to tears upon hearing these stories. We join our military sisters by grieving and lamenting with them for ourselves and for the human race. Together we all find what is common between us, the landscape in which all women live. That is when the healing begins, a bridge is built, a hand is extended . . . in both directions.

Women Family Members

"When my brother enlisted, I didn't know I was enlisting too." Jean is the 32-year-old sister of an active duty soldier who has been serving for 15 years. She has been one of his chief supporters. Barely making ends meet as a restaurant manager and living and caring for her mother, she feels like she has given her entire adult life to the military. Preparing and sending weekly care packages, arranging and rearranging her schedule to attend deployment and homecoming events, emailing uplifting notes and waiting patiently for a word or two in response, checking out social network sites to find out what is happening in his unit and worrying, all the while being there for her mother who does the same, Jean is tired of war.

Having grown up in a liberal community, Jean shunned the concept of war. However, after her brother's stormy adolescent years, she was happy for him when he enlisted in the military. She hoped it would calm him down and help him mature. She never imagined that he would be sent on numerous deployments and very dangerous missions. She had no idea how it would impact her life. Believing that the wars in Iraq and Afghanistan were unnecessary and not justified, Jean is also angry that her brother (and she herself) had to sacrifice so much for what she called "no good reason."

Dora, a single mother, has survived her son's five deployments serving in the Middle East. Although she is very proud of her son's accomplishments, as a peace advocate like Jean, it has been difficult for her to reconcile her son's involvement in the military. This is a complication that many family members face. They want to support their loved one and yet they are not supportive of what he or she must do as a member of the armed services.

Many, if not most of their friends are also peace advocates and therefore unable to give the kind of non-judgmental, empathetic support they need. Military family members who do not support war cannot justify the sacrifices they and their loved ones have to make. They do not have the comfort others may have of believing that their loved one is serving a noble and honorable cause. In fact, just the opposite is the case. They feel betrayed by a government that seems to not care about them or their loved ones, that uses and abuses their troops for questionable ends.

Always concerned about her son's safety, Dora is very careful about placing any requests on his time and focus when he is stateside. She knows he needs to train and stay sharp to prepare for the next deployment. She doesn't want to burden him with family obligations or concerns. Whenever she has the occasional visit with him, she takes her cues about what they do, and when, from him and his needs. She does not feel resentful, but rather offers this kind of support as her motherly responsibility to protect her son.

Dora knows the stress of preparation for deployment very well. Her son becomes super-focused on his training and withdraws emotionally even more than usual. She knows this means he has to stay sharp and focused on his work. Like most troops, he does not want to risk "softening" emotionally, concerned that would be distracting. His primary focus has to be on the next mission. His life and those of his comrades might depend on it. Not knowing for months exactly when he will be leaving, Dora is always on high alert herself. At least when he is on home soil, she knows he is safe. Anticipating another deployment has at times been torture. Then there are the unexpected delays in departure dates, requiring that she change airline and hotel arrangements so that she could be at his new departure point, as well as cancel and rearrange other plans.

At one such juncture, her son yet again packed up, moved out of his apartment and put all of his things in storage. However, the deployment was then postponed. Because he was not yet divorced from a woman who lived several states away, he was not eligible, by military regulation, to live on the base. With nowhere to go and unable to afford to continue to live in a hotel, he began living out of his car. Dora and her daughter (who were also several states away) were outraged at the military's ridiculous regulations. They couldn't bear to let him do that and ran up their credit cards to give him a bed to sleep in and a place to cook a meal.

Eventually Dora realized that she was going to her son's deployment ceremonies more for herself than for her son. The ceremony is usually boring and overly patriotic for her tastes and beliefs. Her son, who also does not enjoy such events, is just one of a very large crowd and doesn't have much time to be with her. Any personal time they might have is stilted because of his emotional distance and her fear of distracting him with her emotional needs. But it affords her one more time, one "last time," before he departs. She knows it may really be the last time she sees him, and it rips her heart open each time. For military family members, each email message, text, letter, Facebook post, or occasional phone call "could be the last." Each time, family members have to once again experience letting go of their loved one who is in harm's way and may not return home.

Stories like Dora's are all around us. Our government sends people off to foreign soil to fight an even more foreign "enemy." To most of us, war is another world, although we have movies and literature that help us comprehend, as well as stories from veterans themselves. We have some idea of the sounds and sights and terror of the battlefield and the boredom and loneliness of camp life.

However, the families and loved ones who our troops leave behind are with us here, on our own soil. They are the cashier at the grocery store, the hygienist at the dentist's office, the college student across the street, the mechanic, the accountant. They are making sacrifices every day right next to us, and yet we have no idea what their lives are like. They are invisible to us, and they know it.

Cassandra's son also served a tour in Iraq. When he was discharged, he went home and settled right down. He got a good job that he seemed to enjoy and saved enough to buy his own house. As a counselor, Cassandra was aware of the emotional problems troops can come home with. She had been on the lookout for them and was very relieved. However, a few years after his discharge, her son began to break down physically as well as mentally.

Cassandra stepped in to find help for him, but his condition continued to deteriorate. He became isolated and could barely get out of bed. He lost his job and his house. Unable to even drive himself to his doctor's appointments, he moved in with Cassandra and her husband. What she thought was a serious depression turned out to be much more. He began having several different bizarre physical symptoms. After 12 years of medical appointments, tests and retests all over the country, fighting for his military records, fighting for VA medical assistance and benefits, Cassandra is exhausted. As his only caretaker, she has files that stack up over two feet. Eventually it was determined that most of his medical problems are linked to his service in Iraq and exposure to toxic materials.

Cassandra is filled with grief for her son and the life that has unfolded for him. Proud that he selflessly wanted to serve his country, she is enraged that neither she nor her son were told that he was risking a life of endless medical problems if he deployed. "There was no informed consent," she laments. She has since discovered that a significant number of veterans face such medical problems. As with the defoliant Agent Orange, which, according to the National Vietnam Veterans Foundation has contributed to the deaths of two-thirds of our veterans who served in the war in Vietnam, her son is facing an early death. She, like many of us, assumed that the military would, of course, protect him. She calls it "criminal" that they didn't.

Valerie is a physician at a VA hospital and the mother of a young man who has recently returned from a tour of duty in Afghanistan. While her son, who was an excellent soldier, was deployed, he sustained a foot injury during a routine exercise. Although he reported it to his commander and asked for permission to seek medical assistance, he was told to "stop whining and tough it out." When the injury did not heal and he could barely walk, he again asked his commander for permission to obtain medical attention and was again admonished for being a wimp for displaying behavior unbecoming a soldier and was accused of being a slouch just attempting to get out of his duties. Finally, when a dangerous infection developed, he was cared for. Valerie was furious.

Not only had the military refused her son necessary treatment, but they also put his life and the lives of his comrades in danger. Had he been unable to perform well because of his injury, others could be at risk. As a mother, Valerie was naturally concerned about his health and angry that he had such difficulty getting the attention he needed. As a physician, she was appalled that commanders in charge of soldiers' welfare would be so inept and unconcerned about the physical health and wellbeing of their troops.

Valerie's situation is unique in that she also works for the VA. She sees veterans all day long and laments the great inefficiencies and frustrations present in the system, for patients and caregivers alike, that lead to veterans experiencing difficulty in gaining timely access to care and caregivers experiencing great stumbling blocks in being able to provide the high quality care they wish to give veterans. She describes the hospital conditions as chaotic and inefficient. She states that although the clinical staff people are hardworking, talented, and devoted professionals, the overall working conditions are very frustrating. Deficient ancillary support in clinics often impedes the type of effective, efficient, and comprehensive care of veterans that they justly deserve. Because of her experiences, both at the VA and with her son's injury, Valerie has seen a side of the military that she regards as inhumane and disrespectful of the soldiers, veterans, their families, and their health care professionals. As a concerned citizen and taxpayer, she is outraged at our nation's policy makers for their treatment of our troops and veterans. First they ask them to do unthinkable things at great personal sacrifice to themselves and their families, and then they don't take proper care of them when they are emotionally or physically broken.

Valerie, like so many family members, also had difficulty with the loss of control to the military. Just as our troops soon learn that "the military owns me," family members must quickly adapt as well. Johnnie and Jane are at the mercy of the military, and so are their families.

As any typical mother of a soldier whose son is in a war zone, Valerie worried about what her son was being asked to do and how safe he was. However, because he had gotten married just before deploying, it was his new wife who was kept informed about news of their soldier and his unit by the family readiness support group. Valerie and her family felt completely left out of any and all news about their loved one. Her new daughter-in-law was not friendly and did not share information with her. Valerie was reluctant to put pressure on her son and upset him in any way while he was deployed and always in imminent danger. And she didn't want to appear to be a "whining mother" to the military command. Valerie and her family were left to worry in silence during his lengthy deployment, only to gain news about her son and his unit on the rare occasions he was able to e-mail or phone them.

From the time her son left the country, Valerie felt like a *persona non grata* to the military. Parents, those who lovingly and carefully raise our children and make great sacrifices for them, are expected to just turn them over to the military and walk away. Like the old adage says, "If the military wanted you to have a family, they would have issued you one." For Valerie and her family, that was a very difficult pill to swallow.

Most of the family members I have worked with express this same loss of control to the military. This is true whether or not they lived on a base. However, military bases do provide many more supports for families and, of course, families have each other. But in the post-9/11 wars, most of our troops do not live on bases. This means that families are often totally alone with their experiences. They complain that their friends are focused on other things and have little tolerance for listening to them or giving real emotional support. And family members often have difficulty talking about the trivialities of life with others when they have a loved one serving in a war zone. This sometimes gets so frustrating that family members give up and stop socializing, which furthers their isolation.

When they reach out to family member groups, many women have shared that they find the encounters superficial and more focused on supporting the troops than on supporting themselves and each other. They feel conflict behind the faulty but common refrain that "if you don't support the war, you are not supporting our troops." Dora and many others know this is not the case. She feels caught between those who think she should support the war because her son is serving and those who considerate it hypocritical to have a son serving while advocating peace. There is no place for her and others like her.

Denise was a short perky young woman who, in the late 1970s, fell in love with a local boy in her community. This boy enlisted in the Marines and was eventually sent to Vietnam as a helicopter machine gunner. When his helicopter was shot down he was lucky to have survived. However, his best friend, his "battle buddy" riding next to him, was not. Believing he had caused the crash tortured him. From the time he recuperated and returned home he began devoting himself to atoning for his actions in the field. Helping other veterans became his life's mission, so much so that he was rarely available for Denise and their children.

Although Denise knew that her husband was doing good, important work with other veterans, she felt jealous of his devotion to them. His sense of the "brotherhood" seemed to be impenetrable. His experience had been so horrendous and formative, it seemed like he was permanently "stuck" in the rice paddies with his comrades. He was not the same man Denise had fallen in love with. Needless to say, there were many conflicts over the years about his loyalties. Denise, whose anger and disappointment were always just under the surface, almost left him on several occasions. But, as a Vietnam veteran who had been exposed to Agent Orange, he was the one who ended up leaving her by an early death.

The health and medical problems our veterans have to contend with are astronomical. Even when they are not physically wounded, the toll that living and fighting in the war zone takes on them, their bodies, souls, and psyches, often last a lifetime. Family members inevitably become the primary caretakers for them, and yet the rest of us are usually oblivious.

In a time when endless war seems to be the future, it is more important than ever that we, as a nation, pay attention and listen to those who serve in the military and to their families. Their stories alone are enough for a nation to no longer consider war an option.

References

Boyd, M. A., Bradshaw, W., & Robinson, M. (2013). Mental health issues of women deployed to Iraq and Afghanistan. *Archives of Psychiatric Nursing, 27*, 10–22. Retrieved from http://www.psychiatricnursing.org/article/S0883-9417(12)00149-5/abstract

Democracy Now. (2008, July 23). Suicide or murder? Three years after the death of Pfc. LaVena Johnson in Iraq, her parents continue their call for a congressional investigation. *Democracy Now!*. Retrieved from http://www.democracynow.org

McLagan, M., & Sommers, D. (Producers); McLagan, M., & Sommers, D. (Directors). (2006). *Lioness* [Motion picture]. United States of America: Room 11 Productions.

Rand Report. (2014). Sexual assault and sexual harassment in the U.S. military: Top-line estimates for active-duty service members from the 2014 RAND Military Workplace Study. *Rand Corporation*. Retrieved from http://www.rand.org

Shay, J. (2002). *Odysseus in America: Combat trauma and the trials of homecoming*. New York, NY: Scribner.

Tick, E. (2014). *Warrior's return: Restoring the soul after war*. Boulder, CO: Sounds True.

Ziering, A., Barklow, T. (Producers), & Kirby, D. (Director). (2012). *Invisible war* [Motion picture]. United States of America: Cinedigm/Docurama Films.

CHAPTER FIVE

Warrior Rage: The Many Dimensions of Anger in Our Military and Veterans

Kate Dahlstedt and Edward Tick

"Anger be now your song, immortal one. . . ." So begins Homer's *Iliad*, the classic story of the Trojan War (trans. 1974). The epic's very first word is *minin*, which in ancient Greek does not mean ordinary anger, but rage or wrath so severe and destructive that it seems beyond the mortal and to come from gods, demons, or spirits. Warriors in combat are "possessed" by it. Today they call it "the Beast" or "the mad moment." Almost three millennia ago Homer told us what such anger portends; it was "doomed and ruinous, that caused loss on bitter loss/ and crowded brave souls into the undergloom/ leaving so many dead men—carrion . . ." (trans. 1974, lines 1–5). Jonathan Shay (1994), who demonstrated the extreme degree of similarity between Homer's ancient warriors and our veterans of today, wrote that the proper name for the epic is *Rage*.

Women and men who have served in the military, who have experienced or been victimized by it, know this rage all too well.* Far beyond

* In the following pages, we will hear about several of the military troops and veterans whom the authors have come to know through their work running war healing retreats, veteran talking

the scope of everyday stress and irritation, it has many sources. It surfaces in the combat zone, especially in combat toward foes and over intolerable losses. It sometimes propels troops to fight for revenge and can be one source of atrocities toward others or violence toward oneself. And those who have felt it lose their anger gradient. In the combat zone, they learn to "go from zero to sixty" in a nanosecond or they may not survive. They learn to feel wrath rather than irritation, irksomeness, miffed, annoyed, disturbed, or all the other gentler gradations of the emotion of anger. Rage becomes their song and they carry it home from the war zone into everyday dealings with family and society. Without intervention and healing, rage may remain their primary song through life.

As rage-evoking as combat is, it is only one source of our troops' anger and, as survivors testify, not necessarily the most disturbing. The anger that our troops and veterans feel may go in various directions—why, how, where, against whom they fought; how they were trained; how they were treated upon homecoming; at the politicians who sent them; toward former foes with whom they are still not reconciled; at themselves for actions taken or not taken; toward our country, the Department of Veterans Affairs (VA) system, unknowing or uncaring citizens, and many other sources, up to the ultimate—anger at God and life itself.

Anger can poison. Anger unexpressed or unacknowledged can go underground and cause much psychological, interpersonal, physical, or social distress. Deep anger may be involved in the epidemic of suicides, currently over 22 a day, that our veterans are experiencing. And outbursts and explosions of anger are among the most difficult trauma symptoms to live with. Anger management is often a recommendation, but it is a limited response that may not be adequate to the enormity of emotion it is meant to control.

Anger Entering Service

Both men and women who serve in our military often carry much anger from pre-service experiences. Some earlier anger may be directly related to their reasons for serving. Bob enlisted in the Marines and volunteered for Viet Nam[1], not for any elevated political reasons, but over anger that his next-door neighbor had been killed there. Michael was an 18-year-old man in Connecticut when the World Trade Center was attacked. Angry at

---

circles, reconciliation journeys to Vietnam, personal counseling and workshops. With permission and to preserve confidentiality only their first names have been used. Any use of full names has been at their request.

this attack on his homeland and believing that a wide-scale terrorist attack was coming, he became the first person in his state to enlist.

Sometimes people like Bob enter the service solely motivated by anger and the hunger for vengeance. Often, people like Michael enter the service with goals of obtaining a position and performing duties that they can feel proud of, which earn them honor. However, once they enlist, the military can use them however they need to. Michael enlisted for the most patriotic reasons but after a deployment in Afghanistan came home physically and psychologically wounded, declaring that "war is sick and makes everyone who participates sick as well." Many troops and veterans are disappointed and angry because they are often assigned positions they did not want or were asked to give other service than they were interested or believed in. Thus, Rene volunteered to serve as a radio and telephone operator, believing and promised he would receive job training that would prepare him for a civilian career. But he was made a combat infantryman in the most dangerous and hostile conditions. His service caused lifelong disability and he remained baffled, frustrated, and angry his entire life that he did not become the technician he had intended to be and the military had lied to him and used him for its own ends.

Many recruits enter military service after earlier life experiences that had already drenched them in much anger. Without interventions or healing, they are likely to carry this anger into their service, and the military does not offer pre-service rehabilitation. A high percentage of the women joining the military today do so to escape dangerous or abusive households and relationships. Many people join to escape violent inner cities or depressed rural neighborhoods. For example, on one of our largest U.S. military bases, we overheard a conversation between two African American recruits straining to achieve their physical fitness requirements in the gym:

"Another fucking day of pain, sweat, boredom, and orders."

"True, brother, but remember where we come from. This beats the hell out of picking crops."

"Right. Weren't no other future at home."

"Yeah. We got food, clothes, work, and salary. So let's count our fucking blessings."

Finally, many young people enlist because there are few civilian jobs and because college is not otherwise affordable. All these groups carry anger from challenging and dangerous social conditions into military service. This anger can make it more difficult to train them, more difficult for them to conform to military demands and discipline, and more likely that they may act out old anger against their fellows, the rules, or in stressful situations, especially combat.

It is common for young men to want to prove themselves. Throughout millennia, military service has given them such a proving ground. In fact, it has been a primary male rite of passage throughout the ages. Today, when they enlist, young men might convince themselves that it is for noble purposes, as it may have been in past wars. However, once they are in the military, they discover that their high ideals cannot be achieved. Thus, Nick wanted his entire life to be in one of the great wars saving civilization, but after serving in our modern wars he came home in despair, saying, "All they gave me was that dirty, shitty little war of lies—Iraq."

Disadvantaged social groups entering our military already carry anger, frustration, confusion, and feelings of hopelessness and betrayal from previous life experiences. They may have histories of abuse and abandonment, trouble with authorities, and previous traumas. The military has a more difficult time effectively training them. Command officers report that much of military training has become basic socialization, education in civics, and remedial education for basic learning and life skills, all skills that should have been learned in childhood. The military finds it hard to inculcate a positive warrior identity into this challenged population. They are more primitive, do not receive adequate remedial upbringing, and are much more likely to act out anger and other dangerous emotions on foes or their comrades.

Sometimes family members are in disagreement about their loved one's enlistment. It might be difficult for them to be fully supportive when they think enlistment or the cause is a mistake or are anxious about deployment. Leave-taking for deployment is often complicated for family members. Sometimes it is easier for couples to separate if they are angry at each other. This can lead to a lot of remorse and regret afterward, and/or continued anger that may be harbored throughout the deployment, endangering the troop and festering in the family.

Anger in the Service

There are a great many triggers that might awaken old or new anger during service. Basic training is difficult, demanding, painful, and exhausting. Unfair and sometimes brutal drill instructors often use intense anger and other demeaning practices to train recruits. Their goal is to enrage their recruits but teach them to contain that rage and release it later against a foe. Thus, instructors purposely create angry warriors who are immature and frustrated at their inability to release pent-up rage and frustration. And let us not make the mistake of thinking that this rage is necessary for training good warriors. Greg, who served 23 years as a Green Beret and was in many battle zones of the modern world, states, "I'm satisfied that fighting and even killing from a sense of duty or protection carries much less baggage than using hatred of the enemy as a motivator. Military trainers lacking wisdom tried to instill hatred in our training." In contrast, other world cultural traditions that were rooted in spirituality and religion and also nurtured a warrior class taught compassion and humanity toward foes. "Pray for your enemies that all may be well with them," said Confucius. Jesus taught, "Do good to them that hate you." Both Asian and Christian cultures developed warrior traditions over the millennia with these values embedded in them. Think, for example, of St. Francis, who was a traumatized warrior before he became the spiritual master we honor. Or think of the Jesuit Order, founded by another wounded warrior, St. Ignatius of Loyola, and a handful of his fellow soldiers. And when we lead healing and reconciliation journeys to Viet Nam, as we have annually for the past 15 years, we find that there is no post-traumatic stress disorder (PTSD) there (see Tick, 2014, pp. 132–139). Further, Vietnamese veterans retain and express deep compassion and respect for their American counterparts and do not retain the anger over decades that characterize so many Americans. These post-war accomplishments can be attributed in large part to the spiritual values permeating the culture. We see that many warrior traditions create deadly effective warriors without teaching them to hate or awakening this primitive rage and frustration. We also see that much spiritual wisdom bequeathed to humanity can emerge in the aftermath of war's suffering.

We cannot overstate the degree to which our troops are demoralized by poor command. They are willing to give their lives for a worthy and honorable mission. However, all too often they find themselves placed in situations where they are required to do things that they know are morally questionable, if not reprehensible. These can range from participating in black market activities to knowingly taking the lives of innocent people. Anger at these conditions often leads to illegitimate violence, such as the fragging of officers or atrocities against the foe or civilians. Greg remarks, "I remember being mad at the way the Vietnam War was mismanaged and under-resourced by politicians, leading to so many needless deaths." And Forrest, who served for over 30 years in the Air Force said, "Even if the war is wrong, you can't tie the hands of troops but must let them fight. Otherwise, not only are you sure to lose but sure to contribute to killing our own people. Many of us who served harbor anger that we were given both wrong wars and wrong management of them."

Former Army Ranger and combat survivor Glen Miller explains it this way: "I have been aggressive and angry when I feel that anyone—myself or others—are being exploited by those in authority. This anger is an appropriate reaction to authority from my point of view. I was not impressed with my officers' courage or judgment when I served and it was worse in corporate America."

Many women troops do not end up in combat zones. However, as women they often face discrimination so severe that it sometimes puts their lives in danger. Military sexual assault is a different kind of battlefield. Over 50% of military women report some kind of sexual assault or harassment, oftentimes repeatedly. This makes it difficult for them to do their jobs and often erodes their confidence in their will.[2] Male troops are also often sexual abuse victims as well, with as many as one third of men serving reporting some form of abuse. Several members of his squad sodomized one young Marine we worked with because they accused him of being too effeminate. He felt anger at the Corps and the individual Marines who, he rightly declared, were supposed to treat him as brothers.

Troops can feel angry at other forms of oppression and persecution in the military as well. Murray Tick was a military policeman at the end of World War II. Seventy years after service he recalls two sources of deep wounding that are still with him. First, though the military is supposed to be a melting pot, he recalls with pain the anti-Semitic abuse he received from some fellow soldiers.[3] Second, stationed stateside just after the war, his unit was mobilized against the Kentucky coal miners in their 1940s strikes against the "bosses" and abuses of the mining corporations. He laments so many decades later, "How could our own government order us to turn our bayonets against our own working people only struggling for a living wage and decent treatment for their families?" These are but a few examples of hurt and anger our troops feel when victimized by the military; they rightly declare that the military is supposed to be the vessel serving the American melting pot and bringing diverse peoples together in cooperation. When that fails from comrades, command, or mission, anger results.

Veterans often declare that they were enraged by their lack of control. Whether it was orders they disagreed with or death and injury to their peers, as combat medic Al says, "To me the foundation of my anger is my mistrust of my adequacy and control of the life-threatening situation." With other people's lives in their hands and combat raging around them, troops feel extremely vulnerable, yet must act responsibly, all the while knowing that there is no controlling combat. Thus, they may rage at themselves, their foes, their commanders, their mission, their country, the ones they are fighting, and life itself.

Finally, many troops express their anger and frustration with the dull military routine that it is most often tedious and boring. Although training is necessary, people's primitive emotions have been stirred and they are anxious to use them in real world demanding situations. Much wild behavior—drinking, high-speed driving, wild sex, drug abuse—can be understood as frustrated attempts to burn off this angry energy that has been aroused and has accumulated without release.

Anger in the Combat Zone

It is easy to imagine the anger one would feel upon seeing his or her fellow troops injured or killed. We can understand the human reaction to want to lash out in anger at the enemy. This anger at our own losses causes a hunger for retaliation and revenge. We have heard stories from veterans about such instances that they either participated in or witnessed. The urge to retaliate, to get revenge, can be overwhelming, especially in the heated moments of battle. Hanh, a Vietcong veteran explained to us, "Both my parents were just peasants farming our fields when they were killed by American bombers, so during the war hatred was my best weapon." Failure to cash in on this hunger for revenge can itself be a source of anger. Steve was a navy Seabee in Viet Nam. "I volunteered for 'Nam after my cousin was killed there," he said. "I did not care about politics or anything else but getting revenge by killing as many of them as I could." But Seabees are non-combatants. "I failed on my mission of revenge. For my entire life since I've been trying to kill my rage with alcohol."

In the American and many other militaries, troops are trained and encouraged to dehumanize the enemy. They are taught during training and in combat to turn the foe into something sub-human so that they can be more comfortable harming and killing them. It is easier to direct lethal anger at a thing than at a person.

There is another kind of anger released in the combat zone. We often refer to combatants as having a "killing rage." We often refer to them going berserk. The popular belief is that this is rage in its purest form. However, it may have another source.

Willy was a reconnaissance sergeant in fierce combat in the jungles of Viet Nam. Describing what veterans often call the "mad moment," he explained, "It isn't killing rage really. It's a rage to save your own life. The rage we direct at others is really our fierce rage to protect our own existence."[4] It is a rage against death and anything that would impose it upon us. We remember that Spinoza (*Ethics*, 1996/1677) taught that every being seeks to persist in its own existence. Our sheer existence is protected by this existential rage.

Glen Miller, a Ranger leading long-distance reconnaissance missions, says, "I believe that rage is a survival instinct. The adrenaline fires up the spirit and shit happens. It is not controlled. It is pure violence, hell bent on staying alive and preserving one's little tribe." Sebastian Junger (2016) confirms Miller's observations about all warriors: They seek and practice utmost loyalty to their "tribe" and choose loyalty to that small band over all others, satisfying a basic human need to belong that in our modern world is, ironically, most satisfied in life-threatening conditions. Miller describes a fellow team leader on a particularly difficult mission:

> Part of Joe's team was wounded. Enraged, Joe stood, jumped onto the trail, and emptied his clip into the fighting NVA [North Vietnamese Army]. All the while he was yelling and firing. His rage was apparent and his wrath bestowed death on at least three of the five enemy soldiers. Joe's eyes were intense and his blood vessels bulged as he screamed and delivered death. There was no slowing or stopping his fury. And then it was quiet except for a moan from our wounded.

Anger in the combat zone is also often misdirected. As Glen witnesses, the wrath is often so intense that it is impossible to control. Civilians, animals, houses, schools, and any other innocent target may be attacked with accumulated anger due to fear, loss, frustration, or other such conditions. The innocent are often victimized by anger at the immoral conditions in which our troops must serve. The Abu Ghraib prison abuse in Iraq, the My Lai massacre in Viet Nam, the No Gun Ri massacre of the Korean War, and so many other atrocities are not solely actions of disturbed individuals. Rather, they are explosions of anger after much accumulated pain under immoral conditions. Vice President Al Gore observed that the Abu Ghraib prison atrocity occurred only because of the larger immoral context of the Iraq war, a context created by national leadership that inevitably trickled down throughout the military and to front line troops (Gore, 2004). M. Scott Peck (1998) observed the same about the My Lai massacre in the Vietnam War. Dr. Peck was a military psychiatrist, achieved the rank of lieutenant colonel, and served in Viet Nam. He resigned from the army because he was so angry himself over the immorality of the war. As Gore, Peck, and others observe, wartime atrocities are not usually individual pathological reactions but expressions of the immorality in the whole as set in motion by leadership. This conforms to our definition and understanding of moral injury. Our troops are angry because they are morally wounded in having to take actions they find are against their individual and our collective value systems.

Peter, another Vietnam War combat veteran states in a letter written to us:

> Lt. Calley is my brother. And once again I told my story of being berserk and blowing away farmers and water buffalo and fishermen and sampans and how I only saw gook-foe. . . . I'm angry with vets and others who see atrocity as aberration when in my experience it was routine and routinely accepted. There's only a difference of degree in intensity and proximity.

The frustrations mount. Modern technology has made it possible for troops to have 24-hour access to loved ones at home. Although this can be wonderful for sharing special events and encouraging one another, it can also be a detriment in that couples often discuss problems going on at home. They may end up arguing with one another about how to handle things. Or deployed troops may feel angry about having to carry the burdens of home life, which usually seem trivial compared to the missions and dangers they face. Trying to figure out how to manage money or what to do about a child's failing grades back home can be both distressing and trivial when one has to then go on a mission where their own and their comrades' lives are at stake.

Beyond the Zone

Many veterans leave for the combat zone believing in their service, the patriotic reasons behind it, and its present-day political and historical necessity. But many, likewise, return home disillusioned. As one therapy patient of Ed's once said, "At age 18 I went to Iraq as an American patriot. When I came home at age 19, I realized I was nothing but a mercenary for the corporations." In morally ambivalent, economically, and politically motivated wars, veterans return feeling anger and disgust at the particular service to which they were assigned and the actions they had to perform— ultimate actions rendered shameful, rage-producing, and illegitimate by the morally questionable situation they were in. And they may also feel enraged at the conditions of the society at home that they risked all to protect.

Feeling an important sense of purpose is an essential component of becoming a mature adult. We all look for purpose and are willing to sacrifice a great deal, even life itself, for it. However, often our troops come home feeling as though they not only did not gain their own personal or collective sense of purpose, but rather the opposite. Their ability to create a meaningful sense of self and purpose has been shattered.

We have found it useful to call this an identity crisis. When troops come home from the war zone, they are no longer the person they were, changed forever by their experience. For many, the struggle to redefine themselves is daunting. They are confused and disoriented when they return home. Still in battle mode, they are on high alert. Their perceptions of and reactions to everyday things can be far from ordinary. They have lost interest in things that used to matter to them, things that once defined them, but have not found others things to replace them.

Questioning purpose and mission, and feeling anger at their disillusionment, veterans can question everything they previously experienced, including their beliefs. They look back not only at why they were sent and where, but also how they were trained, what they were told, what promises were kept or broken, how they were sent overseas, how they lived while overseas, and what they had to do. They look at what was going on in American popular and political life at home, the shape the country was taking at home, how they were returned from the war zone, and what happened to their comrades. They consider how they were mustered out of the military, whether they had any support that was reliable and accurate upon homecoming, and everything that happened to their family and friends and country while they were gone. Every one of these conditions can evoke frustration, anger, grief, and confusion that can coalesce into an overpowering and undifferentiated wrath against self, others, society, or life itself.

Further, our veterans are often left to struggle with their memories and feelings about their war or other military experiences without any understanding, compassion, patience, or interest on the part of the nation that they believed they were serving. Many not only isolate from those who did not serve, but also from one another, depending on what their service was and how they feel about it. Peter's letter expresses it like this:

> Ironically, I have anger toward other veterans who seem to remain tied to the military apparatus and embrace all the hoorah bullshit, attending reunions, recounting or retrieving some measure of glory and valor. My combat experience was not valorous and I feel no glory. Having experienced my berserker, I am separate from vets who did not go berserk. So I often feel outside the veteran community.

These issues proceed beyond self and nation back overseas to the people against whom they fought. Many veterans remain un-reconciled with their former foes. They may still feel anger at the old pain and losses incurred in combat. They may still judge the former adversary in inhumane, inhuman, or demonizing ways. Upon looking at photos of Iraqi citizens doing ordinary daily activities, one veteran of the Iraq War we worked with shook his head and simply said, "Scum, all of them, scum!"

As part of our war healing work, our organization Soldier's Heart leads annual reconciliation journeys back to Viet Nam. Some veterans will not consider going because they are still enraged at the Vietnamese. Others will not go because they are afraid of their own rage that might be unleashed if they saw Viet Nam again. Many veterans also fear, wrongly, that the Vietnamese are just as enraged at them and will attack, arrest, punish, or even execute them upon return. This is never our experience in Viet Nam; rather, this is a projection of the veterans' own unconscious self-judgments and beliefs that they did deserve punishment and that they harbor unconscious rage toward themselves and our country. However, those Vietnam War veterans who do go and meet the Vietnamese in openhearted and compassionate ways find that the Vietnamese in fact harbor no rage but consider American and Vietnamese veterans, as Vietcong veteran Tam Tien said, "brothers and sisters who survived the same hell." After such reconciliation encounters, American veterans' rage completely dissipates. It is now only forgiveness and acceptance. They perceive no threat and so no longer retain the need for protective or vengeful rage. Our veterans often say to us with huge smiles, "This is the first time I can walk through a jungle—without a rifle and with no fear!"

Shrapnel

From our work with veterans and their families, we have learned many of the determinants of warrior rage and bitter anger from before, during, and after service and all of its hidden causes and conditions. This anger stealthily accumulates, like a time bomb waiting to explode. The public often hears the worst stories of explosions from around the country, and this further alienates them from veterans. We must understand that many of our veterans feel such seething anger and that it often explodes from them, scattering through their families, communities, and throughout society like shrapnel flying everywhere and causing more pain to all.

Veterans' emotional and psychic shrapnel of rage can fly at any source, any target, at a moment's notice, and is often turned against the self. Veterans feel anger at who they have become, their post-service condition, what they did, why they served, and a host of other conditions. Anger itself results in self-destructive behavior that can range from substance abuse and domestic and public violence, to homelessness and all the way to suicide. Epidemic veteran suicide can be understood as rage against oneself, one's homeland, and one's destiny.

Anger can also be directed outward, of course. We hear about extreme veteran anger against the VA system. Much of their anger is justified, as veterans encounter difficulty getting appointments, mistreatment, misdiagnosis, lack of resources, overdependence on medications, lack of know-how, and all the other ills of that system. And veterans are angry at the VA system because it is the representative of the government that should care for them but fails in its promise and responsibility.

Even veterans who do not act out can feel like Peter:

> Yeah, anger is right up there with sadness and regret and grief. My anger for having acquiesced to being drafted then finding myself trapped in the inescapable situation of snipers, incoming mortars, rockets, and artillery; poncho-covered bodies and stuffed body bags. For me, anger is fear's companion. I respond to fear with anger. In 'Nam my fear-anger birthed the berserker and I hit back with exhilaration. Over these decades since my 'Nam, I've been quietly angry and envious of men who've had the wonderful good fortune of NOT having had combat happen to them, were able to avoid it. Reading James Hillman's *A Terrible Love of War* recently I drew some smug satisfaction from his understanding that we veterans are "initiates among innocents."

It is a familiar refrain from veterans that the rest of us "just don't get it." The truth is that most of us do not want to know and understand what they have been through. Most civilians make no effort to really understand where vets have been and how hard it is to come home. Consequently, veterans feel alone with their pain. They feel ignored at best and betrayed at worst, betrayed by the citizenry they wanted to serve.

Unable to feel "at home" again, feeling ignored by their society, and afraid of their own rage, they often isolate themselves from family and friends. Those with families often find it difficult to contain their anger, acting out at inappropriate times and emotionally injuring those around them. Wives and other family members are dismayed, frustrated, and grievous about how their loved ones have been changed by their military experience. The veteran's distance, moodiness, and outbursts of anger all contribute to family disharmony. Veterans may turn to drugs and alcohol to help them sleep at night or to numb their feelings, especially anger, during the day. Veterans have been trained to respond instantaneously to sights and sounds that could be the enemy, a necessity in a war zone. However, in civilian life such training, which involves muscle memory, can result in serious domestic violence.

It has been extensively documented, and a 2013 Rand report indicates, that the divorce rate for veterans is greater than for the general population and that the risk goes up with every month of deployment (Rand Resources, 2013). Not only does this lead to broken homes and children without parents, but it also often leads to homelessness and suicide.

More troops are surviving mortal wounds than ever before due to improved medical advances. Although saving more lives in and from the war zone is a marvelous accomplishment, it also means that a greater percentage of veterans are coming home to live with lifelong disabilities, some of which are massive. Our service people commonly come home with traumatic brain injuries (TBIs), which makes daily functioning difficult and frustrating for veterans and their loved ones. Many have also lost limbs, and have vision, hearing, spinal cord and other life long injuries. Some have suffered such severe burn wounds that they have literally had parts or all of their faces burned off. Still in facilities, being cared for because of the severity of their wounds, these victims have thus far been out of public view.

Anyone who enlists in the military is aware of the risk to life and limb. Although that threat may be with them in some way throughout deployment, most troops do not believe they will be casualties. Although they have agreed to give their lives if necessary, most cannot fathom the realities of living with the kinds of injuries some come home with. Lifelong disabilities, especially ones that require being dependent on physical care from others, are difficult enough for any of us. But for those who have devoted themselves to being in top physical condition and have prided themselves as tough and capable of great physical feats, such injuries can be totally devastating. They may blame themselves, the enemy, or fellow troops on the ground. Or, they may blame poor command or Pentagon officials.

Finally, any account of the impact of military service on our troops would be lacking if it did not include the spiritual dimensions, especially of the combat experience. The battle zone is the ultimate spiritual arena. Life and death, right and wrong, good and evil are ever present. Troops are given the power of God, right in their own hands, over the lives of other human beings. Whether or not they are conscious of this reality, they live it and must deal with its implications.[5]

For many, the horrors of war, the death and slaughter on both sides of the battle are such that any belief in God they may have had is completely destroyed. Troops return home alienated from their spiritual connections that might have otherwise provided solace. When religious belief is offered to them to ease their pain, they often reject it. They are angry with a God that would allow such destruction, especially when there is no clear and imperative justification.

It is common, and has been throughout history, for nations and militaries around the world to believe that "God is on our side." Indeed, such righteous beliefs often serve as motivation for the mission. However, when units sustain high casualties, the horrors of combat are upon them, or innocents are maimed and killed, such sentiments are much harder to believe in. "How could a just God allow this?" is a common question troops ask. Many express anger at God for the horrendous experiences during and outcomes of war. They experience a betrayal by the God they thought of as loving and righteous.

Combat is so horrendous that it seems a belief in divinity is necessary to even survive it. We have all heard the adage, "There are no atheists in the foxhole." It is true for many combatants. However, the opposite is also true. When we quoted this adage to a group of World War II veterans, three who were concentration camp liberators protested. One said, "There are horrors worse than combat. When you see the evil human beings can do it is impossible to believe anymore." Another shouted in anger, "No atheists? Bullshit! The foxhole creates atheists." And we hear from a later war Chaplain William Mahedy (1986) reporting that Viet Nam troops screamed in anguish, "Where was God in Viet Nam? AWOL!" Such anger often results in veterans alienating themselves from their religious origins, beliefs, values, and communities that might otherwise have been supportive. It leaves them floating without grounding in an existential universe in which there are no bounds to the human capacity for evil and no higher guiding principle to help them through. This is the condition the Existentialists labeled despair. We suggest that many veterans are in existential and spiritual despair but that in mental health treatment it is often reduced to and misdiagnosed as depression and then treated with medications and a protocol that does not address or heal such pain.

From Wrath to Righteousness

What is our veterans' fate after its inevitable and multi-determined arousing? Can the Beast be soothed again? As a brigadier general said to us, "Whether its roots are buried in memories lost and actions deliberately forgotten or the crippling effect of a moral injury—an injury to my soul that says I should not have done what I did—the anger is there. Whether it exists to save me, or exists to damn me, the anger is there."

We hear that warrior rage is far beyond the scope of ordinary civilian anger. We hear that it has many sources, comes from many experiences, both legitimate and illegitimate, moral and immoral, is experienced with superhuman intensity, and accumulates over time so that without interventions, explosions may be inevitable. We also hear that ordinary medications and traditional coping mechanisms such as anger management are inadequate to address this warrior rage. Further, we know that many otherwise well-meaning clinicians will call security or refuse to see vets in counseling if they need to express such rage. Clinicians do not commonly feel safe or prepared for dealing with it. But clearly, healing will not occur through medications, censoring, avoidance, or punishment. What then might be some positive and hope-filled responses to such anger?

First of all, warrior rage must be understood as normal and inevitable given all the conditions that created it and all it is trying to express. It must not be pathologized. Rather, we must let the symptom speak. Care providers and the general public must be able to develop the courage and listening skills necessary to receive warrior rage without threat. The expressive arts and other expressive forms of therapy can be helpful tools and, in fact, there is presently an artistic renaissance among younger veterans. People become dangers to themselves or others not when they need to express anger, but when others are unable or refuse to hear them such that their frustration accumulates and finally erupts.

We have been taking veterans of the Vietnam War, and younger vets as well, to Viet Nam for reconciliation and healing since 2000. It has been our experience that when former enemies embrace one another and see each other's humanity, all projections of the "evil other" disappear along with the rage that once consumed them. This demonstrates the necessary principle of re-humanization of self and other. Rage comes from the beast, the primitive parts of us. When we see the "others" as human, we realize that we all experienced hell together and we honor our own and our former enemies' histories and the forces that brought us all together. Then anger dissipates and there are no more enemies. As the African proverb states, "An enemy is someone whose story I have not yet heard." Understanding and forgiveness unify us in our common humanity.

Another step necessary for healing warrior rage is for veterans to tell their stories, reclaim and express the feelings connected with those stories, and have them witnessed and affirmed by the people they served. This means that reconciliation not only between former foes but also between veterans and the civilians they served is necessary to heal warrior anger. Traditional cultures practiced such reconciliation in community ritual. At our Soldier's Heart retreats, we replicate such rituals. Those who have not served in the military tell our warriors, "I sent you. I paid for your bullets. Everything you did was in my name. I take responsibility." When warriors hear this, the tonnage of anger, grief, and responsibility they have been carrying suddenly lifts, they are no longer alienated from civilians or angry with them, and the two groups are reconciled and carry the burdens together. Again, there is no one left to be angry at. When veterans and non-veterans unify, bridges are crossed and true healing can happen.

Another critical step is for veterans to reconcile with their pasts. This is true for any of us, but especially important for veterans. As long as they are stuck in the anguish of thinking it should not have happened, or should have happened a different way, they cannot move forward. We focus on what we call acceptance of destiny, not in any preordained sense, but rather in what actually unfolded out of all other possibilities. As some Native American elders asked their new warriors during initiation ceremonies, "Did you not wish to be a warrior in your people's service? Can you accept the many hardships of the journey?" Only when veterans can affirm their life's unfolding and their determination to thrive can they begin to accept responsibility for their future selves.

Warrior rage can be directed for positive and constructive purposes. Anger is energy. Warriors are angry for good reasons and at good causes; they are filled to bursting with "righteous indignation." When their anger about injustice can be directed for positive change and action, much good can be accomplished. Thus, veteran groups are rebuilding schools and water systems in Iraq and Afghanistan. Veteran groups are defusing old mines and bombs in the Middle East and Southeast Asia. Our organization Soldier's Heart does much philanthropic work in Viet Nam and we always have our veterans present the works—schools, houses, Agent Orange facilities, livestock, fishing sampans. They contribute to their acquisition and present the donations where they actually fought.[6] Thus, people who destroyed become creators, and life takers become life givers. Again, they see that there is nothing and no one in Viet Nam to be angry at anymore. And even more, a new positive identity is achieved. Acts of atonement heal anger. Buddhism teaches that, "Donation is the best consolation." As veterans donate, they heal themselves, their own anger, and the people and places they harmed. They thus fulfill Isaiah's prophecy; "And they that shall be of thee shall build the old waste places: thou shalt raise up the foundations of many generations; and thou shalt be called, The repairer of the breach, The restorer of paths to dwell in" (58:12).

It is not only by doing good that warrior rage can heal. Because their rage is aimed at many of the outrageous social conditions veterans suffer, they often direct it in positive ways into political and social action stateside. Thus many veterans groups—Veterans of Foreign Wars (VFW), American Legion, Military Order of the Purple Heart, Vietnam Veterans of America, Vietnam Veterans Against the War, Iraq and Afghanistan Veterans of America, Iraq Veterans Against the War, Veterans For Peace, and many others, all do important social action and are involved politically in both the causes they value most highly and those that impact the care of their brother and sister veterans. All this is fueled by righteous indignation. It is the directing of anger in appropriate ways through the political process for the good and for us all.

With some of these methods—expressive arts, expressive therapies, caring and listening audiences, reconciliation with civilians and with former foes, philanthropy, and meaningful social action—warrior rage can indeed heal. It will not completely leave the heart, for a soldier's heart does carry anger after such experiences. However, it no longer has to dominate the character, personality, or social actions of the veteran. With the anger dissipated, the entire personality transforms for the better.

At one of our recent Soldier's Heart retreats, many new young veterans of "the sand box" who had not previously done storytelling in front of a receptive audience told some traumatic combat tales for the first time. They expressed much anger and were emotionally supercharged from the overload they were carrying. After some storytelling, these newer veterans asked for stories from those who had already been through this process several times. Both Magoo, a Vietnam War combat veteran, and Dave, a Desert Storm Navy veteran, sat back, smiled, open their arms peaceably, and said, "Thank you, but I don't need to tell my story now . . . 'cause I'm not angry anymore."

Notes

1. Vietnamese is a monosyllabic language, so when referring to the country of Viet Nam, we use the proper Vietnamese spelling in two words rather than the Americanized combination into a single word. We retain the spelling of the Vietnam War as that has become standard American usage. The Vietnamese refer to it as the American War.

2. For a full analysis of military women's anger issues, see Kate Dahlstedt, "The Anger of Women Warriors" in this volume.

3. Among many other sources, the 1946 play *Home of the Brave* by Arthur Laurents documents such anti-Semitism in the combat zone and the disastrous psychological impact it could have on targeted troops and unit cohesion and morale.

4. This incident, along with Willy's full story, is told in Edward Tick's *Sacred Mountain: Encounters with the Vietnam Beast* (1989).

5. To fully explore military service and the combat zone as spiritual arenas, see Edward Tick's *War and the Soul: Healing of Nation's Veterans from Post-Traumatic Stress Disorder* (2005) and *Warrior's Return: Restoring the Soul After War* (2014).

6. For a full presentation of this practice, its philosophy, and many actual projects, see Edward Tick (2011).

References

Gore, A. (2004, May 26). Al Gore links Abu Ghraib prison abuses to deep flaws in Bush policy [speech in New York City]. Retrieved from http://www .prnewswire.com/news-releases/al-gore-links-abu-ghraib-prison-abuses -to-deep-flaws-in-bush-policy-74232392.html

Junger, S. (2016). *Tribe: On homecoming and belonging,* New York, NY: Twelve.

Mahedy, W. (1986). *Out of the night: The spiritual journey of Vietnam vets.* New York, NY: Ballantine Books.

Peck, M. S. (1998). *People of the lie.* New York, NY: Simon and Schuster.

Rand Resources (2013, September 3). Lengthy military deployments increase divorce risk for U.S. enlisted service members [press release]. Retrieved from http://www.rand.org/news/press/2013/09/03.html

Shay, J. (1994). *Achilles in Vietnam: Combat trauma and the undoing of character.* New York, NY: Athenaeum.

Shay, J. (2002). *Odysseus in America: Combat trauma and the trials of homecoming.* New York, NY: Scribner.

Spinoza, B. (1996). *Ethics.* New York, NY: Penguin. (Original work published in 1677).

Tick, E. (1989). *Sacred mountain: Encounters with the Vietnam beast.* Santa Fe, NM: Moon Bear Press.

Tick, E. (2005). *War and the soul: Healing our nation's veterans from Post-traumatic Stress Disorder,* Wheaton IL: Quest Books.

Tick, E. (2011). Atonement practices after war. In P. Coussineau (Ed.), *Beyond forgiveness: Reflections of atonement* (Chapter 9). San Francisco, CA: Jossey-Bass.

Tick, E. (2014). *Warrior's return: Restoring the soul after war.* Boulder, CO: Sounds True.

CHAPTER SIX

"A Bad Counselor": Anger in the Bible[1]

David A. Salomon

In the midst of writing this essay, my mother passed away after a battle with diabetes and dementia. Her death compelled me to think about my own relationship with the Bible, particularly as it relates to feelings of anger. I began reading the Bible as a child, *The Children's Bible* at my bedside, and reveled in *The Ten Commandments*, the 1956 Hollywood version of the Exodus story, which I once dragged my father to see in a theater in the Bronx, only to discover it was being shown dubbed in Spanish with English subtitles (not a problem—I had the entire dialogue committed to memory by then).

I recall reading stories from my *Children's Bible*, particularly in the Old Testament, in the morning after waking, and fantasizing about being the heroes of those stories, particularly Moses. (I'd even made my own robes and staff to replicate his—or Charlton Heston's—appearance in the desert.) The anger in the Old Testament, whether experienced by individuals or by God, never really occurred to me until my grandmother died when I was 13. Having just been bar mitzvah'd, in an Orthodox synagogue no less, I had a close relationship to my Jewish faith and culture, so much so that many in my young life thought I might become a rabbi. My grandmother's death changed that.

As Elisabeth Kübler-Ross tells us, denial quickly turned to anger, and I discovered that looking to the Bible for exemplars on that emotion was not helpful. The lessons taught in Hebrew School focused almost exclusively on the triumphs of the Israelites as well as the overwhelming support and encouragement of a beneficent God. Even Moses's anger at the Israelites' building of the golden calf was framed more as frustration than as rage. Ultimately, my anger went unresolved and shifted to God as its object as I grew older and more disenchanted with my faith.

Now, as my mother has passed away, I work on this essay to shed light on the depictions and approaches to anger in the Old and New Testaments of the Judeo-Christian Bible. I first looked to the story of Moses with which I was intimately familiar as a child. I discovered that anger can be confused with fear, and fear can be confused with reverence as in Exodus 15:31: "the people feared the Lord; and they believed in the Lord."[2]

I returned to the *Children's Bible* of my childhood (having recently purchased a copy for my daughter) to look at the Exodus story, as its editors redacted it for children. In fact, the anger of God and the anger of Moses are both prominently mentioned. Why then did I not remember either clearly? As that question is beyond my area of scholarship, I will leave that up to my colleagues in psychology. I do, however, posit that there is a clear Old Testament connection among anger, fear, and reverence. That connection shifts in the New Testament to a focus on anger as sin and wrath as punishment.

Introduction

In *The City of God,* Augustine writes, "The poets give such a distorted picture of the gods that such deities cannot stand comparison with good humans" (Augustine, 2003, p. 169). Nowhere is that comparison more evident than in discussions of the anger or wrath of God in the Judeo-Christian Bible. Augustine here highlights the problem of anger for religious writers: anger is sinful, and the anger of God seems inconsistent with his beneficence. Elsewhere, Augustine writes, "We do not worship a God who is repentant, jealous, needy or cruel" (McCarthy, 2009, p. 865). Nonetheless, God's "anger" or "wrath" is mentioned repeatedly throughout the canonical texts of the Old and New Testament. As Michael McCarthy writes, "The radical dissociation of divine wrath and human anger, for instance, represents a strong refusal to allow Scripture to legitimate destructive, hateful human behavior, while admitting the possibility of acting on divinely inspired anger" (2009, p. 848). The ancient philosophers clearly viewed anger as a vice that resulted in physical and psychological distress. In *On Anger*, Seneca writes, "when the sea is stormy, you can see nothing clearly" (Seneca, 2007, p. 28). He continues, "many men have been incapacitated by their anger, many disabled" (p. 42). The Stoics in general assessed anger as an evil (Holmes, 2004). The Old Testament text is no different: "A fool gives full vent to his anger" (Proverbs 29:11 Revised Standard Version). And the New Testament echoes: "In your anger do not sin" (Ephesians 4:26). The Old Testament, however, presents anger in quite a different light; whereas God's anger in the New Testament seems aimed at the sin, the Old Testament God's anger focuses on the sinner (Mattison, 2007).

Nonetheless, other than the occasional news story reporting a copy of the Bible protecting a victim from a shooter's bullet, or in the pages of theological linguists studying Hebrew, Latin, and Greek etymological roots in biblical texts, anger and the Bible are not conventionally discussed together. In fact, in many pastoral situations, priests and ministers are encouraged to downplay the anger of God in their interpretations and sermons (Augsburger, 1993). Certainly the relationship of the Judeo-Christian Bible with radical fundamentalism (in any religious tradition or sect) raises ire and has often inspired anger and violence. In this essay, I attempt to frame the presence of anger in the Judeo-Christian Bible with a mind to contextualizing that anger for the contemporary political, social, and religious issues the other essays in the volumes at-hand address. I will focus on the anger of God and only touch peripherally on human anger, as a comprehensive study of the question would fill its own volume (Baloian, 1992; Schlimm, 2011).

Anger plays a central role in several central narratives in the Judeo-Christian Bible, particularly in the Hebrew Bible, or Old Testament. Perhaps that is because anger has traditionally been so closely connected with discipline and judgment, with which much of the Old Testament is concerned. By contrast, the New Testament, with Jesus as the physical representation of redemption and forgiveness, hardly relates characters or tales of anger at all but instead includes sermonizing, mostly in the epistolary writing of Paul, on the dangers of anger. From the anger of Yahweh to the anger of Moses, the Old Testament is rife with stories of dissatisfaction, dismay, and downright rage. In the figure of Jesus, on the other hand, the exemplar for human behavior as Thomas Aquinas would later write, anger itself might be considered a sin and thus contrary to the nature of the sin-free Jesus of Nazareth, particularly as a model for ideal human behavior. It is not until the Book of Revelation, the final book of the New Testament, that the wrath of God returns as a key player.

Although Jesus teaches in the New Testament that the meek will inherit the earth, it is also clear that it is the aggressive Old Testament figure, an often-angry figure such as Samson (whose achievements include slaying an army with the jawbone of an ass and destroying a pagan temple with his bare hands), who achieves advances for the people in the name of God. In fact, an early judgment must be made on the value of anger, positive or negative; it is clearly not an absolute in that the very ethos embedded in many biblical texts encourages the *via media* or middle way between absolute anger and absolute passivity. A qualified anger therefore plays an important role in the history of western thought.

The Old Testament presents three types of anger: anger toward individuals (e.g., Cain and Abel); anger of an individual toward God (e.g., Job); and the anger of God at his people (e.g., the Flood). The New Testament, on the other hand, rarely indicates the anger of Jesus; instead, when anger is mentioned, it is more likely in the context of a lesson or teaching, and not as an exemplar. Anger most frequently appears in the New Testament in narratives related to God's wrath at the apocalypse in Revelation. Human anger is clearly a sin and is almost always portrayed as such, particularly in the Pauline epistles. Divine anger is often interpreted as "wrath" (Hanson, 1957, pp. 36–40; MacGregor, 1961).

Anger was not understood as explicitly psychological by the ancients, but was viewed as a physical ailment. Most often, as in the work of Galen and others, anger is categorized as one of several "passions of the soul": "anger, wrath, fear, grief, envy and violent lust" (Galen, 1963, p. 32). Such passions, he writes, "arise by an irrational impulse" (p. 31). Seneca regarded anger as a form of madness. In *Rhetoric*, Aristotle defines anger as "an impulse, accompanied by pain, to a conspicuous revenge for a conspicuous slight directed without justification towards what concerns oneself or towards what concerns one's friends" (Aristotle, p. 2195). It seems, however, that these readings of anger apply only to human beings. It was left to the early rabbinic and patristic writers to explicate the anger of God in the biblical texts. In the second century, Tertullian would argue that human and divine emotions are radically different; thus, "God's wrath must be distinct from what we generally understand as anger" (McCarthy, 2009, p. 861).

Studies of anger in the Bible have conventionally focused on one character or book, and such studies have rarely examined the New Testament. Is there something about anger that is particularly Hebrew or Jewish? Maimonides noted that "our sages refer to anger as idolatry." And, of course, Sigmund Freud categorized anger as a form of displacement. The "angry Jew" is almost a stereotype in theater.

Rather than merely catalog instances of anger in the Judeo-Christian Bible (a feat that can be easily accomplished with online concordances and wonderful biblical scholarship aids such as the BibleWorks software package), I attempt in this essay to first give a broad overview of the types of anger in the Bible and then focus on the anger of God. The theological debate, played out on the pages of the Church Fathers and the Talmudic scholars, often questions the appropriateness of anger in the holy text. Although interesting as philosophical and linguistic discussions, these writers often get caught up in abstraction, sometimes ignoring what is clearly evident in the text: both humans and God, regardless the possible anthropomorphic heresy, experience anger. All anger has ramifications and consequences, some good, many not. Behind the stained glass windows of modern churches and synagogues, there has developed an awkwardness, an embarrassment, regarding particularly the anger or wrath of God in the Bible. Many apologists attempt to compensate for this liturgically through a kind of avoidance, often by omitting "offending" passages from readings and sermons.

The wrath of Yahweh in the Old Testament and the anger of Jesus in the New Testament are not as easily contrasted as assumed in the work of late-nineteenth century biblical scholars. The traditional assumption of Old Testament wrath versus New Testament mercy is actually flawed. This assumption, which dates to the heresies of Marcion in the second century CE, claims two divinities: "an inferior Hebrew God, who created the world but behaves in a reprehensible manner, and a supremely good God, whom Jesus came to reveal" (McCarthy, 2009, p. 857). In other words, the love and mercy of the New Testament (the Beatitudes, for example) correct the stern, authoritative voice of the Law handed down at Mt. Sinai in Exodus. As a result of this, Marcion dropped the Old Testament entirely from his Bible, choosing instead to focus exclusively on the "supremely good God" of the New Testament (Lieu, 2015). Origen of Alexandria, quite concerned with linking the New Testament to the Old, would eventually posit a way of reading the Bible "spiritually" in order to justify—some would say correct—interpretation inconsistent with the apparent beneficence of the divinity. Marcion himself was later corrected by Tertullian in the third century in his argument that God's justice requires God's anger. We might suggest the equation "anger balanced by justice tempered by mercy."

To be sure, it is easier to find Old Testament examples of God's anger with man's sin since the Old Testament is an account of thousands of years of living, whereas the New Testament recounts a much shorter history (Aloysia, 1946). The anger of God in the Old Testament is immediately felt, whereas it is most often delayed in the New Testament. Thus, we are able to see God's wrath more clearly in the Old Testament in a cause-and-effect relationship, whereas the New Testament wrath of God appears later, generally delayed until Revelation. A mere catalogue of Bible verses on anger is not needed here, as such an enterprise is now easily accomplished with databases. Suffice it to say that the word "anger" appears in some form in the New Revised Standard Version no fewer than 450 times. In the first part of a three-part essay on anger, David Powlison writes, "The Bible is about anger. Who is the angriest person in the Bible? *God*" (1995, p. 4).

Old Testament

There are ten Hebrew terms used 714 times in the Old Testament to describe anger (Baloian, 1992). Of these, the majority—518—refer to divine wrath with the remaining 196 describing human anger. Divine anger differs greatly from human anger in the Old Testament, with the latter innately being of a more visceral nature—individuals "burn" with anger, or anger is reflected in blushing or flushing of the skin; the Greek Septuagint uses *orgē* for anger, a word related to the Greek *ragō*, denoting a swelling, reinforcing the etymological connotation of anger as a physical manifestation. Thus, the word's derivation implies that anger may result in a physical change to the individual as in Moses's "hot anger" at Pharaoh in Exodus 11:8.

Although, by a ratio of more than two-to-one, the word is used to describe the anger of God, the first explicit appearance of anger in the Old Testament is the story of the murder of Abel by his brother Cain in Genesis. While God appears displeased with Adam and Eve after their transgression in Genesis 3, his punishments of the pair (and the snake) are expressed calmly, some might say "flatly," and the writer indicates nothing of the divine wrath we find later in the book. For one explanation of the "flaming sword" as God's wrath, see the English Puritan Thomas Watson's 1650 *A Body of Practical Divinity*.

The outward manifestation of anger is often displayed violently and swiftly, as in Cain's anger with his brother. And that physical manifestation is often reflected in a physical change in the angry individual. Anger's effect on the physical body of human beings is illuminated in the work of early writers on physiology such as Galen, who warned that anger in infants was a precursor to severe disease and disfigurement. In the biblical account of the first murder, Cain's offering to God is rejected, and the writer claims, "Cain was very angry, and his countenance fell" (Genesis 4:5); the text, however, provides no elaboration on what "angry" means here. The Hebrew word used is חָרָה, a word that can also mean to burn or be kindled with fire (Schlimm, 2011). Schlimm notes this as the "most common verb" for anger in Genesis, appearing 93 times (Schlimm, 2011, p. 197). Suffice it to say that Cain's anger has a visceral quality to it, and God uses the same word in the next verse in an attempt to calm Cain where he questions Cain's anger and advises him, "If you do well, will you not be accepted? And if you do not do well, sin is couching at the door; its desire is for you, but you must master it" (Genesis 4:6–7). Cain's fallen countenance implies his behavior or demeanor has shifted as a result of his emotional distress. The image of sin "couching at the door" is a startling one that evokes a Freudian sense of repressed anger and memories, ready to reveal themselves and pounce at any moment. Cain's identification as the first murderer and the first person physically affected by anger is elaborated in Regina M. Schwartz's insightful study, *The Curse of Cain*, where she argues that "the origins of violence" can be found in "identity formation" (1997, p. 5). Anger clearly forms an integral aspect of that identity formation in the Old Testament.

Stephan A. Martin expresses well the Jungian dichotomy of the archetypal complex of anger particularly as it relates to the physical manifestations:

> One aspect of this dichotomy is characterized by a seething, red-hot emotionality that pumps blood into our faces and hands and pushes us ever closer toward impulsive and regrettable acting-out. Its complement is a quite different hardness of heart, a disturbing stillness of icy emotional withdrawal that shuts us down and in. (1986, p. 31)

The latter is reflected in God's response to "the wickedness of man" in Genesis 6: "And the Lord was sorry that he had made man on the earth, and it grieved him to his heart. I will blot out man . . . for I am sorry that I have made them" (Genesis 6:7). After explaining to Noah that he will "destroy all flesh in which is the breath of life from under heaven," God tempers his anger with an offer to "establish my covenant with you" (Genesis 6:17, 18).

An interesting contrast to God's calming covenant with Noah is his punishment of Cain, who is to be "a fugitive and a wanderer on the earth" (Genesis 4:12). God's anger with the collective group is expressed in more reflective sorrow in the Noah story: "I am sorry that I have made them" (Genesis 4:7), whereas his anger with Cain's murder of his brother is marked by focused and external anger resulting in exile. The two stories, which follow each other in Genesis, seem to note a shift in the anger of God from impulsivity to reflexivity and thoughtfulness. In fact, the writer does not indicate God's protection of Noah, only that, once the waters begin to recede, "God remembered Noah," "remembering" often a euphemism through the Old Testament that indicates God's care for and protection of his creation (Genesis 8:1). That remembrance, and Noah's successful sacrifice (Genesis 8:21) cause God to promise never again to destroy the creatures of the world "as I have done" (Genesis 8:21). Nevertheless, the anger and resulting punishment are immediate: a flood kills instantly.

The recurring pattern in the Old Testament of sin, repentance, and deliverance seems to come to an explicit head in God's commandment in Exodus prohibiting idol worship: "for I, the Lord your God, am a jealous God" (Exodus 20:5); the second account, in Exodus 34, even notes that God's "name is Jealous" and that he "is a jealous God" (Exodus 34:14). In fact, the noteworthy relationship of jealousy to anger in the Old Testament God is clear from early in the Old Testament where the Hebrew Yahweh is one of many available deities and that Yahweh is indeed jealous, a jealousy that leads to anger and seems to evoke fear in his creations.

God's anger is not always released externally. As the Old Testament progresses, God's anger becomes more repressed, reflective, thoughtful—less impulsive and instantly putative. Curiously, the golden calf episode, occurring late in Exodus 32:14, evokes not palpable anger but instead contemplative anger: "And the Lord repented of the evil which he thought to do to his people." This echoes God's reaction to man's corruption (leading to the Flood) in Genesis 6:6: "And the Lord was sorry that he had made man on the earth, and it grieved him to his heart." Gary Heiron among others refers to "the overall anthropopathic character of Hebrew descriptions of Yahweh," that is, God's actions are described through human emotion, something early Christian writers such as Marcion found heretical (Heiron, 1992; for discussion of the Numbers verse "God is not like humans," see the opening chapter of Sheridan, 2015).

The Exodus passage on the golden calf is followed by Moses's anger, which "burned hot" and compelled him to throw "the tables out of his hands" (Exodus 32:19). It almost seems here that Moses's anger has become the physical manifestation of the anger of God, who has by Exodus removed himself from much direct interaction with his creation. The entire episode evokes the language of the Flood. Here God said to Moses, "Whoever has sinned against me, him will I blot out of my book" (Exodus 32:33), resulting in "a plague upon the people, because they made the calf" (Exodus 32:34). Moses's punishment for destroying the tablets is indeed harsh: God will no longer speak with Moses "face to face, as a man speaks to his friend" (Exodus 33:11), a punishment patristic and Talmudic writers also noted in Adam and Eve's expulsion from the Garden of Eden. Again, God's anger is immediate and tangible.

God's anger in the Pentateuch is vindictive and vengeful, and, although there is anger between human beings, examples pale in comparison to God's anger and punishment that is not only paternalistic, but also fatalistic. One finds a disappointment in God's anger, often including mention of the broken covenant, followed by judgment and punishment or penalty. That disappointment evokes the psychological guilt of a child toward a parent. Divine anger, "the wrath of God," is almost always a response to the breaking of the covenant and is clearly less immediate than earlier cause-and-effect anger (as in the story of Cain and Abel) but is more overwhelming and overarching. Dennis McCarthy notes one of the few examples where divine wrath results in "reaffirmation of covenant": 1 Samuel 12:8–12, where the transgressions of the Israelites are recalled. Samuel recalls his people's history since Moses and notes "if you will not hearken to the voice of the Lord, but rebel against the hand of the Lord, then the hand of the Lord will be against you and your king" (1 Samuel 12:15). Samuel then instructs, "Only fear the Lord, and serve him faithfully with all your heart . . . . But if you still do wickedly, you shall be swept away" (1 Samuel 12:24, 25). The wrath of God is directly related to the people's actions, implying a clear cause-and-effect relationship between human sin and divine anger.

This causal relationship is nowhere more evident than in the book of Leviticus, a compilation of rules and regulations regarding ritual and law. Leviticus 26 outlines the punishments beginning with an "if" statement in verse 3 and changing tone to a sequence of "but if" statements in verse 14 and after: "But if you will not hearken to me, and will not do all these commandments . . . I will appoint over you sudden terror." The breaking of the covenant in verse 15 will cause the estrangement of God from his people: "I will set my face against you" (26:17). Once again, God's anger is manifested in a literal turning away from his creation.

This ramification of God's anger is also clear in the earliest biblical story of sin. After Adam and Eve have eaten of the Tree of Knowledge, they are expelled from the Garden of Eden, prompting many patristic writers to read the estrangement from God as representing God's anger. God will no longer walk with Adam as he did earlier in the Garden. In the early books of the Old Testament, especially, God's anger is depicted as disappointment, regret on God's part for having created sinful beings, but also disappointment on the part of humans. Interestingly, in Genesis 3, once Adam and Even admit their sin, implicating the serpent who "beguiled" Eve, the rest of the chapter is given to God to lay out punishment. God "drove" Adam and Eve out of Eden (Genesis 3:24). The separation, noted later in Exodus 33 ("Thus the Lord used to speak to Moses face to face, as a man speaks to his friend" [Exodus 33:11]), is the direct consequence of human transgression and God's anger.

It is important to note that God's anger in the Old Testament is always tempered with justice, recalling the ethos behind Dante's *Inferno*: God created Hell for justice. This tempering is indicated by contrition and confession even in Leviticus 26: "But if they confess their iniquity. . . . then I will remember my covenant" (26:40, 42). It is also interesting to note that God never becomes angry in the opening chapters of Genesis; through the Fall of Adam and Eve, the sin of Cain, the travesty of Sodom and Gomorrah, God's "anger" is never explicitly mentioned. Not to belabor a metaphor, but if we look at the earliest characters in the Old Testament as humanity in its infant and toddler stage, then God fulfills the parental role. As anyone who has raised children can testify, those early years are not only filled with education but with frustration. Like the parent guiding the crawling child away from the stairs, God in these early tales attempts to adjust the course of humanity. By the time we reach the story of the Flood, it seems that humans have entered adolescence and must endure punishment for their transgressions—humanity is sent into a "timeout." The parent whose child runs out into traffic will react with anger, although it is an anger tempered by love and justice.

At the same time, we must recall early rabbinic and patristic discussions of the linguistic and theological inaccuracy of attributing human traits (i.e., anger) to the divinity. This anthropathosing (that is, using the concept of human emotion/pathos on a non-human being) of God is viewed as dangerous by many and as openly heretical by others. Perhaps one of the most important voices here is Lactantius, the fourth-century North African theologian whose "Treatise on the Anger of God" warns about the arrogance of boasting that human beings can ever know the same emotional sensations as the divinity, particularly anger (Lactantius, n.d.).

Lactantius also posits that if we decline to attribute anger to God, we can neither attribute kindness: "both alike must be taken from Him" (Lactantius, n. d., p. 392). But he also suggests that as humans cease sinning, God's wrath declines (McCarthy, 2009, p. 864). Lactantius actually suggests that "the loving of the good arises from the hatred of the wicked" (Lactantius, n.d., p. 395). One of his more startling conclusions reiterates Proverbs 9.10: "there can be no religion where there is no fear." Lactantius clearly links fear to divine wrath (p. 406).

Anger is a human emotion. Thus, the chief problem with discussing God's anger is the question of anthropomorphosis. Can we attribute a human emotion to a divine being? Or is it, as Augustine would argue, that God's anger is of a different character and definition? Augustine also suggests that we look at concepts such as God's anger as metaphors, reading such passages in Origen's *sensus spirtualis*. Essentially, Augustine argues that the language of the bible is necessary so that human beings might understand it: "If scripture did not employ such words, it would not strike home so closely, as it were, to all humanity" (Augustine, 2003, p. 643).

When considering the role of anger in the Bible, we might be prone to default to the story of Job and his anger at a God who seems to be using him as a pawn in a game. For Jung (1973), this was the prototypical discussion of anger in the western world. But we can see anger in the Hebrew Bible as early as Adam and Eve when, in Genesis 3, God doles out his punishments for Adam, Eve, and the serpent. However, the first mention of anger occurs in the Cain and Abel story when we are told that "Cain was very angry" (Genesis 4:5) when God "had no regard" for Cain or his offering. God asks Cain, explicitly, "Why are you angry" (Genesis 4:6) and warns him that "sin is couching at the door" (Genesis 4:7). Thus, at its first mention, anger is comingled with sin. To be angry is, if not a sin, then certainly not a positive attribute.

As Regina Schwartz mentions, the sacrifices of Cain and his brother "suggest propitiation, that is, an offering to ward off divine wrath" (1997, p. 2). But, we might ask, at this point in the Hebrew Bible, is there an underlying assumption of divine anger that must be placated, as Schwartz continues, "to invoke his blessings of prosperity"? Schwartz echoes our frustration when she asks, "What kind of God is this who chooses one sacrifice over the other?" (1997, p. 3). This can all be contrasted with the thought of the ancient Greek Jew Philo of Alexandria, following Plato, who wrote that because God is without passion or emotion, he cannot be angry (van der Horst, 1993).

The result is an atmosphere of fear in which the Israelites constantly anticipate the wrath of the father. Nonetheless, as exhibited in the stories in Judges, they continually displease God, endure his wrath, suffer through punishment, experience redemption, and begin the cycle anew. As just one example, in Judges 2 the angel of God tells the Israelites, "I brought you up from Egypt and brought you into the land which I swore to give to your fathers. I said, 'I will never break my covenant with you, and you shall make no covenant with the inhabitants of this land; you shall break down their altars.' But you have not obeyed my command. What is this you have done? So now I say, I will not drive them out before you; but they shall become adversaries to you, and their gods shall be a snare to you" (Judges 2:1–4). In response, the people "lifted up their voices and wept" (Judges 2:4).

There seems to be no summative effect of this transgressing, as God's anger, exhibited in his consistent plaint that the Israelites have "transgressed my covenant," seems quelled with each new generation. Even the worshipping of other gods, in the form of the Ba'als, which would seem a gross transgression and violation of the first of the commandments, results perhaps in severe immediate punishment, but no enduring punishment.

Ultimately, God's anger in the Old Testament is not entirely literal, but instead implies what Rudolf Otto termed something more "numinous," *mysterium tremendum et fascinans*, a fearful and tremendous mystery. Otto (1958) is keen to relate the *tremor* root of *tremendum* to shutter or fear, noting that the ineffable divine evokes fear in human beings, partially due to its ineffability; we fear what we do not or cannot know. Otto addresses "the wrath of God": "'Wrath' here is the 'ideogram' of a unique emotional moment in religious experience," a moment Otto imagines must be "gravely disturbing" to those who "recognize nothing in the divine nature but goodness, gentleness, [and] love" (1958, p. 19).

The anger or wrath of the Old Testament God has had a particular impact on the philosophies and theologies related to the Holocaust. In a 1999 speech in Washington, D.C., Elie Wiesel noted the sentiment of many survivors: "Rooted in our tradition, some of us felt that to be abandoned by humanity then was not the ultimate. We felt that to be abandoned by God was worse than to be punished by Him. Better an unjust God than an indifferent one. For us to be ignored by God was a harsher punishment than to be a victim of His anger. Man can live far from God—not outside God." So, given the choice of God's wrath or God's indifference, Wiesel chooses anger. We need also remember that Wiesel is the author of *The Trial of God*, a drama in which prisoners (not unlike concentration camp prisoners) put God on trial (cf. Maitles, 2002).

Perhaps one of the most confusing instances of God's anger in the Old Testament occurs in the story of Uzzah and the Ark of the Covenant in 2 Samuel 6 where "The anger of the Lord was kindled against Uzzah" after he "put out his hand to the ark of God and took hold of it" (2 Samuel 6: 6–8). The ark, according to Numbers 4:15, was untouchable by humans. The punishment of death seems extreme in the case of Uzzah, who reached out to steady the ark because "the oxen stumbled." Early rabbinical interpretations of the passage merely attribute the incident to the anger of the deity, claiming that Uzzah should have been aware that the Ark of the Covenant could easily have borne its weight and did not require the assistance of human hands. The Uzzah incident in 2 Samuel is especially problematic when read in the light of the mercy of God. How could Yahweh be so vindictive as to react angrily to what is clearly a misstep on the part of a minor character moving to prevent the ark from crashing to the ground? How indeed. The message would appear to be more closely aligned with the dictates of established rules and the consequences of violating those rules. The writer first claims it is "the anger of the Lord" that was "kindled against Uzzah" (2 Samuel 6:6). Then, in a clear one-to-one relationship, "God smote him there because he put forth his hand to the ark" (2 Samuel 6:7).

Uzzah's fault is that he has treated the Ark has if it were any ordinary box and not the base of God's throne.

Oftentimes, it is difficult for moderns to fully appreciate what Rudolf Otto called "the idea of the holy" in the ancient world, particularly when it comes to the holiness of objects and their connection to the divinity. The Israelites understood that wherever the Ark of the Covenant was, Yahweh was present. The Old Testament prohibition from seeing God certainly extends to physical contact as well. Thus, Uzzah violates several edicts in his efforts to prevent the Ark from crashing to the ground. God's anger at this—the death of Uzzah—is then followed by the anger of David, who refuses to continue the trip to Jerusalem with the Ark, fearing the power of its very presence.

To be sure, in early books of the Old Testament, divine wrath is roused by the willful disobedience of God's creation (Numbers 32:13) and by worship of other gods (Deuteronomy 32:19). Later, outside the text of the Pentateuch, God's anger is especially provoked by the sin of the people (Isaiah 47:6; Psalms 89:30).

The effects of divine wrath in the Old Testament clearly illuminate the poor choices and actions of the Israelites. In what sounds like a Zen Koan, Jung cites the Midrash on Genesis 18:23: "If thou desirest the world to endure, there can be no absolute justice, while if thou desirest absolute justice, the world cannot endure. Yet thou wouldst hold the cord by both ends, desiring both the world and justice" (Jung, 1959, p. 59). This paradox is at the heart of the "problem" of a divine wrath often expressed in parental terms and many times implying shame and disappointment. We need only compare the anger expressed by Cain in murdering his brother Abel with Yahweh's reaction to Moses's destruction of the ten commandment tablets to see both the differences. It would seem that man was created in Genesis without the ability to express anger. Biblical exegesis, both Jewish and Christian, indicates that the Fall introduced an unnatural conflict between body and soul and, with that conflict, anger.

Perhaps, ultimately, the paradox of anger in the Old Testament is part of the *mysterium tremendeum* in that it is consistently inconsistent with the loving nature of the being who gave life to Adam and Eve. And perhaps it is a paradox akin to theodicy, the phenomenology of perception, and the inability of the Chicago Cubs to win a World Series. God's loving anger in the Old Testament is one of his defining traits; without it, Yahweh would transform into the Christ of the New Testament. Just as John Hick recalls that the human attempt to understand theodicy is "a foolish pretension . . . under the illusion that [humans] can judge God's acts by human standards," so too is comprehending God's anger at his creations (1966, p. 6).

Anthony Hanson suggests that in the Old Testament, "where the divine wrath is met with, it is thought of as not necessarily accountable or rational, or morally motivated" (1957, p. 3).

New Testament

Anger presents quite differently in the New Testament. Jesus is only explicitly angry in one verse in the New Testament: after critics accuse him of healing on the Sabbath, he "looked round about on them with anger" (Mark 3:5). Perhaps this scene is most succinctly explicated as follows: "Compassion fueled it. He was both angry at the Jewish leaders' hypocrisy and grieved at their hardness of heart" (Elliott, 2006, p. 214). In fact, the Greek word ὀργή used here suggests more frustration or exasperation than true anger. In fact, "the reason for anger in this situation fits the pattern for God's anger" (Elliott, 2006, p. 214). Jesus's anger here is, as Elliott writes, "to set things right, it had a constructive purpose" (p. 214).

Otherwise, discussions of divine anger or wrath are confined to the Pauline Epistles and the Book of Revelation, a fact that should not come as a surprise given the merciful stories recounted in the Gospels compared with the many horrific events experienced by the Israelites throughout the books of the Old Testament. Even when, in Matthew, John the Baptist urges the crowd to "flee from the wrath that is coming" (Matthew 3:7), it is to the eschatological day of judgment that he refers and not to an immediate manifestation of that wrath. Again, as C. H. Dodd reminds us, Rudolf Otto's *tremendum mysterium* is relevant here: "When religion reaches the point of personifying the objects of numinous feeling, such phenomena [i.e., natural phenomena such as earthquakes] are explained on the analogy of the irrational passion of an angry man: they are the anger of the gods" (1932, p. 22). Thus, the "wrath of God" is the thunder and the pestilence of the Old Testament, and it is, as in Romans 1:18, "God's anger . . . revealed from heaven against all the impiety and wickedness of those who hinder the Truth by their wickedness."

What of Jesus's displays of anger? The most notable instance of Jesus's anger appears when he overturns the tables of the moneychangers in Mark 11:15; however, the gospel writer does not make Jesus's anger explicitly clear (cf. Hengel, 1989, chapter 4). As Stephen Voorwinde notes, "In point of fact, however, none of the Synoptic accounts attributes any emotion whatsoever to Jesus in connection with this incident" (Voorwinde, 2014, p. 31). In John's account (2:17), Jesus's anger is interpreted as "zeal." "Zeal is more than anger. It is the ardor of red-hot passion" (Voorwinde, 2014, p. 31). The Synoptics describe "an incident of well managed outrage," not anger in the traditional sense (Voorwinde, 2014, p. 32).

As G. H. C. MacGregor notes, "it is with Paul that the conception of the 'wrath' of God becomes prominent" (1961, p. 102). Jesus's anger is, as noted, rarely alluded to. Instead, it is Paul who, looking back to the God of the Old Testament, evokes God's wrath anew in the Christian world. This suggests, from the New Testament perspective, that God uses his anger as a threat, punishment in the future for current transgressions, whereas in the Old Testament, the anger of God is felt almost immediately: for example, Adam and Eve are expelled from Eden, Moses is forbidden to enter the Promised Land. MacGregor argues for "wrath" as an "attribute of God, but, if we may so put it, an attribute held in reserve" (1961, p. 104). Although God's wrath is certainly effectuated by human sin, it is a wrath immediately present in the Old Testament, whereas it is delayed, perhaps until Judgment, in the New Testament.

John suggests in 3:26 that those who do not "obey the Son shall not see life, but the wrath of God rests upon him." Divine retribution in the New Testament is long-term, whereas the Old Testament God might immediately lament his creation fresh on the heels of his transgression. The Old Testament sinner has violated an explicit law and is so punished in a cause-and-effect relationship. "We shall remind ourselves that, according to the New Testament, God vindicates his own justice and righteousness . . . not through his 'wrath,' but through his forgiving love" (MacGregor, 1961, p. 100). So then, the relationship between anger and justice, a pairing so often evident in the Old Testament, shifts in the New Testament to connect justice with love. After all, it is the New Testament God who grants man redemption (out of love) for his sin, instead of dooming man to an eternity of pain and punishment. And so John 3:16, "For God so loved the world that he gave his only Son" in order to, as the poet John Milton writes, "end the strife/Of Mercy and Justice" (Milton, 1998, p. 428).

The Pauline Epistles have much to offer on the question of anger. In Ephesians 4:26–27 Paul counsels to "be angry but do not sin"; however, that anger is not to percolate beyond the end of the day: "do not let the sun go down on your anger" (Ephesians 4:26). In Galatians 5:19–23 Paul lists anger as one of the "works of the flesh," a list that includes "fornication, impurity . . . drunkenness, carousing." Paul warns "those who do such things will not inherit the kingdom of heaven." As Denney put it, "In the NT itself there are far more warnings against anger than indications of its true place and function" (1906, p. 60).

The connection of divine anger to the Day of Judgment harkens to the Old Testament Prophets who suggested that God will "sit to judge all the nations round about" (Joel 3:12) at which "the terror of the Lord" (Isaiah 2:10) will be present. Certainly it is in the book of Revelation, a text Carl Jung (1973, p. 76) called "a veritable orgy of hatred, wrath, vindictiveness, and blind destructive fury," that the divine wrath is clearly felt, although it does differ in nature and tenor from the Old Testament divine wrath in one significant way: the wrath of God in the Old Testament (outside the books of the prophets) is recounted historically, whereas the divine wrath in Revelation is a fiction, something yet to come. This and this alone may account for the more elaborate and involved descriptions of the anger of the deity in Revelation, particularly considering its author, John, was in prison on Patmos at the time of writing. His own bitterness and anger are palpable from the opening verses. However, the wrath in Revelation is not purely eschatological: "it is a process, stretching from the Cross to the Parousia" (Hanson, 1957, p. 170). Hanson goes on to argue that in the New Testament, wrath is never disciplinary: "The wrath is not an attitude of God, but a condition of men" (p. 180). In fact, biblical scholars have consistently drawn parallels between the divine wrath in Revelation and the representation of divine wrath in the Old Testament, almost as if the writer of Revelation is looking to the Old Testament and not the Gospels for inspiration and influence.

Conclusion

This essay has certainly not aimed to be a comprehensive study of anger in the Bible. Instead, I hope to have provided the reader an introduction to the issue, encouraging that reader to consider the Bible in the greater context of cultural history. Greater insight and understanding of anger in the Bible can certainly help us to better grasp the nature of anger in the Judeo-Christian traditions, but also speaks to a larger context: the role of anger in Western religion in general, although the significance seems to differ in Islam. For mainstream Christianity, anger is one of the seven deadly sins. In Rabbinical Judaism, the Babylonian Talmud identifies anger as one of the characteristic traits of an individual: "Rabbi Ila'i said: A person is known by three things: his cup (by how he holds his wine), his pocket (by his generosity) and his anger" (Babylonian Talmud, *Eruvin* 65b).

For several centuries, human beings have often credited natural evils to the anger of God, most notably after the 1755 earthquake in Lisbon. God's wrath, derived from the myriad stories in the Old Testament in particular, is, they claim, evident as punishment of human beings for perceived transgressions. However, as we have seen, the Old Testament stories of divine wrath lack moralizing and often seem the impetuous reaction of an impatient character.

As a result of the varied representations of anger in the Bible, it is difficult indeed to emerge from study of this issue with a broad or general conclusion. The Old Testament God is wrathful and impetuous; the New Testament God is more understanding and delays his wrath until the end times. That assessment is too black and white and does not account for the many shades of gray in the text. We might look instead at a progression of divine behavior, implying growth of the divinity from the punishment in Eden—part of an historical narrative of the Israelites, birth and growth—to the apocalyptic end in Revelation—a fictional progression of an event yet-to-come.

What does all of this mean for contemporary conceptions of anger as they relate particularly to religion and religious groups in the West? I might suggest that the especially Jewish approach to the anger of God is an immediate reaction, within one's very lifetime. Perhaps the Christian perspective is more a delayed response, in either the next life or at Judgment. This could explain the very different approaches to action in Jewish and Christian societies and governments, the Jewish approach more immediate, the Christian more nuanced.

Much of the hermeneutic complexity comes not in the canonical Bible but in the multitude of peripheral interpretive texts produced in more than 2,000 years. Anger is a concern in western philosophy dating to the pre-Socratics, and volumes on anger and its intersection with religious and spiritual sensibilities continue to be popular enough to appear on bestseller lists. If indeed the Bible text is meant to serve as an exemplar for human behavior, it is confusing and spurious on the issue of anger. Perhaps that is why the topic has been central to patristic and rabbinical writing for some two centuries. The same text-based religious tradition that purports to exemplify love, forgiveness, and mercy has to wrestle with apparent inconsistencies.

The ancients as well as modern psychologists concede that anger operates as a necessary, if unpleasant, aspect of human being. Seneca notes that some examples are to be avoided while others are to be imitated (Seneca, 2007, p. 36); one wonders whether some instances of anger in the Bible are intended as examples to avoid. As he notes, "many men have been incapacitated by their anger, many disabled, even when their victims have yielded to such treatment" (p. 42).

In fact, I have found Seneca to be most helpful on the question of anger in the Bible. During the first century CE, Seneca's sentiments seem to parallel much of the teaching in the New Testament while reflecting the memory of the collective past. In his tract, Seneca reminds us of the contrary and unproductive nature of anger.

In his study of the decline of violence, Steven Pinker notes that the Old Testament is rife with violence and anger, almost from the opening pages

(2011, pp. 8–10). Perhaps this can be explained by the multiplicity of gods the ancient Israelites were dealing with. In order to express the dominance of Yahweh as *the* only God, the writers of Old Testament tales are pressed to display that dominance through a metaphorical battle with the other gods (not unlike similar conflicts amongst the Greek and Roman gods). As the text of the Old Testament progresses, and the New Testament arises, the need to exert power through anger and violence is reduced. Countries battle for primacy only when they are threatened by each other; in times of peace, both the rhetoric and the actual events are smoothed over/made more calm.

Notes

1. My title comes from a French proverb: "La colère est mauvaise conseillère" ("Anger is a bad counselor").
2. The Revised Standard translation will be used throughout this paper.

References

Aloysia, M. (1946). The god of wrath? *The Catholic Biblical Quarterly, 8*(4), 407–415.

Aristotle. (1984). J. Barnes (Ed.), *Rhetoric. The complete works of Aristotle* (Vol. 2, pp. 2152–2269). Princeton, NJ: Princeton University Press.

Augsburger, D. W. (1993). Anger and aggression. In R. J. Wicks, R. D. Parsons, & D. Capps (Eds.), *Clinical handbook of pastoral counseling, Vol. 1* (pp. 482–501). Mahwah, NJ, Paulist Press.

Augustine. (2003). *Concerning the city of God against the Pagans.* (H. S. Bettenson, Trans.). New York, NY: Penguin.

Baloian, B. E. (1992). *Anger in the Old Testament.* New York, NY: Peter Lang.

Denney, J. (1906). Anger. In J. Hastings (Ed.), *Dictionary of Christ and the Gospels* (pp. 60–62). New York, NY: Charles Scribner's Sons.

Dodd, C. H. (1932). *The epistle of Paul to the Romans.* New York, NY: Harper and Brothers.

Elliott, M. A. (2006). *Faithful feelings: Rethinking emotion in the New Testament.* Grand Rapids, MI: Kregel.

Galen, C. (1963). *On the passions and errors of the soul.* (P. W. Harkins, Trans.). Columbus, OH: Ohio State University Press.

Hanson, A. T. (1957). *The wrath of the lamb.* London, UK: SPCK Publishing.

Heiron, G. (1992). Wrath of God (OT). In D. N. Freedman (Ed.), *The Anchor Bible dictionary* (pp. 989–996). New York, NY: Doubleday.

Hengel, M. (1989). *The zealots: Investigations into the Jewish Freedom Movement in the period from Herod I until 70 A.D.* (D. Smith, Trans.). Edinburgh, UK: T&T Clark.

Hick, J. (1966). *Evil and the god of love.* Norfolk, UK: Collins.

Holmes, M. H. (2004). The importance of being angry: Anger in political life. *European Journal of Social Theory, 7*(2), 123–132.

Jung, C. G. (1959). *Aion: Researches into the Phenomenology of the Self* (R. F .C. Hull, Trans.). Princeton, NJ: Princeton University Press.

Jung, C. G. (1973). *Answer to Job* (R. F .C. Hull, Trans.). Princeton, NJ: Princeton University Press.

Lactantius. (1885). *De Ira Dei* (A treatise on the anger of God), (P. Schaff, Ed.). Retrieved from http://www.ccel.org/ccel/schaff/anf07.html

Lieu, J. M. (2015). *Marcion and the making of a heretic: God and scripture in the second century.* New York, NY: Cambridge University Press.

Maitles, H. (2002). Surviving the Holocaust: The anger and guilt of Primo Levi. *Journal of Genocide Research, 4*(20), 237–251.

Martin, S. A. (1986). Anger as inner transformation. *Quadrant, 19*(1), 31–45.

MacGregor, G. H. C. (1961). The concept of the wrath of God in the New Testament. *New Testament Studies, 7*(2), 101–109.

Mattison, W. C., III. (2007). Jesus' prohibition of anger (MT 5:22): The person/sin distinction from Augustine to Aquinas. *Theological Studies, 68*(4), 839–864.

McCarthy, M. C. (2009). Divine wrath and human anger: Embarrassment ancient and new. *Theology Studies, 70*(4), 845–874.

Milton, J. (1998). Paradise lost. *The riverside Milton.* (Roy Flannagan, Ed.). New York, NY: Houghton Mifflin.

Otto, R. (1958). *The idea of the holy* (J. W. Harvey, Trans.). London, UK: Oxford University Press.

Pinker, S. (2001). *The better angels of our nature: Why violence has declined.* New York, NY: Viking.

Powlison, D. (1995). Anger, part 1: Understanding anger. *The Journal of Biblical Counseling, 14*(1), 40–53.

Schlimm, M. R. (2011). *From fratricide to forgiveness: The language and ethics of anger in Genesis.* Winona Lake, IN: Eisenbrauns.

Schwartz, R. M. (1997). *The curse of Cain: The violent legacy of monotheism.* Chicago, IL: University of Chicago Press.

Seneca. (2007). On anger: Book 3: To Novatus. In (J. Davie, Trans.), *Dialogues and Essays* (pp. 18–52). Oxford, UK: Oxford University Press.

Sheridan, M. (2015). *Language for god in patristic tradition: Wrestling with Biblical anthropomorphism.* Downers Grove, IL: IVP Academic.

Van der Horst, P. W. (1993). Philo van Alexandrie over de torn Gods. In A. de Jong & A. de Jong (Eds.), *Kleine Encyclopedie van de Toorn* (pp. 77–82). Utrecht, NL: Utrechtse Theologische Reeks 21.

Voorwinde, S. (2014). "Jesus and anger: Does he practice what he preaches?" [Online document]. Retrieved from http://www.baylor.edu/content/services/document.php/235701.pdf

Watson, T. (1650). *A body of practical divinity.* (Subsequently published in 1660, Glasgow, UK: Lochhead). Retrieved from https://ia802604.us.archive.org/15/items/1826abodyofprac00watsuoft/1826abodyofprac00watsuoft.pdf

CHAPTER SEVEN

Anger and Conflict in Cinema

Rob Edelman

Whether a film is a pulse-pounding thriller, a mind-massaging drama, or a quick-witted romantic comedy, conflict is one of the key components of successful storytelling. It is essential to the establishment and development of the central characters and the flow of the storyline. And, usually, feelings of anger are a byproduct of conflict. Whether hero, heroine, or villain, characters will be spurred on by anger as they embark on their efforts to achieve their objectives or seek revenge against those who have thwarted those endeavors.[1]

In any serious analysis of film, it is essential that several points about the moviemaking process be established. Most importantly, within the boundaries of mainstream American cinema, films are a "product." (Hollywood is an industry town and, within that industry, motion pictures are known as "products." They are no different from automobiles, lightbulbs, or bathroom tissue. This was true in 1925, and it remains so now.) At the same time, many films are created by talented, serious-minded individuals who wish their output to be successful financially but also want to create meaningful entertainment and cinematic art. These aspirations give rise to the creative approaches they take as they choose the stories they wish to tell, select camera angles, and decide how and when to move the camera, collaborate with cinematographers to determine the most effective lighting design, or determine when one shot will end and the next will begin. In particular, editing plays a powerful role in this process and in expressing the conflict and anger that is inherent to the storyline.

According to Sergei Eisenstein (1949), each shot in a film is a unit with a dynamic visual charge. The goal is to successfully connect one shot with the next, resulting in a contrast and collision of images, and what might be described as conflict on a purely visual level.

As we study the history of cinema, we also can analyze specific films for the manner in which they record the past or reflect the prevailing culture at the time in which they were made. And with all this in mind, a successful film—whether it was produced to provoke thought or merely to entertain—will grab onto and hold the attention of audiences while transporting them into realms that are far from everyday reality. If, for example, two individuals meet, share an attraction, begin dating, marry, start a family, and remain a contented couple for decades to come, that certainly is a real-world ideal. It can be said that individuals who are raised by loving parents, complete their schooling, find gainful employment, pay their taxes, take vacations, and eventually enjoy quiet retirements are living peaceful, productive lives. But scenarios that feature such happy beginnings, middles, and endings will not translate into compelling storytelling. Where is the conflict? Where is the anger? Where are the issues? Without them, audiences quickly will become bored with what is unfolding onscreen.

To be sure, a scenario that is rife with conflict will feature the problem-solving that is an intrinsic part of forceful storytelling. The anger-related issues exhibited by the characters will be resolved, leading to the happy-ever-after endings that permit the movie-going masses to exit the theater with smiles on their faces. And if there is no resolution by the final credit roll—if the conflict and anger issues are not settled—the audience will be left to ponder the plights and fates of the characters.

Anger and Romance

The plotlines of myriad romantic comedies and musicals are spun into motion by anger and conflict. The central characters may hear wedding bells at the finale, but they often are at odds upon first meeting. They even may intensely dislike each other and, as the story progresses, they will clash over serious issues or personality differences. But eventually, as their stories unfold, they will develop feelings for each other as they strive to overcome those obstacles. Such is the tried-and-true formula employed in boy-meets-girl storytelling.

Take, for example, the 1930s Fred Astaire-Ginger Rogers musicals. In most of them, when Fred and Ginger meet, there is an intense dislike on the part of one or both of their characters. In *Top Hat* (1935), Fred plays Jerry Travers, a musical revue star who practices his tap dancing while ensconced in a London hotel. The resulting noise enrages Dale Tremont (Rogers), who occupies the room below. Upon meeting Dale, Jerry is smitten, but she rebuffs him. What follows is a cat-and-mouse scenario involving various misunderstandings. At the finale, of course, the struggles disappear, Dale's marriage to a less-suitable suitor is sabotaged, and Fred and Ginger merrily glide down a flight of stairs and across a dance floor. In *Swing Time* (1936), Fred is John "Lucky" Garnett, a dancer-gambler; he meets Penny Carrol (Rogers), a dance instructor who misconstrues his friendliness for an unwanted sexual come-on and even accuses him of thievery. Yet again, Fred's character is infatuated but rejected. Yet again, Ginger's character is set to wed an inappropriate suitor, but the union is disrupted. Yet again, a host of additional complications are resolved. And at the finale, Ginger agrees to wed Fred and the two overlook a picturesque window view of snow falling over a Big City vista while briefly, sweetly reprising Jerome Kern and Dorothy Fields's "A Fine Romance."

One of the classic modern-day romances in which an oil-and-water encounter evolves into love is found in *When Harry Met Sally . . .* (1989). At the outset, twenty-somethings Harry (Billy Crystal) and Sally (Meg Ryan) meet while sharing a ride from Chicago to New York. To Harry, Sally is superficially happy; to Sally, Harry is a slob with a "dark side." They disagree over the plot of *Casablanca*. They have different approaches to ordering meals in restaurants. They argue about everything and, at the end of the trip, Harry tells Sally, "It was nice knowing you," while Sally tells Harry, "Have a nice life." But over the years, they keep encountering each other in bookstores and airports and eventually forge a friendship. They date others, sleep with others, and commiserate over their failed romances. They squabble, and they apologize—but will their connection somehow segue into romance? Is true love in the picture for Harry and Sally? Of course it is and, at the better-late-than-never finale, the pair acknowledge they indeed are more than friends.

If anger and conflict are not keys to the scenario when the boy and girl first meet, they are fated to factor into the plot as the story unfolds. In *Annie Hall* (1976), Alvy Singer (Woody Allen) and the title character (Diane Keaton) meet and begin a romance. At the outset, they get along famously—but in order for the storyline to resonate, the two must quarrel. Alvy's and Annie's relationship is destined to nosedive: Alvy is, like Woody Allen, a confirmed New Yorker, while Annie chooses to move to Los Angeles to advance her career. Upon rejecting him after he jets off to California to visit her, Allen expresses Alvy's anger visually by having him smack his rented car into one auto after another in a restaurant parking lot. At the finale, they meet by chance on a Manhattan street. Their romance clearly will not be rekindled, but they share happy memories of their union. However, if the scenario did not progress beyond Alvy's and Annie's initial attraction, *Annie Hall* would not have been much of a film.

Similarly, in other Woody Allen films, the central characters become involved with women who are attractive, supportive, devoted: idealized romantic partners who would be coveted by any sane male. But Allen's males are irrational and highly neurotic, and conflict enters the storyline as they sabotage their relationships. In *Deconstructing Harry* (1997), the title character (played by Allen) is paired with the ever-adoring Fay (Elisabeth Shue), but Harry implores her to not take their bond seriously. So when Fay meets, dates, and marries Larry (Billy Crystal), angst-ridden Harry is devastated. In *Manhattan* (1979), Allen is forty-something Isaac Davis, whose girlfriend is beautiful, sensuous—and is all of 17. However, Tracy (Mariel Hemingway), despite her age, is up front with her feelings in a manner that eludes Isaac, who constantly disappoints her and even advises her to try dating boys who are her contemporaries. A conflicted, disappointed Tracy eventually distances herself from Isaac.

Anger in Drama

If the film in question is a drama, mystery, or thriller, the hero or heroine will face off against the machinations of a villain who is exploiting all those in his or her path; in this regard, anger and conflict are the central aspects of the storytelling. In a Western, the crooked, all-powerful cattleman or saloon owner will be fleecing the town and its citizens. In a crime tale, the underworld overlord will be robbing banks, dealing drugs, selling illegal liquor, and committing murder. In a spy or sci-fi tale, the megalomaniacal villain will be scheming to dominate the world. The victimized masses are powerless to protest; anyone who is angered enough to do so— the newspaper editor in the Western town who prints editorials damning the crook or the newly installed district attorney who promises to rid the corrupt city of the crime syndicate—is assaulted or murdered by the villain's henchmen. The conflict escalates upon the arrival of the hero: the federal marshal who is assigned to clean up the town; the G-man who is determined to eradicate the criminal element; or the representative of law, order, and decency who takes on and subsequently crushes the world domination-obsessed rogue.

Some of the very best dramatic films, those that offer piercing psychological portraits of the central character, veer away from these formulas. One of the all-time-great American films is *On the Waterfront* (1954), which, despite its thinly veiled rationale for "naming names" before government committees, is a poignant tale that stresses the anger and conflict that are an intrinsic part of everyday life. The central character is Terry Malloy (Marlon Brando), a none-too-bright former boxer who, once upon a time, "coulda been a contender" for a boxing crown. However, upon the urging of Johnny Friendly (Lee J. Cobb), a thuggish union boss, and Charley the Gent (Rod Steiger), Terry's brother and Johnny's right-hand-man, Terry thoughtlessly allowed himself to throw the fight that might have landed him a shot at the title. And so Terry is not so much a has-been as a never-was.

The conflict and subsequent anger on the part of Terry results from his unknowingly becoming an accessory to the murder of a dockworker who had agreed to testify before a waterfront crime commission. Terry begins questioning the motives of Johnny and Charley, and his festering, all-consuming anger is expressed in the film's legendary taxicab scene. Here, Terry has realized that his shot at the title was stripped away from him solely because of the greed of Johnny Friendly and the support of Charley. Terry might have been a champion. He might have risen out of the exploited working class. But instead, he is nothing but a self-described "bum," on a "one-way ticket to Palookaville." This is his present, this surely will be his future, and at the heart of Terry's plight is his sibling's deception. Terry faces off verbally and emotionally against his brother, his pent-up anger coming to the surface as he excoriates Charley for not looking after him. In *On the Waterfront*, the core of this brother-brother relationship is greed and deceit, which segues into the conflict between the two men and Terry's justifiable, all-consuming despair.

The Best Years of Our Lives (1946), another Hollywood classic, is the story of three World War II veterans and their plights as they return to their fictional Midwestern hometown. If these men were to reunite with their wives, girlfriends, or parents and seamlessly blend into the American mainstream, the result would not be much of a film. But each man faces a specific issue, one in which conflict and anger are at center stage. Homer Parrish (Harold Russell) arrives home missing both his hands, and the questions facing him are: How will he be accepted by his family? Will he be treated as an invalid, and will he be a burden to Wilma (Cathy O'Donnell), his childhood sweetheart? Meanwhile, how will Al Stephenson (Fredric March), a middle-aged former bank officer, readjust to civilian life? Will he be allowed to employ his military experiences and meet the special needs of the veterans who request loans from his bank? And what of the plight of Fred Derry (Dana Andrews), a bona fide war hero who lacks education and is unable to secure lasting employment? What will be his future? How will he react when the skills he acquired as a GI—skills that were intrinsic to the war effort—now are shown to be worthless? Also, how will he respond when Marie (Virginia Mayo), his self-absorbed wife, cheats on him? *The Best Years of Our Lives*, released during the first full post-war year, is at once a portrait of life in America in 1946 and an exploration of the varying degrees of anger and conflict that affected veterans.

Occasionally, mainstream dramatic films directly examine provocative, controversial social issues. For example, *I Am a Fugitive from a Chain Gang* (1932), the story of an innocent man (Paul Muni) incarcerated for a crime he did not commit, exposes the mistreatment of prisoners on Southern chain gangs; its storyline is representative of American social conscience films at their most compelling. To varying degrees, a host of films—the list begins with *Fury* (1936), *Black Legion* (1937), *They Won't Forget* (1937), and *The Ox-Bow Incident* (1943)— lambaste lynching and other offshoots of mob justice. *Gentleman's Agreement* (1947) and *Crossfire* (1947) are condemnations of anti-Semitism. Dozens of films whose productions parallel the beginnings of the civil rights movement denounce racism American-style; these titles only begin with *Intruder in the Dust* (1949), *Home of the Brave* (1949), *Lost Boundaries* (1949), *Pinky* (1949), *No Way Out* (1950), *The Jackie Robinson Story* (1950), and *Bright Victory* (1951). By their very nature, all these films feature characters who are conflicted for a range of reasons: They are innocent individuals who are unfairly imprisoned and abused within the criminal justice system; they are victimized by the out-of-control, vengeance-seeking masses; or they are persecuted because of their race or religion. These storylines emphasize the conflicts and resulting anger that are directly related to the victims' maltreatment. Simultaneously, they are meant to provoke anger in viewers, anger on the part of the fair-minded filmgoer who will respond to the injustices being perpetrated against the characters, and perhaps even anger on the part of those who would justify the actions of lynch mobs or the mistreatment of Blacks and Jews and summarily blame "liberal Hollywood" for the content of these films.

However, it must be acknowledged that countless films produced before the advent of the civil rights movement feature characters who are not allowed to express their feelings simply because of their race. Prior to the late 1940s, African Americans were endlessly stereotyped in Hollywood movies as thick-witted souls who wrecked the English language. They referred to every white person as "Boss," and the purpose of their onscreen presence primarily was for comic relief. But what was going on inside these characters? How did they feel about their second-class American citizenship? Did they resent the manner in which they were patronized by Caucasians? Were they ever conflicted? Were they ever angry? Because of the accepted mainstream view of African Americans, their issues and feelings were ignored simply because of race.

The Denial of Anger

In recent decades, countless films include reaction shots of children who are dazed, confused, and traumatized as they stand off to the side in quiet shock while their parents scream at each other, or even physically abuse each other. But such was not always the case. In particular during the 1950s, various scenarios put forth what then was an accepted idea about children: They are half-formed human beings, incapable of being conflicted or angered; their feelings somehow are not real, and are not to be considered within the realm of the "adult world."

For example, in *The Big Heat* (1953), big city cop Dave Bannion (Glenn Ford) is determined to bust open an all-powerful crime syndicate. Bannion, who values the love of his devoted wife and sweet young daughter, is plunged into anger and despair when his mate is murdered. But the impact on the child, who logically is just as equally damaged, is completely ignored. In the first scene after the killing in which she appears, the girl merrily greets her dad and asks him to read her a story. Later on, she clutches a ragdoll and kisses her father goodnight. While the adult is embittered, the child's pain is nonexistent. She is not allowed to ask: "Where is mommy?" "What happened to mommy?" "Will I ever see her again?"

At the finale of *Between Midnight and Dawn* (1950), a psychotic bad guy is dangling a little girl out of an apartment window and threatening to drop her to her death. The child is screaming hysterically, as one would expect. But after she is rescued amid additional violence and chaos, she is shown to be oblivious to what has just happened—and the now-relaxed, smiling child is carried off by her mother. But what about her ordeal? It is as if what she has just experienced never occurred; the following morning, she will wake up from a peaceful slumber and play with her toys or head off to school. The message here is that she will not be scarred by this experience or even remember it, simply because of her youth.

The Marrying Kind (1952) is the story of Florrie and Chet Keefer (Judy Holliday and Aldo Ray), a New York couple who are seeking a divorce, with their case being argued in the city's Court of Domestic Relations. The scope of their relationship unfolds in flashback and, at one point, their young son accidentally drowns. Both parents are anguished. Florrie cries hysterically, while Chet is in shock. But the Keefers also have a daughter, and she is not allowed to express any emotion over the tragedy. In her first appearance after the accident, the child pesters her mother for a soda, just as any kid might. Next, she excitedly greets her father after a separation, just as any kid might. Then she helps her mother set the dinner table and sounds off on her favorite desert, just as any kid might. Is she in any way traumatized by the tragedy? No. Does she question the fate of her sibling? No. Is she shown to miss him? No.

The Marrying Kind may be progressive in its portrayal of gender roles: The wise, patient judge who hears the case is a woman. (At this time, myriad post-war American movies depicted women as subservient figures who were expected to toss their conflicts, ambitions, and feelings aside, all in the name of marriage and family life.) But the Keefers' daughter is a half-formed character. She expresses emotion after her brother's death only in one scene: Her parents are loudly fighting, and the sleeping child is awakened by the "mad people" who are hollering. But her hysteria has nothing to do with her state of mind. It only is present in relation to her parents and their issues.

For decades, children who had grown into adolescence were acknowledged to be old enough to deal with anger and conflict. Often, however, those feelings were linked to class. In innumerable films, ghetto kids—particularly those who were lacking positive role models—joined gangs and broke laws. One example: In *Angels with Dirty Faces* (1938), the Dead End Kids, a band of scruffy, surly teen boys, idolize neither parent nor educator nor religious figure but Rocky Sullivan (James Cagney), a notorious hoodlum. Meanwhile, in other films, the children of the American middle class, as personified by Andy Hardy (Mickey Rooney) in a series of popular MGM features released from the late-1930s to mid-1940s, were solid citizens-in-training whose conflicts were of the "who shall I take to the prom" variety. The very real feelings of young people who were born into outwardly respectable families finally were acknowledged in *Rebel Without a Cause* (1955), a landmark exploration of teen angst. The central character is Jim Stark (James Dean), a troubled product of the American middle class. His hapless, clueless parents constantly toss mixed messages in his direction, and at one point the seething teen admonishes them by lamenting that they are "tearing me apart." Jim Stark's anger and conflict were—and are—ever-so-relatable to young people who are coming of age in a less-than-hospitable culture.

Anger, Conflict, and the New American Cinema

Keeping in mind that films are products of the time in which they were made and the prevailing culture, a new kind of motion picture emerged from Hollywood in the late 1960s and 1970s. These films mirror the uncertainty that existed in the United States at this time while exploring the issues of the day: the civil rights movement, the anti–Vietnam war movement, and the sexual revolution. They feature characters who are angered, conflicted, and alienated for a range of reasons. They are misunderstood by their parents, for example, or they feel powerless as the world around them is engulfed in chaos.

Benjamin Braddock (Dustin Hoffman) in *The Graduate* (1967), Bobby Dupea (Jack Nicholson) in *Five Easy Pieces* (1970), and Travis Bickle (Robert De Niro) in *Taxi Driver* (1976) are three classic characters who embody the era. Ben Braddock refuses to embrace the "plastic" world of his parents and commences a sexual relationship with the infamous Mrs. Robinson (Anne Bancroft), a woman old enough to be his mother. Bobby Dupea rejects the elitism of his family and his classical music background, toils in an oilfield, and quietly seethes as he mixes with individuals of all classes. Travis Bickle, an alienated, psychologically scarred Vietnam veteran, complains about the lowlife scum who inhabit the Manhattan streets. So what does he do in his spare time? He watches porn movies in a sleazy movie house. Plus, he plots an assassination. It does not matter to Travis if he murders a presidential candidate (which would label him a villain of Lee Harvey Oswald–like proportion) or a pimp (which he does, and which earns him heroic status in the media). Travis is angry. He is aimless. He is alienated and conflicted. And he is a product of his era.

Meanwhile, the struggles and feelings of women that resulted in the feminist movement were explored in *A Woman Under the Influence* (1974), *Alice Doesn't Live Here Anymore* (1974), *An Unmarried Woman* (1978), and *Kramer vs. Kramer* (1979). These films spotlight women of varying backgrounds and life experiences: respectively, a psychologically unhinged wife and mother (played by Gena Rowlands), a recently widowed mother (Ellen Burstyn) attempting to build a new life for herself and her son, an upscale Manhattanite (Jill Clayburgh) who is unceremoniously dumped by her cheating husband, and another wife and mother (Meryl Streep) who feels stifled by the expectations thrust upon her and who abandons both her mate and her offspring. Collectively, these women are angry and conflicted; they share a frustration with a male-dominated culture that devalues them solely because of their gender.

Bonnie and Clyde (1967) is yet another landmark film of its era. A fictionalized, highly romanticized biopic chronicling the stories of Bonnie Parker (Faye Dunaway) and Clyde Barrow (Warren Beatty), the infamous Depression-era criminals, the film reflects on the conflicts and angers that were enveloping the nation three decades after the Great Depression. The scenario portrays the title characters not as amoral lawbreakers, but as modern-day Robin Hoods who literally take from the rich while sparing the poor. In one sequence, while hiding out in an abandoned farm-house, Bonnie and Clyde are joined by the former owner and his family: hard-working, salt-of-the-earth Americans who have been thrown off their land by the cruel, insensitive government. Bonnie and Clyde are sympathetic to the farmer's plight, but they cannot steal the farm back. However, before the sequence ends, they provide the farmer with a gun and encourage him to vent his anger by shooting at the bank ownership sign. The farmer then introduces an African American who for years helped him work the land—and he too is permitted to shoot up the joint. In other words, the Black man is allowed a symbolic equality.

All of this may be translated into 1967 terms. In *Bonnie and Clyde*, a heartless, indifferent government tosses hard-working citizens off their farms. Compare this to a heartless, indifferent government that was sending off young Americans to their deaths in Vietnam. Unlike World War II, Vietnam was controversial; America's presence in Southeast Asia was the subject of a growing national debate. And by playing into the farmer's anger, and his conflict with a system that was indifferent to his and his family's plight, *Bonnie and Clyde* becomes politicized. Even though it is set in the 1930s, the film mirrors the then-escalating angers and conflicts of the late 1960s.

Anger-Conflict Variations

Certain filmmakers employ satire to comment on the very real angers and conflicts of their characters. Quentin Tarantino is one writer-director whose cinematic sensibility allows him to brilliantly lampoon the cruelty and idiocy of the Holocaust and the history of slavery in the United States. In *Inglourious Basterds* (2009), Tarantino depicts a Jewish American GI who relishes bashing in the skulls of Nazis with a baseball bat; at the finale, Hans Landa (Christoph Waltz), a sadistic Nazi, ends up with a swastika etched onto his forehead. *Django Unchained* (2012), set prior to the Civil War, charts the story of the title character (Jamie Foxx), an escaped slave who morphs into the "fastest gun in the West." In these films, Tarantino is making light of the anger and conflict that were very real in Europe during the 1930s and 1940s and in the United States prior to the 1860s. But he is not doing so in an insensitive or disrespectful manner. *Inglourious Basterds* and *Django Unchained* are revenge fantasies in which caricature is employed to expose and condemn piggish Nazi swine and sadistic slave owners.

Other anger-centric films are especially relatable to viewers in that they touch on tragedies that may befall anyone in the audience. One of the keys to the enduring popularity of Alfred Hitchcock is his penchant for spot-lighting characters who are neither cops nor soldiers nor spies; they are, like most viewers, not in the "business of danger." But by fate or accident, they find themselves accused of committing heinous crimes and often are hounded by the authorities as well as the real culprit. Such is the plight of a nondescript Canadian Everyman (Robert Donat) on vacation in England in *The 39 Steps* (1935); a suave New York advertising executive (Cary Grant) in *North by Northwest* (1959); a blue collar Glendale, California, aircraft fac-tory worker (Robert Cummings) in *Saboteur* (1942); a nice-guy Washing-ton DC-based tennis player (Farley Granger) in *Strangers on a Train* (1951); and a Queens, New York, musician (Henry Fonda), a workingman who rides the subway to and from work like millions of city dwellers, in the aptly titled *The Wrong Man* (1956).

Occasionally, onscreen anger and conflict may be taken to an extreme. *Death Wish* (1974) follows the plight of Paul Kersey (Charles Bronson), an educated New Yorker with liberal inclinations who is transformed into a one-person vigilante squad after street punks brutally murder his wife and rape and traumatize his daughter. In its day, *Death Wish* was highly con-troversial. At its core, it offers the point of view that victims of brutality (or, extending this further, any kind of injustice) will be so enraged that they will place their ideals aside and fight violence with violence.

The manner in which issues relating to anger and conflict are resolved in *Death Wish* may be contrasted to the actions of one of the central char-acters in *Network* (1976), penned by the estimable Paddy Chayefsky. At one point, network news anchor Howard Beale (Peter Finch) begins a lengthy on-air tirade that touches on the exasperation of any and all average Johns or Janes as he comments on everything from rising crime rates to unemployment, inflation to air pollution. What is Beale's solution? How might the seemingly powerless, conflicted masses demonstrate their ire? For openers, he implores them to open their windows and loudly yell what has become one of the more celebrated bits of dialogue of recent decades: "I'm as mad as hell, and I'm not going to take this anymore!"

In *Network*, Chayefsky employs the anger and conflict that are intrinsic to everyday life and places them within a higher realm. Simply put, one does not have to internalize anger. One does not have to accept conflict as an inevitable aspect of everyday living. One can take action. And in this regard, a film like *Network* is more than just a Hollywood entertainment. As Howard Beale pontificates, Chayefsky's words—just as those in *On the Waterfront* as Terry comes to understand and articulate his issues relating to his brother—become readily identifiable to the average viewer.

Notes

1. Anger portrayed in film focuses on depictions of individuals rather than groups for effectiveness in this medium. The apprehensions of onscreen characters may reflect on group anger or deal with the real-world concerns of the masses of individuals. In this regard, the characters' plights and fates may be relatable to the masses. But for the sake of clarity and narrative cohesion, cinematic storylines spotlight individual behavior, individual feelings, and the specific issues faced by specific characters within the framework of their story arcs.

On the Waterfront is not the tale of a group of dockworkers and how they collectively respond to their exploitation by the corrupt union. It is a drama about one man—Terry Malloy—and how he comes to realize that he is being oppressed. *The Best Years of Our Lives* may touch on the challenges faced by countless World War II veterans who were transitioning from wartime to peacetime, but the scenario would lack power and poignancy if it generalized about these issues. The film works because it focuses on the specific problems of three men.

I Am a Fugitive from a Chain Gang is an exploration of prison abuse. Countless films produced during the late-1940s and into the 1950s (*Intruder in the Dust, Home of the Brave, Lost Boundaries* . . .), acknowledge racism American-style. Films such as *The Graduate, Five Easy Pieces*, and *Taxi Driver* mirror the alienation felt by young Americans in the late-1960s and 1970s, while *A Woman Under the Influence, Alice Doesn't Live Here Anymore, An Unmarried Woman*, and *Kramer vs. Kramer* explore the pre-feminist frustrations of women. These films can be relatable to audiences only because they are potent portraits of the plights of individual characters.

Romantic dramas or comedies may deal with issues faced by myriad couples as they establish and define their relationships. But the films will connect with the masses only if they are clever and original—and if their storylines spotlight specific couples: Harry and Sally in *When Harry Met Sally . . .* , for example, or Annie and Alvy in *Annie Hall*.

Reference

Eisenstein, S. (1949). The cinematographic principle and the ideogram. In *Film form: Essays in film theory* (pp. 37–40). New York, NY: Harcourt, Brace & World.

CHAPTER EIGHT

Anger, Connection, and Activism: Coming of Age in *Harry Potter*

Sybillyn Jennings

This volume addresses groups organized around the emotion of anger, whether anger is the impetus for the group's formation or whether an association, organized by other characteristics, has experiences that result in anger. Anger may arise temporarily in many different associations without those inside or outside the group viewing anger as its defining feature. Anger that sustains an association of adults over time may not be observable as an attack, though it may rouse the group to action and serve to remind its members of what has so insulted, injured, or threatened them. There are groups and anger aplenty in the *Harry Potter* novels, but are there angry groups? Anger, as Lazarus (1991) describes the adult emotion, is provoked by "a demeaning offense against me and mine" (p. 222). Parents may surely strike out in anger if their children are threatened, and there are many family groups in Rowling's panoramic series of novels. Some groups are separated from each other by culture, as are wizards and non-magical people, or *muggles*, and such differences can engender anger. Some groups, such as wizards and goblins, have been set against each other by historical events. But what of angry groups in childhood? What does it mean for a child to grow up in a family that hates the child for burdening them, as is the case with Harry Potter? What does it mean for a child to figure out that his mother rejected him and so hate her for abandoning him, as with Tom Riddle? How do these early emotional experiences shape associations with others later in childhood and in adolescence, and how do these associations, in turn, shape emotional development? Anger can erupt in the face of having one's identity questioned and one's word not being believed, whether by dyadic groups or by larger groups that have power to enforce their interpretation, as happens with Harry. A group initiated to accomplish one function may evolve into an angry group, as is the case with Dumbledore's Army.

Of what use is a series of novels in informing these developmental and social psychological questions? In recent years psychology has been exploring narrative methods of research, borrowing, in part, from the accepted and essential use of biography in clinical case studies (e.g., Bakan, 1996; Kegan, 1994; McAdams, 1993) along with Erikson's (1958) pioneering work in psychohistory. In current psychology, Lewin's (1939) dictum that behavior is a function of person X environment, although expressed and examined through different conceptual frameworks, has become a taken-for-granted assumption. Then too, studies of the development of mental life including emotions, memory, and most especially, consciousness (e.g., Lewis, 2014) lend credence to the importance of how people make meaning and how meaning changes or becomes crystallized as people develop resources to think about situations and their experience across time in the contexts of their lives. J. K. Rowling has given her readers an amazing story of a boy growing up, a wonder in itself. She has also given readers and fans a well from which they can draw to generate their own questions and musings about the many characters whom readers meet and learn about at different moments across their lives. Rowling herself extends Harry's story by following the path of Harry and Ginny's son, Albus Severus, to Hogwarts in *Harry Potter and the Cursed Child* (Rowling, Tiffany, & Thorne, 2016). Along with my students[**], I have been experimenting with the novels as though they were a database to explore well-known concepts in developmental psychology such as attachment, loss, identity, friendship, reasoning, and issues of risk and resilience. In this chapter, I will explore pathways of anger in a number of characters and discuss how their associations with others intensify, deflect, or transform their emotional

---

[**] I offer thanks to my seminar students for their delight in studying the novels, to Sara Schuman and Michelle Napierski-Prancl for their helpful suggestions, to Kenneth Jennings for sharing the Harry Potter journey, and, of course, to J.K. Rowling for making it all possible.

expression and understanding. Rowling's fictive world, more capacious even than Hermione's beaded bag, offers perspective on how divergent pathways in developing consciousness influence experiences of anger and their sequelae.

Rowling's *Harry Potter* Novels

The story of Rowling's series of novels is widely known so I offer a simple version here. Voldemort, a dark wizard, learning of a prophecy that a baby will rival his rule of the wizarding world, hunts down the likely baby, murdering him and his parents. But the one-year-old Harry Potter does not die. Voldemort's curse backfires, causing Voldemort to vanish, leaving the scar of his attack on Harry's forehead. The baby is taken to live with and be brought up by his aunt and uncle, who have no traffic with the wizarding world and treat Harry miserably as a freak to be shut away. At 11 years of age, for the first time, Harry learns that he is a wizard and has been enrolled in Hogwarts School of Witchcraft and Wizardry. The seven novels follow the adventurous, often impetuous and clueless, but kind, Harry through his schooling at Hogwarts as he learns about his past and the likelihood of his future troubles upon the return of Voldemort.

We begin with an overview of the magical world, which is structured, though incompletely, along the lines of a non-magical, or *muggle,* world. Although the magical world Rowling describes extends through history across countries and nations, one estimates that its total population is quite small owing, no doubt, to the fear and persecution of wizards and witches through the centuries. (Population estimates are offered in harrypotter.wikia.com.) According to Bagshot's *History of Magic,* in 1689 wizards retreated into secrecy, hiding in "knots" of families in small English villages (Rowling, 2007, pp. 318–319). Across the seven novels readers are introduced to a number of wizard institutions including businesses (e.g., wand makers), governance (e.g., Ministry of Magic), media (e.g., *The Daily Prophet*), as well as many face-to-face groups. Rowling paints the Ministry as a typical, perhaps stereotypical, bureaucratic institution with a minister anxious about his political status and department heads working to gain the favor of those above them while civil servants conduct the chores of the quotidian. There is, however, no description of a parliament with organized, opposing political groups. The Ministry bumbles along in the enterprise of keeping the social order and, for the most part, the social good. At urgent times (i.e., the return of Voldemort), the Minister of Magic communicates with the British Prime Minister, much to the discomfort of the latter.

Hogwarts School of Witchcraft and Wizardry, the only wizarding educational institution in England, brings together members of the wizarding community and is the heart of the novels. The school is maintained and overseen by the Ministry of Magic. Its headmaster is Albus Dumbledore, a wizard of wide acclaim, greatly honored in the international magical world. Eleven-year-olds who are deemed somehow to be magical, receive letters from the headmaster inviting them to enroll in the seven-year course of study. Students are organized by their year in school, and any magical activity is traced when they are away from school because they are seen as not yet having control over their magical talents and may violate the 1689 law of secrecy, intended to maintain muggles' ignorance of magic. Students purchase their first wands, robes, books, and school supplies in Diagon Alley in London.

At Hogwarts, differences within the magical community of birth status (pure blood wizard or half-blood wizard, *mudblood*, a racial slur describing a wizard with muggle parentage), economic class, and more importantly character and intellect, find some expression through the organization of four houses, each with its own space, faculty head, ghost, and the historical legacy of its founder. Students live in their respective houses, but they attend classes together, convene in the great hall of the castle for meals, ceremonies, and celebratory feasts. Houses compete throughout the year, gaining and losing points for behavior, for academic performance, and for their teams' performances in the wondrous, magical team sport of *quidditch*; however, anger is not a feature that characterizes any one house. During an opening ceremony, the ancient Sorting Hat is placed on each entering student's head in turn. The Sorting Hat tells students the house they will be in and sings of Hogwarts's history and current concerns.

Angry Groups in the Magical World

The world Hogwarts students study extends beyond wizards to *muggles* and nonhuman, non-wizard groups of centaurs, elves, giants, goblins, *merpeople*, beasts and magical creatures with whom they live in an apparent, though uneasy, peace. A fountain in the Ministry of Magic (Rowling, 2003) portrays the racial hierarchy of "The Magical Brethren" in "a group of golden statues" (p. 127). Tallest is a wizard with wand directed upward, then a witch looking up at him with her wand poised upward. They are surrounded by those they have subjugated; a centaur, goblin, and house-elf all gaze up at them.

Wizards and witches are identified by their ability to do magic. This ability becomes evident in childhood, and can then be developed through training. Children born to wizards who do not demonstrate the ability to do magic are referred to as *squibs*. At 11 years of age, children obtain their first wands in a complex transaction between the child and the wand overseen by an established wand maker (Rowling, 1997). Wandlore is an esoteric and difficult area of study addressing the special relationship between wand and wizard (Rowling, 2007). Wizards who violate wizarding law may have their wands broken. Goblins refer to wizards as *wand carriers*, noting the essential role wands play in identifying this group. Wands serve as the sort of artifacts that Caporael (1997, p. 290) discusses as linking individuals to their world culture and supporting a shared reality.

Centaurs want no traffic with wizards, whom they view as inferior to them in contemplating the universe. Centaurs maintain their distance from human groups and their role in protecting the beasts of the forest. Centaurs become angry when a member of their group, Firenze, helps Harry, a human. Later, their anger at Firenze's agreement to teach Hogwarts students, and so violating the distance between centaurs and humans, results in his being banished from the forest.

In the magical world, goblins offer the clearest example of an angry group. Vanquished by wizards in ancient wars, goblins' distrust and enmity toward wizards, though kept at bay, continues. Wizards accord goblins respect and admire their craftsmanship. They depend on goblins to manage and to safeguard the impenetrable Gringotts Bank, where wizards keep their wealth. Bill Weasley, who works with goblins at Gringotts, warns Harry, who is planning a transaction with the goblin, Griphook, that goblins and wizards do not live in a shared reality. For goblins, an object belongs to the one who has crafted it; whereas, for wizards, the purchase of an object determines ownership.

House-elves, who are also capable of magic, present a different situation, from the standpoint of angry groups. House-elves belong to, and live to serve, their wizard families and other wizard institutions, as slaves do their masters. Both house-elves and wizards view this relationship as the received state of affairs. Some masters are kind; others cruel, but the relationship of house-elf to wizard is not questioned. House-elves identify with their families, and their emotional feelings appear to depend, not entirely on their identification as house-elf, but on the particularity of the relationship. For example, the house-elf, Dobby, upon being set free from his master, pledges allegiance to the wizard who freed him (Rowling, 1998). Turning from these larger social aggregates, we will examine anger as it appears in the smaller, face-to-face worlds of Rowling's characters.

Family Groups

Rowling introduces her readers to many families, over 20 by my count, across the seven novels. Some families we barely glimpse; others we come to know rather well. The families come in a variety of arrangements; some, like the Weasleys, function well and happily, others, like the Gaunts and the Crouchs, are bitterly dysfunctional. A central theme of the novels is the responsibility of families to protect and to care for their children. In the magical world as in ours, life is full of risks in bringing up children. Some families, for different reasons, are unable to protect their children. Severus Snape's parents are so caught up in argument and poverty that they neglect their son. Tom Riddle's father deserts his mother. Remus Lupin's family could not prevent their child from being bitten by a werewolf, or Adriana Dumbledore's family from her being attacked by a gang of muggle boys. Some parents die, as did James and Lily Potter and Remus and Tonks Lupin, or are tortured into madness in fighting the war against the Death Eaters, as were Neville Longbottom's parents. Then too, children may rebel against their family's beliefs, as does Sirius Black, creating lasting strife and anger. Children can reject family responsibilities that fall to them, leading to self-hate, remorse, and lasting grief, as happens to Albus Dumbledore.

Protecting children can have hard consequences. Percival Dumbledore violated the wizarding law of secrecy to avenge an attack on his young daughter and died in prison. Lily died trying to protect her son from Voldemort's curse, Narcissa Malfoy lied to Voldemort that he had indeed killed Harry to protect her son, Mrs. Crouch saved her son from prison by going in his stead, and Aunt Petunia abandoned her possessions to protect her son. With seething, cold rage Molly Weasley fought and killed Bellatrix Lestrange to protect her children. Some of these actions are generated by anger; others are cause for anger and revenge. Circumstances that create risk for the development of children in families are topics of extensive study in the psychological literature (e.g., Goldstein & Brooks, 2006) and of deep concern in applied fields (Garbarino, 1982; 1999). Rowling's array of fictional families and their troubles can help readers broaden their appreciation of stress that families experience. The range of risk (except for divorce, which Rowling does not include) also provides a perspective from which to analyze and to critique inventories and interview protocols used in researching resilience in families (e.g., Sroufe, Egeland, Carlson, & Collins, 2005).

Protection takes a somewhat more complex turn in the dyadic relationships among adults that Rowling describes. Severus Snape makes an unbreakable vow to Narcissa Malfoy to protect Narcissa's son, Draco.

Severus, the long unknown protector, has vowed to Dumbledore that he will protect Lily's son, Harry, whose father Severus detests. Later, Severus gives Dumbledore his word that he will protect Draco by killing Dumbledore. Both Dumbledore and Snape protect what Dumbledore describes as Draco and Harry's "undamaged" souls by keeping them from committing murder (Rowling, 2007, p. 683).

Throughout the novels many individuals protect Harry. I focus here on Dumbledore, who protects Harry directly, by saving his life in a number of episodes, and indirectly, through teaching him. Most importantly, Dumbledore protects and cares for Harry by supporting Harry's friendships. Dumbledore reveals information to Harry and assigns Harry various tasks, pledging him not to divulge this information except to his friends, Ron and Hermione. Thus, the group of friends is strengthened by Dumbledore. In the next-to-last conversation between Harry Potter and the deceased Dumbledore, at an empty King's Cross Station of the mind, Dumbledore describes "the true magic" of Harry's invisibility cloak as its ability "to protect and shield others as well as its owner" (Rowling, 2007, p. 716). The cloak has been passed down to Harry through generations; it connects him to his family and reveals his courage in protecting those who have protected him. In Rowling's novels, the fascinating stories of protecting adults weave in and out as finely as the threads of Harry's invisibility cloak, the cloak under which Harry, Ron, and Hermione come of age.

Friends and Enemies

If Privet Drive, Diagon Alley, and the Forbidden Forest set boundaries between non-magical and magical human groups, and Hogwarts reveals the stratification among wizards, the scene on the train as students travel to Hogwarts (Rowling, 1997) introduces what will become the core group of the novels, the trio of friends, Harry, Ron, and Hermione. The three first-years are united in this scene by Draco Malfoy's rejection of them. Ron's family, though pureblood, is large, identifiable as Weasleys by their red hair, hand-me-down make-do robes, second-hand books, and no spending money for a treat. On top of that, Ron's father holds an undistinguished position in the Ministry of Magic. Hermione is a witch, but the daughter of muggles, thus from Draco's perspective a disgusting mudblood, and Harry is rejected because he declines Draco's offer to join his group of companions. Harry's pronouncement to Draco that he thinks he knows who the right kind of people are with whom to associate is the first time we hear Harry expressing his beliefs. Later, at the opening ceremony, when the Sorting Hat distributes the first-year students across the four houses, anxious as Harry is in this completely unfamiliar world, he asks the sorting hat not to be placed in Slytherin, Draco's ancestral house. At the time of this assertion, Harry is unaware that his parents were in Gryffindor, only that he is choosing away from Draco. Thus the inimical peer groups are set—Draco and his companions against Harry with Ron, and soon after Hermione, reinforced by the institutionalized competition between Slytherin and Gryffindor. Draco's rejection of Harry's friends because of blood and economic status do indeed anger Harry, as does Draco's presumption in telling Harry what to do.

Readers quickly recognize how essential each member of the trio is in maintaining a sense of purpose and in accomplishing any task (what current psychologists refer to as distributed cognition, Hutchins, 1995, and social cognition; Caporael, 1997; Resnick, Levine, & Teasely, 1991). Though Harry is identified as the nominal "hero" of the story, without Ron and Hermione, Harry could not succeed. And should Harry fail, as Harry much later in the story discovers Dumbledore's calculations, there would still be Ron and Hermione to carry out the mission to defeat Voldemort. The importance of their friendship cannot be overestimated. For Harry, the bond among the three of them offers the care he has been without for 10 years in his aunt and uncle's home and provides security as he finds his way at Hogwarts.

All four functions of friendship, so clearly laid out by Bukowski (2003), are evident in this group. Friends know they are valued for themselves. Being with a friend reduces anxiety in the face of threat and protects against continuing adverse effects of earlier rejections one may have experienced. Friends encourage exploration and support each other in trying out new skills. They are co-constructors of knowledge. Friends can speak openly; they can challenge each other. Friends create an environment with its own expectations—a culture. Across the novels, the friendship group expands to include the awkward, late-bloomer, Neville Longbottom, and the insightful oddball, Luna Lovegood. It is in this group that Harry comes to care for others and to know what it is like to be cared for. This is always the back-story of the novels—love, that ancient magic, deflecting anger and transcending power. Voldemort lacks what Harry holds dear—friends. This is the word, repeated a thousand times, in a wreath Luna paints on her ceiling encircling and joining portraits of her friends. The enchanted ceiling in the great hall at Hogwarts is made of stars, sometimes stormy, sometimes bright. Luna paints the heavens as the constancy of friends.

In the last novel of the series (Rowling, 2007), the trio does not return to school. Instead, they set out on the secret mission Dumbledore has given Harry, with Ron and Hermione, to find and to destroy the remaining *horcruxes*. These are objects in which, through acts of murder and dark magic,

Voldemort has implanted parts of his soul. The trio is resolute in not sharing the information Dumbledore has asked them to keep to themselves. This exclusivity is irritating to others, especially Ron's family and the Order of the Phoenix, the group of adult wizards led by Dumbledore to oppose Voldemort and his Death Eaters. From the trio's perspective, it is essential that they protect their families and supporters from attempts by Voldemort to gain information, thus their secrecy. They are on their own without the protection of family, away from the familiar Hogwarts, and absent Dumbledore's guidance. Hermione's wit and care do much to provide protection for the three friends. She applies her magical skills to enlarge a beaded bag to hold everything they need: books, a tent, essential potions, clothes, even toothbrushes. It is she who casts the protective spells about their encampment while they are on the run. The three friends are often discouraged and become angry and jealous. They blame each other for not having a plan or knowing what direction to take. They have little knowledge to work from and even less experience in taking care of themselves and living together. The tasks Dumbledore sets them are daunting, and they are challenged in every way: their belief in Dumbledore, their sense of purpose, their everyday needs for food and shelter, their magical skills, and most of all their friendship. There are serious breaks—Harry's impulsive acts, Ron's leaving, Hermione's curse that breaks Harry's wand. Still the connection holds. Rowling shows her readers how repair work gets done, how anger can be transcended by taking responsibility, by reflecting on the situation, and by joined action. In close relationships, as Sullivan (1940/1945, p. 20) reminds us, "When the satisfaction or the security of another person becomes as significant to one as is one's own satisfaction or security, then the state of love exists."

Anger, Loss, and Trust

Harry's anger stems from the loss of his family. As readers we imagine Harry's despair; we detest his ill treatment by his aunt, uncle, and cousin, and observe the hatred he returns to the Dursleys early on in the books. But in the last novel when he visits the place where his parents were murdered, the place where he survived, we hear his lashing out at the situation he has inherited and the enduring sadness his deepening realization brings. Why couldn't he have died along with his parents? Why was he saved? Why didn't Dumbledore tell him? Why hadn't he asked Dumbledore for more complete explanations? Why had he trusted Dumbledore? What if he had a normal family who would love and protect him, a family like that of his friend Ron, a mother who would make his birthday cake (Rowling 2007, p. 321)?

Like Harry, abandonment in infancy is at the core of Tom Marvolo Riddle's (Voldemort) anger. It catalyzes his single-minded drive to punish muggles, to control wizards, to conquer death, and blinds him to all other motives. Voldemort tells Dumbledore that, "There is nothing worse than death" (Rowling, 2003, p. 814); after all, it is death that has cheated him from having a mother. As Dumbledore tells the story of Voldemort's origins (Rowling, 2007), the hapless witch, Merope, lives with her abusive father and brother on the edge of the country estate of the wealthy, muggle Riddle family. She falls in love with their handsome son, Tom, and bewitches him into marriage. The enchantment, however, breaks, and Tom leaves Merope, pregnant and penniless, to fend for herself in London. What Voldemort cannot reconcile is that Merope, a witch, fails to use her magical powers to control the unfamiliar environment and to stay alive to care for the baby she births. Instead, she dies, leaving him to endure growing up in a muggle orphanage with a muggle's name. Whereas others might view Merope's situation with more generosity, for Tom Riddle no explanation will excuse his mother, nor will murdering his wizard grandfather and his muggle father and family make up for their offenses against him, what Lewis (2014, p. 248) discusses as a conversion of shame to blaming others. Here then is the source of Voldemort's continuing anger and bitter rejection of love as a deeper, more ancient magic. Merope failed to survive. Unlike Harry's mother, she even failed to give him the protection of her love.

The two babies, Tom and Harry, have their physical needs attended to, though it would seem grudgingly on Aunt Petunia's part. As toddlers and young children they must have been engaged and talked to by their caregivers, whether unkindly for Harry and indifferently for Tom; we have no details and do not know. Harry is described as a small boy with unruly hair and glasses, his forehead marked by an ugly scar. He has no way of countering the Dursleys' account of his past, nor their negative view of him. He has a running inimical relationship with his cousin, Dudley, which for all its unhappiness, seems to give Harry a sense of what he hates and what he does not want to be (Abecassis, 2003). Tom is described as handsome. He appears to be attractive to his caregivers and other children in the orphanage, but as he gets older other children are wary, even fearful, of him (Rowling, 2007). Tom senses he is different from and better than the other children. Dumbledore's interaction with Tom at 11 years of age shows Tom priding himself on his skill in taking care of himself, on not needing anyone. Tom is eager to be gone from the orphanage and off to Hogwarts, a more fitting place for him.

The seeds of disbelief and mistrust are sown early on in the Dursley household and have lasting repercussions, as we observe in Harry and learn from psychological theory, whether Erikson's (1982), Bowlby's (1980, 1988), or Ainsworth's (1995) accounts. Countering these experiences of mistrust is Harry's earliest experience as the beloved infant son of Lily and James. By 15 months, Harry has surely formed an attachment to his parents, and his development is proceeding in a positive, healthy manner. Then, with Voldemort's curse, separation strikes, leading to ultimate loss; the anchors of Harry's security are yanked up, and Harry is set adrift. The pathways of loss at this age have been well described in the psychological literature (e.g., Bowlby, 1980, 1988), and we turn to these descriptions to imagine Harry's experiences in late infancy and toddlerhood, especially his interactions with Petunia. Petunia remains angry toward her sister, Lily, for being a witch when she is not and for abandoning her by attending Hogwarts. There may well be threads of connection provided by similarities in the sisters' voices and touch that soften the baby's loss of his mother. It is hard to conceive of Petunia's complete rejection of her older sister's baby, though favoring her own son of the same age. Still, smiles and hugs for Dudley and scowls and inattention to Harry seem more likely than not.

In the course of the series Harry discovers that he has a godfather who cares deeply for him. But this hope of family is cut off when his godfather is killed in a duel. Losing his godfather, who has died coming to help Harry, makes fresh the loss of his parents and intensifies his anger in the face of loss. Harry does not consciously hold anger against his own parents, who died trying to protect him. Instead he seems to have displaced his anger, raising it to a general, unbending principle, as we see in an interaction with Remus Lupin in the last novel. Remus, who had been their teacher of Defense Against the Dark Arts in their third year at Hogwarts, suggests that, even not knowing the task they have been set by Dumbledore, he might accompany them. He reminds the trio that they have no idea of the powerful magic they are likely to be up against and that he could be helpful. While Harry is taking in this possibility, Remus acknowledges that Tonks, his young wife, is expecting a baby. At first the news is greeted with customary congratulations. But Harry becomes enraged and lets go a tirade of assaults that end with Harry calling Remus a coward for abandoning his child. At this last insult, Remus vanishes by *disapparating*, and Hermione and Ron, distressed at Harry, tell him that he has gone too far. Harry acknowledges that he should not have called Remus a coward, and then rationalizes, "But if it makes him go back to Tonks, it'll be worth it, won't it?" (Rowling, 2007, p. 215).

Remus is angry with himself, a werewolf fathering a baby, and has reached out to these young friends, offering them skills he knows he has. Remus feels, though he does not say, his own parents' grief and anger. They did not, could not, protect him as a young child from being bitten by a werewolf. For Harry, there is no competing emotion, understanding, or action: Parents do not abandon their children. Parents protect their children, as his father and mother protected him with their lives. Remus is able to deflect his own anger with Harry, and later honors Harry by asking him to be the baby's godfather. In a later scene, Harry struggles trying to resolve in his own mind the choice Remus and Tonks have made to leave their baby in his grandmother's care and join the battle for Hogwarts, the battle in which they die. As Harry walks into the forest to meet Voldemort and his own death, he is accompanied by *shadows* of his parents, godfather, and Remus. Harry tells Remus that he is sorry, that he did not want him to die. Remus responds, "I am sorry too . . . . Sorry I will never know him . . . but he will know why I died and I hope he will understand. I was trying to make a world in which he could live a happier life" (Rowling, 2007, p. 700). This degree of commitment, whether one looks at it from the standpoint of self-development (Kegan, 1983), the progression of reasoning (Belenky, Clinchy, Goldberger, & Tarule, 1986; Perry, 1970), or the development of moral reasoning (Colby et al., 1983; Gilligan, 1982) is something Harry has not yet internalized.

Anger at Not Being Believed

Harry grows up in an environment of lies intended to protect him. Here is a basis for the oscillation between belief and doubt in his identity that will trouble Harry throughout his adolescence and will fuel his anger in not being believed, particularly by those who have power over him. Dumbledore seeks to protect Harry from Voldemort, who was unable to kill him, and also from knowing that he is a cause célèbre among wizards. His aunt and uncle seek to protect themselves from the fact that they have a wizard in their home. Harry's "abnormality" is a cause of anger and fear to Aunt Petunia and an embarrassment to Uncle Vernon. They take in the 15-month-old Harry, but treat him badly in an effort to wipe out all tendencies toward wizardry, which they hate and view as disgusting and evil. Unable to completely quash these tendencies in the 10 years they have neglected, more than nurtured, Harry and kept him in a cupboard under the stairs, they become ever more angry at their situation when Harry, at 11, learns his identity as a wizard.

For the young Harry, the revelations delivered by the kindest and most trusting of wizards, Rubeus Hagrid, amaze him. Hagrid asks him, "Never wondered how you got that mark on yer forehead? That was no ordinary cut. That's what yeh get when a powerful, evil curse touches yeh . . ."

(Rowling, 1997, p. 55). Harry, "the boy who lived" (Rowling 1997, p. 1), is also the boy marked by anger. But Harry has to grow into his anger at Voldemort. The scar elicits the sensory experiences of light and sound when his mother was murdered, and it comes to signify a conflict he is caught up in. Harry's emotions deepen as his awareness of the meaning of his scar changes from what others have told him has happened to his own experience. As the story progresses, Harry sees and then physically experiences Voldemort's rage against others through the pain produced by the scar that Voldemort's curse stamped on his forehead. The lightning scar unites the physical-emotional-cognitive-social experience of anger; it is always there. Learning to interpret the pain his scar produces helps Harry subordinate his growing hatred toward Voldemort to the purpose of defeating him, a mission the 16-year-old Harry chooses.

Initially, however, he is more enchanted with the new world of magic to which he learns he belongs than angered by the lies that have tied him to the cupboard under the stairs. Hagrid offers explanations that normalize feelings and experiences Harry had, but did not understand and so denied. Such actions were taken as evidence of Harry's abnormality by his aunt and uncle, and Harry had little ground for not believing their account of him and his actions. Not being believed, denying, and so not trusting either his aunt and uncle or, most especially, his own experience, is all too frequent for Harry.

The 11-year-old Harry is often mute; he does not disclose what he thinks and feels. He does not appear curious about the world; he has little experience with books, though he has gone to school. Harry's reactions to others and to events can be swift. Speed has been his major resource in protecting himself from his cousin Dudley and Dudley's bullying gang. Seldom does Harry initiate interaction; silent acquiescence has been the safest response to being ordered about and put down by his Uncle Vernon, much as house-elves are treated in the wizarding world. It is unlikely that anyone in the Dursley household has asked Harry what he thinks about anything, what he likes or does not like, what opinions he may have; Harry has few opportunities to practice conversation, much less reflection, and there is nothing he can call his own. It is something of a miracle that he has glasses, broken though they are. No wonder he cannot believe Hagrid's announcement that he, Harry, is a wizard and his name has been down to attend Hogwarts since he was born.

The first three novels of the series play on issues of trust and doubt organized around identity—true identity, false identity, mistaken identity. Identity is a central, organizing concept in developmental psychology following Erikson's (1958, 1968) accounts of adolescence as a time in which one works through a sense of who one is, and who one is not, in relation to others. Harry is learning about, questioning, and coming to settle into the belief that he is a wizard and that he belongs in Gryffindor House. For the first time in his life he sees his parents in the *Mirror of Erised*. Though dead, they become real to him. Harry is impulsive and quick to defend others, for example, against Draco's continuing taunts (Rowling, 1997). He is learning what it means to acquire skills and use them properly. He experiences the house-elf, Dobby's, good intentions to protect him using magic that goes awry. He and his friend, Ron, discover the false identity of their teacher, Lockhart, who uses magic to gain his own ends (Rowling, 1998). Harry is finding that he cares for others and that they care for him. He has moments of intuitive awareness, for example, when he protects his father's friends by preventing them from committing murder (Rowling, 1999).

The experience of not being believed intensifies in Harry's fourth year at Hogwarts (Rowling, 2000). Unbeknownst to Harry and in violation of the rules of the contest, his name has been entered into the international tournament being hosted at Hogwarts. Although Hermione believes Harry and fears for him because the tasks the school champions must compete in are so dangerous, Ron doubts Harry, as do most of the Hogwarts students. Ron, his best friend, accuses Harry of secretly putting his name in the goblet. Harry's feeling of security in being Harry Potter, a fourth year student in Gryffindor, is deeply shaken.

In the last task of the tournament, Harry and his fellow Hogwarts competitor, Cedric Diggory, decide together to take the tournament prize cup. Neither is aware that a charm has been put on the cup, turning it into a *portkey*, which transports them instantly from the maze at Hogwarts to a country graveyard where almost immediately Cedric is murdered. In a gruesome scene Voldemort creates a body for himself from a potion rivaling the witches' brew in *Macbeth*, requiring his servant's arm and Harry's blood. Voldemort, now embodied, calls his followers, the Death Eaters, to observe him murder Harry. In fright and horror of what he is witnessing, Harry summons enough strength to fight Voldemort. They duel, revealing a secret connection between their wands. Harry narrowly escapes through a *portkey*, returning him, with Cedric's body in his arms, to Hogwarts. Harry, exhausted, appalled by what has happened and deeply distressed, tells Dumbledore all that he has witnessed. Harry's direct experience is critical because it arms him against falling prey to others' doubts and to the ensuing efforts by the Ministry to cover up Voldemort's re-appearance. Dumbledore, who believes Harry's word, and the Minister of Magic, who denies Harry's report that Voldemort has returned, part ways. The event also intensifies enmity between the paired trios, Draco with Crabbe and Goyle, who take the Ministry's side, and Ron and Hermione, who do not doubt Harry. Draco goads Harry by again scorning his choice of mudblood and blood-traitor friends. Harry's anger erupts on the train home, and his friends and supporters join him in a retaliatory hexing attack on Draco and company.

In his fifth year (Rowling, 2000) Harry is caught in a tangle of distrust. Over the summer vacation, in the neighborhood of his aunt and uncle's home, Harry and his cousin are attacked by *dementors*, who guard the distant, secret wizard prison, Azkaban. Violating the rule against using magic outside of school, Harry produces his *patronus* to ward off the dementors, thus saving his cousin's life. Harry's violation leads to a hearing at the Ministry to determine whether he may return to Hogwarts. The Ministry continues to deny that Voldemort has returned, and they consider even less likely that dementors could appear in a suburban muggle community. Only a thread of testimony absolves Harry at the hearing. Upon returning to Hogwarts, Harry is called a liar for his insistence that Voldemort has returned and has re-called his force, the Death Eaters. Harry refuses to take back what he knows to be true, which leads to multiple detentions during which he undergoes the torturous punishment of writing over and over again in his own blood on his hand, "I will not tell lies." Harry wears the faint outline of these words as a continual reminder of not being believed, much as his scar reminds him of the loss of his parents.

Then, through a combination of his own forgetfulness, impulsiveness, and betrayal by the house-elf, Kreacher, Harry is led into a trap. His friends are injured, and his newfound godfather, Sirius Black, is killed in a duel with Voldemort's loyal Death Eater, Bellatrix. Harry comes undone. He attacks Bellatrix, and for the first time in his life he throws at her the forbidden curse, *Crucio*. His curse is deflected, and Bellatrix throws back in his face his underage magical skills and derides his fit of fury. Later, back at Hogwarts, angry at himself and beside himself with grief at the death of his godfather, Harry rages against Dumbledore, hating him, wanting to hurt him, displacing his fury at Bellatrix and the situation he cannot control onto his kindly and understanding mentor.

Deflecting Anger: Dumbledore as Mentor

It is not so hard to understand Harry's anger at the loss of his godfather and in response to not being believed. It takes just another step to see how not being believed leads Harry to question Dumbledore. Harry counts on Dumbledore's integrity, and Dumbledore, from their earliest encounters in Year 1, has assured Harry that he will tell him the truth, though he may not be able at that particular time to disclose all that he knows.

Dumbledore struggles in his relationship to Harry, questioning himself as to the timing of letting Harry know what is likely to be in store for him. Rowling offers up the adult's dilemma of how much to tell a child and how much to hold for the child to learn by him or herself. In contrast to Dumbledore, for Molly Weasley, witch and mother of seven children, the boundary between adults and children is clear; wizards come of age at 17. By then they will have completed their schooling and will be accorded the privileges and responsibilities of adult wizards. But Harry is not an ordinary underage wizard. Dumbledore, though he is well aware of the wizarding world's need for the extraordinary Harry, is anxious for Harry to learn, to be "trained up," as Hagrid says, to make friends, and to enjoy his school years. And slowly, five novels' worth to be exact, Dumbledore comes to grips with disclosing to Harry, in the sixth novel, the extraordinary circumstances that make him "the chosen one." The need for disclosure is made urgent by Dumbledore's imminent death from encountering a deadly curse. Believing Dumbledore and believing in Dumbledore are paramount in Harry's understanding his own identity and in choosing that he will be faithful to Dumbledore. This is Erikson's (1961, 1982) notion of fidelity, the virtue or personality strength that takes on increased importance in adolescence. When our mentors are found to be imperfect, believing in them can swiftly engender anger, doubt, and repudiation.

Rowling's insight into the widening and deepening of consciousness is a marvel. I sometimes think she has read and digested much of developmental psychology. She employs adult characters in what Vygotsky (1962) has described as the zone of proximal development, where development is encouraged by challenges just a little beyond where the learner is, with the help of models and guidance. For example, during a rough patch when Harry and Ron are irritated with Hermione and are not speaking to her, Hagrid invites the two boys to his cabin. He lets the boys know how Hermione has found time to help him with the *hippogriff*, Buckbeak's, defense; the boys know they have not helped, and Harry, chagrined, apologizes. Hagrid doesn't sermonize, but he says, "I gotta tell yeh, I thought you two'd value yer friend more'n broomsticks or rats. Tha's all" (Rowling, 1999, p. 274).

Through the pensieve, Harry has opportunities to look into the earlier lives of people he knows only as adults. The *pensieve* is an external memory store that allows wizards to capture and to exchange their personal, episodic memories. Physically, the pensieve is a stone basin into which a wizard pours an event extracted from memory, whether his own or another's, that has been captured in a flask. For example, by looking deep into the basin Dumbledore and Harry can experience a remembered episode in its time and space. These glimpses raise questions in Harry's mind and lead to greater awareness of individuals' feelings and actions. In his later lessons with Dumbledore, Dumbledore follows up his trips with Harry into the pensieve by quizzing Harry about what Harry has noticed and how he is analyzing what he has seen (Rowling, 2005).

Harry's early history with the Ministry of Magic is clouded by the scrapes he has gotten into, not all by his own doing. But his distrust of the ministry is intensified by the Ministry's failure to believe that he has indeed seen Voldemort and that Voldemort has returned. When the Minister of Magic finally acknowledges Voldemort's return, he asks Harry to become part of the Ministry's media blitz to reassure the wizarding community that the Ministry is mobilizing against Voldemort. Harry rejects the Minister's request outright; Harry has no use for the Minister of Magic. The Ministry has failed by not believing him and by not taking steps to prepare for Voldemort's return when it should have. Instead, the Ministry tried to protect itself. It removed Dumbledore as Headmaster and perpetrated destructive decrees at Hogwarts, interfering with students' education. Now, following Dumbledore's death and funeral, when the Ministry has been seriously weakened and is on the brink of collapse, again Harry rejects the Minister's request for assistance. Harry reminds the Minister that he is, as the Minister has dubbed him, "Dumbledore's man" (Rowling, 2005, p. 348).

Harry's distrust, enmity, and anger come to a peak when the Minister arrives at the Weasleys' home demanding to meet alone with the trio. In this scene, the Minister explains that he is there about Dumbledore's will. The three had no idea that Dumbledore had a will, and even less that they would be included in it. Harry angrily refuses the Minister's plan to meet with each of them separately, and they pepper the Minister with questions about why he has taken so long to inform them of Dumbledore's will. Hermione catches the Minister off-guard when she explains, to the benefit of her clueless chums, that according to wizarding law, the ministry is obliged to notify beneficiaries and distribute what they have been given within a time certain. She expects that the delay gave the ministry time to probe the objects, examining them for information they imagine Dumbledore may have left in hidden protections. Anger and distrust at the Ministry fuels this group of 17-year-olds' resistance to the Minister of Magic's demands that they reveal the mission Dumbledore has given them.

Injustice: Activism

So far I have suggested that anger arises from loss: the loss of protection in childhood, without physical or moral power to defend oneself, and loss of trust in oneself, when one's experience, and later one's word, are doubted. Tom Riddle's defense, as he builds it, is to make himself powerful, unbeatable, immortal. Harry's defense is connection. The path Hermione, the only child of loving parents, presents is different from both Tom's and Harry's. As we meet Hermione's parents, they are supportive of their daughter, different from them though she is. Hermione's security in her family and her schooling allows her to cross boundaries between muggle and wizard worlds. Her interests are not so much in their technologies; rather Hermione's concerns are with social arrangements and moral principles that have evolved in the history of the cultural groups. Hermione's defense is in learning rules, in caring for others, and applying her analytical skills when these two principles come in conflict. When we meet Hermione at 11 years of age, she is a bright, self-confident young girl and an observant, questioning student, eager to learn all that she can as she enters the wizarding world. Her classmates tend to resent her outstanding performance in class and view her as a know-it-all. Hermione does insist on checking facts, following rules, and telling the truth. She has become friends with Harry and Ron early in their first year at Hogwarts, joining them in their adventures, and pretty much protecting them from failing their classes by correcting their homework.

Hermione's social action stems from her awareness of and care for others and a sense of righteous anger about slavery, based on the principles she has acquired in the muggle world. But her first attempt at activism is a dismal failure. Unfamiliar with the magical world's master/slave relationship between wizard and house-elf, the 12-year-old Hermione is outraged when she learns that there are house-elves at Hogwarts who live unseen in the kitchen preparing meals and serving the staff and students. She also learns through the incident in Year 2 (Rowling, 1998) between Lucius Malfoy and Harry concerning the house-elf, Dobby, that house-elves can be freed from service if clothes are extended to and accepted by the house-elf. Armed with this knowledge, Hermione forms the Society for the Protection of Elfish Welfare (S.P.E.W) and teaches herself to knit so that she can make small hats, which she leaves about the Gryffindor rooms for house-elves to pick up. Her efforts to persuade her classmates, even her closest friends, to join S.P.E.W. fail, and the house-elves do not pick up the hats.

Hermione does not give up the cause, and her anger at injustice in the magical world, symbolized in the Ministry statue depicting wizard rule over all other beings, intensifies through the novels. She is always subject to taunts, especially by Draco Malfoy, and at one point, Hermione, her patience at an end, takes an angry and well-directed swing at him. She explains to Harry the likely motivation behind the house-elf, Kreacher's, lies that have led Harry's godfather into the trap where he meets his death. Kreacher, however, meets her compassionate efforts with derision. In the last novel, having endured torture because of her mudblood status, Hermione responds to the goblin's question of who, among wizards, would protest the treatment of those they have subjugated. "We do!" said Hermione. She had sat up straight, her eyes bright. "We protest! And I'm hunted quite as much as any goblin or elf, Griphook! I'm a Mudblood" (Rowling, 2007, p. 489).

Like Hermione, Ron holds the prejudices of the culture in which he has grown up. Although his family does not own a house-elf, Ron takes the view that house-elves like the received arrangement and would be unable to manage otherwise. Dumbledore's, Hagrid's, and Hermione's ideas, respectively, about love over power, the beauty of dragons, and S.P.E.W. earn them Ron's ready quip—"mental." Ron has no illusions about his skills, though he wants to be as good as his older brothers. Ron's sense of loyalty to family and friends is highly developed, and we see his care in not expecting or asking for more than he thinks they can afford, for example, the CleanSweep rather than the more expensive, high-end Firebolt broomstick. Ron's consciousness about social justice takes a bit longer, spurred on as it is by his growing love of Hermione. Ron wins Hermione's embrace at last by reminding her and Harry as the battle for Hogwarts begins that they need to tell the house-elves in the kitchen to get out: "We can't order them to die for us" (Rowling, 2007, p. 625).

Choice: Shared Agency

In a recent paper, Aldwin (2015) poses the question of how free will develops, and she offers two possible sources: (1) experiences of stress that lead to awareness of oneself in relation to others, and (2) experiences of reflection that increase self-awareness, a sense of agentic action. Harry has both of these experiences, the first with the house-elf, Dobby, whom he freed. Dobby's gratitude to and admiration of Harry are boundless. Though he is a free elf, not bound to Harry or any family, against all odds, Dobby chooses to rescue Harry and his friends from the cellar at Malfoy Manor where they are imprisoned. In the successful rescue attempt, Bellatrix stabs Dobby and kills him. Digging Dobby's grave by hand rather than by magic, Harry comes to resolution about his course of action, setting aside his doubts about Dumbledore's motives, and counting on the loyalty and love of Ron and Hermione. Secondly, we observe the impulsive Harry becoming more reflective. Often Harry sees something, hears something, gets an idea in his mind, makes a decision, and acts on it, without thinking it through. Dumbledore's guidance progressing across the series of novels has been essential for Harry to learn what choice entails. It was Dumbledore who explained to the clueless 11-year-old Harry that he had made a choice under the Sorting Hat; he chose not to be in Slytherin. Harry, at 17, carries on a conversation in his mind with the dead Dumbledore. The continuing topic is choice, and Harry, through Dumbledore's voice now internalized in his head, reminds himself that he can choose. He can return to fight Voldemort or he can "board a train" (Rowling, 2007, p. 722). Harry is no Hamlet, and we would not expect to hear him ruminate over the decision. Harry has a task to perform. If he fails, Ron and Hermione will carry on along with Neville Longbottom, whom Harry entrusts with the order to kill the snake. They are joined as friends, and their collaboration as a group creates shared agency.

Resistance: *Protego*

Rowling emphasizes and celebrates practice—practice in learning spells, in quidditch, in friendship. Although the novels feature magic, magic requires practice. In their fifth year Defense Against the Dark Arts class, Hermione is appalled by the instructor's failure to provide hands-on learning and practice. *Protego,* for example, is a spell that inserts a shield between opponents, preventing them from harming each other. In fact, the instructor, the awful Dolores Umbrage, prohibits demonstration as well as practice, claiming that reading the Ministry-approved text is sufficient. Hermione views this situation, in conjunction with ministry decrees that appear to be taking control over the curriculum and faculty, as preventing students from learning to protect themselves. Her concern has intensified with the Ministry's denial of what she knows to be true because she, unlike the Ministry, believes Harry that Voldemort has returned. Thus Hermione's activism emerges in the face of threat to her and her classmates, who will not have the knowledge and experience to protect themselves, and her anger at Harry's not being believed.

But now, three years later, Hermione has become savvy. She has learned the need for more effective strategies to enlist others in joining a movement. Her first and main task is to persuade Harry that he has knowledge and experience that can help his peers, and then that he can teach them some of the defensive spells that have helped him. She also has to address their peers' uncertainty about forming a group when there are students who are unsure that they can trust Harry in the face of the ministry, supported by the wizard newspaper, *The Daily Prophet*, telling their parents not to worry and denying Voldemort's return. Hermione arranges an informational meeting off school grounds, following which interested students can meet and decide to go forward. At this meeting students sign their names and decide on the group's name, Dumbledore's Army or the D.A. Hermione has charmed galleons (the currency used in the wizarding world) so that they will alert the holder as to the date and time of the next meeting without drawing attention to the presence of the secret group. Harry is responsible for finding a meeting space. All goes well until one member reveals the existence of the group to the acting headmistress. However, due to Hermione's planning and her magical skill, betrayers are cursed with a disfiguring skin eruption. Fearing further damage, the student who snitched reports nothing more at a hearing before the minister of magic. Dumbledore's Army succeeds, not only in giving students practice in defending themselves, but also in creating camaraderie and a sense of shared purpose. The skill, cleverness, and thoroughness that Rowling accords Hermione in organizing a group are noteworthy. Hermione uses her outrage at Dolores Umbrage's teaching in Defense Against the Dark Arts to mobilize others to defend themselves by learning what they will need to know.

Rowling does not miss showing that the other side is also skilled. Voldemort has given Draco the task of murdering Dumbledore to redeem his father's name and status among the Death Eaters. Lucius had failed in a task that Voldemort had set him, namely to retrieve a prophecy globe from the Department of Mysteries in the Ministry of Magic offices. Furthermore, the Death Eaters, led by Lucius, had not been victorious in the battle that erupted (Rowling, 2003). Draco, for all his family's wealth and pure-blood status, does not appear a happy boy. He is haughty with his peers. His companions hang on him and follow his directions, but appear to offer little else to the group. Draco falls short of his father's expectations, which increases the importance of carrying out the task set him by Voldemort as the way in which he will earn his father's praise and love. Draco, at 16, is allowed by Voldemort to join the Death Eaters, but Voldemort is no mentor. He hands Draco a heavy burden. If Draco fails to kill Dumbledore, Voldemort will kill him and his parents. Although Draco's planning largely happens behind the scenes, it is not difficult to imagine the difficulty this adolescent has in organizing the more experienced adult Death Eaters, who fear Voldemort's wrath and compete for his favor, to lead an attack on Hogwarts. He works diligently to plan a passage into Hogwarts that will breach the protections placed upon the school, protections that will be lost upon Dumbledore's death. For Draco, the work is about personal success, not collaboration (Sullivan, 1953).

Although aligned on opposing sides, Hermione and Draco plan and mobilize their respective groups to prepare for attacking the opposing force.

These teen-age groups, organized by students within Hogwarts, parallel the re-energized adult forces of Dumbledore's Order of the Phoenix and Voldemort's Death Eaters, the groups that will do battle in the closing, climactic chapters of the last novel. The need to protect themselves, their families, friends, and classmates motivates Hermione and Draco's activism.

In the last novel (Rowling, 2007), the Ministry of Magic has fallen to Voldemort, and his Death Eaters have taken control over Hogwarts. Dumbledore's Army has been re-established under the joined leadership of students who were in the original organization as an underground resistance group at Hogwarts. Dumbledore's Army, now most clearly an angry group with the stalwart Neville Longbottom at its head, undermines the new teaching tactics and does everything it can to oppose the Death Eaters, who respond with outrageous punishments. In the closing chapters of the series, the student-organized group leads the open war against Voldemort and his Death Eaters. Neville's command as he stands, wandless, defying Voldemort is, "Dumbledore's Army!"

Concluding Comments

Rowling's story, though set in a magical world, is of our time with our concerns about power and injustice, our fears and our certainties about what we can and cannot control, as individuals and in multiple associations with each other. Rowling illustrates the slow unfolding of lifespan development with its missteps, stops, and re-starts through glimpses into the lives of different characters with different starting points, who encounter different supports and risks along their way. My effort has been to draw out the paths of but a few characters, examining the course of their anger arising from loss, especially in childhood, and appreciation of injustice with its threats of insult and injury. Rowling affirms what we wish to believe, namely, that connection with others who care for us can buffer anger, making time and space for planful action and strengthening resolve to counter trouble, as we are sure to encounter it. Still, the story is not over. We, readers and psychologists, are left with the lost boys, with groups that do not share realities, with the continuing breach we cannot repair, the flayed thing squealing in King's Cross Station.

References

Abecassis, M. (2003). I hate you just the way you are: Exploring the formation, maintenance, and need for enemies. *New Directions for Child and Adolescent Development, 102,* 5–22.

Ainsworth, M. D. S., & Marvin, R. S. (1995). On the shaping of attachment theory and research: An interview with Mary D. S. Ainsworth. *Monographs of the Society for Research in Child Development, 60*(2–3), 3–21.

Aldwin, C. (2015). How can developmental systems theories cope with free will? The importance of stress-related growth and mindfulness. *Research in Human Development, 3–4*, 189–195. doi:10.1080/15427609.2015.1068042

Bakan, D. (1996). Some reflections on narrative research and hurt and harm. In R. Josselson (Ed.), *Ethics and process in the narrative study of lives* (Vol. 4, pp. 3–8). Thousand Oaks, CA: Sage Publications.

Belenky, M. F., Clinchy, B. M., Goldberger, N. R., & Tarule, J. M. (1986). *Women's ways of knowing.* New York, NY: Basic Books.

Bowlby, J. (1980). *Attachment and Loss. Vol. 3. Loss.* New York, NY: Basic Books.

Bowlby, J. (1988). *A secure base: Parent-child attachment and healthy human development.* New York, NY: Basic Books.

Bukowski, W. F. (2003). Friendship and the worlds of childhood. *New Directions for Child and Adolescent Development, 102*, 93–105.

Caporael, L. (1997). The evolution of truly social cognition: The core configurations model. *Personality and Social Psychology Review, 1*(4), 276–298.

Colby, A., Kohlberg, I., Gibbs, J., Lieberman, M., Fischer, K., & Saltzstein, H. D. (1983). A longitudinal study of moral judgment. *Monographs of the Society for Research in Child Development, 48*(1–2), 1–124.

Erikson, E. H. (1958). *Young man Luther.* New York, NY: Norton.

Erikson, E. H. (1968). *Identity: Youth and crisis.* New York, NY: Norton.

Erikson, E. H. (1961). The roots of virtue. In J. Huxley (Ed.), *The humanist frame* (pp. 145–165). New York, NY: Harper.

Erikson, E. H. (1982). *The life cycle completed.* New York, NY: Norton.

Garbarino, J. (1982). *Children and families in the social environment.* New York, NY: Aldine.

Garbarino, J. (1999). *Lost boys: Why our sons turn violent and how we can save them.* New York, NY: The Free Press.

Gilligan, C. (1982). *In a different voice.* Cambridge, MA: Harvard University Press.

Goldstein. S., & Brooks, R. B. (Eds.). (2006). *Handbook of resilience in children.* NY: Springer.

Hutchins, E. (1995). *Cognition in the wild.* Cambridge, MA: MIT Press.

Kegan, R. (1983). *The evolving self.* Cambridge, MA: Harvard University Press.

Kegan, R. (1994). *In over our heads: The mental demands of modern life.* Cambridge, MA: Harvard University Press.

Lazarus, R. S. (1991). *Emotion and adaptation.* New York, NY: Oxford University Press.

Lewin, K. (1939). Field theory and experiment in social psychology: Concepts and methods. *American Journal of Sociology, 44*, 868–897.

Lewis, M. (2014). *The rise of consciousness and the development of emotional life.* New York, NY: Guilford.

McAdams, D. (1993). *Stories we live by: Personal myths and the making of the self.* New York, NY: Morrow.

Perry, W. (1970). *Forms of intellectual development in the college years.* New York, NY: Holt.

Resnick, L. B., Levine, J. M., and Teasley, S. D. (Eds.). (1991). *Perspectives on socially shared cognition.* Washington, DC: American Psychological Association.

Rowling, J. K. (1997). *Harry Potter and the sorcerer's stone.* New York, NY: Scholastic Press.

Rowling, J. K. (1998). *Harry Potter and the chamber of secrets.* New York, NY: Scholastic Press.

Rowling, J. K. (1999). *Harry Potter and the prisoner of Azkaban.* New York, NY: Scholastic Press.

Rowling, J. K. (2000). *Harry Potter and the goblet of fire.* New York, NY: Scholastic Press.

Rowling, J. K. (2003). *Harry Potter and the order of the phoenix.* New York, NY: Scholastic Press.

Rowling, J. K. (2005). *Harry Potter and the half-blood prince.* New York, NY: Scholastic Press.

Rowling, J. K. (2007). *Harry Potter and the deathly hallows.* New York, NY: Scholastic Press.

Rowling, J. K., Tiffany, J, & Thorne, J. (2016). *Harry Potter and the cursed child. Parts One and Two. The rehearsal script.* New York, NY: Scholastic Inc.

Sroufe, A., Egeland, B. Carlson, E., & Collins, A. (2005). *The development of the person: The Minnesota study of risk and adaptation from birth to adulthood.* New York, NY: Guilford.

Sullivan, H. S. (1940/1945). *Conceptions of modern psychiatry. The First William Alanson White Memorial Lectures.* Lecture 2. The human organism and its necessary environment, (pp. 14–27). Washington, D.C.: The William Alanson White Memorial Foundation.

Sullivan, H. S. (1953). *The interpersonal theory of psychiatry.* New York: NY: McGraw Hill.

Vygotsky, L. S. (1962). *Thought and language.* E. Hanfmann & G. Vakar (Eds. and Trans.). Cambridge, MA: MIT Press.

SECTION II

From a Historical to Geopolitical Context

Revolution, Emigration, and Anger: Angry Exile Groups in the Aftermath of the French and Russian Revolutions

Frank Jacob

Anger is an essential part of emigration movements. Especially so, since the new environment is usually productive of tensions that are the consequence of misunderstandings, cultural differences, stereotypes, and fears for the future. Europe is currently experiencing emigration movements that are the consequence of the so-called Arab Spring (Danahar, 2015) and the reshaping of the Middle East and North Africa (MENA) region. The decline and fall of the regimes in Libya (Prashad, 2012), Tunisia (Willis, 2014), and Egypt (Korany & El-Mahdi, 2014), as well as the Syrian Civil War, are producing waves of refugees trying to cross the Mediterranean to find a safe harbor and a possible future in Europe. This both causes and has caused anger on both sides. The European states and their governments, who are trying to delegate management of the stream of human beings to member territories (Geddes, 2008), and the European populations, fearing an increase in terrorism as a consequence of the arrival of hidden terrorists (Newton, 2015) as part of the refugee groups—all are struck by a fear that also causes anger. On the other hand, those who have risked their lives to reach the "promised land" of Europe also manifest anger, especially when they are treated in an inappropriate way, accused on the basis of stereotypes, and told to return to fight the Islamic State in Syria instead of trying to survive (Stone, 2015).

The elemental changes that have been achieved during the last five years in the MENA region deserve to be denominated revolutionary. It is not surprising that emigration and anger are the results. Historical examples show us that both of these factors are highly interrelated and usually appear as a consequence of revolutions. The French Revolution of 1789 and the Russian Revolution of 1917 produced anger in several ways. The aim of the current chapter is to analyze why and how anger was created in the course of these two major events in the "long nineteenth century" (Rosenberg, 1995). I will first try to give a short definition of the three interrelated factors of emigration, anger, and revolution. The emigration movements that were caused by the French Revolution in the late 18th century as well as those caused by the Russian Revolution in the early 20th century will then be analyzed and compared. This comparative approach will help us understand the basic interconnectedness of revolutions, emigration movements, and the creation of several different types of anger. In addition, it will also help us better understand the roots of the actual emigration movement from the MENA region to Europe, and hopefully explain the anger on both sides.

Emigration, Anger, and Revolution

Nancy L. Green has highlighted that "emigration even more than immigration defines the outer boundaries of the state" (2005, p. 266), and thereby also provokes a struggle at these borders. Although emigration seems to be the sole solution for refugees, states are frequently restrictive in sharing their idea of a nation, as well as its physical and legal expression, the nation state, with other interest groups. In other cases, existing nation states seek to prevent their citizens emigrating, whether for political or economic reasons. In general, there are different forms of emigration (Weiner, 1995) that can be created by the economic, political, religious, and/or social aims of the emigration group. The 19th and 20th centuries saw major migration movements, caused by war and persecution; however, as the present chapter will show, emigration extends much back further, yet is still a severe problem for international relations and with regard to the humanitarian needs of the refugees (Green, 2005).

Green states that the "history of emigration . . . needs to range from the laws governing departure and the formal ties that bind (such as passports, consulates, and military service) to research into attitudes on the part of those who stay home" (2005, p. 269; on passports, cf. Torpey, 2000); it also has to consider the personal and emotional experiences of emigration and its consequences. Anger is one of the human emotions that is stimulated on both sides. Those who become refugees can feel it just as much as those who ought rather to welcome refugees with open arms, but instead, driven by selfish fears and the unreasonable arguments of (modern) demagogues, direct their anger against the exiled people. It has to be made clear that revolutionary emigration is a form of forced exile for those who are leaving, whether due to lack of resources, political threats, or the loss of hope in the new regime, as is the case at the end of so many revolutionary developments.

For those who are forced to emigrate, it is a necessity to leave in order to survive. In 1816, the *Allgemeine Zeitung* of Augsburg (Germany) described the situation in which refugees might find themselves in a foreign exile: "Emigration is a form of suicide because it separates a person from all that life gives except the material wants of simple animal existence" (as quoted in Green, 2005, p. 279). It consequently seems only natural that anger should develop among many people who are forced to emigrate, who search for hope in exile and finally settle in a sometimes hostile and disillusioning environment abroad.

Anger

There is nothing new in claiming "that emotions such as fear and anger can contribute to political attitude formation" and that "anger is elicited when the out-group's actions are perceived as unjust and as deviating from acceptable norms" (Halperin, Russell, Dweck, & Gross, 2011, p. 275). Consequently, anger in many cases is a reaction to changes that seem to be unacceptable by an individual or a particular interest group. It therefore is responsible for the constitution of "a significant emotional barrier to negotiation, compromise, and forgiveness" (Halperin et al., 2011, p. 275), meaning that it limits the altruistic feelings that are usually esteemed in modern societies. Evolutionary biologists, however, have also shown that anger is a basic part of human behavior that "spontaneously appears in infancy, [and] is effectively universal in its distribution across cultures and individuals" (Sell, Tooby, Cosmides, & Orians, 2009, p. 15073). Its function as a human emotion "is to orchestrate behavior in the angry individual that create[s] incentives in the target of the anger to recalibrate upwards the weight he or she puts on the welfare of the angry individual" (Sell et al., 2009, p. 15073).

Where anger and its expression are accepted in a society, this is usually based on cultural tradition and existing social norms (Zagacki &

Boleyn-Fitzgerald, 2006, p. 290). It therefore "is sometimes the emotion we expect people to feel or the rhetorical response we expect them to display and evoke in others" (Zagacki & Boleyn-Fitzgerald, 2006, p. 290), but the image and the appropriateness of such cultural expressions are changeable through time. While numerous philosophers in antiquity seemed to be rather hostile to anger, which was seen as a sign of a loss of self-control, others, such as Aristotle, believed that this particular human emotion could have some positive impact in preventing injustice; attention could be drawn to the latter by the angry reaction of someone who expressed his disagreement with an unjust situation (Kemp & Strongman, 1995). In medieval times, anger was divided into a beastly and a rational form (Kemp & Strongman, 1995).

Revolutions offer plenty of options to develop anger as a reaction to specific developments. It can express "restraint, the blocking or interrupting of goal-directed activity, aversive stimulation, being misled or unjustly hurt, and moral indignation" (Kemp & Strongman, 1995).[1] It is usually stimulated by harm, loss, or threat, especially "a demeaning offence against me and mine" (Lazarus, 1991, p. 221). Revolutions therefore provide plenty of possibilities to develop one or another form of anger for all those who are involved in the revolutionary process.

Revolution

Following my theoretical phase model for revolutions (Jacob & Altieri, 2015), the revolutionary circle or process consists of the following 10 steps:

1. Violation of rights
2. Disagreement
3. Protest
4. Reaction by the ruling power

    a) Ignorance
    b) Compromise
    c) Violence

5. Point of no return (PONR)
6. Struggle between the population and the ruling power/government
7. Change
8. Internal power struggle for the interpretation of the revolutionary aims
9. Violence
10. Establishment of a new regime

There are plenty of points within this theoretical model where anger is able to evolve. It can be triggered by the disagreement (2) of the people whose rights are violated by a government, individual ruler, or ruling elite who, from the perspective of the ruled, is abusing power for an unjust cause. Anger can also be the result of the ignorance about or violence against (4a, c) the protesters on the part of the ruling power. The struggle between both parties (6) is definitely influenced by anger, as is the internal power struggle (8), during which different factions fight for the right of interpretation of the revolutionary events and the form of the new government that has to be established after the successful struggle against the "old regime."

A revolution, however, can also stimulate emigration at several points of the cycle elaborated above. Whereas the violation of rights (1) can lead to emigration on an individual level, the struggle (6) creates fear, leading to an exodus by privileged classes that might fear political turmoil. Those who resist early emigration can be eventually persuaded to leave when the new political system is installed (7), or if they become targets during the internal struggle (8) between the revolutionaries and their political antagonists and former enemies. The fear of violence, as in modern times, might then be the driving force behind an incipient mass migration. It consequently seems to be more than obvious that emigration, anger, and revolution form a trinity of interrelated factors. The analysis of two specific case studies will make this interrelation even more obvious.

The French Revolution

The French Revolution as a historical process would determine European and global history for decades to come. It is therefore also a complex series of events, at the center of which lies a specific problem, namely emigration (Darricau-Lugat, 2001). During the different periods of the revolution, numerous people decided to leave France, hoping that a solution to the political crisis would allow them to return safely as soon as the situation became stable again. The revolutionary events, including the reign of terror by the Jacobins and Maximilien Robespierre (1758–1794), created "victims of change, refugees from readjustment, fugitives from violence, disorder, and economic stress" (Greer, 1966). Most of the emigrants would return to France after the revolution, but the reasons to leave and the time abroad were sufficient to stimulate anger. Having to leave one's home country, with an insecure future ahead, naturally created an anger that was directed against those who were in favor of the radicalization of the revolution.

Emigration was debated in revolutionary France, however, especially because it led to a "tension between human rights and the sovereignty of the nation" (Boroumand, 2000, p. 70). Even in 1791, before the revolution finally radicalized with the execution of the king and the transformation of France into a republic, a discussion arose about the status of the emigrants, who were claimed in the radical political circles to be traitors. These accusations were also stimulated by the idea that the emigrants were plotting against the revolution from the outside. They were reported to have established connections to the king's relatives, and to be demanding an invasion of France to stop the revolution and reestablish the king as the highest and unquestioned authority in the country (Aulard, 1889–1897, Vol. 2, pp. 75–78). The accusations created anger inside and outside France. Those who were still in France, believing such accusations, became angry about those who had emigrated; those who had emigrated were angry about their own image as traitors to the home country.

As a consequence of these debates, some Jacobins demanded stronger legislation to prevent people from leaving the country. The radical political clubs were paranoid about a fifth column inside France that would cooperate with those who had left the country to gain foreign support against the revolution. Pressure was put on the National Assembly by using the anger of the population for political purposes. Public opinion needed to be changed to support an anti-emigration law and a common anger seemed to be the most suitable force to achieve this aim (Boroumand, 2000, p. 74). The rumors of a possible plot by the emigrants never turned out to be real, even though they were cited again and again in the debates of the National Assembly.[2] It might have been an amalgamation of anger at those who left and a projected fear about the emigrants' anger at having to leave that stimulated such controversies.

However, there were also voices that criticized the reasons that had made people leave their fatherland. Jacques Mallet du Pan considered it shameful that people should be forced by fear to leave the country of their birth. (See *Mercure de France,* March 5, June 4, September 3, and October 22, 1791.) As stated above with regard to the relationship between revolution and anger, the French Revolution also provided a number of reasons to become angry: about the need to leave, about those who left, about those who forced others to leave, and so forth. In February 1791 and in July of the same year the National Assembly debated emigration. Because the aunts of King Louis XVI had recently left for Rome, the fear of a plot animated the discussion. Hence it was the king himself who finally crystallized the discussion about the role of the emigrants as a possible dagger against the revolution from abroad.

When Louis XVI tried to escape from France and was arrested in Varennes on June 20, 1791, the assembly decided to prohibit emigration. A law was agreed upon in August 1791 and those who had left the country already were punished by taxes three times higher than the norm (Boroumand, 2000). A month later, however, the freedom to emigrate was restored when the members agreed that such a law would be contrary to the existing constitution. The discussion continued, and emigration again became a matter of high importance when the revolution further radicalized. The king was against a restriction with regard to the right of emigration, but was forced to sign a law that did exactly that in January 1792. Another step in April 1792 allowed the government to confiscate the property of those who had already left the country. Yet while emigration was always considered by the radicals to be dangerous for the revolution, it never actually was.

Those people who had left were "demographically inconsequential, socially disparate, ideologically divided, and militarily weak" (Boroumand, 2000, p. 68). They might have been angry about their fate, but since the emigration took place in several waves, the emigration movement was never politically and socially united enough to pose a threat against Paris.[3] The emigrant groups and their destinations were far too different to reconquer France with a united front.

The first wave of emigrants consisted mainly of French noblemen who feared for their lives. No doubt they were angry about their material losses and their new lives in a foreign environment far from home. These were reasons for them to try to get into contact with the noblemen of their new homes to persuade them to invade France and re-establish the old order (Darricau-Lugat, 2001, p. 232). Of the around 150,000 emigrants (Greer, 1966, p. 18), however, the noblemen never comprised the largest group, and we would do better to understand French emigration in the aftermath of the revolution as a heterogeneous movement. Different levels of fear forced different people to leave the country at different points of the revolutionary cycle (Greer, 1966, p. 3). The emigration lists that were produced by the revolutionary officials were not always accurate, but the noble "fugitives from the burning chateaux" (Greer, 1966, p. 22) were just one group. There were also provinces in France from which a comparatively high number of people emigrated, such as Burgundy, Franche-Comté, Dauphiné, and Languedoc.

As the revolutionary radicalism increased, so did the number of refugees from the *terreur* in France. Those noblemen who had already left certainly stimulated further emigration because they tried to persuade their friends and relatives to leave the country as well. After the king's attempt to escape and his arrest in Varennes, many of the noble officers of the time also fled. Just six weeks after the events, around 6,000 officers, three-quarters of the French officer corps, had reached foreign soil (Greer, 1966, p. 26). The open spots would be later filled by young ambitious officers such as Napoleon Bonaparte, who was more than grateful for the chance the revolution had provided him to pursue his own aims of promotion. A law was signed on November 9, 1791, that demanded the return of all emigrants, under penalty of death for those who refused. The date by which the emigrants had to return was January 1, 1792, but the actual events made most of those who had left stay longer outside France.

Another group that left the country during the revolutionary cycle was those who served the church. Between 1792 and 1795, 5,000 people emigrated from France, most of them forced to do so by their unwillingness to swear loyalty to the Civil Constitution of the Clergy, established in 1790 (Hill, 2004). The secularization of the former church land was acceptable to many members of the clergy, but when the new constitution and the oath came into play, many church representatives considered it to be a danger for the traditional clerical privileges. Consequently, many of them left the country, especially for the British Isles (Burke, 1792, as cited in Greer, 1966). When the Jacobins intensified their rule by using violence as a political tool, the masses also started to leave France—when the revolution began to feed on its own children. Donald Greer was right when he claimed that "No social group was immune to panic" (1966, p. 35), but some panicked earlier than others. Those who had the most to lose were those who left first. The noblemen were followed by the clerics, leaving the wealthy members of the former Third Estate and the commons, who might have accepted the revolution at first, but were driven into exile when they recognized the danger.

In exile those different groups met again. They were angry about the Jacobins and the revolution, angry about their personal loss, and even angry about their fellow emigrants, who might have left earlier or wealthier, or for other reasons. Whereas some had supported the revolution but were forced out by radicalization, others might have detested all the events since 1789, not accepting the late-coming emigrants as equals. The different centers of French emigration consequently became melting pots of different French ideas composed of emigrants of different migration waves in the years after 1789.

The emigration centers in Europe and North America were as disparate as the ideas they contained. Brussels, London, and Hamburg became centers of French exiles, attracted by the urban centers and their infrastructure (Baret, 1935). The counter revolution and its supporters tried to establish a network of support for those who would leave France in the future, in order to influence the nobility abroad to intervene for the sake of the conservative powers in Paris, and to survive as comfortably as possible. However, political hesitation, distance from the homeland, and the cultural differences they faced created several forms of anger. Although Hamburg, for example, was an urban center at the time, it was no Paris (Greer, 1966). The emigrants were consequently disappointed. Hence, another geographical location arose for possible French exile, which transpired to be the most disappointing: the United States (Childs, 1940).

In France the first eruption of the anger of the revolution was directed against the aristocrats, because the members of this class were "the embodiment of everything that was oppressive, unjust, and humiliating in the order of things that was coming to an end, [and they] merited nothing better than hanging, that is, death and dishonor" (Hasanyi, 2010, p. 4). The need to escape death, especially among those who were wealthy, fulfills all the preconditions of exile from a more global perspective. The United States had "offered Europe an ideal chance to export all its virtues and none of its vices" (Hasanyi, 2010, p. 41). There was, consequently, a positive image of the United States in France, and the moderate intellectuals who left as a consequence of fear thought it apt to be a "laboratory for social and political experiments" (Hasanyi, 2010, p. 41). A few years before the revolution, Benjamin Franklin (1784) had written a guide for those interested in immigrating to the United States, and this had been well received. He pointed out that "all who became Americans, acquired precisely the qualities hailed as exemplary by enlightened opinion in France" (Hasanyi, 2010, p. 43). Everyone in France who was looking for democratic and constitutional ideals was attracted by the United States. Moderate and enlightened aristocrats, therefore, tried to leave for the New World to escape the dangers of the old.

The French Revolution was seen as a possibility to create a new form of government. Camille Desmoulins demanded "Neither a despotic republic, nor an aristocratic republic, nor a federative republic . . . We want something unknown until this day" (Aulard, 1901, p. 81). However, instead, it created fear, hate, violence, and anger. The United States was, therefore, an alternative means to achieve the original aims of the revolution that had been corrupted by the radical elements, that is, the Jacobins. The Scioto-Valley Company was founded and tried to buy land in the Ohio River valley, where French emigrants would be offered the possibility to find a new home abroad. Officers of the French army were attracted by the company and took a leave of absence to immigrate to the New World. Other emigrant groups followed, but almost all of them would be disappointed. Far from an enlightened utopia, they found a life that was circumscribed by the hardships of rural work, and battles with the Native Americans who were already living in the new settlement. Anger must have been the natural consequence. Most of the French settler colonists consequently "lost heart and deserted . . . in the face of these unexpected hardships" (Hasanyi, 2010, p. 49).

Other exile experiences were not as disastrous as the one in the United States. Britain provided a better environment for the French nobility, especially because London was internationally well connected and a financial center of the world. It, therefore, could offer all the pleasures a French nobleman could demand. However, the struggle of the exiles was not only related to the place of exile, but also those who shared the fate of emigration. The fact that the emigrants left France in several waves also indicates a variation in political ideas. Doina Pasca Hasanyi points out that "Political defeat, followed by persecutions at the hands of the Jacobin government, lack of money, insecurity, and anxiety over the fate of family members left behind, could have very well embittered the most gracious and stoic nobleman on the run" (Hasanyi, 2010, p. 51). However, some of these men left later than others because they had believed in the ideals of the revolution. When the different political ideas now met in exile, they could elicit anger from within the heterogeneous exile group. The emigrants of the second wave would, therefore, find a situation where they were under pressure both from France and the already existing exile community. Consequently, "feelings of outrage and disappointment" (Hasanyi, 2010, p. 52) must have been common in such an environment.

The French Revolution was an event that caused tremendous changes to the course of human history, but it was also a force that created several forms of anger within and outside of France, within the French population, among the exiles themselves, and in their new environment. The French Revolution is far from the only event in world history that caused such a development. At the end of the "long nineteenth century," the Russian Revolution had similar effects that should be examined in detail.

The Russian Revolution

The Russian Revolution is not only an essential part of the history of the First World War; it also had an impact on the history of 20th century as a whole. Like the French Revolution before, it caused massive emigration; between 1918 and 1921, around one million people left Russia (Johnston, 1988, p. 3). The interrelationship between the revolution and a large exodus of another heterogeneous emigration group between 1918 is clear. Despite the fact that the group of exiles was usually depicted following a stereotype of a former rich aristocrat who is now struggling with his life in exile,[4] the group itself was as heterogeneous as in the French case. In the crisis after World War I, a Russian refugee was defined as "any person of Russian origin who does not enjoy, or who no longer enjoys, the protection of the Government of the Union of Soviet Socialist Republics and who has not acquired another nationality" (Johnston, 1988, p. 4). A large number of exiles resulted from the victory of the Bolsheviks in Russia. Consequently, the "Russian Civil War exiles represented the defeated, the first of the twentieth-century Europe's lost causes" (Johnston, 1988, p. 4).

Before Wrangel's army collapsed at the end of the Civil War and, therefore, destroyed all hope for a return to pre-revolutionary conditions in the near future, those in fear of the new regime left Russia by the thousands. However, the Russian emigrants also saw their exile as a temporary one, because the "political and cultural leaders who got away tended to see themselves, in the early years at least, as constituting a 'Russia Abroad' (*zarubezhnaia Rossiia*), the temporary guardians of their country's interests until the Bolshevik perversion had run its brief, murderous course" (Johnston, 1988, p. 5). They would be disappointed. The exile would last much longer than they thought.

Anger was a natural consequence, especially when the emigrants recognized that they had no way of returning home. Against their wishes, they had to get accustomed to their new situation abroad, even though they were unwilling to integrate and sought to keep their Russian heritage alive, hoping for a possible return to Russian soil in the future. Although large emigration communities were established, as in Paris, where 120,000 emigrants were heading, the majority of those who fled remain unknown, because they were dealing with the "sheer task of surviving" (Johnston, 1988, p. 6). Because many intellectuals left Russia after the revolution, we have plenty of descriptions of the hardships of emigration. Vladimir Nabokov later described the exodus of Russia's intelligentsia in terms heavy with meaning: "The tremendous outflow of intellectuals that formed such a prominent part of the general exodus from Soviet Russia in the first years of the Bolshevist Revolution seems today like the wanderings of some mythical tribe whose bird-signs and moon-signs I must now retrieve from the desert dust" (Nabokov, 1963, p. 8).

The newly founded League of Nations determined the status of those who had emigrated from Russia as "citizens without fatherland" and, in the Western diaspora, the former Russian citizens assimilated pretty quickly

(Kotenev, 1934, p. 563). However, the group itself was as heterogeneous as the emigrants of the French Revolution, leading to anger between the different parts of Russian emigration in exile as well.[5]

The liberal Kadets, as the members of the Constitutional Democratic Party were called, were one part of the Russian emigration wave. After the revolution, their network spread among London, Paris, Berlin, and Constantinople, where leading members had found shelter from the new Russian regime (Weiss, 2001, p. 510). These members were able to establish a personal network sufficient for them to partially influence politics in their new host countries. In Germany, this group was especially active.[6] In Berlin, they founded the daily newspaper *Rul* in 1920, and Russian intellectuals established the Russkij klub in March 1921 (Weiss, 2001). The paper had between 10,000 and 20,000 readers in Europe and the new club provided the Russian intelligentsia with a way to stay in regular contact. When Paris took over the role of the most important Russian emigration center in the late 1920s, the activities in Berlin decreased, but the network of the Kadets still remained active.

Another exile group was the leading Mensheviks, who left Russia in high numbers as soon as the Bolsheviks established their rule and began to extinguish their political enemies. Until 1940, the Mensheviks still acted as a party from exile, especially in the council meetings of the Labour and Socialist International parties. The Mensheviks were bonded by their "social status as intelligents in a working-class party," although that led to antagonism from other elements of the early revolution in exile, who saw them as not pure enough to act on behalf of proletarian interests (Liebich, 1995, p. 6). André Liebich sums up the fate of the Mensheviks in exile pretty well when he states that:

> As Jews, as socialists, and as a defeated party, the Mensheviks were indeed estranged from Russia, past and present. Thanks to their discipline, their resourcefulness, and their ideological faith they succeeded more easily than others in making themselves at home among foreigners. The Mensheviks' survival as a coherent group in exile enabled them to render service to Russia even after their defeat. (Liebich, 1995, p. 13)

The third, larger, exile group consisted of former members of Wrangel's White Army. Although the general demanded the loyalty of all Russian emigrants, he could really rely only on his army (Raeff, 1990, p. 34). This army was not dissolved when it had to leave Russia after the collapse. Even international intervention could not stop the victory of the Bolshevik army against its internal enemies, which is why Wrangel, accompanied by what was left of his force, needed to go into exile as well. The White Army may have been reduced in size, but it still existed abroad until 1927 (Robinson, 2005, p. 720). Once they were abroad, a struggle began between the Zemgor (Russian Zemstvo and Towns Relief Committee) and Wrangel for humanitarian aid, as the Zemgor was interested in providing equal support to all Russian émigrés while Wrangel wanted to use the available resources exclusively for his military personnel (Robinson, 2005, p. 723).

The League of Nations reacted to this struggle by creating the position of a High Commissioner for Refugees, and appointing Fridtjof Nansen to the role. Nansen hoped to solve the refugee crisis by repatriation of the Russian emigrants to Russia, something Wrangel criticized because he did not favor repatriation without a return to the political status quo ante of the Russian Revolution. Anger was the consequence, and the heterogeneity of the exiled Russians assisted the nascent Soviet Union, which had nothing to fear from a disunited refugee movement abroad. The only successful cooperation between the army and Zemgor was achieved with regard to the integration of large parts of the Russian White Army into the armies of Bulgaria and Yugoslavia in 1921. This particular story of the cooperation between the different exile organizations "was a very rare case of everybody pulling together in the same direction, and it brought positive results, enabling the transfer of elements of the Russian Army to Yugoslavia to take place smoothly and without undue complications" (Robinson, 2005, p. 730). As in the case of the French emigration after 1789, we have seen that the Russian emigration consisted of different, sometimes antagonistic elements that in most cases were not able to cooperate, sometimes because of anger. The situations in which the emigration movement as a whole found itself was as diverse as the geographical destinations of the Russian émigrés.

On November 14, 1920, a fleet of Russian ships with around 150,000 Russian refugees crossed the Black Sea from Sebastopol to Constantinople. They were desperate: "ahead, unperceived, loomed a life of exile and an exile's eternal 'what ifs' and 'if onlys.'" (Johnston, 1988, p. 9). With the final victory of the Bolsheviks, more and more refugees would follow their lead. The sheer number of refugees "presented the continent with human tragedy on a colossal scale" (Johnston, 1988, p. 10) and, therefore, caused anger on both sides. At the beginning most of the refugees who had crossed the Black Sea were brought to refugee camps in Constantinople or the Gallipoli Peninsula—something that might remind us of the current refugee crisis in Europe. As today, the living conditions in those camps were anything but pleasant and, thus, the levels of anger naturally increased. And while the refugees were suffering these conditions, the rest of Europe was discussing what to do. Like today, "it was just the sort of international emergency calculated to test the willingness of member states to match with deeds the promises made in setting up the League of Nations" (Johnston, 1988, p. 12). A return to the Soviet Union was impossible without risking one's life, but the actual situation in the rest of Europe was no cause for hope. Anger was natural, especially because the Russian emigrants had lost everything at home and were facing an insecure future. The approximately 800,000 Russians in Europe at the end of the 1920s would finally find new homes in all its countries. Not a few also left for the United States to start a new life there.

In the early 1920s, Berlin became a center of Russian exiles where, as described above, they found new ways of communication with the exile groups in other parts of Europe. Later in the 1920s, the center of Russian emigration in Europe moved to Paris, which would play a "sixteen-year long role as brain and heart of the Russian exile world" (Johnston, 1988, p. 15). Another European city that was famous for the presence of Russian academics and intellectuals after the events of the Russian Revolution was Prague, which would become known as the "Russian Oxford" (Johnson, 2007, p. 372). The new government of Czechoslovakia, led by President Tomáš Garrigue Masaryk, was not entirely altruistic in accepting the large number of Russian exiles. Masaryk believed that Bolshevism would soon collapse and hoped to inculcate pro-Czechoslovakian attitudes among the new leaders who had found shelter in his country. A democratic Russia would be a Czechoslovakian construct and would therefore have no choice but to support the future plans of Prague (Johnson, 2007, pp. 377–381). Sam Johnson brought this interrelationship into focus when he stated that the "Czechoslovak government felt itself incumbent to make practical preparations for the future Russia. The emigration, albeit a human tragedy, could be utilised for the advantage of Russia and the world" (Johnson, 2007, p. 382). The same author described the agricultural and economic measures that were taken to prepare for this future dependence:

> Russian peasants were to be schooled in Czechoslovakia's advanced agricultural technology, new knowledge that would instigate unheard-of progress in the Russian countryside. There was a final aim in Czechoslovakia's policy towards peasant refugees. In directly invigorating Russian agriculture and dragging it out of its medieval past, Czechoslovakia would reap further future benefits by ensuring economic links between the two states. (Johnson, 2007, p. 383)

Another country that had an interest in Russian emigration was Yugoslavia, where the remaining parts of Wrangel's army—alongside those that went to Bulgaria—would be incorporated in the postwar military of King

Alexander. The king had also been in favor of the conservative values of Russia as they were presented by many refugees after the civil war (Johnston, 1988, p. 14; Raeff, 1990, pp. 20–21). The integration of the emigrants posed no problems, as linguistic and cultural similarities were greater than in other parts of the world. The positive attitude of the government with regard to integration also provided the Russian exiles with a new home that received them positively, even if it was still considered a temporary one. Other parts of the world were much more hostile to the Russian refugees, and provoked anger accordingly.

In China—to be more specific, the Manchurian town of Harbin—the Russians had much more reason to become angry. Those who had to flee from the Eastern parts of Russia used the Manchurian borderland as a means to escape the reach of the Bolshevik prosecutors. Despite having reached a safe environment, the refugees now faced new problems. The Chinese government treated the Russians as aliens, leaving them without any legal rights (Kotenev, 1934, p. 564; Raeff, 1990, pp. 22–23). Geographically separated from the other spheres of Russian exile, they were also not able to establish steady contact and an exchange of ideas with the other emigration centers in Europe or the United States. Living in a foreign and rather hostile environment, their anger must have been much stronger than in European Russia.

All in all the Russian emigrants, as the French ones before them, considered their exile to be temporary. They were not only exiles, but they were also refugees who had been forced to leave their home country. Although this already might have led to anger, the situation in the new environment and the treatment of the Russian emigrants played a key role in stimulating anger, or at least preventing already existent anger from dissipating. The hope for a swift return to Russia decreased step by step, and the fear of being de-Russified in the future increased. The Russian emigrants tried hard to keep their heritage alive, still dreaming of a Russia that could recover from Bolshevist rule. As has been shown, the Russian exiles were as heterogeneous as the French exiles before them. Religious, ethnic, intellectual, and economic differences led to tension among the different elements of the emigrants' community, stimulating anger within it. As in the French case, it might have been this disunity that made united action against the revolutionary government impossible. But angry or not, at some point the emigrants simply had to accept their fate.

Conclusion

Refugees in the aftermath of a revolution need "massive help from foreign rescue organizations" (Raeff, 1990, p. 18). European politicians today could learn a lot with regard to the current refugee crisis by considering the Russian and French revolutions. First of all, anger is always associated with any form of revolution, showing itself in the different phases of the revolutionary circle. Although anger was a reason for the outbreak of the revolutions itself, in the course of events it reappeared in several forms and levels. The fact that the refugees had to leave their possessions is definitely an aspect that created anger. The second source of anger relates to their new places of shelter; but if the foreign environment allows the forced emigrants to continue their lives and professions, it may rather quickly be accepted as a new home, and anger might not become a problem.

In contrast, an environment that is hostile to refugees will create anger on both sides, among the refugees as well as within the native population in the emigrants' new sphere of life. The treatment in refugee camps especially caused tension between those who lost everything and those who were not willing to dare to provide the former group with hope for the future. Finally, a particular form of anger inside the emigration movements can be traced. Based on the timing of their exodus, the different exile groups accused each other of political antagonism, or simply competed for the limited resources available in the new environment. The pressure put on the exile community by the host governments in such a situation could also lead to anger against those who, solely by their existence, might worsen the treatment of an already existing emigrant group.

To conclude: Anger is always a cause, component, and consequence of revolutions. It is closely connected to emigration, and different forms of anger evolve therein in relation to a range of factors faced by emigrants. Depending on how host governments manage these factors, levels of anger can be mitigated or exacerbated. What we have to consider with regard to the actual refugee crisis in Europe today are ways to decrease the anger level in the exiled communities to better integrate them and to find ways to make them feel more welcome in our modern, multicultural, and hopefully tolerant societies. In so doing, we would be well advised to draw lessons from successful strategies at anger containment from former revolutions and refugee crises.

Notes

1. Kemp and Strongman (1995, p. 409) name the following reasons for "antecedents of anger: the failure of friends, the failure of strangers, inappropriate rewards, the failure of relatives, inconvenience, and the failure to reach goals." In the particular context of personal relationships, they point to "unjust treatment, the violation of norms, and damage to property."

2. An example would be the works that were published in the journal *Révolutions de Paris* (1789–1793 [1794]).

3. On the different political positions of the emigrants, see Higonnet (1981, pp. 293–295).

4. This image was a construction of the 1920s and was expressed in works such as that of Joseph Kessel (1927).

5. Johnston (1988, p. 11) falsely claimed that the heterogeneity of the Russian emigrants was different in contrast to the French emigration movement.

6. For a survey on Russian emigrants in Germany, see Karl Schlögel (1999).

References

Aulard, A. (1889–1897). *La Société des Jacobins: Recueil de documents pour l'histoire du Club des Jacobins de Paris.* Paris: Librairie Jouaust.

Aulard, A. (1901). *Histoire politique de la Révolution française.* Paris: Armand Collin.

Baret, R. (1935). Bibliographie critique sur les relations du gouvernement britannique avec les emigres et les royalistes de l'Ouest. *La Province du Maine, 15,* 177–186.

Boroumand, L. (2000). Emigration and the rights of man: French revolutionary legislators equivocate. *The Journal of Modern History, 72,* 67–108.

Burke, E. (1792). *The case of the suffering clergy of France: Refugees in the British dominions.* London: s.n.

Childs, F. S. (1940). *French refugee life in the United States, 1790-1800: An American chapter of the French Revolution.* Baltimore: The John Hopkins Press.

Danahar, P. (2015). *The new Middle East: The world after the Arab Spring.* London: Bloomsbury.

Darricau-Lugat, C. (2001). L'Émigration en pays basque pendant la Révolution française: Une question spécifique? *Histoire, Économie et Société, 20,* 231–255.

Franklin, B. (1784). *Avis à ceux qui voudraient s'en aller en Amérique.* n. p.: Printed by Benjamin Franklin.

Geddes, A. (2008). *Immigration and European integration: Towards fortress Europe.* Manchester, UK: Manchester University Press.

Green, N. L. (2005). The politics of exit: Reversing the immigration paradigm. *The Journal of Modern History, 77,* 263–289.

Greer, D. (1966). *The incidence of the emigration during the French Revolution.* Gloucester, MA: Peter Smith [Harvard University Press, 1951]).

Halperin, E., Russell, A. G., Dweck C. S., & Gross, J. J. (2011). Anger, hatred, and the quest for peace: Anger can be constructive in the absence of hatred. *The Journal of Conflict Resolution, 55,* 274–291.

Hasanyi, D. P. (2010). *Lessons from America: Liberal French nobles in exile, 1793–1798.* University Park: Pennsylvania State University Press.

Higonnet, P. (1981). *Class, ideology, and the rights of nobles during the French Revolution*. Oxford, UK: Oxford University Press.

Hill, A. G. (2004). Wordsworth and the émigré French clergy, 1790–1827. *The Review of English Studies, 55*(218), 60–74.

Jacob, F., & Altieri, R. (2015). Einleitung: Die Russische Revolution und ihre Bedeutung. In R. Altieri & F. Jacob (Eds.), *Die Geschichte der Russischen Revolutionen: Erhoffte Veränderung, erfahrene Enttäuschung, gewaltsame Anpassung* (pp. 7–27). Bonn: Minifanal.

Johnson, S. (2007). 'Communism in Russia Only Exists on Paper': Czechoslovakia and the Russian refugee crisis, 1919–1924. *Contemporary European History, 16*, 371–394.

Johnston, R. H. (1988). *New Mecca, New Babylon: Paris and the Russian exiles, 1920–1945*. Kingston/Montreal: McGill-Queen's University Press.

Kemp, S., & Strongman, K. T. (1995). Anger theory and management: A historical analysis. *The American Journal of Psychology, 108*, 397–417.

Kessel, J. (1927). *Nuits de princes*. Paris: Les Éditions de France.

Korany, B., & El-Mahdi, R. (Eds.). (2014). *Arab Spring in Egypt: Revolution and beyond*. Cairo: The American University in Cairo Press.

Kotenev, A. M. (1934). The status of the Russian emigrants in China. *The American Journal of International Law, 28*, 562–565.

Lazarus, R. S. (1991). *Emotion and adaptation*. Oxford, UK: Oxford University Press.

Liebich, A. (1995). At home abroad: The Mensheviks in the second emigration. *Canadian Slavonic Papers / Revue Canadienne des Slavistes, 37*(1–2), 1–13.

Mercure de France. [1791, March 5].

Mercure de France. [1791, June 4].

Mercure de France. [1791, September 3].

Mercure de France. [1791, October 22].

Nabokov, V. (1963). *The gift: A novel*. New York: G.P. Putnam's Sons.

Newton, J. (2015, July 6). ISIS terrorists are arriving in Europe hidden among migrants crossing the Mediterranean on boats, warns EU's top prosecutor. *Daily Mail*. Retrieved from http://www.dailymail.co.uk

Prashad, V. (2012). *Arab Spring, Libyan Winter*. Edinburgh: AK Press.

Raeff, M. (1990). *Russia abroad: A cultural history of the Russian emigration, 1919–1939*. New York/Oxford: Oxford University Press.

Révolutions de Paris, dédiées à la nation et au District des Petits Augustins. (1789–1793 [1794]). 10(119–120), 105–115, 145–149.

Robinson, P. (2005). L'invention d'une politique humanitaire: Les réfugiés russes et le Zemgor (1921–1930) [Zemgor and the Russian army in exile]. *Cahiers du Monde russe, 46*(4), 719–737.

Rosenberg, J. (1995). Hobsbawm's century. *Monthly Review: An Independent Socialist Magazine, 47*(3), 139–157. Retrieved from http://monthlyreview.org

Schlögel, K. (1999). *Chronik russischen Lebens in Deutschland 1918–1941*. Berlin: Akademie Verlag.

Sell, A., Tooby, J., Cosmides, L., & Orians, G. H. (2009). Formidability and the logic of human anger. *Proceedings of the National Academy of Sciences of the United States of America 106*(35), 15073–15078.

Stone, J. (2015, November 16). Syrian refugees should be trained into an army to fight Isis, Poland's foreign minister says. *Independent.* Retrieved from http://www.independent.co.uk

Torpey, J. (2000). *The invention of the passport: Surveillance, citizenship and the state.* Cambridge: Cambridge University Press.

Weiner, M. (1995). *The global migration crisis: Challenge to states and to human rights.* New York: Harper Collins.

Weiss, C. (2001). Die verkannte Elite: Ein Beitrag zum Wirken der russischen Kadetten in der Emigration. *Jahrbücher für Geschichte Osteuropas, 49,* 510–525.

Willis, M. (2014). *Politics and power in the Maghreb: Algeria, Tunisia and Morocco from independence to the Arab Spring.* New York: Oxford University Press.

Zagacki, K. S., & Boleyn-Fitzgerald, P. A. (2006). Rhetoric and anger. *Philosophy and Rhetoric, 39,* 290–309.

CHAPTER TEN

The Extreme Right and Neo-Nazism in the Post-War United States

Ryan Shaffer

Following the Civil Rights movement of the 1960s, political groups shifted language and tactics surrounding race. Groups on the far-right emerged that believed there was a finite amount of rights and that any gains for minorities came at the cost of White males. Those in the working and lower-middle classes who attached prestige to skin color as the physical proof that they were better than others developed new ways of expressing anger at the changing social and political landscape. The more extreme groups saw these changes as a deliberative and destructive transformation led by African American and Jewish people, and they believed the only effective response to the threat was a violent revolution, including the destruction of the United States government and genocide. The extremists developed outreach to youth with abrasive music, political campaigns, and even racist religions. Meanwhile, other groups and figures worked at resurrecting the memory of German Nazism and breathing new life into anti-Semitic conspiracies in U.S. politics. With further societal changes, the extreme right and neo-Nazi movement toward the end of the 20th century was acting out violent ideology in headline-grabbing ways.

U.S. fascism was revived after World War II by George Lincoln Rockwell, a veteran of the war, to create a worldwide National Socialist revolution and seek "a final reckoning with the Jews" (Weinberg & Kaplan, 1998, p. 42). In 1959, Rockwell established the American Nazi Party, which had a significant intellectual influence over a range of contemporary domestic and international fascist and extreme-right groups. Reacting to the Black Power movement, he formulated a reactionary brand of politics and published *White Power* (1967/1996), a work bemoaning racial and sexual equality while denouncing homosexuality and affirmative action, claiming that "[t]he Jews and their colored allies" were behind intentional efforts to destroy the White race (Rockwell, 1967/1996, p. 408). Rockwell's answer to the changes and the threats was "white power," which he described as a revolution "to meet the enemy in the street" and fight Black and Jewish "manipulation" as well responding to "burdensome taxation" (Rockwell, 1996, pp. 472, 444). When he was assassinated by a former supporter in 1967, the party began to fracture without a clear leader, but as scholars Leonard Weinberg and Jeffrey Kaplan explain, "Rockwell's alumni serves as a virtual who's who of the contemporary racist right" (Weinberg & Kaplan, 1998, p. 118). Notably, William Pierce (1933–2002), who earned a PhD in physics, worked with Rockwell and even edited American Nazi Party publications, but most of his fame in far-right circles was for leading the National Alliance from 1974 to 2002 as well as authoring *The Turner Diaries* (Macdonald [Pierce], 1978). By the 1980s, anti-Semitic concepts and Jewish conspiracy merged with anti-government ideology with the idea of ZOG (Zionist Occupation Government), which became the "hallmark of the modern movement," including Ku Klux Klan groups, Christian Identity, and neo-Nazi groups (Weinberg & Kaplan, 1998, p. 105). For these groups, anti-Semitic conspiracy connected the dots in the "destruction" of society and race. This chapter examines the ideology and key groups that promote far-right extremism and violence, and provides analysis about the history of the movements.

Opposition to Democracy and Equality

The core issues for racist movements, Aryan religions, and neo-Nazi youth cultures rest in the rejection of liberal democracy and opposition to equality. Roger Griffin's classic definition of fascism "is a political ideology whose mythic core in its various permutations is a palingenetic form of populist ultra-nationalism," which combines biological, political, and temporal beliefs (Griffin, 2008, p. 186). After World War II, the crisis of capitalism was no longer tenable and the xenophobia of the inter-war era "found an outlet in overly anti-liberal forms of conservatism and revolutionary nationalism" shifted in the post-war era by adopting "an illiberal form of democratic politics" (Griffin, 2008, p. 194). Indeed, more successful radical right parties in Europe have adopted "illiberal" democratic ideas, but the U.S. post-war far-right and fascist organizations oppose all forms of democracy, including Rockwell who stated: "the idea of democracy is a monstrous fraud" promoted by Jews "to hide their own power over these masses" while the "ordinary man cannot know personally the men and issues for which he is allowed to 'vote'" (Rockwell, 1979, p. 417).

Influenced by Rockwell, subsequent U.S. national socialists envisioned a violent rebellion to overthrow the government in novelized depictions of their movement, which is the most popular medium and outlet, surpassing the circulation of the groups' magazines and newspapers. William Pierce's infamous novel *The Turner Diaries* sold 185,000 copies and inspired Timothy McVeigh to destroy the federal building in Oklahoma City. The book's plot depicts the U.S. government being destroyed by "patriots"; then the world drifts into a "war of extermination" based on race with the genocide of the Jewish, African, and Asian populations, leaving only a "white world" (Macdonald [Pierce], 1996, pp. 207, 210; the sales number of 185,000 copies appears on the title page). Pierce's next novel, *Hunter*, sold over 61,000 copies and is about a man opposed to interracial relationships, homosexuality, and immigration, which Pierce connects to "Jewish media control" and "hunts" interracial couples (the amount sold is in Macdonald [Pierce], 1998). William Pierce and the National Alliance were not the only organizations to promote Rockwell's fascist and violent ideas. Tom Metzger founded the White Aryan Resistance in early 1983, having previously been a member of the John Birch Society and leader of the California branch of the Knights of the Ku Klux Klan (KKKK). As the director of the California KKKK, Metzger promoted Rockwell's "white power," but also focused on reaching out to youth ("Gathering of the Klans in Fremont, California," 1979). He first helped develop the Aryan Youth Movement with his son in Southern California, but by the end of the decade focused his energy promoting music with fascist messages. In 1988, Metzger and the White Aryan Resistance organized the Aryan Festival that spread "anti-system music and speeches" with a "white power" band ("Aryan Festival '88," 1988). Metzger warned his followers about "self-inflicted genocide" and told readers to prepare for a White revolution ("Self-inflicted genocide," 1988). In addition to his interest in music, Metzger was a member and minister of the Church of Jesus Christ Christian, a Christian Identity sect that believes Jews "are literal children of Satan" (Barkun, 1996, pp. 189, 196). For the religious and fascist, the religious justification for their beliefs meant that the adherents had God on their side in the future violent struggle for global domination.

Started by Richard Butler (1918–2004), the Church of Jesus Christ Christian's headquarters was established in a secluded "white homeland" in Idaho and the religion's political arm, the Aryan Nations, held annual meetings that drew radicals from throughout the country. The property welcomed an array of extremists over its history where plans were developed and served as a springboard for violent activity. In 1983, Butler invited a man named Robert "Bob" Mathews to serve as security for that year's meetings where he gathered a group of men who would put *The Turner Diaries* goal of a racist revolution into action (Flynn & Gerhardt, 1989, p. 88). Mathews started The Order, mirroring the revolutionary group depicted in the book, with other Aryan Nations and National Alliance supporters, assassinating Jewish radio host Alan Berg and robbing armored cars that netted millions of dollars to fund the racist revolution (Flynn & Gerhardt, 1989, p. 140). After The Order members were arrested and given long prison sentences, Mathews died in a shootout with federal authorities in 1984 and became a martyr for Butler, Metzger, and Pierce. In 1988, just a few years later, 13 people, including Butler as well as The Order members David Lane and Richard Scutari, were charged and later acquitted of sedition for plotting to overthrow the federal government. Metzger praised the accused and called the "sedition trial" a "witch hunt" of White separatists (Metzger, 1988, p. 1).

The group's anger was directed at minorities and the government, which they believed were opposed to their interests, and the extremists were involved with "sophisticated counterfeiting schemes, terrorist bombings, masterful loan fraud operations, daring armored car robberies, theft rings, a raft of murders, and thousands of federal firearms and explosives violations" (Coates, 1988, p. 11). When Timothy McVeigh detonated a truck bomb of ammonium nitrate in 1995 and destroyed the federal building in Oklahoma City that killed 168 people, he carried out the plot from *The Turner Diaries*. In the book, Earl Turner, along with others, destroyed the Federal Bureau of Investigation (FBI) headquarters in Washington, D.C., to eliminate "their new computer complex" by using "100 pound bags" of ammonium nitrate fertilizer in a truck for the bomb (Macdonald [Pierce], 1996, p. 38). When McVeigh was arrested, police found excerpts of the book in his car (Thomas, 2001). Letters from McVeigh to his family revealed that he was distressed about not being able to discuss his " 'lawless' behavior and anti-gov't attitude" and his anger at the government grew following the 1993 raid of the Branch Davidian property in Waco,

Texas (Thomas, 1998). The ideas in an extremist book directly influenced an angry man to commit one of the worst domestic terror acts in the history of the country.

After the Oklahoma City bombing, Pierce expanded to new mediums that expressed anger and hate. Like Metzger in the previous decade, Pierce turned his attention to youth culture and music. When Metzger's White Aryan Resistance began associating with racist skinheads, he unleashed feelings and ideas that young people carried out in violent ways. Ultimately, in 1990, the family of a murdered Black man, represented by the Southern Poverty Law Center and the Anti-Defamation League, successfully sued Metzger and several others, winning a $12.5 million judgment by arguing that the "defendants knew or should have known that the agents whom they had selected were violence prone racists and white supremacists who had themselves committed crimes of violence with racial animus, and who were likely to encourage the Oregon defendants to commit such crimes" (Berhanu v. Metzger, 1989). The White Aryan Resistance's assets were forfeited and Metzger's home was seized to pay the judgment, while items sold by Metzger continue to generate money to pay the family's judgment (Langer, 2003). In contrast to Metzger, the National Alliance's popularity and membership grew during that period. By the late 1990s racist music was a burgeoning business and in 1999 Pierce's National Alliance purchased Resistance Records from Todd Bloggett, who had bought it from founders George Burdi and Mark Wilson, two senior figures in the racist religion Church of the Creator (Michael, 2009). Under the National Alliance's ownership, music sales provided funding and promoted concepts through music, such as RaHoWa (Racial Holy War), a tenant of the Church of the Creator that sought a White world through genocide.

Identity as a Driving Force

The issues that drive an individual or movement to racial separatism and violent revolution are many. At the individual level, some people suffer from the feeling of displacement and alienation in society, which are sometimes caused during childhood, whereas other people become supporters or activists due to a yearning of wanting to belong to a "heroic" movement and be remembered by future generations for carrying out a revolution. Both types are drawn to a particular cause for different psychological and sociological reasons, much as how a person becomes involved in a religion. Some become introduced to ideas through friends or family; others learn about ideology through a search for new philosophies. The more esoteric ideas appeal to those who seek abnormal or "hidden" beliefs, and the ideas are special due to their perceived clandestine or deviant nature. At the group level, the individual's beliefs are reinforced and expanded on by a collection of people and subculture that affirms those attitudes through newspapers, books, and music. For instance, the belief that immigration and the mainstream media were both part of a Jewish conspiracy was supported in a publication edited by revered fascist and academic William Pierce (Pierce, 1995). The xenophobic and extremist ideas are reinforced in an echo chamber where dissenting views or skepticism about conspiracy do not appear. The ideas are mixed with contemporary news to encourage the separation of the races and hostility between communities, such as claims "about the dangers of contracting AIDS through sexual contact with non-Whites" (Pierce, 1999). Consequently, the only evidence that the supporter hears from leaders and authors affirms the beliefs that attracted the supporter to the movement.

One of the most significant frustrations is the changing concepts of race and "White" male preference, which these people see as the source of identity that has lost value. Though race in contemporary terms is merely a social category and science has been unable to find any genetic evidence that supports race or racial hierarchy, fascists and far-right activists continue to see "White" and "Black" as fixed genetic categories.[1] For example, David Duke, a former leader of the Ku Klux Klan, wrote as fact that "dramatic IQ differences exist between Blacks and Whites" (Duke, 2008, p. 55). In earlier eras of racism there were social and legal mechanisms, such as Jim Crow laws, that reinforced poverty with a lack of access to education and political rights. The second wave of feminism in the early 1960s that saw women seeking equalities, such as in the workplace or in education, caused noticeable societal change, including more women receiving higher education to become judges, medical doctors, and professors. Fascists and far-right activists opposed and still remain defiant to these changes, as they perceive them destroying a way of life they want to conserve, and see transformation as part of the latest intentional campaign by long-standing "enemies." Pierce remarked that the Civil Rights movement saw:

> the transformation of the strongest, richest, and most advanced country on earth from a White nation, in which racial minority groups had been effectively excluded from any significant participation in White society except as laborers, to a multiracial pseudo-nation, in which non-Whites not only participated but were a privileged and pampered elite. (Pierce, 2012, p. 324)

For the radicals, the unifying feature of the threat to White male preference is conspiracy. Changes are seen as purposeful negative consequences and borrow from traditional anti-Semitism, including Rockwell's readings of Adolf Hitler. Rationalized through dot-connecting in the infinite constellation of politics, business, religion and race, the "blame" for immigration, racial equality, sexuality equality, and government policies is easier to understand if a small group of people are blamed rather than the reality of disconnected and contradictory actions of a large population shaped by the electorate. As they preach violent revolution, any attempt for the government to create new laws concerning guns is seen as a way by the New World Order to "disarm America" (Pierce, 1994). The anger at these changes can then be directed to specific targets, which, as the thinking goes, can be physically attacked and defeated. A prominent target for the "decay" of society are Jews, who are blamed for everything from media coverage about gun violence to masonic lodges, which Pierce claims is part of "Jewish schemes" (Pierce, 2012, p. 325). Any group that is considered not hostile to organizations with Jewish or perceived Jewish people is seen as aligned with Jewish interests and those who have engaged in activity the fascists or far-right oppose is blamed on Jews or people being manipulated by Jewish interests.

Political Groups, Cultural Movements, and Aryan Religions

There are three types of groups that are significant among the fascist and far-right community. The first consists of political and social activist groups such as National Alliance-allied groups, Ku Klux Klan organizations, and neo-Nazi sects. This category consists of traditional political campaigns, such as the American Freedom Party, or groups such as the National Alliance and White Aryan Resistance, which have an organization that spreads political beliefs through the publication of material. Next, the least organized but no less dangerous grouping consists of youth and cultural-oriented organizations, including skinhead groups, notably the Hammerskins and Blood & Honour, along with virtual online communities. These groups differ from the political-group type because they rarely publish periodicals with political analysis and do not campaign, but are rather devoted to musical expressions of extremism and manifest those ideas into street violence. The last type is extremist religious movements, consisting of racist beliefs, such as Christian Identity and the Creativity Movement. These beliefs and their associated organizations or churches offer a theological backing for extremism, which includes mandates for a Racial Holy War or biblical justification for White supremacy.[2] Although these three categories are used to highlight different roles in the movement, there are significant overlaps, as politically oriented groups are connected to music operations and racist religions, and skinheads also associate and identify with Aryan religions and join political groups. With a simplification of the categories, the groups' roles and practices can be more easily understood.

The Southern Poverty Law Center lists hundreds of "active" U.S. hate organizations, which encompass a range of political, religious, and youth groups (Southern Poverty Law Center, 2015). After the splinter of the American Nazi Party, the most influential fascist organization, in terms of membership, book circulation, and admiration, has been the National Alliance. Though elements of the American Nazi Party continued under various incarnations led by people such as Matt Koehl (1935–2014), its operations became mostly limited to having a post office box and publishing pro-Hitler tracts. In contrast, the National Alliance drew a significant membership for its marginal politics, emerging as a major distributor of fascist magazines, books, and music, including sales of *The Turner Diaries*. Since Pierce's death in 2002, there have been different leaders of the National Alliance, which had slowed and then stopped producing periodicals (Potok, 2012). Former activists have been battling, both on the Internet and in court, over control of the organization and Pierce's legacy (Terry, 2014). Despite its current troubles, Pierce's ideas continue to be spread electronically and the infamy of its violent racist "martyrs" ensures its unrelenting popularity. While Tom Metzger's White Aryan Resistance was associated with skinheads due to his promotion of music and his subsequent civil trial loss, the group was originally started with more traditional political efforts. Since the early 2000s, Metzger's efforts are mostly confined to Internet posts about "lone wolf" activity on his website with no regular physical publication or activism outside the virtual world.[3]

The extremists' traditional political efforts have lacked sustained success. The most notable electoral victory, which has failed to be repeated, was then Republican David Duke's 1989 special election victory for Louisiana's House of Representatives. Duke, a former Ku Klux Klan (KKK) leader who later founded the National Association for the Advancement of White People, is a well-known extremist with inflammatory rhetoric and neo-Nazi associations. He admitted that the image of the KKK was detrimental to his political goals and as a member of the Klan, "[i]t became harder to discuss the critical issues facing our race and nation" (Duke, 2008, p. 633). He subsequently ran for office several times, including the U.S. Senate, but following his criminal tax convictions has mostly confined his activities to self-publishing books and making Internet videos. In *My Awakening*, Duke wrote about his life and ideas, arguing terrorism and violence undermine the "cause" and that there needs to be a "political path" to have "a government and a mass media composed of our own people" (Duke, 2008, p. 692). Yet, the reality of U.S. fascist and racist third-party politics has been a history of failure. The American Freedom Party, previously named the American Third Position Party, nominated Merlin Miller for the 2012 presidential election, earning 2,703 votes compared with President Barack Obama's winning vote of 65,915,796 (Anonymous, 2013). This electoral result demonstrates how marginal these ideas are in the political realm. However outside of the political process, members in their own groups and gatherings give the appearance that they have strong numbers in their ranks.

Fascists have found a community of like-minded people online and at concerts. The most visited extremist U.S. website is Stormfront, founded by Don Black, who had previously inherited leadership of the Ku Klux Klan from Duke in the early 1980s (Duke, 2008, p. 634). Stormfront was launched in 1995 by Black, who learned about computers while in federal prison, in order "to take America back" (Abel, 1998). In 2014, the website was again engulfed in controversy when news outlets reported that the Southern Poverty Law Center connected the website to nearly 100 murders committed by Stormfront forum members, most recently skinhead Wade Michael Page's murder of six Sikhs in 2012 (Newcomb, 2014). Although skinheads have had a decreasing role in politics since the 1990s, music still plays a part in uniting and promoting transnational extremism (Shaffer, 2013, 2014, 2015). The largest national skinhead groups are the Hammerskins and Blood & Honour, with the first being a homegrown organization started in Dallas and the latter originating in London (Shaffer, in press). Both groups at their peak had infrequently published periodicals with concert and album reviews as well as some political news, but currently have an online presence with occasional concerts that can draw a few hundred people. The local branches of these groups as well as other skinhead organizations do not publish magazines, but are instead interested in listening to or performing incendiary music. Despite the declining role of fascist music, which was a successful business for racists, the threat of violence remains as illustrated with Hammerskin Wade Michael Page's 2012 rampage.

The third grouping of extremists is centered on racist religions, which have a more marginal role, but are no less of a threat to minorities and authorities. The oldest contemporary racist religion associated with these groups is Christian Identity. Scholar Michael Barkun's history of the religion explored the origins of belief in British-Israelism in the late 19th century and took root in the United States during the Great Depression. For the next several decades it spread around the country. In 1973, Richard

Butler moved from Southern California to Coeur'd Alene, Idaho, and continued the theology of Wesley Swift, a former Ku Klux Klan member, by establishing the Church of Jesus Christ Christian and the Aryan Nations (Barkun, 1996, p. 70). This was followed by "highly politicized and often violent Identity groups of the 1970s and 1980s" (Barkun, 1996, p. 70). These acts included connections to numerous people who were involved in racist murders, including Robert "Bob" Mathews's The Order as well as Buford Furrow's 1999 Los Angeles anti-Semitic shooting rampage. The following year the Southern Poverty Law Center won a $6.3 million lawsuit, finding Aryan Nations members responsible for the 1998 assault of three minorities (Michael, 2006). Butler lost the Idaho compound that included the headquarters of the Church of Jesus Christ Christian, and two members, Ray Redfeairn and August Kreis, battled for control of Butler's organization. Redfeairn died in 2003 and Kreis continued his efforts to lead the organization, though many activists did not consider him to be Butler's true heir. Kreis made news in 2005 when he "expressed support for al Qaeda and publicly announced that sleeper cells of non-Muslims were ready to fight alongside the organization" (Michael, 2006, p. 185). The claim prompted the federal government to examine Kreis's finances, and this led to fraud convictions over his income, causing him to step down before being charged with child molestation (Associated Press, December 11, 2011; Turnage, 2014). Filling the power vacuum in the early 2000s, several organizations competed for followers, which diluted membership and the ability to organize.

Though Christian Identity's roots predate World War II, it is not the only racist religion followed by extremists. In 1973 the Church of the Creator, which became known as Creativity in 2003, was started by former state Republican politician Ben Klassen. As founder of the religion, Klassen wrote two religious texts about the tents of Creativity, including *Nature's Eternal Religion* (1973) and *The White Man's Bible* (1981). In *Nature's Eternal Religion*, Klassen wrote the belief "reject[s] the Judeo-democratic-Marxist values of today" and praised Hitler "as the brightest meteor to flash through the heavens since the beginning of history" (Klassen, 1973, pp. 7, 290). The religion has 16 "commandments" that tell believers they must "secure the existence of our race" and "destroy Jewish influence" (Klassen, 1973, pp. 269, 279). Klassen's *Racial Loyalty* periodical, which was later included in edited books that preached violence against minorities, told readers that RaHoWa, or Racial Holy War, "is inevitable" and the "ultimate and only solution" (Klassen, 1987).

Unlike Christian Identity believers, young fans of extremist music grew to be a large part of Creativity that was attracted to the radical and violent beliefs. Notably, Canadian George Burdi became a significant member, founding a band called RaHoWa and helping to establish Resistance Records, which achieved large international sales. Skinheads around the world joined the religion and Mark Wilson, who co-founded Resistance Records, briefly replaced Klassen as its leader (Michael, 2006, p. 97). A series of legal fights, criminal convictions, and murders in the 1990s fractured the movement's structure, causing different sects to claim position as the rightful heir to Klassen's leadership. In 1991, an African American Navy veteran was murdered by a church member and the Southern Poverty Law Center filed a civil lawsuit against the church, winning a $1 million judgment (Michael, 2006, p. 107). Several other crimes shook the religion, including member Ben Smith's 1999 attempt to start "RaHoWa" by shooting and injuring several Jewish men near a synagogue, shooting at several African Americans and Asians, killing one before ultimately committing suicide (Michael, 2006, pp. 154, 155). A few years later the religion's then leader, Matthew Hale, was charged in a plot to kill the federal judge who ruled against him in a trademark case over the name Church of the Creator. As revealed at court, Hale solicited a man working for the FBI to murder the judge and was convicted of the crime, receiving 40 years in prison (Michael, 2006, pp. 175, 184). The organization fractured as Hale's successor testified again him. During the following years, others attempted to position themselves as Creativity's leader and a series of other violent acts created further setbacks for the religion (Michael, 2006, pp. 190, 191).

Spreading the Ideas and Direct Action

Fascist and far-right groups exist beyond the mainstream outlets of the media and political establishment. As a result, the groups turned to making public inroads through a range of grassroots political issues, occasional attention-grabbing violence, and outreach through non-traditional media. The first type of action is political efforts, which include mostly unsuccessful campaigns, such as the Populist Party and American Freedom Party running presidential candidates in national elections. The next form of activity is violence to enact direct change, such as The Order's criminal enterprise in the 1980s, the 1995 Oklahoma City bombing, skinhead violence, or Church of the Creator member Ben Smith's 1999 murder-suicide rampage. The final type is propaganda delivered through music, video games, and the Internet. The groups have failed to enact any significant change with these efforts and while the violent outbursts have grabbed headlines, this violence has also led to the destruction of specific groups and provoked law enforcement interest that damaged the extremists' efforts. Yet, the constant battle to spread their ideas has made marginal gains, such as David Duke's successful special election campaign in 1989 or youth recruitment through skinhead music in the 1990s.

U.S. third parties are mostly a story of failure. With a few notable exceptions, the two mainstream parties, Democratic and Republican, have dominated state and national elections. It is not surprising that fascist third parties would be an even more difficult sell as popular post-war memories reflect proudly on the U.S. role of defeating fascist Italy and Nazi Germany, and the horrors of the Holocaust have been an important part of public discourse. Indeed, David Duke ran for office and won a seat in the state government of Louisiana as a Republican in 1989, but he also unsuccessfully ran as a Democrat for president in 1988, as a Republican in 1991 for governor, and then had a 1992 Republican Party presidential campaign (Bridges, 1994, pp. 82, 139, 167, 216, 238). Since World War II, the few attempts for extremist and pro-segregation parties, including the National States' Rights Party and American Freedom Party, failed to have their candidates elected. The parties have used their campaigns not to win elections, but to spread literature and promote particular ideas. This has included getting headlines through attention-grabbing efforts, such as Robert Ransdell's 2014 write-in campaign for U.S. Senate in Kentucky that used the slogan "With Jews We Lose" (Montoya, 2014). Ransdell, a former National Alliance organizer, admitted he could not win the election against then Senate Minority leader Mitch McConnell, but used the controversy about his slogan and the campaign as a platform to spread his views (Montoya, 2014; see also Blackford, 2014).

Unable to make any impact in elections, fascist and far-right individuals and sub-groups have lashed out at critics, the government, and minorities. Violence in politics is nothing new, as several generations of Ku Klux Klan activity have employed terror, assault, and murder to enforce racial lines and retain influence outside electoral politics. There are numerous examples ranging from minor physical and verbal assaults from skinheads to large-scale bombings. The "bible" of extremist violence for the last four decades has been *The Turner Diaries*, which was originally self-published by Pierce and then distributed by a large independent publisher, Barricade Books. Rather than shy away from the controversy, Barricade Books' version stated on the cover: "This book contains racist propaganda. The FBI said it was the blueprint for the Oklahoma City bombing" (Macdonald [Pierce], 1996). Indeed, the actions of Robert Mathews and Timothy McVeigh mirrored the characters of the book to help bring about the violent genocide depicted in the book's final pages. Numerous other crimes have been associated with the book, including local violent crime as well as the murderous 1999 nail bombing spree of David Copeland, a neo-Nazi in Britain (McLagan, 2000). Other people associated with the Aryan Nations, Creativity movement, and White Aryan Resistance have engaged in murder and assault, acting on their beliefs of racial superiority and justifying their actions as being benevolent for their extremist cause (for example, see Anti-Defamation League, 2014). Ultimately, the violence in each group led to its bankruptcy and divisions after losing civil court cases against the Southern Poverty Law Center on behalf of victims or victims' families (Geranios, 2001; Wiley, 2000). Violence had few, if any, short-term gains and proved in the long-run to cause financial ruin and factionalism.

Aside from violence and political campaigns, fascist and far-right groups have been at the forefront of using new mediums to reach people. In the late 1970s, several organizations were started, such as the Anti-Nazi League and Rock Against Racism, in opposition to the electoral gains made by the National Front in England. In response, the National Front started its own music outreach efforts with its own White Noise Records and Rock Against Communism concerts that used skinhead music and style with fascist and racist themes (Shaffer, 2013, p. 467). Since White Noise Records' 1983 release of Skrewdriver's "White Power," skinheads have been a mainstay, with music becoming one of the few money-making aspects of fascist politics when book sales proved to be weaker (Shaffer, 2013, p. 472). Groups such as the National Alliance promoted music with violent racist and fascist ideas, selling thousands of albums (Shaffer, 2013, pp. 474, 481). In addition to music, the National Alliance also created computer games, notably Ethnic Cleansing, where the player's goal is kill minorities and ultimately murder then Israeli prime minister Ariel Sharon (Eng, 2002). Despite sales, the ability to convert youth and retain their long-term involvement in extremist politics is less certain. Nevertheless, youth who would not appear at a political lecture played computer games with racist themes and gathered at concerts. In doing so, the youth brought money and energy to extremism, while the media attention surrounding the extremist youth violence and offensive music further spread their message to larger numbers. Similarly, the use of the Internet by fascist and extreme-right groups has fostered faster and more international contact between radicals, enabling people in marginal groups in the United States to connect and reinforce their beliefs with fellow travelers in Europe. David Duke, for example, wrote that "[e]very Aryan should become computer literate, become connected to the Internet, and learn how to use it to spread our truth and awaken our race" (Duke, 2008, p. 692).

Spreading the extremist message through music and the Internet came at the cost of traditional groups that suffered from the changes brought by the online community. Music sales have been negatively affected due to people's ability to download or stream songs for free. Consequently, this has deprived organizations of money they had earned from music sales. Likewise, the Internet has hurt book and magazine sales, as people can freely download and circulate publications such as *The Turner Diaries* and, in the era of rapid news, people rely on blogs and Internet posts, which causes fewer people to join an organization for a newsletter or subscribe to an organization's magazine. With more people relying on the computer for their activism, these far-right and fascist groups have a harder time producing periodicals, mobilizing supporters, and growing actual membership. That is not to imply they do not have supporters or people willing to act on their beliefs. These groups certainly maintain backing, though in a diminished way. Yet their standing and operations have slowed in recent years. The Aryan Nations and Creativity movement lack a compound for year-around meetings and organizing members and fail to circulate periodicals that generate regular revenue.

Projections and Status of the Issue

Despite persistent activism before and after World War II, U.S. fascist and far-right political groups have failed to come to power or have any significant political influence. Indeed, the Civil Rights movement, the Sexual Revolution and more recently gay rights gains have shown a consistent loss of ideological ground for extremists. Although some elements of the extreme right have arguably drifted into mainstream politics, the call for racial genocide through a White revolution has fallen on deaf ears. As JoEllen McNergney Vinyard (2011, pp. 306, 307) explained in her book about the far right in Michigan, including the Ku Klux Klan, there are new phenomena with traditional concerns that oppose social reforms, distrust the government, and accept conspiracy as they harness support in the midst of economic volatility. Nevertheless, no extremist political organization or religion bent on White separatism had membership beyond a few thousand people. The reason for the failure to gain support for a "whites only nation" in the marketplace of ideas in a multicultural, democratic country is obvious.

Extreme-right and fascist groups in Europe, by contrast, have made electoral gains and in some countries have been members of ruling coalitions. The reasons for these successes are different from the issues the United States faces, including debates about the European Union, long histories with pre-war fascist movements, anti-Semitism in popular culture, the role and history of immigration, and parliamentary systems that give more room to third-party politics. Indeed, the European extremist groups have found support from debates about the nation as the European Union is accused of diluting national identity and superseding member states' governments. Robert Ford and Matthew Goodwin examined the radical right in Britain and discussed the importance of Euroscepticism mixed with domestic issues for people who feel they have no political voice (Ford & Goodwin, 2014, pp. 211, 213).

The importance of the Internet has only grown and will continue to play a dominant role for U.S. radicals. As they seek support, it becomes clear that it is easier to get backing by reaching out to like-minded people in other countries rather than change minds locally. This has fostered new transnational dimensions of whiteness, which is much different from pre-Internet racist groups that stressed strict national identity. David Duke, for example, organized an international conference, and stood with British fascists and National Alliance members for "a Euro-American" meeting in 2004. Several different figures signed the New Orleans Protocol to get different groups to agree on a few basic principles, including repudiating violence. In a panel with Duke, the speakers voiced the need to distance themselves from terrorism. Sam Dickson said, "the idea of *The Turner Diaries* about organizing a revolutionary group and toppling a government that is fighting against us is a complete non-starter" (Discussion Panel, 2004). Similarly, for the last decade the American Renaissance Conference has hosted international fascists, including leaders from Britain and France, who spoke about politics and commonalities with U.S. extremists (Griffin & Fraser, 2006; Taylor & Gollnisch, 2000). Meanwhile, U.S. computer servers have proved to be important for European radicals, whose countries make it illegal to deny the Holocaust, promote hatred, or share fascist books. U.S. extremists have helped their foreign counterparts with Internet postings and websites that could not be produced otherwise.[4] As websites such as Stormfront have grown in numbers, governments like Italy have blocked access and prevented its residents from posting and reading the content (Associated Press, November 16, 2012).

Extremist political ideas, such as the demands for a "whites only nation," have changed little since the era of the American Nazi Party. The physical sale of music, books, and magazines has dropped due, in part, to the Internet harming sales to fund extremist activity. Yet, the ideas are circulated and available for free by downloading a song or digital book. At the same time, the nature of the Internet demonstrates how marginal these ideas are because although one can visit a website and download *The Turner Diaries* in seconds, the information has not ushered in a political change or made extreme-right and fascist terrorism any more likely than earlier decades. Nonetheless, the threat of violence remains as the groups become increasingly marginalized in a multicultural and global world and the groups' members feel helpless in the face of the changes.

Notes

1. For example, "There is great genetic diversity within all human populations. Pure races, in the sense of genetically homogenous populations, do not exist in the human species today, nor is there any evidence that they have ever existed in the past" (AAPA, 1996); "In view of concerns that linking of emerging genetic data and race/ethnicity categories may promote racist ideologies, we emphasize that there is no scientific basis for any claim that the pattern of human genetic variation supports hierarchically ranked categories of race or ethnicity" (Sandra Soo-Jin Lee et al., 2008).

2. William Pierce developed a religion called cosmotheism, but this was not a centerpiece of his mission, in contrast to Richard Butler's Church of Jesus Christ Christian or Ben Klassen's Church of the Creator.

3. For more on "lone wolf" terror, see George Michael (2012).

4. For example, the FBI closed a neo-Nazi website hosted in Arizona for a Polish Blood & Honour branch ("Poland shuts down neo-Nazi site," 2006).

References

2006 AR conference Nick Griffin and Andrew Fraser (Marietta, GA: American Renaissance Conference. [DVD Recording].

AAPA. (1996). AAPA statement on biological aspects of race. *American Journal of Physical Anthropology, 101*(4), 569–570. Retrieved from http://www.physanth.org/about/position-statements/biological-aspects-race

Abel, D. S. (1998, February 19–25). The racist next door. *New Times.* Retrieved from http://www.browardpalmbeach.com/news/the-racist-next-door-6332282

Anti-Defamation League. (2014). Creativity movement. *Extremism in America.* Retrieved from http://archive.adl.org/learn/ext_us/wcotc.html

Aryan Festival '88. (1988). *White Aryan Resistance, 7*(4), 1.

Associated Press. (2011, December 15). Aryan Nations leader gets fraud sentence in SC. *SCNow Morning News.* Retrieved from http://www.scnow.com

Associated Press. (2012, November 16). Italian police block white supremacist website. *The Big Story.* Retrieved from http://bigstory.ap.org/article/italian-police-block-white-supremacist-website

Barkun, M. (1996). *Religion and the racist right: The origins of the Christian identity movement.* Chapel Hill, NC: University of North Carolina Press.

Belluck, P. (1995, May 11). Terror in Oklahoma: Defense strategy; McVeigh said to play role in seeking holes in government's case. *The New York Times.* Retrieved from http://www.nytimes.com

Berhanu v. Metzger. Circuit Court, Multnomah County, Oregon (1989). Retrieved from http://www.splcenter.org/sites/default/files/berhanuvmetzger_amco mplaint.pdf

Blackford, L. (2014, September 18). Racist remarks by write-in U.S. Senate candidate cause a stir at University of Kentucky. *Lexington Herald-Leader.* Retrieved from http://www.kentucky.com

Bridges, T. (1994). *The rise of David Duke.* Jackson, MS: University Press of Mississippi.

Coates, J. (1988). *Armed and dangerous: The rise of the survivalist right.* New York, NY: Farrar Straus & Giroux.

Discussion Panel. (2004). *International European American Unity and Leadership Conference* [DVD]. Mandeville, LA: David Duke Report.

Duke, D. (2008). *My awakening: A path to racial understanding.* Mandeville, LA: Free Speech Press.

Eng, P. (2002, March 4). Racists produce high-tech hate games. *ABC News.* Retrieved from http://abcnews.go.com

Flynn, K., & Gerhardt, G. (1989). *The silent brotherhood: Inside America's racist underground.* New York, NY: Free Press.

Ford, R., & Goodwin, M. J. (2014). *Revolt on the right: Explaining support for the radical right in Britain.* New York, NY: Routledge.

Gathering of the Klans in Fremont, California. (1979). *California Klan News,* 2(3), 1.

Geranios, N. (2001, February 14). Aryan Nations compound sold. *The Columbian* (Vancouver, WA). Retrieved from https://www.highbeam.com/doc/1P2 -23468498.html

Griffin, R. (2008). Fascism's new faces (and new facelessness) in the "post-fascist" epoch. In M. Feldman (Ed.), *A Fascist century: Essays by Roger Griffin* (pp. 181–202). Basingstoke, UK: Palgrave Macmillan.

Griffin, N., & Fraser, A. (2006). *2006 AR conference Nick Griffin and Andrew Fraser* [DVD]. Marietta, GA: Renaissance Audio-Visual.

Klassen, B. (1973). *Nature's eternal religion.* Lighthouse Point, FL: Church of the Creator.

Klassen, B. (1981). *The White man's bible.* Lighthouse Point, FL: Church of the Creator.

Klassen, B. (1987). *RAHOWA!: This planet is all ours.* Otto, NC: Church of the Creator.

Langer, E. (2003). *A hundred little Hitlers: The death of a Black man, the trial of a White racist, and the rise of the neo-Nazi movement in America.* New York, NY: Metropolitan Books.

Macdonald, A. [William Pierce]. (1996). *The Turner diaries.* Fort Lee, NJ: Barricade Books.

Macdonald, A. [William Pierce]. (1998). *Hunter.* Hillsboro, WV: National Vanguard Books.

Martinez, T., & Guinther, J. (1988). *Brotherhood of murder.* New York, NY: McGraw-Hill.

McLagan, G. (2000, June 30). The nailbomber [Transcript]. *BBC*. Retrieved from http://news.bbc.co.uk/hi/english/static/audio_video/programmes/panorama/transcripts/transcript_30_06_00.txt

Metzger, T. (1988). Ft. Smith Inquisition. *White Aryan resistance, 7*(2), pp. 1, 12.

Michael, G. (2006). *The enemy of my enemy: The alarming convergence of militant Islam and the extreme right*. Lawrence, KS: University Press of Kansas.

Michael, G. (2009). *Theology of hate: A history of the World Church of the Creator*. Gainesville, FL: University Press of Florida.

Michael, G. (2012). *Lone wolf terror and the rise of leaderless resistance*. Nashville, TN: Vanderbilt University Press.

Montoya, A. (2014, September 17). US Senate candidate uses campaign to spread slogan: 'With Jews we lose'. *WLWT.com*. Retrieved from http://www.wlwt.com

Newcomb, A. (2014, April 17). Stormfront website posters have murdered almost 100 people, watchdog group says. *ABC News*. Retrieved from http://abcnews.go.com

Pierce, W. (1994, January 29). Gun control: Not what it seems. *American Dissident Voices*. Retrieved from http://web.archive.org/web/20120521095841/http://www.natvan.com/american-dissident-voices/adv012994.html

Pierce, W. (1995). Non-White immigration: Death sentence for America. *Free Speech 1*(5). Retrieved from http://web.archive.org/web/20130510100632/http://www.natvan.com/free-speech/fs955c.html

Pierce, W. (1999). AIDS and the cult of equality. *Free Speech 5*(2). Retrieved from http://web.archive.org/web/20130510101045/http://www.natvan.com/free-speech/fs992c.html

Pierce, W. (2012). *Who we are*. N.p.: Revisionist Books.

Poland shuts down neo-Nazi site. (2006, July 6). *BBC.com*. Retrieved from http://news.bbc.co.uk

Potok, M. (Fall 2012). Ten years after founder's death, key neo-Nazi group 'a joke'. *Intelligence Report* (147). Retrieved from https://www.splcenter.org/news/2012/07/23/ten-years-after-founders-death-key-neo-nazi-movement-joke

Rockwell, G. L. (1979). *This time the world*. Los Angeles, CA: Parliament House.

Rockwell, G. L. (1967/1996). *White power*. Champaign, IL: John McLaughlin.

Self-inflicted genocide. (1988). *White Aryan Resistance, 7*(4), 7.

Shaffer, R. (2013). The soundtrack of Neo-Fascism: Youth and music in the National Front. *Patterns of Prejudice, 47*(5–6), 458–482.

Shaffer, R. (2014). From outcast to martyr: The memory of Rudolf Hess in skinhead culture. *Journal Exit-Deutschland, 2*(4), 111–124.

Shaffer, R. (2015). British, European and White: Cultural constructions of identity in post-war British Fascist music. In N. Copsey & J. Richardson (Eds.), *Cultures of post-war British Fascism* (pp. 142–160). Abingdon, UK: Routledge.

Shaffer, R. (in press). Bonded in hate: The violent development of American skinhead culture. In M. J. Pfeifer (Ed.), *Global lynching and collective violence*. Champaign, IL: University of Illinois Press.

Soo-Jin Lee, S. Mountain, J., Koenig, B., Altman, R., Brown, M., Camarillo, A., . . . Underhill, P. (2008). The ethics of characterizing difference: Guiding principles on using racial categories in human genetics. *Genome Biology, 9*(7), 404. Retrieved from http://genomebiology.com

Southern Poverty Law Center. (2013). American third position gets a makeover following election losses. *Intelligence Report* (150). Retrieved from http://www.splcenter.org

Southern Poverty Law Center. (2015). Hate Groups [Web page]. Retrieved from http://www.splcenter.org/get-informed/hate-map

Taylor, J., & Gollnisch, B. (2000). *2000 AR Conference Jared Taylor and Bruno Gollnisch* [DVD]. Marietta, GA: Renaissance Audio-Visual.

Terry, D. (2014, October 24). In major surprise, Erich Gliebe steps down as National Alliance Chairman. *Southern Poverty Law Center.* Retrieved from http://www.splcenter.org/blog/2014/10/24/in-major-surprise-erich-gliebe-steps-down-as-national-alliance-chairman

Thomas, J. (1998, July 1). McVeigh letters before blast show the depth of his anger. *The New York Times.* Retrieved from http://www.nytimes.com

Thomas, J. (2001, June 9). Behind a book that inspired McVeigh. *The New York Times.* Retrieved from http://www.nytimes.com

Turnage, T. (2014, February 19). Former Aryan Nation leader charged with sexually assaulting child. *WISTV.com.* Retrieved from http://www.wistv.com

Vinyard, J. M. (2011). *Right in Michigan's grassroots: From the KKK to the Michigan Militia.* Ann Arbor, MI: University of Michigan Press.

Weinberg, L., & Kaplan, J. (1998). *The emergence of a Euro-American radical right.* New Brunswick, NJ: Rutgers University Press.

Wiley, J. (2000, September 3). Jury verdict against Aryan Nations. *The Daily,* p. 14.

CHAPTER ELEVEN

Fighting "The System": *The Turner Diaries*

Carmen Celestini

The Turner Diaries has become the "Bible" of right-wing White suprema-cists and a symbol of violence and home-grown terrorism to mainstream media and their audiences. The book, an underground hit since the 1970s, became an overnight symbol of terrorism, homegrown fear, and racist vio-lence when media reports linked the bombing of a federal building in Oklahoma to U.S. White supremacist who was obsessed with the book. Timothy McVeigh, the Oklahoma Bomber, and his accomplice Terry Nich-ols, brought *The Turner Diaries* into the spotlight. In fact, the book has not only had an impact on White supremacist groups in the United States, but it has also become an aspect of their religious mythology, created martyrs, and helped to mobilize and inspire self-envisioned heroes of the right to start what they hope will be their end time, apocalyptic revolution. Crimes have been re-enacted from the novel, groups have adopted names and step-by-step plans from the book, but McVeigh's bombing of the government building was the most easily recognizable enactment from the book, and was also the most deadly/violent act instigated by William Pierce's most famed fictional novel.

The Turner Diaries creates a narrative of a persecuted and marginalized people rising against other races to save the United States, and to save the White race. It has the hallmarks of conspiracy theories, redemption, and revelation. It supports a sense of continuous disaster and a pathway to hope for those currently mired in conspiracy and fear. Why has William Pierce's fictional novel of race wars, revolution, and hatred become the "Bible" of these homegrown U.S. hate groups? More importantly, what has motivated the individuals described within this chapter to become violent murderers, robbers, counterfeiters, and conspiracists to overthrow the U.S. government? In their demise, the heroes to White supremacists call to their fellow racists to never forget and to be the catalyst to the revolution as described in *The Turner Diaries*. What is the impetus to this behavior? One possible answer to this question is fear and an impending sense of disaster. This fear and sense of impending doom crosses the line between secular and religious as conspiracy theories, eschatological myths, and economic downturns. Government laws and programs of equality create an atmosphere where instability in societal institutions, fears, marginalization, and religion allow individuals to easily accept ideas previously held unacceptable, to embrace theories of conspiracy that govern the world and, in their view, ultimately lead to the greatest battle between good and evil. This battle, this need to be an active participant in bringing forth this final holy revolution, is the rationale for this angry mob to mobilize.

The unlikely creator of the ultimate tale of *The Turner Diaries* is Dr. William Pierce, a physicist, a former professor, and, in the end, the leader and spokesperson of the neo-Nazi organization the National Alliance. Pierce graduated from the University of Colorado at Boulder with a PhD in physics in 1962 and from 1962 to 1965 he taught at the University of Oregon (McAlear, 2009). Pierce began moving within the realms of "mainstream" right-wing organizations, and soon became swept up in the extreme right of White supremacists.

Pierce, searching for answers in the late 1950s and early 1960s, wanted to stop the infiltration of Communists in the government. He wanted to stop the growth of both the size of the U.S. government and their power/infringement on the U.S. people. In response to these desires, he joined the John Birch Society (JBS), but soon became disillusioned with the anti-Communism group who did not see Communists as the same enemy as Pierce did. Pierce perceived Jews as the enemy. Both the JBS and Pierce shared in their belief that the Civil Rights Movement was being controlled and instigated by the Communists to cause civil turmoil and allow for martial law in the United States. Yet, Pierce believed that the JBS members' letter writing campaigns, meetings, and quiet rebelling would not stop the Jewish conspiracy (Griffin, 2001). Pierce expanded his search for those who felt as he did about the ills of society and soon ended up among the neo-Nazis of the National Youth Alliance.

Becoming more involved in the White supremacist world, in 1968, Pierce began publishing *Attack!* to build the membership numbers for the National Youth Alliance (Griffin, 2001). The publication contained anti-Semitic and racist cartoons, "journalistic" articles, and bomb-making instructions. These anti-Semitic views gained public notoriety in 1973 when leaders and members of the National Youth Alliance testified before the Senate Committee on Foreign Relations, that Henry Kissinger should not be confirmed as secretary of state, because of concerns that he would put Israel before the United States (Durham, 2007). In 1974, it became the National Alliance (Durham, 2007) and Pierce took over the helm.

One of the inspirations for the book was the John Birch Society's *The John Franklin Letters,* which was given to Pierce by Revilo Oliver, then one of the council members of the Birch Society. *The John Franklin Letters* is a collection of letters from the future from John Franklin to his uncle, about the rebellion/revolution being waged against the Communist government who had taken over the United States. Similar to the *The Turner Diaries, The John Franklin Letters* is written by the single hero who leaps into the fray to save his country, a patriot to the end (Anonymous, 1959). Pierce wrote the book under the alias Andrew Macdonald and published it in his periodical *Attack!* in 1975 (Durham, 2007). In 1978, Pierce self-published it as a novel (McAlear, 2009). Sales figures for the book are not readily available, but it is estimated that as of 2001 at least 300,000 copies had been sold (Griffin, 2001).

Similar to *The John Franklin Letters*, Pierce's novel is portrayed as a manuscript found in the future, the year 2100, after an Aryan revolution had changed the world. It is the diary of a revolutionary hero named Earl Turner, a member of an elite cadre of a group of revolutionaries called The Organization, whose small, violent acts of rebellion were the beginning of this worldwide revolution. As their acts of violence grow, so does the movement itself. The book is a horrific retelling of a revolution that results in a worldwide massacre of all non-Aryans. Focusing on the beginning stages of the revolution, the diary follows Turner and his fellow "Organization" members as they conduct a guerrilla war against "The System" (the ruling government). Within the larger group, there is an elite inner structure known as "The Order," which Earl Turner eventually joins. In the novel, The Organization damages the FBI building in Washington with a truckload of explosives. In *The Turner Diaries*, the explosives in the vehicle were a mixture of heating oil and ammonium nitrate fertilizer—the same mixture used by McVeigh in his attack on the Murrah Federal Building in Oklahoma. The two pages describing the bombing from *The Turner Diaries* were found in McVeigh's vehicle after the bombing (Griffin, 2001). The members of The Organization fund their revolution through robberies of stores, banks, and armored vehicles, as well as using hidden printing presses to counterfeit money to pay for their violent revolution. The world that Pierce, under the alias of Macdonald, creates is one in which the Second Amendment has been erased, where African Americans and Jews were in control, as White people happily gave up their freedoms and "heritage" in exchange for security and a regular paycheck. It was a world where the Jewish-controlled media had fed the White populace strong liberal ideas to the point where their freedoms were gone, their hegemonic position was a thing of the past, and they were now under the control of Blacks, Latinos, and Jews.

The Turner Diaries was the first piece of evidence introduced by the prosecution at McVeigh's trial and witnesses were brought forward to attest to McVeigh's obsession with the book (McAlear, 2009). These witnesses revealed to the court that while McVeigh was in the military, he read the novel repeatedly, and then once out of the military, he began to sell the book at gun shows where he found his clientele (Griffin, 2001). The idea of government control, Second Amendment attacks, and revolution were the basis of McVeigh's terrorism. The date of the Oklahoma bombing supports this because April 19, 1995, was the second anniversary of the 1993 massacre of the Branch Davidians at the hands of the U.S. government in Waco, Texas. Waco and the earlier 1992 attack at Ruby Ridge are considered the ultimate examples of the government infringing on gun laws, the Second Amendment, and the over-involvement of the government in people's lives.

McVeigh is not the only would-be leader of the revolution to be inspired by *The Turner Diaries*. Two past violent groups, as cited by the Anti-Defamation League (ADL), had taken their names from *The Turner Diaries*. Dennis McGriffin and two other individuals were charged with conspiracy to possess and produce machine guns in 1998. FBI agents testified at the three individuals' trials that they were influenced by Pierce's novel. The three had planned to create a "New Order" and had conversations about bombing state capitals and post offices, and poisoning the public water systems with cyanide (Griffin, 2001). In 1996, in Jackson, Mississippi, Larry Wayne Shoemaker killed an African American and wounded several others. Shoemaker's wife said that he had read *The Turner Diaries* in the mid-1980s and that from that point on he had not been the same (Griffin, 2001).

The most well known of the violent groups inspired by *The Turner Diaries* is The Order, also known as Brüder Schweigen or Silent Brotherhood, which was formed in 1983 by National Alliance activist Robert Mathews. The small group took its name from the group of elite leaders of the revolutionary group The Organization in *The Turner Diaries*. What Mathews wanted to create was a group with both the will and the resources to over-throw the government that he believed to be controlled by the Jewish conspiracy, ZOG, the Zionist Occupation Government (Barkun, 1996). Members of The Order had to pledge as Aryan warriors. They engaged in counterfeiting, robbery of three armored cars, a synagogue bombing, and two murders. Alan Berg was one of those murdered, a Jewish radio talk show host who The Order believed had insulted two Christian Identity preachers, Pete Peters and Jack Mohr, on his show (Durham, 2007). Alan Berg was not the original target of The Order; he was a substitute for Morris Dees, the founder of the Southern Poverty Law Center (Durham, 2007).

Prior to this activity, Mathews had a long history with right-wing groups, and had been a member of the John Birch Society since his youth (Durham, 2007). He joined Pierce's National Alliance in 1980. He is also known to have spoken about *The Turner Diaries* long before creating The Order (Barkun, 1996). In fact, on the fateful night The Order was created, he handed out copies of the book to the original nine members (Barkun, 1996). The Order was originally composed of Bob Mathews, Richie Kemp, Bill Soderquist, Ken Loff, David Lane, Dan Bauer, Denver Parmenter, Randy Duey, and Bruce Pierce (no relation to William Pierce) (Flynn & Gerhardt, 1990). Mathews had developed a six-step plan: (1) form a group, (2) set goals (what exactly they wanted and how far they were willing to go for those goals), (3) procure funds, (4) recruit, (5) use these funds for right-wing causes, and (6) form a guerrilla army, "a strike force with the ability to carry out sabotage in urban areas" (Flynn & Gerhardt, 1990, p. 126). Mathews had written an oath for each of the Aryan warriors to take as members of The Order. The oath the nine men took included a promise: "My brothers, let us be His battle axe and weapons of war. Let us go forth by ones and by twos, by scores and by legions, and as true Aryan men with pure hearts and strong minds face the enemies of our faith and our race with courage and determination" (Flynn & Gerhardt, 1990, p. 126). The men decided at first to take a "Robin Hood" approach to step 3 of the plan, procuring funds. They planned to steal the money from pimps and drug dealers. This plan did not gain the funds they required and they soon turned to more lucrative criminal activities. There was one holdout among the group; although committed to the cause and to his brothers in The Order, Loff refused to be involved in anything illegal.

The Order soon started counterfeiting money, much like The Organization in *The Turner Diaries.* Their revolution officially began on December 3, 1983, with the first robbery of an adult sex shop. In the end it was Mathews, Kemp, and Loff who committed the robbery; the rest dropped out and Pierce was jailed for being caught using the counterfeit money. The group soon evolved to committing bank robberies, and graduated to armored trucks. They also had planned on bombing the Olympic Four Seasons Hotel in Seattle because the Baron Elie de Rothschild was going to speak at a Jewish fundraising group (Flynn & Gerhardt, 1990, p. 134), but the group split on turning to assassinations, and focused on armored vehicles. In July 1984 they stole $3.8 million from a Brinks armored car in California. Significant portions of this money were given to right-wing organizations, many of which were Christian Identity organizations. The largest portion of this money has yet to be found (Barkun, 1996, p. 228). This returning of the money to the cause matched The Order oath: ". . . from this moment on, I have no fear of death, no fear of foe, that I have a sacred duty to do whatever is necessary to deliver our people from the Jew and bring total victory to the Aryan race" (Barkun, 1996, p. 229).

"We hereby invoke the blood covenant and declare that we are in a full state of war and will not lay down our weapons until we have driven the enemy into the sea and reclaimed the land which was promised to our fathers of old, and through our blood, becomes the land of our children to be" (Flynn & Gerhardt, 1990, p. 126). Members of The Order soon were laying down their weapons and some were laying down their lives for the war they had vowed to fight. Gary Lee Yarbrough was arrested on November 24, 1984, after a shootout with FBI agents at a Portland, Oregon, motel. The gun that was used in the murder of Alan Berg had been found after a raid of Yarbrough's home on October 16th. Yarbrough was in the hotel room with Robert Mathews, who escaped ("Idaho man held," 1984), only to die later, after a 36-hour siege, on December 8, 1984. More than 60 FBI agents were in the woods of Whidbey Island, north of Seattle, where a heavily armed Mathews hid in one of the cabins on the island and refused to leave. At the start of the second day of Mathews hiding in the cabin, the FBI surrounded the house and fired tear gas into it, attempting entry. They were met by heavy gunfire from Mathews. That night the FBI fired flares into the house to illuminate it and the house caught on fire. Mathews's ammunition exploded as the house burned to the ground, keeping the FBI agents at bay, and his charred remains were found later in the home (Parker, 1984). A tribute to Mathews was published by William Pierce's National Alliance via an audio recording of one of his speeches under the title of "A Call to Arms" (Durham, 2007, p. 102). Other members of The Order were apprehended throughout 1985 and 1986. Some reached plea agreements with the government; others were tried and convicted for their criminal activities as Aryan warriors in Mathews's The Order (Barkun, 1996, p. 228). Members of The Order were put on trial in Fort Smith, Arkansas; the indictment stated that the accused had tried to overthrow the government and form a new Aryan Nation (Durham, 2007, p. 69). David Lane, who was the driver of the car in the murder of radio talk show host Alan Berg, is currently serving a 150-year sentence for racketeering, conspiracy, and violating Berg's civil rights. Lane is famous among the extreme right for his "14 Words": "We must secure the existence of our people and a future for White children" (Durham, 2007, p. 73).

For The Order, there was a crossing over of religion and politics. Their oath was similar to that of Earl Turner in *The Turner Diaries*. The men wanted to be "His battle axe and weapons of war." That war was to return their country to how they racially envisioned it, overthrowing the government in the process. There were two religions within The Order, which eventually split the group. The Order was composed of both Christian Identity and Odinism believers (Durham, 2007, p. 73). Odinism spread among the Aryan extreme-right groups with the support of the Wotansvolk group run by Katja Lane, the wife of David Lane (Durham, 2007, p. 73). David Lane and Robert Merki attended Pete Peters's Christian Identity church, Church of LaPorte. Lane was a prolific writer of Identity works prior to and after his incarceration (Barkun, 1996, p. 231). Mathews's religion seems to have been a mix of Odinism and Identity, but a large portion of the eventual 30 members of The Order had direct links with Aryan Nations or the Christian Identity Church of Jesus Christ Christian associations (Barkun, 1996, p. 231). Eventually there was a split in The Order based on religion; the Identity branch (consisting of 16 men, women, and children) was led by Bruce Carroll Pierce, who was an Aryan Nations member (Barkun, 1996, p. 231). These religious aspects and their complementary viewpoints will be explained next.

It is not precisely clear where Odinism originated, but it seems to have risen in popularity in the Weimer Republic. The German Youth Movement, which was composed of displaced or disillusioned German youth who developed into wandering groups, began to make sacrifices to Wotan. These wandering groups and their sacrifices were soon given up as the Third Reich started to develop. As National Socialism was rising, the occult implications of the Nazis were gaining the attention of those outside of Germany. One such person was an Australian named Alexander Mills, a Nazi sympathizer. Mills penned the book *The Odinist Religion: Overcoming Jewish Christianity*, in the 1930s. He believed that the ills of contemporary society were due to Jewish influence (Kaplan, 1997, p. 15). In his view, the rise of Christianity was a victory for the Jews over the Nordic religion. The Jews had created a sinister plot to convince Aryans to worship the Jews as the chosen people. The Aryans became weakened because of immigration and miscegenation, and succumbed to the Jewish plot. This paved the way for an effeminate Christianity and claims of the equality of all (Gardell, 2003, p. 167). In the 1920s and 1930s, Mills helped establish polygamist Odinist groups in Australia, the United Kingdom, South Africa, and North America. The Church of Odin did not survive, but his tracts did. Odinism believes that Europe is the true birthplace of modern civilization, not the Middle East, and that Whites descended from a common ancestor. These descendants were responsible for the building of the pyramids and founded empires. From this imagined history, Mills added conspiracy theories, warning against usury and miscegenation, and most radical of all, that Christ did not die on the cross (Kaplan, 1997, p. 16). In the 1960s, Else and Alex Christensen rediscovered Mills's book and Odinism. In 1970 Else, now a widow, formed the Odinist Fellowship and her group began publishing a journal in 1971 called *The Odinist*. Odinists hold a conspiratorial view of history, a warrior ethic that is pronounced in a hope to strike back at the dominant culture for the injustices they perceive to exist, and racial mysticism (Kaplan, 1997, p. 16). Wyatt Kaldenberg has cultivated a more political Odinism characterized by lone-wolfism and calls for violence (Gardell, 2003, p. 177). Kaldenberg wanted to establish Odinism as the White Nation of Islam (Gardell, 2003, p. 178). Kaldenberg started publishing *Pagan Revival*, where he openly dehumanized his racial enemies, referred the White masses as sheep, and called for war and stealing from the rich, White upper- and middle-classes to pay for this war. He argued that the only hope for survival of the White race is through violence and terrorism (Gardell, 2003, p. 181). From Odinism, Wotansvolk was developed, which has become the most influential in racial Odinism (Gardell, 2003, p. 177). Established in early 1995 by David and Katja Lane (David Lane of The Order), and Ron McVan, it has been influential with Aryan groups and has spread throughout the United States, being very successful in outreach programs to U.S. penitentiaries. Lane claimed that the U.S. government had come under ZOG control; his religion calls for a White revolution and a leaderless resistance, similar to The Organization in *The Turner Diaries* (Lewis & Petersen, 2005, p. 389).

Where Odinism holds that Christianity is the conspiratorial plan of the Jews to have Whites worship them as the chosen people, Christian Identity believes that the Bible narrative actually made the Whites the chosen people. In the 1870s, a movement in Britain known as British Israelism was founded by Edward Hine, who wrote of his theory in a book *Identification of the British Nation with Lost Israel* (1871). The doctrine states that European Jews are not descendants of ancient Hebrews but are descendants of Khazars, a warlike nation of southern Russia who converted to Judaism in the 8th or 9th century. As a result, they are not from the lineage of

Abraham, Isaac, and Jacob, and are not the people of the covenant (Flynn & Gerhardt, 1990, p. 71). Hine's book developed the "two seed theory," which states that Eve was seduced by the serpent and bore him a son, Cain. Adam, the first White man, passed his seed to another son, Seth, who became the father of the White race, God's chosen people. Cain's descendants were the Jews according to Hine, and in this book they are literally the seed of Satan (Hine, 1878). This movement claimed that Jews were only part of the people once inhabiting Israel, and that many Israelites had been taken captive by the Assyrians, 700 years before the birth of Christ, and did not return to their homeland but rather disappeared from history. Yet, they note, at the same time these individuals seemed to disappear, another new group of people suddenly appeared, namely the British. This group seemingly did not know their true identity, but now it was known that the British were the missing sons of Isaac (Durham, 2007, pp. 66–67). The United States was seen as the child that had broken away from Israel as representative of the United States breaking away from Britain, but that it would be reunited in pursuit of their rightful dominion (Durham, 2007, p. 67). British Israelism privileged the British, strongly believed that the United States had an important and crucial role in God's plan, and advocated that the Jews should be returned to Palestine. This belief persisted until the 1930s when Christian Identity appeared as an offshoot of British Israelism. Mainstream British Israelism was not anti-Semitic. Jews were understood to have been cursed by God for rejecting Jesus, but salvation was still available for them if they converted (Barkun, 1990, p. 123). In contrast, under Christian Identity, Britain's role diminished in theological significance; the Jews were now understood as the enemy and the United States became the Promised Land, the New Jerusalem (Durham, 2007, p. 67). Leaders such as Wesley Swift, William Potter Gale, and Bertrand Comparet fostered a belief in the hatred of Jews who were conspiring through desegregation to destroy the United States. In time, National Identity impacted Rightist groups such as the KKK (Durham, 2007, p. 67). Christian Identity claims that the lost tribes crossed the Caucasus Mountains and settled in the Western European countries. Their descendants eventually sailed to America on the Mayflower and after settling in this new Promised Land, God inspired the founding fathers to write the Declaration of Independence, the Constitution, and the Bill of Rights. According to the Christian Identity beliefs, any changes and amendments to these documents are Satanic additions dictated through contemporary Jews to undermine the White race (Flynn & Gerhardt, 1990, pp. 71–72). Christian Identity is a purely U.S. movement, appealing to the religious identity of the rightists as well as emphasizing the importance and destiny of the

United States. It tries to remove Judaism and the Jews from Christianity while substantiating the specialness of their White race (Durham, 2007, p. 82). Christian Identity followers believe that the apocalypse is nigh, seeing signs in contemporary news as direct confirmations of the Book of Revelation (Flynn & Gerhardt, 1990, p. 72). In contrast to other groups, Identity believers are not preoccupied with dates of the return of Jesus, nor are they preoccupied with interpreting signs in the news. Instead, they focus on racial struggle and conflict. They see their role in the return of Jesus as the victors of an earthly battle against the Jewish conspiracy that they believe dominates the United States, the media, and the government (Barkun, 1990, pp. 126–127).

Christian Identity is a millennial movement but is very different from the millennialism espoused by Fundamentalist Christians. Theirs does not accept the belief that Jews must return from diaspora to Israel. An anti-Semitic group would not hinge their millennial beliefs on a group whom they believe to be the spawns of the seed of Satan. Theirs is a racial apocalypse that reads both secular and sacred history from the perspective of racial reason and a promise of racial redemption (Barkun, 1990, p. 126). The Christian Fundamentalist view of the end times sees the coming of God's Kingdom as a time of peace where believers will be awash in heavenly bliss. The Christian Identity believers see a world of racial redemption where the Whites, as God's chosen people, are the majority in power. Christian Identity links politics with religion, linking the political enemy with Satan, the rise of the Anti-Christ, and the imminence of the end times (Barkun, 1996, p. 50). We can understand this crossover between religion and politics here, where we see the movement's anger and resentment toward the Civil Rights Movement and affirmative action programs (blamed for taking their jobs, ensuring their poverty and loss) being understood in religious end times stories (Barkun, 1990, p. 126). They are infused with the idea of a Jewish conspiracy controlling the world—what some Aryan churches refer to as ZOG, or "Zionist Occupation Government." This is the powerful Jewish group who securely controls the United States, including media, banks, and the government. Christian Identity is built on the idea of loss. There is less emphasis on the visions of natural disaster in the end times, so less fear of earthquakes, floods, and so on. Their idea of disaster resembles ideas of revenge. Their vision of the end times reflects retribution for the Aryan loss of inheritance through the theft of their "chosenness" by the Jews, and God's punishments for sins of their fathers (Barkun, 1990, p. 128).

Both of these faiths, which were a part of The Order, play an important role in explaining the movement, in particular, why they are angry and why they are violent. The religions both link a mythology of race with politics, violence, and overthrowing the government. Religion and politics become one. For the Christian Identity movement and the Odinist, "the Jew as absolute evil confronts the absolute good of the "Aryan" racial adversary, which must inevitably lead to a final conflict in which the issue of racial dominance is settled once and for all" (Barkun, 1990, p. 128). This is the plot of *The Turner Diaries*. The main character of Pierce's novel, Earl Turner, writes about the current state of the United States as, "We have allowed a diabolically clever alien minority to put chains on our souls and our minds" (Pierce, 1978, p. 33). Although the novel itself makes only passing reference to religion, it fulfills many of the pillars of these two faiths: the ultimate battle of good versus evil, the lone wolf among a small, leaderless group that rises up and through violence destroys "the system" and creates a new Aryan world. Much like Earl Turner, Robert Mathews became a martyr to the cause, a lone-wolf hero who led his people. As Mathews emulated the group in *The Turner Diaries*, soon other people and groups began to follow in his footsteps, and the power of Pierce's novel continues to inspire violent acts.

The Aryan Republican Army (ARA) was a group of six men who robbed a series of banks in the Midwest. The ARA was composed of Peter Langan, Richard Lee Guthrie Jr., Scott Anthony Stedeford, Kevin William McCarthy, Michael William Bresica, and Mark Thomas. With Langan as its leader, the group netted over $250,000 in its bank-robbing spree (Michael, 2012, p. 41) of approximately 20 bank robberies between 1992 and 1996 (Michael, 2012, p. 182). In one bank, they left behind a lunch box with a pipe bomb and a Hostess Twinkie. In another, they left a bomb in an Easter basket. In yet another, one of the robbers wore a Santa Claus suit and left a bomb behind in a Santa hat. The ARA was dedicated to the violent overthrow of the U.S. government and the death of all Jews, and proceeds from the bank robberies were to be used to fund the revolution. The robbers left a newspaper article about McVeigh on the seat of the getaway car they used in Bridgeton, Missouri. The car had been rented and the name they used for the rental was Wayne Manis, the FBI agent who had led the hunt for Robert Mathews, founder of The Order. When police searched their house they found 13 pipe bombs, seven homemade grenades, a pistol, assault weapons, components for making explosives, and a two-hour video, "The Aryan Republican Army Presents: The Armed Struggle Underground." In this video, Langan tells his viewers to read right-wing material like *The Turner Diaries* and he praises Mathews of The Order, saying, "Come on, guys the war's been going on for 10 years. Learn from Bob. Learn from his methods" (Thomas, 1997, p. A01). Guthrie, who began cooperating with the government after he was apprehended, hung himself in his jail cell in Kentucky.

In June 1998, John William King (also known as "Possum"), Shawn Allen Berry, and Lawrence Russell Brewer chained James Byrd Jr., a disabled African American man, by his ankles to the back of their pickup and dragged him. This act ultimately ripped the man's head and his right arm from his body. Berry, in a statement to the police, said that King had said the words "We're starting 'the Turner Diaries' early" as Byrd was dragged to his death (Pressley, 1998, p. A01). According to the prosecutors at his trial, King had wanted to create his own chapter of a White supremacist group, and believed he needed a dramatic event to put him into the public eye to get members. Police found in the three men's apartment an article from *Esquire* about the 1955 lynching of Emmett Till. They also found a collection of King's racist writings, including a constitution for his future group called The Texas Rebel Soldiers Division of the Confederate Knights of America, a code of ethics, bylaws, membership applications, and a letter for new members of the group (Lyman, 1999, p. A01).

William Pierce, in his National Alliance magazine *Vanguard,* wrote, "No purely political program can have any real value for us in the long run unless we get our souls back, unless we learn once again how to be true to our inner nature, unless we learn to heed the divine spark inside us and base all our decisions on a clear and comprehensive philosophy illuminated by that spark" (Pierce, 1976). With this statement, he is separating the Whites from the government of the United States, stating that no political program can truly represent a lost people. Yet, the call to overthrow the U.S. government is symbolized in the acts of the government. These acts are interpreted by some as a sign, or another symbol of the persecution of the White race, and it draws people into groups like the National Alliance. In *The Turner Diaries,* the U.S. government bans the private ownership of guns and staged raids to arrest gun owners. These gun raids were assigned to "special deputies" who were Black men. Many see this as prophetic and see the new laws restricting gun ownership or Second Amendment changes as the beginning steps of what is depicted in Pierce's book. The Supreme Court's decision in *Brown vs. Board of Education* impacted not only the Civil Rights Movement, but also the backlash from Whites (Durham, 2007, p. 3). Many of those who opposed *Brown* have been drawn into the world of the extreme right (Durham, 2007, p. 3). These individuals have a sense of powerlessness and disenfranchisement, viewing the lack of jobs, women's liberation and rights, Black power, LGBTQQIP2SAA rights, a perceived moral decline in society, jobs outsourcing including factory jobs sent to other countries, and affirmative action programs as a death of the American dream. Their culmination creates a sense of disaster, both real and imagined. There is a lack of hope and a lack of understanding as to why there is a continuous loss and as an explanation, an enemy is created to blame for all that is occurring to them. ". . . *everything* will be lost—our history, our heritage, all the blood and sacrifices and upward striving of countless thousands of years." "If we fail, God's great Experiment will come to an end, and this planet will once again, as it did millions of years ago, move through the other devoid of higher man" (Pierce, 1976, pp. 34–35).

With Christian Identity and Odinism and in the words of *The Turner Diaries*, we see stigmatized knowledge that binds all these subjects together. There is a commonality of conspiracism that something or someone, an evil power, is controlling human destinies (Barkun, 2013). Most importantly, once this common conspiracy and enemy are exposed to those who know the truth, then a plan can develop, a plan to destroy the enemy and set the world straight. Conspiracists believe that the universe is governed by design and that nothing is random. The conspiracists' view magnifies the power held by the evil ones (Barkun, 2013). What we see is that this evil is most powerful, not simply because of their master plan or their control, but because of the inactivity and lack of response by the masses. The masses have been controlled or bribed into submission, yet this gives the impression that evil is in the supreme position. There is hope that good will rise up and will eventually win the ultimate battle, but at this moment it appears as though evil is winning and is the more powerful. This battle and this enemy give the believer a life with purpose (Barkun, 2013). This purpose can be seen in the words of Pierce, "The acceptance of our truth not only burdens us with the responsibility that other men have shunned throughout history, it bestows on us a mantle of moral authority that goes along with the responsibility, the moral authority to do whatever is necessary in carrying out our responsibility" (Pierce, 1976).

Although much of the violence described above is quite terrifying, we must remember that these groups are fragmented and there is no central organization. They are suspicious of government and of the involvement of others, and experience the continual breaking and reestablishing of internal alliances within their structure. Despite this, the core ideas among these groups seems to be uniform (Barkun, 1996, p. 60). It is reassuring that these small groups of people remain disconnected as a whole from similar groups. They are outsiders, the marginalized, who find each other, who share ideas and beliefs, build upon each other's ideas, and introduce and accept new ones. The media is the enemy, controlled by their enemies (the Jews). The very fact that the mainstream media discounts them and their beliefs provides proof, to their adherents, of their enemies' control and the legitimacy of their beliefs. Their ideas are shared by mediums such as magazines, ezines, websites, forums, cassettes/DVDs, mail order book services, and gun shows, all of which are interconnected, citing each other (Barkun, 1996, p. 60). These groups are becoming less and less isolated by two bridge phenomena. Michael Barkun, a scholar of religion, conspiracies, and millennialism, argues that the isolation members feel society is reduced by "bridge" phenomena that link mainstream and fringe. The members present themselves as patriots and representatives of constitutional fidelity and link themselves to core U.S. values. This makes them appear attractive to individuals who would otherwise be unlikely to join such organizations. Once they become members, they are made aware and bombarded with right-wing materials and networks . . . bridging the mainstream (patriotism, U.S. value systems) and then to activities and memberships that were once outside of the norm (Barkun, 1996). The violence of these groups is strategic in that it is targeted at enemy groups, the racial enemy or the government (Blee & Creasap, 2010, p. 276).

The Turner Diaries remains the "Bible" of the right-wing extremists, and even though Pierce died of cancer and kidney failure in July 2002 (Durham, 2007, p. 33), his work continues to influence. The National Alliance still publishes his writings and his speeches on its website. Before his death, Pierce purchased an Aryan Nation record company and this continues to draw in new recruits to the movement. The mobilization of these right-wing movements is increasing through the use of alternative media, such as virtual communities on blogs, websites, forums, and discussion boards. Some argue that these virtual communities are used to recruit new members, but others argue that to bring people into groups that are marginalized in society, there needs to be personal contact (Blee & Creasap, 2010, p. 277). Women are joining right-wing groups in larger numbers, although women are perceived as non-political wives and mothers by these hypermasculinized groups. Research into why U.S. women are joining these groups seems to show that they are being recruited to work for what appears to be mainstream causes (Blee & Creasap, 2010, p. 278).

To fully understand the issue of right-wing extremism, research needs to focus on the areas of religion, conspiracy theory, and terrorism. These three areas would help us to understand political violence and social movement theory. Such investigations would benefit from the inclusion of those who feel marginalized in the public sphere. For these groups, politics is something that is inaccessible and non-representative. It would also help to overcome the self-imposed exclusion from society that these individuals insist is part of their path, their religion, and their mission.

References

Anonymous. (1959). *The John Franklin Letters.* New York, NY: Bookmailer.

Barkun, M. (1990). Racist apocalypse: Millennialism on the far right. *American Studies, 31*(2), 121–140.

Barkun, M. (1996). Religion, militias and Oklahoma City: The mind of conspiratorialists. *Terrorism and Political Violence, 8*(1), 50–64.

Barkun, M. (2013). *Culture of conspiracy: Apocalyptic visions in contemporary America, Vol. 15.* Berkeley, CA: University of California Press.

Blee, K. M., & Creasap, K. A. (2010). Conservative and right-wing movements. *Annual Review of Sociology, 36,* 269–286.

Durham, M. (2007). *White rage: The extreme right and American politics.* London, UK and New York, NY: Routledge.

Flynn, K., & Gerhardt, G. (1990). *The silent brotherhood: Inside America's racist underground.* Dell City, OK: Signet.

Gardell, M. (2003). *Gods of the blood: The pagan revival and white separatism.* Durham, NC: Duke University Press.

Griffin, R. S. (2001). *The fame of a dead man's deeds: An up-close portrait of white nationalist William Pierce.* Bloomington, IN: Authorhouse.

Hine, E. (1871). *Identification of the British Nation with Lost Israel.* Manchester: J. Heywood. Retrieved from https://archive.org/stream/cihm_44746/cihm_44746_djvu.txt

Hine, E. (1878). *Forty-seven identifications of the Anglo-Saxons with the lost ten tribes of Israel founded upon five hundred scripture proofs.* New York: James Huggins, Printer and Publisher. Retrieved from http://www.thechristianidentityforum.net/downloads/47-Identifications.pdf

Idaho man held after shoot-out with FBI agents gun that killed radio host found in Neo-Nazi's home. (1984, December 14). *The Los Angeles Times,* p. 5.

Kaplan, J. (1997). *Radical religion in America: Millenarian movements from the far right to the Children of Noah.* Syracuse, NY: Syracuse University Press.

Lewis, J. R., & Petersen, J. A. (2005). *Controversial new religions.* New York, NY: Oxford University Press.

Lyman, R. (1999, February 17). Dragging death is called signal for racist plan. *The New York Times.* Retrieved from http://www.nytimes.com

McAlear, R. (2009). Hate, narrative, and propaganda in *The Turner Diaries. The Journal of American Culture, 32*(3), 192–202.

Michael, G. (2012). *Lone wolf terror and the rise of leaderless resistance.* Nashville, TN: Vanderbilt University Press.

Parker, L. (1984, December 12). U.S. alleges overthrow plot. *The Washington Post.* Retrieved from https://www.washingtonpost.com/archive/politics/1984/12/12/us-alleges-overthrow-plot/55f2b675-fc38-4617-b14b-ae1030a2cab4/

Pierce, W. L. (1976). Our cause. Available at: http://nationalvanguard.org/2010
    /09/our-cause/
Pierce, W. L. (1978). *The Turner Diaries*. Arlington, VA: National Vanguard Books.
Pressley, S. A. (1998, June 13). Down a dark road to murder: Three accused tied
    to hate groups. *The Washington Post,* p. A01.
Thomas, J. (1997, January 9). Bank robbery trial offers a glimpse of a right-wing
    world. *The New York Times*. Retrieved from http://www.nytimes.com

The Institutionalization of Political Anger: The Case of the Affordable Care Act

Terry Weiner

During the August recess of Congress in 2009, legislators came home to meet with constituents, as they often do, in town-hall-type settings. These members of Congress expected to be asked about a range of topics; however, one topic seemed to dominate most of these meetings—the Affordable Care Act (ACA; referred to derogatorily as "Obamacare"). Members were certainly expecting questions on this topic and were prepared to handle them. What they experienced, though, was far from the usual give-and-take of a question-and-answer session with constituents. Instead, it was more like an ambush by citizens who had apparently been encouraged by radio talk-show hosts and other conservative grass roots organizations to show up at these meetings and demonstrate their opposition to the president's health care plan. Indeed, at some of these meetings, there were fistfights, arrests, and even some hospitalizations (American Civil Liberties Union, n.d.). Most of the Congress members ambushed were Democrats, but Republicans were not spared, either. A taste of what happened can be garnered from the two descriptions below:

At the beginning of a rowdy forum hosted by Rep. John Dingell, D-Mich., Mike Sola pushed his wheelchair-bound son up to the podium where Dingell stood and began to yell, "I'm his father and I want to talk to you face to face." Dingell was only accepting questions written in advance on notecards. Sola went on to loudly claim that Obama's health care plan would provide "no care whatsoever" to his son, who has cerebral palsy. "You've ordered a death sentence to this young man," he shouts before being escorted out of the room by police.

Rep. Kathy Castor, D-Fla., struggled to keep a health care town hall meeting in Tampa under control as protesters crowded the room and the struggle turned physical. Hundreds of people showed up for the meeting to protest Obama's plan and many were not allowed into the room. That didn't stop them from banging on the door and drowning out the congresswoman's remarks with shouts of "You work for us" and "Tyranny." (Shanahan, 2013)

To many "policy wonks" who follow the history of public policy and its progress from ideas to legislation, this reaction was difficult to understand. To be sure, the legislation that President Obama was proposing was filled with compromises and had many flaws that would trouble legislators on both sides of the aisle. Indeed, many health care experts had raised some concerns, particularly about the likely success of holding health care costs down with the large expansion of coverage. But, and even more importantly, the president's plan had its origins in conservative think tanks and Republican alternatives to the ill-fated Clinton plan in the mid-1990s (ProCon .org, 2012). Ironically, the first real consideration of an individual mandate for health care came out of the Heritage Foundation, a conservative think tank, in 1989 (Krugman, 2011). The Heritage Foundation set up "Heritage Action," a political action wing of the Foundation to encourage these very protests described earlier. They were campaigning against their own ideas! And, as we all know, the Republican presidential candidate in 2008, Mitt Romney, had implemented a plan not too different from the Obama plan in Massachusetts, and the plan was seemingly quite successful in significantly expanding coverage at an affordable cost (Robertson, 2011).

Also, it was strange to see that many of the participants in the protests were likely over 65 and benefitting from Medicare, a program entirely funded by the federal government. In the town-hall vignette with the disabled child who had cerebral palsy, it was very likely that the education of the child and his medical needs were partially funded by Medicaid, a joint state and federal program. So why was this citizen outraged at a proposal to expand this type of coverage to millions of others who did not have insurance?

It is difficult to explain the reaction many citizens had to the president's plan. This level of anger and rage is rarely seen in most legislative proposals considered by Congress. However, it is not unusual in proposals to reform health care. Surprisingly, the outrage we witnessed in the summer of 2009 was indeed similar to the politics we observed in 1993–1994 with the consideration at the time of the proposal from President Clinton (also referred to as "Hillarycare"). Health care reform inevitably strikes at an industry that is one sixth of our economy and consumes currently almost 18% of our gross domestic product (GDP). The number of interest groups that could be impacted and the amount of money at stake is often unimaginable. So, when President Clinton proposed his plan, which also had its origins in a moderate think tank led by the so-called "Jackson Hole group" that proposed managed-competition and managed-care solutions to our troubled health care system, there still were claims that we were going down the road to socialism, that it was a government takeover of health care, and that citizens would lose choice and be at the mercy of uncaring federal bureaucrats for their health care needs (Skocpol, 1997). When the president or first lady hit the campaign trail to push for their plan, they were met with similar expressions of anger. Again, this was not new in the history of health care reform; when President Truman proposed a national health care plan, the American Medical Association (AMA) organized an effort to have doctors lobby their patients in their offices to oppose the plan.

Health care reform is different in another way from popular welfare proposals such as Social Security or unemployment insurance. Most Americans have health care insurance and, although most agree that the "system" needs reform, they report being happy with their providers and often content with their insurance. So, reform is often threatening in that it can raise fears that to extend coverage to the uninsured, the government is going to reduce the quality of the coverage or increase the cost of coverage for the many who are insured (Skocpol, 1997). Those with coverage are often not aware that the coverage they have is often not comprehensive and leaves them at risk for catastrophic health events, for example, cancer or the birth of a baby with serious complications. Consequently, the marketing of health care reform has always been difficult due to the large number of impacted interest groups and the inclination of those who have coverage to be wary of change.

Yet, something still felt different this time. The anger was not just about Obamacare, and the political context in which this anger was expressed was different from past reactions. The United States was in the midst of a "great recession" and was being guided by its first African American president. Public support and trust in government and Congress were at all-time lows. Possibly, this anger was quantitatively and qualitatively different from what had gone on before. In this chapter, we will consider a few possible explanations for this "rage over Obamacare" and consider whether this is indeed something new in our politics.

The Role of Anger in Politics: Some Observations

Anger is not new to politics and many political theorists have observed that it is indeed essential to political action. Lyman, in his work on the "domestication of anger," says "anger is often described as a wild emotion . . . and yet anger is an indispensable political emotion—for without angry speech the body politic would lack the voice of the powerless questioning the justice of the dominant order" (Lyman, 2004, p. 133) Indeed, many critical theorists in political science believe conflict is the "engine of change" and that anger is essential to the motivation of those suffering injustice to engage the system (Holmes, 2004).

The dominant political order often uses stereotypes and images of anger by marginalized groups to create fear and delegitimize their complaints. For instance, feminists and Black males who angrily protest injustice are perceived as challenging conventional notions of their roles in society or raising fears among the dominant group (Holmes, 2004). For this reason, many critical theorists are quick to defend the role of anger in politics as a way of challenging both injustice and conventional norms of behavior. They see efforts to repress expressions of anger as part of the tools of domination employed by the powerful.

Democratic theorists, however, have been less supportive of the role of anger because it is seen as inhibiting the ability to compromise, a goal that is essential in a complex and diverse society living under constitutional forms of government. Hattam and Zembylas (2010), in their study of conflict in Australia and Cyprus, point out that anger can "create a backlash against rights for the oppressed" and call for a third way in response to those who wish to silence anger or "cultural workers who call for the mobilization of anger." In particular, they show that "racism continues to grow in new and alarming ways that demand new conceptual tools."

When we look at anger in the context of the debate about health care, race will play an essential role in how we explain what has been happening. Interestingly, in one study of the Tea Party movement by Sparks (2015), she points out that the movement gave freedom for Black males and White females to express anger in the public arena. It is likely that this freedom is given to minorities who support the views of the dominant group, but not those who oppose it. The role of race is heightened in this debate because many of the beneficiaries of the Affordable Care Act are citizens of color and the leading proponent of the reform is the first Black president of the United States.

The Racial Resentment Hypothesis

Several political scientists have examined the possibility that race and ethnocentrism played a role in the attitudes of White voters toward the Affordable Care Act. Maxwell and Shields (2014) describe this hypothesis and its relationship to the "anger" we are addressing in this volume:

> Many defenders of "Obamacare" insisted that the angry criticism was racially motivated. For example, Jim Winkler (2009), General Secretary of the United Methodist Church, noted that opposition to healthcare reform had "transmogrified into something far deeper, far more elemental." "Anger" he observed, was "its salient feature" and racism and fear is at the core of the anger. (p. 293)

New York Times columnist Frank Rich also states bluntly that this anger we observed was not about health care. He says:

> If Obama's first legislative priority had been immigration or financial reform or climate change, we would have seen the same trajectory. The conjunction of a black president and a female speaker of the House—topped off by a wise Latina on the Supreme Court and a powerful gay Congressional committee chairman—would sow fear of disenfranchisement among a dwindling and threatened minority in the country no matter what policies were in play . . . When you hear demonstrators chant the slogan "Take our country back" those are the people they want to take the country back from. (Rich, 2010)

If this is so, it would help us understand why the opposition worked so hard to reframe the proposal as "Obamacare" so as to increase the linkage with the Black president. Before the research was done, there was room for some skepticism about this hypothesis because President Clinton failed as well and of course he was White. So if race is a factor, we need to explain how a "non-racial" issue such as health care reform can in fact increase the divide between Black and White voters.

In their research, Maxwell and Shields (2014) describe three processes by which a non-racial issue can in, fact, be "racialized." They point first to "racial cues" that link policies with race because they deal with the poor, inner city life, welfare, or crime, all of which imply African Americans as a prime beneficiary of the legislation (p. 294). Supporting this point, Banks, in his study of White racial attitudes toward reform, says:

> Because the public mostly associates blacks with welfare, racial attitudes dominate their opinions (Gilens, 1995; Winter 2006). Williamson et al. (2011) suggest that the health care debate has produced similar appraisals and is viewed as another sign of government redistributing resources from hard working Americans to undeserving individuals. (Banks, 2014, p. 493)

In the context of health care reform, then, the focus on the problems of the large number of uninsured in the United States may seem to link the policy with the improvement of conditions for minorities more than Whites. It is probably the mistaken view that the uninsured are not working and undeserving, that they are overwhelmingly living in poverty and on welfare, or just choose not to pay for insurance, that this policy may be linked in the minds of White voters to race and the undeserving poor. However, in fact, the majority of the uninsured are either working or are children or spouses living in the household of an employed individual who has no insurance (Majerol, Newkirk, & Garfield, 2015).

A second mechanism, according to Maxwell and Shields, linking health care policy to race is the strong association of the reform proposal to the Democratic Party. Because the Democrats have been unsuccessful in attracting support from moderate Republicans, health care reform is linked with a party that contains greater numbers of minorities in leadership positions and with overwhelming support from Black voters.

Finally, a third mechanism for linkage is "personal cues" and in this case this means the strong and obvious association of this proposal with the president. The fact that a strong minority of White voters who identify with the Republican Party held extreme views toward President Obama would suggest this was likely a factor in their attitudes toward the plan. For instance, in August 2010, just a few months after the passage of the ACA, 41% of Republicans still believed President Obama was probably not born in the United States (Maxwell & Shields, 2014). To a minority of very active White conservative voters, the president was a "foreigner," "un-American," and ineligible to hold the presidency.

In his work on the racial resentment hypothesis, Tesler answers the question whether or not the opposition to health care reform was quantitatively different by race in the Clinton years compared to the Obama presidency. In fact, he shows that the racial divide did grow substantially and was

20 points greater under Obama than under Clinton on health care reform. His work seems to support the idea of the impact of the "personal cue" discussed by Maxwell and Shields. He says:

> Aside from polarizing the electorate by racial attitudes, our first African-American president may also drive the political opinions of blacks and whites farther apart. For, as Kinder and Winter put it, "Issues can be formulated and framed in such a way as to light up or downplay racial identity, and therefore, in such a way as to expand or contract the racial divide in opinion" (2001, 452). Attributing policies to black sources seems likely to "light up" racial identity, and therefore expand the racial divide in public opinion. (Tesler, 2012, p. 700)

Tesler also shows that when the provisions of the ACA were identified in an experiment as a proposal from former president Clinton, it had more support than when identified as being from President Obama. Indeed, when survey respondents were asked directly if President Obama's race was a factor in the health care debate, PEW reported in November 2009 that 54% of all respondents agreed it was at least a minor factor and 52% of African Americans thought it was a major factor (Tesler, 2012, p. 690). Clearly, these studies lend some significant weight to the role that race played in opposition to the ACA and most likely in explaining the anger that many conservative White citizens had regarding it.

Banks, however, in a slightly different take on the relationship of race and the anger observed on the health care debate, argues that anger is, or can be, independently aroused and that anger once produced enhances racial polarization. Here we have a claim that the anger comes first or is activated somehow by other processes and that it then pushes views on policy toward racial polarization:

> I contend that anger makes thoughts about race more accessible in many white Americans' minds—thereby enhancing the effect of their racial attitudes on health care policy opinions. That is anger should push racial liberals to be more supportive of health care and racial conservatives to be more opposing of health policy—adding to the racial polarization over health care reform. I argue that this process occurs because anger is tightly woven into the fabric of whites' racial predispositions—so that the two are fused together in memory. (Banks, 2014, p. 494)

In his experiments, Banks (2014) shows that when anger is elicited as compared to other emotions, that anger uniquely moves racial conservatives toward opposition to reform. This work I believe is a bridge to other theories that demonstrate that to motivate protest and demonstrations of anger, we need a third force, possibly from elites, to energize average citizens to show up at town hall meetings. It raises the question, how do we make people angry enough to act?

A Vast Right Wing Conspiracy: Elite Mobilization and the Process of Victimization

It is important to ask how the town hall meetings described earlier came to be filled with hundreds of protestors in the first place in August 2009. Was this a spontaneous display of legitimate outrage and anger over a significant and badly flawed health care reform proposal being "rushed" through Congress? Or was this a movement mobilized by conservative elites and media stars who used disreputable tactics to encourage a barrage of incivility at these meetings?

In her thesis on the role language and communication strategies played in the health care debate in the summer of 2009, Duffy (2013) argues that elite conservative organizations headed by Dick Armey, a former Republican congressional leader, and the billionaire Koch brothers, worked to "frame" the debate by vilifying the proposal and the president. She says:

> I argue that the rhetorical strategies utilized by these two conservative groups in the weeks and months leading up to the health care town halls relied predominantly on the use of victimage rhetoric to inflame the anxiety of the conservative public. FreedomWorks and Americans for Prosperity complete the two steps of the victimage ritual by first systematically constructing the Obama Administration and the broader health reform movement as the enemy; and second by constituting an ethic of action, imploring the conservative audience to storm the town halls to prevent the constructed dangers posed by the vilified health reforms. (Duffy, 2013, p. 45)

The key to the process Duffy describes is that the audience must begin to see themselves as "victims" of actions by evil and immoral actors such as President Obama and Nancy Pelosi:

> The vilification portion of the ritual requires the opponent be cast as "a violator of the ideals of the social order" (Blain, 2005, p. 34). In the instance of the health care debate, these ideals revolve around the notions of individual liberty and patriotism. A key aspect of the vilification step revolves around the use of hyperbolic language to transform a proposed foe into an evil, immoral other that creates group solidarity through opposition to the adversary, an example of Burkean congregation through segregation (Blain, 1994, p. 820). This emphasis on hyperbole to dramatize the "evilness" of

the proposed foe is a dominant element of the conservative groups approach to vilifying the Obama Administration. (Duffy, 2013, p. 47)

So those protestors at the town hall meetings were seeing themselves as victims and challenging leaders that for them were un-American, unpatriotic, and a real threat to the values they held dear. But how did conservative elites transform the health care debate into this life and death struggle for the soul of the United States? Well, it helps to have a popular radio talk show, for example, as Sean Hannity does. On this show, Hannity called on his listeners to "become the party of the mob" and storm the town halls.

However, even before the health care debate, the conservative media from Fox News to Rush Limbaugh had worked hard to delegitimize the new president by challenging his constitutional right to hold the office on the basis of his place of birth, which for some talk show hosts varied from Kenya to Indonesia. The constant emphasis, which continues really through his entire term, on President Obama being the "other," not really an American, someone who might have been educated in a "madras" in Indonesia, made it easier to oppose him and his proposals.

The process of vilification of the President was followed by the use of hyperbole and distortion of the health care proposal so that the legislation was seen as a threat to the core values conservative Americans cherish, such as autonomy, choice and freedom, as well as limited government. The first and probably most successful use of hyperbole in the debate started with Sarah Palin's and Rush Limbaugh's characterization of the Advanced Care Planning Consultation for seniors as a "death panel" (Duffy, 2013, pp. 13–43).

This use of hyperbole by Palin took on a life of its own. It had the impact of turning opponents of the law into both victims (the government is trying to convince Grandma to commit suicide) and heroic actors seeking to defeat this evil and immoral legislation. Conservatives were able to convince large numbers of Americans that the president of the United States was actually proposing that government bureaucrats force the elderly into consultations to convince them to either commit suicide or refrain from medical care in the case of serious illness in order to save money (Duffy, 2013). The idea was preposterous on the face of it, but lies told often enough can seem true. Indeed, the media gave more attention, as it usually does, to covering the conflict than sorting out the substance of the debate. Of course, none of this was true and advanced planning consultation was already being done and encouraged by Medicare policies for years. In fact, the idea for this provision had its roots originally in a proposal by a Republican conservative senator (Jacobs & Skocpol, 2012, p. 84). The purpose was to have patients sit with their doctors, not bureaucrats, and consider the options they may face at the end of life. These decisions would be between doctors and patients.

The "death panel" lie also had the added benefit of diverting the debate away from health care security for all to a debate about government over-reach, intrusion into personal autonomy, and an effort to strip seniors of choice about their care. Doing this encouraged conservatives to see them-selves again as victims and as defenders of cherished values under attack.

After the death panel diversion, other techniques followed, including the claim repeated over and over again that the plan was really a "govern-ment takeover" of the health care system and an attempt to impose a "Euro-pean style" socialized system on the United States (Duffy, 2013, p. 5). As the plan was similar to the one passed in Massachusetts by then Gover-nor Mitt Romney, it was unclear how Republicans could make this argu-ment, but it is one that has been used by opponents of universal coverage for 100 years. Of course, in reality, Obama was delivering millions of Ameri-cans into the hands of private insurers with government subsidies flowing to those insurers to help pay for the premiums, which certainly is not social-ism by any definition.

To sum up this argument, then, the protestors at the town halls who were filled with anger and moral outrage were there because they had fol-lowed a "call to arms" from conservative media outlets and other grassroots organizations who, through the use of web sites, email, and mailings and, frankly, distortions and lies, as described by Duffy, got conservative lis-teners out to protest the health care reform proposal. But the main object of attack was really the president and the effort to delegitimize and weaken him and to position the Republicans for a major electoral victory in the upcoming congressional elections, as they had done to President Clinton in 1994 by scuttling his proposals (Jacobs & Skocpol, 2012, p. 85). Conse-quently, the anger was not just expressed at the grassroots level. It appeared in the halls of Congress and even at the State of the Union address when Representative Joe Wilson cried out "you lie" in the middle of President Obama's speech when he claimed that illegal immigrants would not be covered by the health care proposal. The anger and incivility of the protestors was merely a reflection of what they were observing on Capitol Hill. Inci-vility had become a political tactic to mobilize the base. How did this hap-pen? Is the anger we have observed in our politics really a symptom of a much larger problem?

Anger as a Symptom of Political Dysfunction: A Macro Perspective

Although historians are quick to point out that partisanship and strong language have been part of U.S. politics for most of our history, it seems to many observers that the level of hostility and anger that exists in modern politics is at an all-time high. Some political scientists have set out to look at whether or not the level of partisanship has indeed increased. It turns out it has. As Mann and Ornstein point out in their book *It's Even Worse Than It Looks*:

> Political polarization is undeniably the central and most problematic feature of contemporary American politics. Political parties today are more divided and more internally unified and ideologically distinctive than they have been in over a century. (2012, p. 44)

Mann and Ornstein locate the two major causes of the current dysfunction:

> The first is the serious mismatch between the political parties, which have become as vehemently adversarial as parliamentary parties, and a governing system that unlike a parliamentary democracy, makes it very difficult for a majority to act . . . The second is the fact that, however awkward it may be for traditional press and nonpartisan analysts to acknowledge, one of the two major parties, the Republican Party, has become an insurgent outlier—ideologically extreme, contemptuous of the inherited social and economic policy regime, scornful of compromise; unpersuaded by conventional understanding of facts, evidence, and science; and dismissive of the legitimacy of its political opposition. (2012, p. xiv)

There are many structural factors that help us understand how this polarization occurred. For example, the move toward a candidate nominating system that weighs primaries very heavily and reduces the roles of party elites, which gives advantages in both parties to the most active wings of each party due to the fact that so few voters participate in primary elections. Secondly, the rise of cable news channels and talk shows that allow room in the market for a greater amount of adversarial and partisan platforms such as Fox and MSNBC are also a way of ensuring that many Americans hear the news and views through a filter that conforms to their predispositions. Finally, the Citizens United decision by the Supreme Court equating corporate donations to candidates as a form of "free speech" unleashed a windfall of money to Republican candidates. The growth of the role of money in attaining and keeping political offices has impacted politics so as to give enormous influence to individuals and corporations that support the conservative cause (Mann & Ornstein, 2012, pp. 31–80).

However, it was also during the last health care reform debate, during the Clinton administration, that we saw the origins of the kind of political warfare that was to come. Under the leadership of Representative Newt

Gingrich, the newly elected Republicans pledged to kill health care reform. Gingrich made it clear that he thought any successful bill would hurt Republicans for a generation, as it would put Democrats in charge of another "welfare benefit" that millions would depend on. It was Gingrich's wish to kill any bill, including any potential compromise, even if it included Republican ideas:

> Gingrich and Armey turned out to be forerunners of a burgeoning right wing crusade—a campaign to counter not only the Clinton Health Security Plan but also the premise that America faced a "health care crisis" and needed any sort of comprehensive reform through government legislation. In late 1993, insurgent antigovernment Republicans realized that their ideological fortunes within their own party, as well as the Republican partisan interest in weakening the Democrats as a prelude to winning control of Congress and the presidency, could be splendidly served by first demonizing and then defeating the Clinton plan, along with any compromise variant. (Skocpol, 1997, pp. 144–145)

Fifteen years later, Senator McConnell would say much the same thing as he essentially promised to defeat any bills that might lead to the re-election of President Obama in 2012. It was now more important to defeat Obama than to pass any legislation, even if it was based on Republican principles such as individual mandates and private insurance that might provide 50 million uninsured Americans with some health security. The Republicans tried to use the same playbook on the Obama plan as they did on Clinton. But this time the plan would pass anyway.

During the Obama administration, we saw the rise of the Tea Party as a response to the efforts of the administration to help out homeowners who had found that their subprime mortgages left them, as a result of the housing bust and great recession, with homes worth less than their mortgage and many with an inability to pay the new higher rates. The Tea Party saw these homeowners as individuals who took advantage of low rates to buy houses they could not afford and that it was not the responsibility of the government to bail them out. In fairness, most "Tea Party" leaders were also opposed to the bailout of the banks. The Tea Party originally represented a new conservative movement opposed to the growth of government under President Obama, particularly manifested in policies such as the stimulus bill, the bailout of General Motors, and the effort to help homeowners. The Tea Party would grow and elect members of Congress who, though Republican in political identification, were committed to a new style of politics. They wanted no compromises and were willing to shut down government over issues such as raising the debt limit or passing the federal budget.

Because they threatened established leaders in the primaries, they pushed the already conservative Republican Party even further to the right.

These events led to what I would call the *institutionalization of political anger*. Anger became normalized. Republican activists in Congress and in the media were *always angry* and expressing outrage. Rarely did they provide alternatives or offer compromises when policy disputes existed on health care or immigration. Instead, they would toy with impeachment over disagreements about the use of executive orders by the president on immigration, and they continued to challenge his legitimacy, his place of birth, and his patriotism.

This institutionalization of political anger also can be seen in the effort to reverse the Affordable Care Act even five years after its passage. The Republicans in the House have passed dozens of bills to repeal the bill, only to have it die in the Senate where 60 votes were needed to stop a filibuster. The effort to delegitimize the bill continued even after its passage, with several court cases to challenge parts of the bill or its constitutionality. Anger, for example, was stoked over the provision in the law to require all employers to offer insurance that covers contraception and birth control to women. Religious organizations claimed the law violated their First Amendment rights to religious freedom by making them offer coverage they felt violated church doctrine. Of course, the employers were not paying for the contraception; insurance companies were. The fact that many religious organizations employ thousands of workers, many who may not share the same religious faith, was not seen as relevant. As of now, the Supreme Court has not taken this case, but the government is under restraining orders not to enforce it.

Though the Supreme Court upheld the individual mandate in the law in a narrow 5–4 decision and also rebuffed, by the same margin, the challenge that the law did not allow for subsidies except in states that had their own marketplaces and websites; further, technical challenges are to still be decided. As of this writing, it is unclear if the efforts to undo the Affordable Care Act by a thousand cuts will succeed, though the permanence of the law is increasingly likely.

Anger on the Left

While liberal Democrats did not storm town halls or question the president's legitimacy to hold office, the health care plan was not popular with many liberals, and the concern that later was confirmed was that the president was seeking a plan that would be bipartisan in nature and gather at least some Republican support.

Liberals were clearly expecting more. They had supported Barack Obama over Hillary Clinton not only because of his opposition to the war in Iraq, but because he was seen as more likely to govern from the left than Hillary. Bill Clinton's presidency was filled with political compromises, including the unpopular campaign among liberals to "end welfare as we know it" that ended some of the federal guarantees created in the 1935 Social Security Act for mothers of dependent children.

Most liberals, as in 1993, wanted the United States to adopt a plan that was either similar to Canada's single payer system or one like many European systems that provided guaranteed health care for all. President Clinton rejected that path because he felt it could not pass and would never get the support of key constituencies such as physicians, hospitals or insurance companies. It was clear early on that President Obama felt the same way.

President Obama was also constricted, ironically, by the success of the Democratic Party's decision to run competitive races in all 50 states. The result was the Obama tide in 2008 that swept in senators and representatives from states where Obama actually lost or were traditionally "red." These members of Congress would often try to steer a middle course in voting so as to stay close to the views of their constituents. Thus, a substantial number of Democrats would not have supported any plan like what the liberals wanted. Nonetheless, liberals were frustrated because the president early on abandoned one of the main objectives liberals had, which was to create a "non-profit public option" that consumers could choose over private plans and that would compete with these plans in the health exchanges or marketplaces to be created. Liberal columnist Paul Krugman spoke for many on the left:

> Paul Krugman hammered Obama, not even six months in office, for "searching for common ground where none exists" and negotiating "with himself" for policies that are far too weak. Zeroing in on Obama's unwillingness to endorse a public option, Krugman derided him delivering a "gratuitous giveaway in an attempt to sound reasonable" and warned that "reform isn't worth having if you can only get it on terms so compromised that it's doomed to fail." (Jacobs & Skocpol, 2012, p. 80)

Liberal scholars also agreed that the president had missed understanding the "smoldering public anger over the health system" as demonstrated by public opinion polls and as Gottschalk described:

> Obama and the Democrats may have squandered an exceptional political moment. There are not many times in US history when the previous administration, the ruling party, and the financial sector have been so thoroughly discredited. (Gottschalk, 2011, pp. 398–399)

Clearly, many felt that the crisis presented by the "great recession" and the huge margin of victory by Obama and the Democrats in 2008, had opened a "window of opportunity" for a health care reform that was not "minimalist" in its approach. They were disappointed that the Obama administration was so concerned to have a bipartisan bill with at least some Republican support. Ironically, in the end, not one Republican would vote for the ultimate legislation.

However, the anger we observed from liberals was quantitatively and qualitatively different from that expressed on the right. Unlike the right, there was no effort to delegitimize the president or see themselves as victims. Liberals tried to pressure the president through conventional methods of advertising, letter campaigns, lobbying, and some threats of non-support for the final bill. Rather, this anger stems from the structural conditions described earlier. Democrats are far more ideologically diverse than the Republicans. Because the Senate is required to essentially have a super majority of 60 votes, typically some support is necessary from the other side. If that support is not forthcoming, it is necessary to have all Democrats united. In 2009 the Democrats had the 60 votes but had at least three to five conservative senators who could not support a public option. The current system of governance prevents majority rule and works to the disadvantage of the Democrats, who are less ideologically homogenous. So liberals, though frustrated, ultimately had to accept a reform that really was quite moderate in approach and filled with provisions that have their origins in conservative proposals of the 1990s.

Are the Three Theories Compatible?

Each of the three theories described above is a window on the problem of anger in the context of the debate on the Affordable Care Act. The first theory sees anger as a "trigger" that releases the racial resentment and prejudice lurking among many conservatives who opposed the reform. The level of analysis is at the micro level and focuses on the predispositions of the actors involved. The second theory looks at how important elites and those able to utilize important resources such as the media and other grassroots mobilization strategies were able to create a sense of victimization and sense of loss among conservative voters and delegitimize both the president and the plan. Here the focus is on the effectiveness of political organizations and conservative activists to create a social movement. Finally, the last model looks at the structural causes of the anger and sees it really as a byproduct—almost inevitable really—of the current political system that ensures partisan polarization. It sees the cures for the polarization in the reform of the political system, including expanding the vote, reducing the role of money, and changing the rules of Congress to restore majority rule (Mann & Ornstein, 2012, pp. 31–80). Much of the anger on the left was clearly a result of the structural forces at work on the politics of the health care reform bill.

So these theories work at different levels of analysis but together form a picture of what went wrong in the summer of 2009. But it is also important to remember that not all anger is bad and some of the anger in the case of the Affordable Care Act was probably fair.

Legitimate Anger?

Obviously, we would all agree that anger is legitimate in the case of gross injustice and poor treatment or in cases where citizens are deceived. Did any of this happen in the case of the Affordable Care Act? Indeed it did.

After the act was passed, conservatives made much of the fact that the president had promised during the campaign and through the debates on the bill that "if you liked your insurance, you would be able to keep it." However, it turns out that this was not entirely true, and after the ACA was implemented, thousands of Americans found they were dis-enrolled from their current insurance plans and had to seek new plans. The ACA required insurance companies to meet certain conditions and plans had to have a minimum of benefits in order to be certified. Often these plans had poor coverage, high risks for out-of-pocket payments in the case of serious illness, and other similar problems related to adequate coverage. Consumers would in many cases be eligible under the ACA for subsidies to buy better insurance. So they lost their current insurance but still had access to insurance and could not be refused (Robertson, 2014). However, it was likely that the coverage in some cases would still cost more and in other cases might mean the doctors and hospitals that participated would differ from the consumer's previous plan. There can be no sugar coating of the fact that the promise was not kept and indeed the promise was deceptive.

Of course, conservative organizations like Americans For Prosperity and other opponents of the law launched a political storm over this apparent deception. It was a mistake by the president to offer this promise and he needed to be clearer and more transparent on how the plan would impact millions of Americans with substandard insurance. The irony here is that conservatives seemed to be defending the right of consumers to have poor and substandard insurance instead of the ability to upgrade to better coverage with support from the government if they could not afford it.

Summary

This chapter reviewed the events surrounding the rage and anger expressed at town hall meetings and in other forums regarding the Affordable Care Act, particularly in the summer of 2009. The anger has really never let up as we showed with the continuing efforts of the now Republican majority, swept into office in 2014, to overturn the law in Congress and the courts.

All the theories reviewed to explain the phenomenon, including (a) the effect of racial resentment and prejudice that leads citizens to reject ideas proposed by the first African American president, (b) the work of conservative organizations and media outlets to create a social movement against the plan by turning conservative voters into "victims" of a "government takeover" of health care, and (c) a structural perspective that sees the anger as a result of new institutional arrangements in our politics that makes political polarization inevitable, are described as being relevant to help us understand the rage over Obamacare. However, the argument put forth in this chapter concludes that anger and rage have been "institutionalized" and are now a continuing feature of the polarized political system. The anger has been manifested most clearly in the debates over health care, but the fact is the political right would have chosen any issue that President Obama put forward that had the potential to mobilize the grassroots in order to further its cause to take the White House and Congress back, and more importantly to control the political agenda.

Unfortunately, we have a political party now that actually does not accept the legitimacy of rule by the opposition, even when the opposition wins the election by a large margin. Going forward, Americans will either have to find a way to reform the political system by increasing voter turnout, reducing the role of money, and encouraging the adoption of rules that allow congressional majorities to act—or face a future in which the politics of anger is normal. Without these and other possible structural reforms to our politics, it is hard to see how the Republican Party can be encouraged to move closer to the center and restore a commitment to compromise and dialogue with those with whom they disagree that is essential for a democratic form of governance to survive.

References

American Civil Liberties Union. (n.d.). Challenges to the federal contraceptive coverage rule. Retrieved from https://www.aclu.org/challenges-federal-contraceptive-coverage-rule

Banks, A. J. (2014). The public's anger: White racial attitudes and opinions towards health care reform. *Political Behavior, 36*(3), 493–514.

Duffy, C. (May 2013). Vilifying Obamacare: Conservative tropes of victimage in the 2009 health care debates. [Master's thesis]. Wake Forest University, Winston-Salem, NC.

Gottschalk, M. (2011). They're back: The public plan, the reincarnation of Harry and Louise, and the limits of Obamacare. *Journal of Health, Politics, Policy and Law, 36*(3), 393–400.

Hattam, R., & Zembylas, M. (2010). What's anger got to do with it? Towards a post-indignation pedagogy for communities in conflict. *Social Identities, 16*(1), 23–40.

Holmes, M. (2004). Feeling beyond rules: Politicizing the sociology of emotion and anger in feminist politics. *European Journal of Social Theory, 7*(2), 209–227.

Jacobs, L. R., & Skocpol, T. (2012). *Health care reform and American politics: What everyone needs to know* (Revised and Expanded Edition). New York, NY: Oxford University Press.

Krugman, P. (2011, July 27). Conservative origins of Obamacare [Web log post]. *New York Times*. Retrieved from http://krugman.blogs.nytimes.com

Lyman, P. (2004). The domestication of anger: The use and abuse of anger in politics. *European Journal of Social Theory, 7*(2), 133–147.

Majerol, M., Newkirk, V., & Garfield, R. (2015, November 13). The uninsured: A primer—Key facts about health insurance and the uninsured in the era of health reform. Kaiser Family Foundation. Retrieved from http://www.kff.org

Mann, T. E., & Ornstein, N. J. (2012). *It's even worse than it looks: How the American constitutional system collided with the new politics of extremism*. New York, NY: Basic Books.

Maxwell, A., & Shields, T. (2014). The fate of Obamacare: Racial resentment, ethnocentrism and attitudes about healthcare reform. *Race and Social Problems, 6*(4), 293–304.

ProCon.org. (2012, February 9). History of the individual health insurance mandate, 1989–2010: Republican origins of Democratic health care provision. Retrieved from http://healthcarereform.procon.org

Rich, F. (2010, March 27). The rage is not about health care [Opinion page]. *New York Times*. Retrieved from http://www.nytimes.com

Robertson, L. (2011, March 25). "RomneyCare" facts and falsehoods. *FactCheck .org*. Retrieved from http://www.factcheck.org

Robertson, L. (2014, April 11). "Millions" lost insurance. *FactCheck.org*. Retrieved from http://www.factcheck.org

Shanahan, M. (2013, August 7). 5 memorable moments when town hall meetings turned to rage [Web log post]. Retrieved from http://www.npr.org

Skocpol, T. (1997). *Boomerang: Health care reform and the turn against government*. New York, NY: W.W. Norton & Company.

Sparks, H. (2015). Mama grizzlies and guardians of the republic: The Democratic and intersectional politics of anger in the Tea Party movement. *New Political Science, 37*(1), 25–47.

Tesler, M. (2012). The spillover of racialization into health care: How President Obama polarized public opinion by racial attitudes and race. *American Journal of Political Science, 56*(3), 690–704.

CHAPTER THIRTEEN

Anger and Political Action by Cubans in Florida since 1959

Trevor Rubenzer

Almost 25 years after the end of the Cold War, the Cuban embargo remains one of the most enduring features of United States foreign policy history. It is clear that there is much more to the embargo, and other elements of U.S. foreign policy toward Cuba, than sociopolitical anger on the part of Cuban Americans in Florida. However, the intense feelings of hatred toward the Castro regime, and feelings of betrayal by that regime, and at times by the U.S. government, have fueled a small but politically powerful domestic interest group that has managed to maintain, and in some cases strengthen, the embargo in the face of growing calls for normalization of U.S. relations with Cuba. This chapter examines the sources and nature of anger within the Cuban American community, and discusses the ways that the generational ebbing of this anger will likely contribute to the end of the embargo. It is important to recognize that, although the United States and Cuba have renewed diplomatic ties at the highest levels, the bulk of the economic embargo, which is controlled by Congress, remains in place as of this writing.

The Cuban Revolution began on July 26, 1953, and intensified into a full-scale armed rebellion in 1956 (Lievesley, 2004, pp. 10–11). In 1959, the defeated Fulgencio Batista fled Cuba for the Dominican Republic, resulting in victory for the forces of Fidel Castro. As Castro consolidated his power, the nationalization of several key industries, the emergence of a dictatorial government structure, and the nature of agrarian reform led nearly a quarter million Cubans to flee for the United States (Garcia, 1996, pp. 13–14). As with subsequent waves of Cuban exiles, most of these individuals settled in the area around Miami, Florida. Recent estimates suggest that the total number of Cuban Americans in the United States is approximately 2 million, with approximately 57% of that population having been born in Cuba (Lopez & Krogstad, 2014).

Sources of Cuban American Anger

The Castro Regime as a Source of Cuban American Anger

The most obvious source of anger and resentment among the Cuban American community in the United States is the Castro regime. As Fidel Castro consolidated his social, economic, and political bases of power in Cuba, the number of political exiles increased. While Cuban Americans concentrated in Florida and New Jersey have never reached consensus with respect to their visions of a potential post-Castro Cuba, first-generation Cubans in the United States have been united by their intense anger at what they feel is a betrayal by the Fidel Castro and the 2nd of July Movement (Garcia, 1996). The perceived betrayal took many forms, two of the most salient being the implementation of agrarian reform, which included significant land confiscation, and government structure, which upset Cubans who had hoped for a milder form of authoritarian government or for procedurally democratic government reforms.

Agrarian Reform

Given the nature of the Cuban revolution, it should come as no surprise that some of the first Cubans to flee the island were supporters of the Batista regime. This group included members of the landed elite, who benefited from Batista-era rules relating to coffee, sugar, and tobacco exports, as well as to beef production. Cuba enjoyed favorable terms of trade with the United States at the time, and the concentration of land ownership generated significant wealth for plantation owners and cattle ranchers. One of the first goals that Castro expressed during the revolution was to create a more equitable land distribution system. The promise of significant agrarian reform won the support of a significant number of Cubans who viewed the Batista regime as corrupt and overly supportive of the entrenched landed elite.

Fidel Castro established the National Institute of Agrarian Reform (INRA) to develop rules for land redistribution. Although almost no land-owners resisted land redistribution by force, many responded to impending land confiscation by not making plans for subsequent years of production. These practices led the Cuban government, spearheaded by the INRA, to expand the pace of land redistribution (O'Connor, 1968). Landowners were offered compensation for seized territory. However, the compensation was normally in the form of bonds enumerated in Cuban currency with extended maturity dates. Land reform efforts originally targeted only the largest farms and estates, but over time, the amount of land seized from medium-sized farms increased (O'Connor, 1968).

Land confiscation, coupled with some of the initial human rights abuses outlined below, meant that many of the original Cuban immigrants to the United States were upper-middle class, possessed considerable entrepreneurial skills, and were White (Garcia, 1996). As a result, this first wave of Cuban immigrants received considerable sympathy in the United States. The exiles as a group were angered, not only by the loss of political power during the Cuban Revolution, but by the loss of a considerable source of wealth at the hands of the Castro regime. At the same time, those exiles who were able to deposit money in banks outside of Cuba, including banks in the United States, were able to flee Cuba more easily. They were also able to pursue economic prosperity in the United States with less difficulty than subsequent waves of immigrants, including those of the middle/professional classes and the working class.

Agrarian reform, led by INRA leader and famous revolutionary Che Guevara, also had a more direct impact on United States agricultural interests. U.S. corporations owned some of the most fertile land in Cuba. Most of this land was used for sugar cultivation. The revolutionary government in Cuba viewed small land-owners and tenants as critical supporters of the Castro regime. Nationalizing the sugar industry by confiscating land and transferring ownership to small-holders would serve the twin purposes of decreasing United States influence on the island nation and consolidating Castro's support among a key interest group. Overall, the INRA confiscated close to 500,000 acres of land formerly owned by U.S. corporations (Kellner, 1989, p. 58). As a result, Cuban American anger over land expropriation was combined with anger on the part of powerful U.S. agricultural interests. This anger, coupled with the realities of Cold War politics, led the United States to pursue several steps to topple the Castro regime.

Agrarian reform in Cuba even led some of the rural proletariat (small farmers and wage workers on plantations), who had originally stood to be some of the chief beneficiaries of the revolution, to become disillusioned by the Castro regime. Some of these workers ultimately fled Cuba during later waves of immigration. There were two main sources of disillusionment. First, the Cuban government, for a variety of logistical, practical, and political reasons, was slow to turn over land to small-scale farmers (O'Connor, 1968, p. 185). Under the first Agrarian Reform Law, which was promulgated in 1959, "excess" land holdings were seized by the government with the stated intent of redistributing at least part of the land to the peasants. This reduced the possibility for the rural proletariat to prosper by holding slightly larger amounts of land.

Second, though this policy was not universal, the INRA converted large portions of expropriated land into large, state-owned, collective farms (Valdes & Foster, 2014). For many of the working-poor in rural Cuba, this meant a transition from being a wage laborer on a large farm owned by a Cuban family or a corporation, to being a wage laborer on a state-owned farm. The Second Agrarian Reform in Cuba increased the amount of land controlled by the state and began to roll back some portions of the First Agrarian Reform that had caused some peasants to become land owners for the first time (Kay, 1988). Labor shortages on the state-owned farms also led to "voluntary" labor recruitment programs. These programs led to further disillusionment and labor dislocations, especially among the volunteers who had to seasonally relocate over long distances for no pay and/or those forced to work during the difficult sugar cane harvest (Kay, 1988). The lack of change in basic material conditions was an important source of disenchantment and anger with the Cuban government. Over time, some of these rural workers were able to leave Cuba and immigrate into the United States.

Human Rights Abuses

It is important to recognize that the Batista regime in Cuba was a known and significant abuser of human rights, especially in the area of civil and political liberties. To many Cubans, the Batista regime and the United States, which supported the dictatorship, were betrayers of Cuban national ideals such as the individual liberty fought for under national hero José Martí. To these Cubans, the supporters of Batista, including the landed elite, were the cause of many of the socioeconomic problems facing Cuba. In this context, the revolution became more popular with its promises of land reform, equitable pay, and worker control of the means of production. Summary trials and summary executions of war criminals and counter-revolutionaries were also very popular in Cuba at the time.

From the perspective of early members of the Cuban exile community, the trials, executions, land seizures, and nationalization processes represented a grave violation of human rights. Nationalization of agriculture, education, hospitals and medical practices, housing, and retail establishments caused many upper class and upper middle class Cubans to lose their property. Though these reforms were also popular among the Cuban population, they lead many Cuban professionals, in addition to the landowners and other Batista supporters mentioned above, to flee the country (Martinez-Fernandez, 2014, pp. 71–72). As human rights abuses increased, including summary executions, forced labor, restrictions on assembly and protest and systematic harassment of counter-revolutionaries, the number of Cuban immigrants settling in South Florida increased to about 250,000 by 1962 (Martinez-Fernandez, 2014, p. 72). Some of these exiles included moderates who had originally supported the revolution, but became disenchanted when it was clear that Cuba would become a dictatorship. Most of those who applied to leave Cuba were allowed. However, their property and any other personal possessions were confiscated by the government, further fueling their anger.

Internal critics of the Cuban revolutionary government lacked a basic political space in which to operate, which increased anger among moderates and led to more emigration from Cuba into the United States. The Cuban Constitution, much like the constitutions of the former Soviet Union and of the People's Republic of China, appears to provide for fundamental liberties including freedom of speech and assembly. However, these rights are limited by an overarching prohibition on any form of political activity that runs counter to the purpose and goals of the revolution (Covarrubias, 2010, p. 172). Basic economic rights, such as free labor association and entrepreneurialism, were classified as capitalist acts and prohibited. The Cuban penal code was amended in 1991 to reclassify capitalist acts as formal crimes, carrying a penalty of up to eight years in prison (Bunck, 1994, p. 75). Dissidents who remained in Cuba and spoke out against the government were subject not only to the penal code and its punishments for political crimes, but also to coercive action by "citizen's brigades" organized by the government to systematically punish political opposition (Bunck, 1994, p. 178).

The Cuban penal code also contains a provision relating to "dangerousness." According to human rights groups such as Human Rights Watch, the dangerousness portion of the penal code serves as a justification to try individuals for pre-criminal offenses (Steinberg, 2009, pp. 28–30). In the event that an individual is found to have engaged in dangerous behavior, even if no other crime has been committed, the person in question can be assigned to a "reeducation group." Re-education can include imprisonment and/or forced labor. Many times, dangerousness offenses are used to target the unemployed or those who associate with other members of the dangerous community (Steinberg, 2009, pp. 52–53). In effect, the dangerousness provisions in the Cuban penal code make both political dissent and unemployment into crimes against the state. Many of these forced laborers are sent to sugar plantations, where outdated equipment often necessitates labor-intensive harvesting practices that are not coveted by other plantation workers.

Human rights abuses of various sorts in Cuba also arouse anger among the exile community in South Florida because of practices relating to family separation. At various points during the Castro era, the Cuban government has allowed free exit to political dissidents. Many of these dissidents flee the county to join relatives in the United States. However, Human Rights Watch estimates that 57,000 political prisoners remain in prisons and labor camp within Cuba (World Report 2014: Cuba, 2014). Many dissidents who desire to leave Cuba to seek political refugee status in the United States are prohibited from doing so out of national security concerns on the part of the Cuban government. When political prisoners from Cuba are freed and allowed to leave for the United States, their arrival can also lead to increased anger within the Cuban American community in the United States as a result of providing new and often graphic information on human rights abuses in Cuba.

United States Action and Inaction as a Source of Cuban American Anger

The revolutionary regime of Fidel, and later, Raúl Castro, has been in power for over 55 years in Cuba. The durability of the regime has been a shock to the first generations of Cuban exiles, many of whom expected to return to Cuba in relatively short order as a result of their own paramilitary action, U.S. military and paramilitary action, or both. Many members of the exile community blame the relative popularity and surprising durability of the Castro regime on the unwillingness of the United States to more directly intervene in the affairs of the island nation. The United States has undertaken a variety of indirect, normally clandestine, activities over time. However, the country has generally stopped short of directly invading the island or providing direct military support to Cuban groups attempting to overthrow the existing government. Even in the case of the 1961 Bay of Pigs invasion, the U.S. government did not provide the level of support initially promised to Cuban paramilitary units.

The most famous example of Cuban American anger at lack of sufficient direct U.S. intervention is the disastrous Bay of Pigs invasion of April 1961. The failure of the invasion resulted in the death or imprisonment of over two-thirds of the Cuban exile force (Martinez-Fernandez, 2014, p. 79). The Cuban government arrested over 100,000 potential collaborators and scored a major public relations coup within the international community by providing direct evidence of aggression on the part of the United States. It is also worth noting that the invasion was hindered by several factors unrelated to the lack of significant U.S. air support, including a poor landing site, poor communication and training between combatants and their trainers, and the fact that the Cuban exile community learned many of the details of the invasion, which made it difficult to hide the operation from the Cuban government ("The Bay of Pigs," n.d.). Several U.S. newspapers ran stories on various elements of the planned invasion as well. As a result, Cuba was well prepared to counter the relatively small offensive on the island.

From the Cuban American exile perspective, the Bay of Pigs invasion could have been successful with more support from the U.S. military (especially the U.S. Air Force). According to one Cuban exile interviewed by González (2007, p. 32), landing and combat vehicles provided by the United States were enough to ensure the success of the operation had those initial forces been backed by U.S. airpower. However, the lack of U.S. airpower (initial air aids only grounded about half of Castro's air force and were not followed up with additional air raids) resulted in the failure to establish an effective beachhead (2007, p. 33). As a result, Cuban dissidents felt betrayal and anger toward the Kennedy administration. The decision by the Kennedy administration to forswear direct intervention in Cuba as part of an agreement that led to the end of the Cuban Missile Crisis, constituted a significant blow to Cuban exile hopes of an early return to the island under more hospitable conditions.

The Bay of Pigs invasion, however, did not mark the end of U.S. intervention designed to topple the Castro regime. In part because of guilt, and in part as the result of pressure from the Cuban American community, President Kennedy launched Operation Mongoose. Operation Mongoose was designed to topple the regime by targeting the economic and social pillars of Castro's Cuba ("The Bay of Pigs," n.d.). Targets would include sugar plantations, communications infrastructure, perceived psychological weaknesses of the Castro regime, and many other activities designed to create instability in Cuba. Specific Cuban American exile actions with regard to the Bay of Pigs Invasion and Operation Mongoose, as well as U.S. actions, will be outlined below. For the purpose of the current section of this chapter, the important takeaway from Operation Mongoose, as well as associated paramilitary activity, is that Cuban American exiles remained angry that the U.S. government would not involve itself more directly and forcefully in the removal of Castro and the establishment of a new regime (Garcia, 1996, p. 131).

At various points, the Cuban American community in South Florida has expressed dissatisfaction and anger with the willingness of the United States government to negotiate with the Castro regime on certain issues. For example, when the Ford and Carter administrations established limited diplomatic relations with Havana, a significant split emerged within the exile community over whether or not to support negotiations over issues such as prisoner releases, family visits, and immigration issues. The *dialogue-ros*, as Garcia (1998, p. 8) calls them, favor at least some form of rapprochement between the U.S. and Cuba. Most Cuban exiles, however, are angered by the dialogue process. They view it as strengthening Castro's hand and, in some cases, providing the regime with much-needed hard currency through emigration tourism (Garcia, 1996, p. 51).

One prominent case of U.S. actions that drew the ire of the Cuban American community was the Elián González saga. González had been discovered on a small raft 3 miles off the Florida coast. His mother, and several others on the raft, had drowned in the attempt to flee Cuba. The case became a media sensation. González's father filed a complaint with the United Nations with the goal of being reunited with his son in Cuba. After a series of court hearings, and negotiations between the United States and Cuba, Elián was taken from his maternal relatives in Florida and returned to his father's custody ("A chronology of the Elian González saga," n.d.). Most members of the Cuban American community in Florida were furious that González had been seized by a predawn government raid and returned to Cuba. Eighty-three percent of the Cuban American community in South Florida favored the idea of González staying in Miami as opposed to his being returned to Cuba (Forero, 2000). At the time the poll was taken, the percentage of Cuban Americans desiring that González stay in the United States was even greater than the percentage of Cuban Americans who desired to maintain the architecture of the Cuban embargo (Forero, 2000).

Cuban Immigration as a Source of Anger among Other Groups in the United States

Each of the waves of Cuban immigrants into the United States has managed to adapt to life outside of Cuba. The ability of Cuban exiles to partially assimilate into U.S. culture while maintaining a strong and unique Cuban identity has been cited as a significant source of strength for the Cuban American ethnic lobby in the United States (Uslaner, 1998). This partial assimilation process has not always been smooth, however. Many Cuban immigrants, for example, were initially unable to gain licensure to practice law, medicine, or teaching, as they had in Cuba. This led to an explosion in the supply of skilled workers willing to work in unskilled positions, which posed issues for the job market in the Miami area. Over time, and with the help of accelerated licensure programs, many of the new Cuban Americans came to prosper in the United States. However, the road to prosperity did draw a reaction from existing U.S. citizens in South Florida.

One source of anger within the existing South Florida community was benefits that Cuban exiles received in the United States. Cuban refugees, for example, received higher social welfare stipends than other individuals for qualified for federal assistance (Garcia, 1996, p. 29). Coupled with competition in the unskilled and semi-skilled labor markets, the amount of welfare payments to Cuban refugees became a source of resentment among members of various impoverished communities in Miami. Subsequent waves of immigrants added to the level of resentment. In a partial response to growing resentment, refugee programs made considerable effort to encourage exiled Cubans to consider settling outside of Miami (Martinez-Fernandez, 2014, p. 75). In spite of incentives, including relocation assistance, job assistance, and the offer of free transportation back to Miami in the event that Castro ever lost power, the vast majority Cuban refugees chose to stay in South Florida.

Property owners in Miami-Dade County, including owners of rental properties, at times also expressed anger at the Cuban American community. The waves of Cuban immigration did create more demand for apartments, which was positive for rent prices. However, Cuban exiles often lived as large, extended family units within relatively small apartments. When new groups of political refugees would arrive, they would normally stay with relatives, friends, or other charitable individuals until they could gain financial footing in the area. Property owners with rooms for rent sometimes responded in anger by prohibiting Cubans, or at least Cubans with children or extended families, from renting units (Garcia, 1996, pp. 29–30). Much of this anger, however, was temporary. As Cuban Americans flourished in South Florida, they began to open their own businesses and thrive in a variety of professional environments. As a result, they contributed in very significant ways to the local and regional economy.

The Mariel Boatlift of 1980 represented a significant departure from previous ways of Cuban immigration into the United States. During the 1970s, it was not uncommon for Cubans seeking to flee the country to request asylum in one of the several foreign embassies in Havana. A group of six Cubans attempting to flee the country created an international crisis when they used a bus to crash through the gates of the Peruvian embassy. When the Peruvian embassy refused to turn the refugees over to the Cuban government, over 10,000 Cubans attempting to leave the country filed asylum requests at the embassy (Hawk, Villella, de Varona, & Ciphers, 2014, pp. 29–30). Ultimately, the Castro regime sought to turn this crisis into an advantage by announcing that ships entering the port at Mariel would be allowed to pick up refugees and bring them to the United States. By the end of the episode, nearly 125,000 Cubans had entered the United States in under six months (Hawk et al., 2014, pp. 31–32). While the vast majority of these refugees were working-class and poor Cubans seeking a better life, a small percentage of the Mariel Boatlift members were either criminals, mentally ill, or both. These stories became sensationalized in the U.S. media, which spread fears about the boatlift. In reality, a majority of those with criminal records who were part of the boatlift had been convicted of offenses that would not have been considered crimes in the United States (Garcia, 1996, p. 64).

From the perspective of the Castro regime, getting rid of a large number of potential critics who also tended to be poor was an optimal situation. For the existing Cuban community in Florida, the Mariel Boatlift presented a variety of challenges. The Mariel Cubans tended to be poorer than the previous waves of Cuban immigrants. Whereas previous waves of exiles had been predominantly White, many of the Mariel Cubans were Black or of mixed racial heritage. The Mariel exiles had also tended to come of age in Castro's Cuba without significant working knowledge of what Cuba was like before the revolution (Hawk et al., 2014, pp. 233–234). This final factor proved critical, as it made it very difficult for the new immigrants to make ties with previous waves of Cuban refugees.

As one might expect given the conditions described above, the Mariel Boatlift resulted in a great deal of fear and anger. This anger existed at the national level, in South Florida as a region, and specifically within the Cuban American community in South Florida and elsewhere. In the United States as a whole, many states worried about the resettlement of Mariel Cubans within their borders. In South Florida, members of the African American community believed that the influx of low-skilled Cubans would increase competition for scarce jobs during the recession. Rioting within the African American community increased the level of racial tension (Mohl, 1990, p. 39). Among members of the existing South Florida Cuban community, opinions varied. On one hand, the Mariel Cubans were fleeing from some of the same hardships encountered by previous waves of Cuban immigrants. On the other hand, the new Cuban immigrants were much more ethnically diverse, as well as much more likely to struggle economically for longer periods of time. Many Cuban Americans feared that the new wave of immigrants would damage the reputation of the existing exile community (Garcia, 1996, p. 72). This fear and anger became stronger when a small number of Mariel refugees who had entered the U.S. prison system began to riot at the prospect of being returned to Cuba.

As was the case with previous generations of Cuban Americans, the Mariel Cubans have adjusted to life in South Florida. As the new wave of Cuban immigrants integrated into the larger economic community, they were aided by the existing Cuban enclave in the Miami area. As a result, much of the anger related to the initial displacement abated over time. In 2010, the Miami Herald noted that the Mariel Boatlift had, in the final analysis, made the Cuban American community stronger (Chardy, 2010). As we shall see later in this essay, however, there are differences in the way that different generations of Cuban Americans view the Castro regime, the comprehensive U.S. embargo against Cuba, and the opportunities for normalization. These fissures within the Cuban American community combine to create the potential for significant changes in the relationship between the United States and Cuba moving forward.

Cuban Americans Acting on Their Collective Anger

The Paramilitary and Propaganda Phase

The initial period of exile activity in South Florida was based on the twin goals of removing Castro from power and returning to Cuba as soon as possible. In furtherance of these goals, the Cuban refugees engaged in a series of paramilitary activities both off the coast of Cuba and, when the opportunity afforded itself, inland as well. The Central Intelligence Agency (CIA) funded a portion of this activity. When American funds were not forthcoming, the Cuban exiles financed their own activities, at times with and at times without tacit U.S. approval. As mentioned earlier, Cubans in South Florida believed they could bring down the Castro regime by discrediting it internationally and by destabilizing its internal pillars of economic support.

In the 1960s and 1970s, paramilitary groups led by Cuban exiles invaded Cuba on numerous occasions. One of the first paramilitary attacks occurred when a paramilitary group caused an explosion on a French ship in port in the processing of bringing arms to Algeria (Heindl, 2003). The attack resulted in the deaths of a large number of dockworkers as well as members of the ship's crew. Other paramilitary operations targeted infrastructure such as railroads and ports. Attacks from inside Cuba also occurred on sugar and tobacco plantations, as well as other sites of economic importance to the Castro regime. Many of these attacks had the opposite effect of what was intended. Castro referred to the exiles as "worms," and used the attacks as a catalyst to enlarge his own paramilitary units (Garcia, 1996, p. 58).

Although the Bay of Pigs invasion represented a major U.S. foreign policy debacle as well as a source of anger on the part of Cuban Americans against the Kennedy administration, it also represented the largest scale raid of the paramilitary era. The Bay of Pigs invasion as a source of Cuban American anger at the U.S. government was investigated earlier in this chapter. It is important to recognize, however, that the Bay of Pigs Invasion was, at least in part, a result of anger on the part of the Cuban exile community. In the context of the unfolding Cold War, Cuban exiles may have been pushing on an open door when it came to pressuring the U.S. government to take actions to topple the Castro regime. That said, the invasion could never have taken place without the willingness of Cuban exiles to form the vanguard of the invasion force. The United States, after all, did not want to enter into direct conflict with Cuba given the possibility that direct action might trigger a direct response from the Soviet Union (Jones, 2008, p. 17).

Planning for what ultimately became the Bay of Pigs invasion began during the Eisenhower administration. A variety of exiles from different backgrounds were recruited into Brigade 2506, which was to spearhead the invasion (after Cuban forces were softened by U.S. airpower) (Martinez-Fernandez, 2014, p. 76). One of the problems that immediately emerged during the planning phase was recruitment. The number of recruits was not growing fast enough to complete a strike before the end of Eisenhower's term (Jones, 2008, p. 42). Ultimately, the plans for an invasion were inherited by the Kennedy administration. Eventually, the CIA gathered and trained the roughly 1,500 men that it was thought would be needed for an invasion. However, recruiting delays resulted in an inability to launch the invasion by March 1st, the latest optimum date for an invasion suggested by military advisors (Jones, 2008, p. 42).

The basic plan for the Bay of Pigs invasion was to use Cuban exiles, trailed primarily in Guatemala, as the main ground force for the invasion. Exiles would launch diversionary strikes in the days leading up to the invasion. As the CIA became less confident of underground resistance within Cuba, the proposed role for the exiles grew (Vandenbroucke, 1984, p. 474). U.S. air support would be used to take out large portions of the Cuban Air Force, leaving the exiles to establish a foothold on the island for further incursions. Various forms of propaganda, including leaflet dropping and subversive radio broadcasts, were also part of the plan. Finally, the plan would rely on various forms of sabotage undertaken by Cubans who had remained in Cuba in concert with Cuban exiles (Martinez-Fernandez, 2014, p. 86). The Cuban American exile community had come to believe that the invasion, which was a very poorly kept secret, would be the optimum way for Cubans to take the lead in liberating Cuba from Castro and returning the country to its former glory.

A complete review of the battles that were part of the Bay of Pigs invasion is beyond the scope of this chapter. The Bay of Pigs invasion failed for a variety of reasons, including the lack of second-stage airstrikes, the lack of secrecy that enabled Castro to imprison many of those who may have been inclined to participate, and the relatively small size of the invasion force (Martinez-Fernandez, 2014, p. 86; Vandenbroucke, 1984, pp. 478–479). The salience of the Bay of Pigs invasion in a discussion of the results of political anger lies not in its failure, but in the fact that many Cuban exiles were willing to participate across social and ideological lines. Batista supporters, Batista opponents of the upper and middle class, and even working class exiles put aside, at least partially, their various differences in an act of defiance against the Castro regime. In this sense, it can be argued that anger toward Castro and his supporters overcame some of the collective action problems that often arise in cases of protest and rebellion.

As noted above, the failure of the Bay of Pigs did not represent an end to Cuban exile paramilitary activity in Cuba. Cuban exiles participated heavily in those portions of Operation Mongoose that were actually carried out. The actions included assassination attempts on Castro, destruction of economic and government facilities, and launching "false flag" operations designed to provoke Cuba into aggressive action against the United States (Martinez-Fernandez, 2014, p. 81). The success of each of the ventures was very limited, in part because the exile community in South Florida and the United States government underestimated Castro's popularity, counterintelligence ability, and general charisma. Once again, however, it is important to understand the paramilitary within the broader context of Cuban American anger. The United States was unwilling to intervene directly in Cuba. Without a willing and motivated group of exiles, the paramilitary activities of the 1960s and 1970s would have been unlikely to occur.

Paramilitary activity was not the only result of Cuban Americans in South Florida during this epoch. There was also an organized propaganda campaign against the Castro regime led by exiles. For example, planes dropped leaflets of an overweight Castro designed to show that he was growing fat and wealthy while the rest of the population suffered (Martinez-Fernandez, 2014, p. 81). Cuban exiles wrote editorials in U.S. and Latin American newspapers, and testified to the atrocities of the Castro regime as a means of pressuring the United States to tighten economic sanctions and to pressure other members of the Organization of American States (OAS) to initiate sanctions, tighten existing sanctions, or otherwise ostracize Cuba in as many different ways as possible (Garcia, 1996, p. 133). Cuban exiles, with the cooperation of the U.S. government, also developed anti-Castro radio and television in the hopes that this would sway Latin American opinion and be heard in those parts of Cuba where signals are more difficult to block (Lohmeier, 2014, pp. 68–69). In some cases, Cuban American pressure did seem to coincide with a desired outcome from the exile perspective. The Kennedy administration did tighten the Cuban Embargo in 1962. The OAS also excluded Cuba from voting as a member of the organization in 1962. Whether the actions of Cuban exiles played a decisive role in these decisions is an empirical question that is beyond the scope of this chapter. What is clear is that anger within the exile community was the impetus for attempts by the community to use propaganda and political pressure as a means to discredit and isolate the Castro regime.

The Cuban Missile Crisis also served to limit somewhat the impact of the propaganda campaign. Although the sanctions established by the United States and the OAS remained intact, the Kennedy administration made qualified assurances that the United States would not invade Cuba or facilitate the invasion of Cuba in exchange for the removal of Soviet missiles and missile bases from the island (Oberdorfer, 1992). It did not become clear until after the end of the Cold War that Kennedy's assurances were qualified enough to provide a great deal of continual operational flexibility. Nonetheless, this agreement between Kennedy and Khrushchev was seen as somewhat of a defeat by Cuban exiles wishing to translate their political anger directly into U.S. foreign policy outcomes.

The Political Action Phase

Over time, the Cuban exile community in South Florida transformed from a group primarily concerned with participating directly in the fall of Castro through paramilitary national liberation efforts to a more organized ethnic identity interest group (Haney & Vanderbush, 2005, p. 33). Several factors contributed to the evolutionary transformation of outlets for Cuban American anger. In the first instance, the Castro regime has proven to be much more durable than the exile community had originally anticipated. Absent full-scale U.S. involvement, it was unlikely that Castro could be toppled by military force alone. The results of the Cuban Missile Crisis made this sort of direct U.S. intervention a remote possibility. Although various paramilitary activities continued for more than a decade, they were mostly unsuccessful. By contrast, Cuban American efforts to strengthen the comprehensive economic embargo had not fallen on deaf ears, demonstrating the political, as opposed to military, organization, had its benefits.

In addition, the Nixon, Ford, and Carter administrations had moved, in certain limited ways, toward rapprochement with Castro's Cuba. Whereas the U.S. embargo against Cuba remained, the OAS nearly voted to drop its embargo against Cuba in 1975 (Garcia, 1996, p. 138). The era of détente that began during the Kennedy administration and came of age during the Nixon administration, made further rapprochement with Cuba possible. The Carter administration also increased diplomatic negotiations by reopening the U.S. Interests section of the Swiss embassy in Havana. Though the process was not immediate, Cuban exiles came to recognize that they would have to increase the power of their collective political voice outside of South Florida in order to keep pressure on the Castro regime. This would include cultivating influence in Washington.

The most critical development during the political action phase was the formation of the Cuban American National Foundation (CANF). The CANF was formally established in 1981. The impetus for the formation of the CANF came from two primary sources. First, Cuban exiles such as Jorge Mas Canosa, the founder of the CANF, recognized the need to create an organized interest group that could influence policy makers in the nation's capital. Second, the Reagan administration played a key role in the formation of the CANF. The Reagan administration, including National Security Advisor Richard Allen, took a more hard line stance toward Cuba than Nixon, Ford, or Carter (Haney & Vanderbush, 2005, p. 35). Allen provided space and logistics for initial CANF meetings. The idea was to use the CANF as a lever push for a harder line toward Cuba and beyond.

One of the keys to the success of the CANF since its founding is the fact that the organization is modeled after the highly successful American Israel Public Affairs Committee (AIPAC). For example, the CANF has followed the successful strategy of formal separation between its activities as an educational advocacy organization and those as a lobbying group (Haney & Vanderbush, 1999, p. 349). The CANF also influences a variety of political action committees (PACs) that contribute money to congressional and presidential campaigns. As a nonprofit, the CANF cannot contribute directly. The CANF, like AIPAC, also does not directly endorse candidates. However, the CANF is able to mobilize its members through letters to the editor, statements on its websites and (later) in social media, and direct community education and organization. As a result of all of these factors, the CANF is generally considered the second-most powerful ethnic lobbying group in the United States, trailing only AIPAC and its affiliated organizations (Rubenzer, 2008).

In cooperation with the Reagan administration, the CANF came to influence many aspects of U.S. foreign policy toward Cuba. The initial establishment and pressure to continue funding for Radio and TV Martí, was a product of CANF influence. CANF also developed a special relationship with the National Endowment for Democracy (Haney & Vanderbush, 1999, p. 352). This enabled CANF to help direct the activities, and money, of the organization, toward efforts to free Cuba from Castro. In essence, the CANF was able to translate Cuban exile anger directly into public policy.

The collapse of the Soviet Union and the end of the Cold War created a new set of challenges. The loss of its Soviet patron made Castro's Cuba much less of a perceived threat to the national security elite. Presidents H. W. Bush and Clinton, while they did not necessarily favor full normalization of U.S. relations with Cuba, did favor varying levels of rapprochement. It is against this backdrop that Cuban Americans in South Florida, especially those who harbored significant anger toward the Castro regime, achieved two of their most important foreign policy successes: passage of the Cuban Democracy Act during the Bush administration and passage of the Cuban Liberty and Democratic Solidarity Act (also known as the Helms-Burton Act) during the Clinton administration.

Successful Cuban American mobilization on these two pieces of legislation owes itself to many factors. First, it is well known that Congress has taken a more active role on foreign policy issues since the end of the Cold War. In some ways, the trend toward what is sometimes called "congressional entrepreneurialism" began during the latter part of the Vietnam era of U.S. foreign policy. Second, the Cuban American community had become successful enough to get some of its members, such as Ileana Ros-Lehtinen, elected to Congress (Haney & Vanderbush, 2005, p. 85). Third, the Cuban American community had grown large enough to provide a potential key swing vote in close pivotal races in Florida or New Jersey. Although the Cuban American community had been known to identify primarily with the Republican Party, Democrats in swing states, as well as presidential candidates, saw the potential to chip away at this advantage by taking a harder line on Cuba. This was especially the case during the first Bush administration.

The Cuban Democracy Act and the Helms-Burton Act had several key ramifications for U.S. foreign policy toward Cuba. First, while the president still maintained important discretionary power, the two laws passed by Congress shifted responsibility for the maintenance of the embargo from the executive to the legislative branch. This was important to the Cuban American community as a result of the fact that Congress is generally seen as more permeable to ethnic interests than is the executive branch. In addition, both laws served to strengthen the Cuban embargo. The Cuban Democracy Act strengthened the embargo by making support for sanctions against Cuba a partial condition for the receipt of U.S. foreign assistance ("Cuba Democracy Act," n.d.). The Act also prohibited vessels that had entered Cuba from trading with the United States for 180 days. Finally, the Act prohibited foreign-based subsidiaries of U.S. companies from trading with Cuba ("Cuba Democracy Act," n.d.). In addition to other provisions to strengthen the Cuban embargo, the Helms-Burton Act went a step further by, in effect, forcing companies to choose between trading with the United States and trading with Cuba (Helms-Burton Act, 1996).

It should be recognized that there are many reasons beyond Cuban American mobilization around a shared sense of anger toward the Castro regime that made maintaining and strengthening the Cuban embargo possible. First, for most of Castro's reign, the executive branch has controlled the mechanics of the Cuban embargo. Especially during the Cold War, presidents were willing to maintain the embargo for political and geostrategic reasons. Second, there are interests beyond Cuban Americans, such as the U.S. sugar industry that benefits from the competitive buffer against Cuban imports provided by the embargo. Third, outside events have sometimes intervened to create or solidify anti-Castro sentiment. For example, passage of the Helms-Burton Act was predated by the Cuban Air Force shooting down two civilian aircraft from the United States ("Clinton moves to punish Cuba," 1996). In spite of these outside factors, it is clear that the Cuban American community, especially those who have expressed the most anger at the Castro regime, have been a significant player in U.S. foreign policy toward Cuba.

Generational Changes in Cuban American Anger

Generational Changes in Attitudes toward the Cuban Embargo

The Florida International University (FIU) Cuba Poll is considered the best source of data on Cuban American attitudes toward the Castro regime as well as a barometer of Cuban American opinion on U.S. foreign policy options. FIU has run the Cuba Poll each year since 1991. Trend data, coupled with results from the 2014 Cuba Poll, reveal several key changes and generational divides in attitudes related to the Cuban embargo. For example, support for the Cuban Embargo has gone from a high of 87 percent in

1991 to 48 percent in 2014 (Florida International University, 2014). Support for unrestricted travel to Cuba has also increased (Florida International University, 2014). Finally, there is a clear generational gap in the data. Immigrants from 1995 to the present are much more likely to support various forms of normalization than their older counterparts (Florida International University, 2014).

These results are not entirely surprising given the previous discussion of waves of Cuban immigration into the United States. The first generation of immigrants lost their property and, in their view, their country, to the Castro regime. Later generations came of age in Castro's Cuba, and left for a wider variety of reasons. The most recent, more moderate generation of Cuban American immigrants, as well as the children of older generations of immigrants, is likely to be a continued source of pressure for change (Haney & Vanderbush, 2005, p. 163).

There are, however, continued sources of strength for the more hardline policy. Cuban American representatives in the U.S. House, for example, have been outspoken proponents of the Cuban Democracy Act and the Helms Burton Act. This does not appear to have changed since the passage of both of these laws in the 1990s. In part, this may be a function of electoral responsiveness. In general, older generations of Cuban Americans are more likely to vote than their more youthful counterparts (Florida International University, 2014). As a result, older Cuban Americans continue to wield influence that is disproportionate to their numbers. In addition, the succession between Fidel and Raúl Castro does not appear to have resulted in significant changes in Cuban foreign policy. As a result, many of the grievances that have been sources of anger for the Cuban American community remain important sources of anger.

Current Status and Future Projections

The Obama Administration's Departure

On December 17, 2014, the Obama administration outlined the most significant foreign policy departure since the severance of diplomatic relations between the United States and Cuba in 1961. The president made several proposals that, if implemented, would radically alter the existing relationship between the United States and Cuba. The most significant departure would be re-establishing ties at the ambassador level. In addition, President Obama has altered several aspects of the Cuban embargo that remain under executive control. These include some travel restrictions and restrictions on remittances from U.S. citizens to relatives and friends in Cuba (The White House, 2014). In May of 2015, Cuba was removed from the State Department list of state sponsors of terrorism.

Although each of the elements of the Obama administration's proposal is significant, it is critical to recognize that much of the machinery that governs the relationship between the United States and Cuba remains under congressional control. Neither the Cuban Democracy Act nor the Helms Burton Act can be altered without Congressional approval. The president has the constitutional authority to name and receive ambassadors, but any U.S. ambassador to Cuba would have to be confirmed by the U.S. Senate. In practice, this means that full normalization of U.S. relations with Cuba depends both on reactions within the Cuban American community and on partisan trends in Congress.

Reaction to Obama's Departure

Reactions to the Obama administration's departure have been mixed. CANF, which at one time had been at the vanguard of maintaining the toughest possible stance on Castro's Cuba, delivered a rather muted response. CANF expressed concern that the Castro regime would take advantage of the political opening and change in economic policies to further consolidate its hold on the island ("CANF Responds," 2014). On the other hand, the CANF statement did not denounce any of the policy changes by name or by substance, and expressed gratitude toward Pope Francis for facilitating the negotiations ("CANF Responds," 2014).

Reactions from directly within the Cuban American community have been far less charitable. Protestors viewed Obama's announcement as a key lifeline to the Castro regime and as a betrayal to all that Cuban Americans have worked for since 1959 (Madigan, 2014). At the same time, one professor interviewed by the *New York Times* noted that the most visceral reactions come from the oldest Cuban Americans, many of whom possess a significant amount of hatred for the Castro government (Madigan, 2014). A poll commissioned just after the announced policy change found a distinct split among Cuban Americans. A majority of Cuban Americans born in the United States support the president's policy, whereas a majority of Cuban Americans born in Cuba oppose the policy of partial normalization (Caputo & Flechas, 2014).

Response from members of Congress has largely fallen along partisan lines. Republicans, especially 2016 presidential hopefuls, have strongly opposed President Obama's policy and have promised to use the power of the purse to defund it. Democrats have been more supportive overall, noting that the existing policy has not resulted in the fall of the Castro regime or in nearly any of the changes desired by the proponents of a strong embargo. Democratic representatives in South Florida, by contrast, have been more muted in their support of Obama administration proposals (Baker, 2014).

Future Projections

Over the long term, it is hard to imagine a situation in which Cuban American anger can continue to drive U.S. foreign policy toward Cuba. Signs of generational divisions within the community are already apparent. Those divisions are bound to increase over time. As the number of Cuban Americans born in the United States increases, it is likely that the amount of anger will continue to abate. As the anger ebbs, it is likely that the younger generation of Cuban Americans will call for fundamental change in U.S. foreign policy toward Cuba. Much of this, of course, is contingent on whether or not the ultimate transition away from the Castros leads to the type of political reform that the younger generations desire. Even if the transition is not smooth, younger generations of Cuban Americans appear to desire increased economic cooperation with their homeland.

In the short term, the prospects for significant change are much dimmer. Although a majority of Americans support some form of normalization, Congress is divided along partisan lines. When the architecture of the Cuban embargo was largely transferred to Congress in the 1990s, the level of difficulty inherent in any attempt to fundamentally alter the relationship between the United States and Cuba increased significantly. Currently, the U.S. Congress is controlled by the Republican Party. Republicans tend to favor maintenance of the embargo in its current form. Even if Democrats controlled the House, the Senate, and the presidency, the prospect of a filibuster in the Senate would make it difficult to alter the embargo. Only the long-term alteration of the electoral incentive to maintain the embargo will result in the collapse of the embargo. This will require either time for anger on the part of Cuban Americans to subside, or a fundamental change in the governmental structure in Cuba.

In the next 1 to 2 years, then, we should expect to see changes at the edges of the Cuban embargo and somewhat more significant changes in other aspects of the U.S. Cuba relationship. Assuming that the Castro regime does not increase its crackdowns on political dissidents, or take aggressive action toward the United States, one would expect to see travel restrictions, restrictions on remittances, restrictions on the provision of humanitarian aid, and restrictions on low-level trade continue to erode. The 2016 presidential election season is likely to make it difficult to establish the type of diplomatic relationship that the Obama administration desires. An appointment of a U.S. ambassador to Cuba would draw significant opposition in the Senate. In this context, one would expect lower level diplomatic contact to slowly increase over the coming years. Many Cuban Americans remain very angry at the Castro regime in Cuba, and at the United States for not doing as much as possible to bring down Fidel or Raúl Castro. Anger, however, tends to fade over time.

References

Baker, P. (2014, December 17). U.S. to restore full relations with Cuba, erasing a last trace of Cold War hostility. *The New York Times.* Retrieved from http://www.nytimes.com

The Bay of Pigs. (n.d.). *John F. Kennedy Presidential Library & Museum.* Retrieved from http://www.jfklibrary.org/JFK/JFK-in-History/The-Bay-of-Pigs.aspx

Bunck, J. M. (1994). *Fidel Castro and the quest for a revolutionary culture in Cuba.* University Park, PA: Pennsylvania State University Press.

CANF responds to today's announcement regarding U.S.–Cuba policy. (2014). *Cuban American National Foundation.* Retrieved from http://canf.org/?news-item=canf-responds-to-todays-announcement-regarding-u-s-cuba-policy

Caputo, M., & Flechas. J. (2014, December 19). Poll: Cuban-Americans split on Obama's Cuba policy. *Miami Herald.* Retrieved from http://www.miamiherald.com

Chardy, A. (2010, April 25). Mariel boatlift tested Miami's strength, then made it stronger. *Palm Beach Post.* Retrieved from http://www.palmbeachpost.com

A chronology of the Elian González saga. (n.d.). *Frontline.* PBS: Public Broadcasting Service [Web page]. Retrieved from http://www.pbs.org/wgbh/pages/frontline/shows/elian/etc/eliancron.html

Clinton moves to punish Cuba for downing planes. (1996, February 27). *CNN U.S. News.* Retrieved from http://www.cnn.com/US/9602/cuba_shootdown/27

Covarrubias, A. (2010). Human rights in Cuba and the international system. In M. Serrano & V. Popovski (Eds.), *Human rights regimes in the Americas* (Chapter 8, pp. 170–188). Tokyo: United Nations University Press.

Cuba Democracy Act ('CDA') United States Code, Title 22. Foreign Relations and Intercourse, Chapter 69. (n.d.). Wayback Machine Internet Archive. Retrieved from http://web.archive.org/web/20041108140907/http://www.treasury.gov/offices/enforcement/ofac/legal/statutes/cda.pdf

Cuban Liberty and Democratic Solidarity (LIBERTAD) Act of 1996. (1996). U.S. Government Publishing Office. Retrieved from http://www.gpo.gov/fdsys/pkg/PLAW-104publ114/html/PLAW-104publ114.htm

Florida International University. (2014). 2014 FIU Cuba Poll: How Cuban Americans in Miami view U.S. policies toward Cuba. Retrieved from https://cri .fiu.edu/research/cuba-poll/2014-fiu-cuba-poll.pdf

Forero, J. (2000, April 28). The Elian González case: The Cuban-Americans; in Miami, some Cuban-Americans take less popular views. *The New York Times*. Retrieved from http://www.nytimes.com

Garcia, M. C. (1996). *Havana USA: Cuban Exiles and Cuban Americans in South Florida, 1959–1994*. Berkeley, CA: University of California Press.

Garcia, M. C. (1998). Hardliners v. "Dialogueros": Cuban exile political groups and United States-Cuba policy. *Journal of American Ethnic History, 17*(4), 3–28.

González, E. (2007). *Cuban exiles on the trade embargo: Interviews*. Jefferson, NC: McFarland.

Haney, P. J., & Vanderbush, W. (1999). The role of ethnic interest groups in U.S. foreign policy: The case of the Cuban American National Foundation. *International Studies Quarterly, 43*(2), 341–361. Retrieved from http://www .jstor.org/stable/2600759

Haney, P. J., & Vanderbush, W. (2005). *The Cuban embargo: The domestic politics of an American foreign policy*. Pittsburgh, PA: University of Pittsburgh Press.

Hawk, K. D., Villella, R., de Varona, A. L., & Cifers. K. (2014). *Florida and the Mariel Boatlift of 1980: The first twenty days*. Tuscaloosa, AL: University of Alabama Press.

Heindl, B. S. (2003). Debating the embargo: Transnational political activity in the Cuban-American community, 1959–1997. *Berkeley Journal of Sociology, 47*, 76–104. Retrieved from http://www.jstor.org/stable/41035582

Helms-Burton Act. (1996). An Act to seek international sanctions against the Castro government in Cuba, to plan for support of a transition government leading to a democratically elected government in Cuba, and for other purposes. Public Law 104–114, 104th Congress. Retrieved from http:// www.gpo.gov/fdsys/pkg/PLAW-104publ114/html/PLAW-104publ114 .htm

Jones, H. (2008). *The Bay of Pigs*. Oxford, UK: Oxford University Press.

Kay, C. (1988). Economic reforms and collectivization in Cuban agriculture. *Third World Quarterly, 10*(3), 1239–1266. Retrieved from http://www.jstor.org /stable/3992290

Kellner, D. (1989). *Ernesto "Che" Guevara*. New York, NY: Chelsea House Publishers.

Lievesley, G. (2004). *The Cuban revolution: Past, present and future perspectives*. Houndmills, Basingstoke, Hampshire: Palgrave Macmillan.

Lohmeier, C. (2014). *Cuban Americans and the Miami media*. Jefferson, NC: McFarland & Company.

Lopez, M. H., & Krogstad, J. M. (2014, December 23). As Cuban American demographics change, so do views of Cuba. *Pew Research Center*. Retrieved from http://www.pewresearch.org

Madigan, N. (2014, December 20). Exiles at Miami rally denounce Obama for rapprochement. *The New York Times*. Retrieved from http://www.nytimes.com

Martinez-Fernandez, L. (2014). *Revolutionary Cuba: A history*. Gainesville, FL: University Press of Florida.

Mohl, R. A. (1990). On the edge: Blacks and Hispanics in metropolitan Miami since 1959. *The Florida Historical Quarterly, 69*(1), 37–56. Retrieved from http://www.jstor.org/stable/30148998

Oberdorfer, D. (1992, January 7). Kennedy qualified pledge not to invade Cuba. *The Washington Post*, pp. A12.

O'Connor, J. (1968). Agrarian reforms in Cuba, 1959–1963. *Science and Society, 32*(2), 169–217. Retrieved from http://www.jstor.org/stable/40401340

Rubenzer, T. (2008). Ethnic minority interest group attributes and U.S. foreign policy influence: A qualitative comparative analysis. *Foreign Policy Analysis, 4*(2), 169–185.

Steinberg, N. (2009). *New Castro, same Cuba: Political prisoners in the post-Fidel Era*. New York, NY: Human Rights Watch.

Uslaner, E. M. (1998). All in the family? Interest groups and foreign policy. In A. J. Cigler & B. A. Loomis (Eds.), *Interest group politics*. Washington, DC: CQ Press.

Valdes, A., & Foster, W. (2014). The agrarian reform experiment in Chile: History, impact, and implications. *International Food Policy Research Institute* [Discussion paper 01368]. Retrieved from https://books.google.com/books/reader?id=mZRmBAAAQBAJ&printsec=frontcover&output=reader&pg=GBS.PR1

Vandenbroucke, L. S. (1984). Anatomy of a failure: The decision to land at the Bay of Pigs. *Political Science Quarterly, 99*(3), 471–491. Retrieved from http://www.jstor.org/stable/2149944

The White House. (2014). *Fact sheet: Charting a new course on Cuba*. [Press release]. Retrieved from https://www.whitehouse.gov/the-press-office/2014/12/17/fact-sheet-charting-new-course-cuba

World Report 2014: Cuba; Events of 2013. (2014). *Human Rights Watch*. Retrieved from http://www.hrw.org/world-report/2014/country-chapters/cuba?page=3

CHAPTER FOURTEEN

Nixon, Latin America, and the Politics of Anger

Jeffry M. Cox

By late morning of May 13, 1958, Vice President Richard Nixon and his retinue knew they were in trouble as their cars were forced to a stop in the streets of Caracas, Venezuela. On cue, an angry mob poured out of the side streets and a wave of sticks, pipes, fists, and spit slammed into the motorcade. For 12 minutes, the mob did its best to vent years of frustration with U.S. policies in a spirited but ultimately ineffective attack. As Venezuela's police and security forces stood by, a handful of Secret Service agents did their best to protect the passengers. A path was finally cleared; the motorcade sped past the mob and, abandoning the rest of the planned activities, took refuge at the U.S. ambassador's residence.

Vice President Nixon's May 1958 tour of Latin America exposed significant problems with President Eisenhower's Latin America policy. Nowhere was this more apparent than in Caracas, where the trouble began as soon as Nixon got off the plane. Ceremonies were cut short, drowned by angry shouts from the waiting crowd, while the Nixon group was showered in spit from the angry Venezuelans there to greet this representative of the United States and U.S. foreign policies. Demonstrations became increasingly violent, leading Nixon to cancel many of the planned activities and leave a day early.

In this chapter, I will do five things. First, I will demonstrate the historical context of this anger toward the United States: a history of paternalism and intervention in the internal affairs of Latin American nations. Second, I will address the specific frustration that aroused their anger: U.S. Cold War foreign policies that privileged anticommunism over democracy or economic development, leading to U.S. support of dictators. Third, I will describe Venezuelan history under the U.S.-supported dictator Marcos Pérez Jiménez to further explain the individuals involved and the sources of their anger. Fourth, I will describe the violence committed against Nixon in an attempt by Latin Americans to draw attention to their grievances and effect change. Finally, I will describe the effects these expressions of anger had on the issue: the serious discussions and reappraisals of U.S. policies that resulted.

The violence Nixon encountered in Caracas shocked the Eisenhower administration, though there was ample warning. Nixon experienced less violent demonstrations earlier in his tour of South America, and received threats of serious violence in Caracas. Yet, even without such warnings, the demonstrations should have come as no surprise. Latin American expressions of discontent with U.S. policies far predated the Nixon tour or even the Eisenhower administration. Throughout the history of U.S.–Latin American relations, the United States has sought political, economic, and cultural hegemony at the expense of Latin Americans.

I

Beginning with their struggles for independence from Spain, Latin Americans have looked up to the United States as an inspiration and an example of what capitalist democracy could achieve. Shortly after Latin American independence movements succeeded, President James Monroe issued the Monroe Doctrine in 1823, declaring the entire Western Hemisphere off limits to Europeans. This was to protect the new republics from attempts to reassert European imperialism.

Though it waxed and waned, this pro-United States sentiment remained a strong, even dominant theme in Latin American perception of the United States throughout the history of U.S.–Latin American relations. Yet not all felt this way. The first significant problems began in 1847 with the United States–Mexican war, a clear land grab by a superior power. This war, and the land seizure that resulted, reflected U.S. perceptions of Latin Americans that would endure well into the 20th century. The United States viewed Latin Americans as inferior, demonstrating an attitude of race-based paternalism. This attitude justified the war with Mexico, as well as many subsequent interventions in Latin American affairs.

After the war with Mexico, the United States was consumed with sectional differences that resulted in the Civil War, and afterward focused on reconstruction and subduing the West. By the end of the century, the United States had recovered and emerged as a power, demonstrated by their unsolicited intervention in the Cuban war for independence, leading to the Spanish–American-Cuban–Filipino war of 1898, commonly called the Spanish–American War. This marked a significant change in U.S. policy regarding Latin America, inaugurating an era of intervention.

President Theodore Roosevelt's infamous "Big Stick" diplomacy embodied this new approach. The Roosevelt Corollary to the Monroe Doctrine was designed to compel "uncivilized" nations, by any means, to live up to their agreements with "civilized" nations, thus justifying U.S. intervention in Latin America in any form, at any time, for any reason. President Taft followed with Dollar Diplomacy. This policy shifted from strategic to commercial considerations. Taft hoped to promote political stability in Latin America through financial stability by encouraging the export of capital through loans to Latin American countries. This increase in financial interventions was paired with continued military interventions. Interventions continued under President Wilson, including the Pershing Punitive Expedition to hunt Pancho Villa.

Throughout this era of interventions, U.S. policy makers believed they had the right to intervene in the internal affairs of other sovereign nations, to redirect the course of other societies. Conversely, they believed that, as part of inferior cultures, Latin Americans did not have the right to conduct their own affairs in their own ways. U.S. policy makers convinced themselves that Latin Americans actually welcomed U.S. influence.

Throughout the 1920s, U.S. presidents sought to limit interventions and end occupations. They were largely successful, though the Marines were still sent in on occasion. Finally, in 1929 President Herbert Hoover announced a new approach to U.S.–Latin American relations: the Good Neighbor Policy. Hoover continued to improve the relationship with Latin America, but it was under President Franklin Delano Roosevelt that the Good Neighbor Policy fully fledged. Roosevelt announced "an end to U.S. interference in the internal affairs of other nations and a cooperative approach to the Monroe Doctrine" (Coerver & Hall, 1999, p. 87). Finally, a U.S. administration pursued a Latin America policy that was pleasing to Latin Americans. The commitment to treat them as equals lasted through FDR's lengthy presidency, and President Harry S. Truman took it up after him.

The Cold War proved to be the death of the Good Neighbor Policy, though the roots of its demise can be found in the end of World War II. In spite of their support of the war effort, with two countries actually contributing troops, Latin America was left out of the peace process. The Truman administration began to hear rumbles of discontent, claims that the Good Neighbor Policy was not being followed with the same vigor as before. Latin Americans felt that the Good Neighbor Policy was pursued during the war because it was expedient, but since the end of the war the Truman administration did not fully appreciate the value of continental solidarity (Confidential Memorandum on Latin America, n.d.). With the advent of the Cold War, global policies superseded regional policies such as the Good Neighbor Policy. With the advent of the Eisenhower administration in 1953, the Good Neighbor Policy was abandoned.

Throughout the 19th and early 20th centuries, the U.S. view of Latin America was racial and gendered. This can be seen in political cartoons: Latin America is consistently shown as either a White woman in need of rescue, or as Black children in need of guidance. This view began to change in the 1930s. Under the Good Neighbor Policy, the United States began to see and treat Latin Americans more as equals. However, under Eisenhower's Cold War–oriented policies, the overt racism was gone, but the paternalistic attitude toward Latin America remained, reasserting itself in Cold War policies.

II

Although these policies provide the historical context for the Latin American view of the United States at the time of the Nixon trip, the frustrations that led to the violence were based on more recent Cold War policies that favored anticommunism, in any form, over all other considerations. The United States was looking for Cold War allies. To this end, the Eisenhower administration's three main foreign policy objectives in Latin America were increasing private investment, building hemispheric solidarity, and promoting anticommunism.

Latin America had been suffering from economic problems since the end of World War II, and Eisenhower's emphasis on loans and private investment was not helping. "Latin Americans felt that the United States owed them economic aid, either because they blamed the United States and U.S. investors for the state of their economy, or because they felt that the United States had the resources, and that both sides would benefit from a stronger Latin American economy" (Cox, 2012). "Where's our Marshall Plan?" became a common refrain in Latin America, referring to the massive economic aid program to assist Europe after World War II. "Latin Americans blamed the US not only for not assisting, but for implementing policies that actually harmed Latin American economies" (Cox, 2012).

These policies included tariffs on some Latin American exports that had deep, adverse effects on Latin American economies. While in Argentina, Nixon repeated the party line, reminding Argentines that "it was incumbent upon the Argentine government to create an atmosphere and incentives to attract that capital" (Zahniser & Weis, 1989, p. 172). The Eisenhower administration recommended that Latin Americans weather the present economic crisis by spending less and delaying economic development programs (Rabe, 1988, p. 101). *New York Times* correspondent Tad Szulc reported that Latin Americans "take exception" to the policy of focusing on private investment, rather than grants or more favorable loans. Szulc argued that the "problem is that where money is most needed is for such unprofitable yet fundamental projects as railroads, ports, highways and dams, for which private investments are not forthcoming" (Szulc, 1956, May 30, p. 25). Thus, Eisenhower's rigid policy of consistently favoring private investment was unable to meet the needs of the majority of Latin Americans. Administration officials warned of "the desire of Latin Americans to have the U.S. assume a larger share of the financial burden involved in solving their economic problems than the U.S. is willing to bear" ("Progress Report on NSC 5432/1," Feb 3, 1955, p. 2).

The Eisenhower administration also insisted on hemispheric solidarity, by which they meant Latin Americans always had to agree with the United States. A primary goal of the Eisenhower administration in its Latin America policy was "hemispheric solidarity in support of our world policies, particularly in the UN and other international organizations" ("Progress Report," 144, p. 2). Latin American governments were judged by the Eisenhower administration in part based on how closely and how willingly they supported U.S. agendas in both the Organization of American States and the United Nations. Essentially, the United States evaluated its neighbors by its own standards on their willingness to be "Cold Warriors," constraining their ability to construct their own foreign policies.

The issue that led to the strongest anger among Latin Americans was the U.S. policy of privileging anticommunism over any other feature of a Latin American government, leading to U.S. support of repressive dictatorships, as well as a return to direct intervention in the internal affairs of Latin American nations. The greatest example is the intervention in Guatemala, in which the Central Intelligence Agency (CIA) aided a handful of rebels in overthrowing a popularly elected president and inserting a repressive military dictator, because of fears of Communist influence. Though it was a covert operation, it was no secret that the United States chose a leader, trained some rebels, and then embarked on a campaign of psychological warfare that ultimately led to the removal of the Guatemalan president. The U.S. role was known throughout the region, and the backlash was strong. Though it did not adversely affect official relations, it accelerated the growing anti-U.S. sentiment in the region.

While the Eisenhower administration was creating problems in the Latin American relationship with the United States, they also demonstrated remarkable ignorance as to the nature and source of these problems. Many U.S. policy makers believed that the root of the problem was in public relations, with the solution being a greater effort by the United States to tell its side (Zahniser & Weis, 1989, p. 165). The Nixon trip was designed in part to address this perception. In fact, the Eisenhower administration made numerous and varied efforts to influence Latin American public opinion, all directed at the masses. These included films, pamphlets, posters, cartoons, exhibits, books, radio programs, and so on ("Progress Report," 1955, p. 20). However, these efforts ultimately met with limited success, and problems in the relationship with Latin America continued to grow.

Eisenhower administration officials continued to blame Latin Americans for the problems. Hard-liners in Washington "found a large measure of self-pity in the hemispheric cries for help and a growing determination to place on U.S. shoulders the burden for economic problems that stemmed from natural and historical causes or that persisted through a lack of national economic and political discipline" (Zahniser & Weis, 1989, p. 168). This diagnosis of "self-pity" demonstrates that paternalistic feelings toward Latin Americans remained prevalent in the Eisenhower administration. Secretary of State John Foster Dulles was even more condescending, telling President Eisenhower, "you have to pat them a little bit and make them think that you are fond of them" (John Dulles to Dwight Eisenhower, quoted in Rabe, 1988, p. 33).

Policy makers in Washington rarely took Latin American critiques of U.S. policies seriously, preferring instead to attribute them to ignorance or foreign influence, usually Soviet. Historian Alan McPherson demonstrated that "anti-Americanism seeped down from literary and other elites into the political consciousness of ordinary people as it also percolated up from the poor to shape mainstream politics" (McPherson, 2003, p. 11). U.S. citizens badly wanted to know, "Do they like us?" But they had no wish to know the real answer to the question, preferring to simply believe they were well liked while simultaneously denying that such opinions even mattered (McPherson, 2003, p. 21). U.S. policy makers believed that Latin American leaders who criticized U.S. policies were "out of touch with popular opinion" (McPherson, 2003, p. 25). United States–Latin American relations got progressively worse after World War II, reaching a new low by the beginning of 1958 (Zahiser & Weis, 1989, p. 168).

III

The Pérez Jiménez administration, both for the Venezuelans who experienced it and for foreign observers such as the Eisenhower administration, represented a dilemma: the ends, or the means? Under Pérez Jiménez, Venezuela experienced the greatest concentrated economic growth in its history. It saw massive public works projects designed to increase the standard of living for all. In many ways, it was the high point of Venezuelan history. But all of this came at a price.

The military government, of which Marcos Pérez Jiménez became the leader, came to power in 1948 following three years of democracy in Venezuela. The Pérez Jiménez regime embraced the notion of a technocracy, a governmental philosophy that de-emphasized political and social progress in favor of economic and material growth. The plan the Pérez Jiménez administration put forward was called the "New National Ideal," which consisted of using Venezuela's mineral wealth to benefit all Venezuelans. Pérez Jiménez himself declared that the goal for his nation was the "moral, intellectual, and material improvement of the inhabitants of the country and the rational transformation of the physical environment, in order that Venezuela occupy the rank that corresponds to its geographic situation, its extraordinary riches, and glorious traditions" (*Servicio Informative Venezolano, 1954*; quoted in Mayhall, 2005, p. 126).

Unfortunately for most Venezuelans, the benefits of this period remained concentrated among a few sectors of society, especially the military and foreign investors. Journalist Tad Szulc reported, "civil liberties and the United States conception of democracy have fallen by the wayside in this attempt by the Venezuelan Government to give the country generations' worth of material progress in less than a decade" (Szulc, 1956, March 17, p. 6). The Pérez Jiménez government made no effort to improve the lives of the rural poor, whose standard of living had been in decline since World War I. The Pérez Jiménez regime returned to a policy of catering to U.S. oil companies, in an attempt to boost production and revenues. Under Pérez Jiménez, U.S. direct investments in Venezuela more than doubled (Rabe, 1982, p. 128). "The oil industry provided the government with over half of its revenues, about 75 percent of its income taxes, and almost 95 percent of its export earnings" (Rabe, 1982, p. 131). Yet, it employed less than 2% of the workforce.

The profits went into massive public works projects, centered in Caracas, which became an impressive, modern-looking city. The repressive Pérez Jiménez government, with U.S. encouragement, squandered the nation's oil revenues and the great opportunity they represented. Meanwhile, U.S. businesses applauded the Pérez Jiménez government, praising "progressive" and "forthright" policies (Rabe, 1982, p. 130).

In 1948, shortly after they took power, the military government banned the political party *Accion Democrática* (AD). AD was by far the most popular party in Venezuela and had just won a massive victory in the 1947 national election. Still feeling threatened, the military government began hunting down *adecos* (members or supporters of *Accion Democrática*). In 1950, when Pérez Jiménez took control, the oppression of opposition expanded and accelerated.

Illegal imprisonment, concentration camps, torture, and murder became the favorite tools of the Pérez Jiménez regime. The tortures inflicted were as imaginative as they were terrible: "prisoners were slashed with razors, burned with cigarettes, forced to sit for hours on blocks of ice. Some prisoners were force-fed harsh laxatives and then, in a chamber of horrors awash with blood, excrement and vomit, they were forced to walk naked around a razor-sharp wheel rim" (*Time* magazine, August 23, 1963, quoted in McMaughan, 2011, p. 22). These activities were the domain of the new *Seguridad Nacional*, and its head Pedro Estrada quickly became the most hated man in Venezuela.

In 1952, the Pérez Jiménez regime felt the time was right to confer at least some legitimacy to their government by calling for an election. One hundred and four members were to be elected to a constituent assembly, which would then elect a president. AD was not allowed to run, leaving Venezuelans to choose between the government party or the two remaining opposition parties. Copei was a conservative, religious party associated with the Catholic Church. The Democratic Republican Union (URD) was the other opposition party, "generally considered a left-of-center nationalistic party," associated with anti-U.S. tendencies, which it denied ("Venezuela vote lead," 1952). The government party was the Independent Electoral Front (FEI). The military regime strictly controlled the activities of Copei and URD, forcing them to turn over all of their materials and even jailing their leaders. Government interference became so great that URD seriously considered simply boycotting the election.

Nevertheless, the opposition parties, especially URD, continued to campaign hard. In spite of their progress, it came as complete shock to all when early returns showed URD with a full 50% of the vote, with FEI at 35% and Copei at 15%. Just as these returns were being reported, the government suddenly imposed a complete media blackout. In one case, a telephone call was taking place, in which a reporter in Caracas was relaying totals. He gave the URD totals at the time, and the Copei numbers, then as he "started to give the next figure—probably for the Government coalition—he was interrupted. When he resumed, he said 'I cannot talk about the election'" (Bracker, 1958). This is an extraordinary example of censorship in action.

While it was initially hoped the blackout was just to avoid further embarrassment, it soon proved to be far more sinister. The blackout remained in place for two full days. When it was finally lifted, the regime announced they had tallied the results. The URD candidate claimed his party had received enough votes to grant it 70 of the 104 seats, but the government later announced that FEI had won 56 seats, URD only 27 seats, and Copei 14 seats. The day after the election the URD candidate and six other party leaders were arrested and deported to Panama. Though both Venezuelans and members of the international community were outraged, the fraudulent election was an insufficient catalyst for revolution, and after a brief period of unrest, it was back to business as usual for the Pérez Jiménez regime.

For the next five years, the military government continued to torture and murder its opposition, while the highest ranking members of the government and the military amassed gigantic personal fortunes through rampant graft and corruption. Venezuela continued to enjoy an oil boom, but the profits continued to flow into showy but ultimately ineffective public works projects, into the pockets of the rulers, or out of the country and into the hands of foreign investors.

By and large, Venezuelans chose to bide their time, waiting for the next opportunity to remove Pérez Jiménez from power. A handful of poorly organized revolts were easily put down, and everyone began turning increased attention to the scheduled 1957 election. Pérez Jiménez was of course also aware that his term was coming to an end, and that he was even less popular in 1957 than he had been in 1952. The regime could not risk the likely embarrassment of another free election. Something needed to be done.

The Pérez Jiménez regime announced a plebiscite, a simple yes or no answer to the question of whether or not Pérez Jiménez should remain in office. Still, even this sham of an election was deemed too risky to proceed freely. A "YES" card and a "NO" card were mailed to all voters. They were to mail their vote back. The day after the election, government workers and employees of businesses friendly to the regime were required to come to work with their "NO" card to prove they had not voted against the regime, or risk losing their jobs.

Unsurprisingly, Pérez Jiménez won the December 15, 1957, plebiscite, though many Venezuelans simply refused to vote. The U.S. ambassador to Venezuela reported, "In the absence of democratic traditions, the majority of Venezuelans have developed what appears to be an apathetic or acquiescent attitude toward their authoritarian governments." He went on to say, "In the present political situation, the typical mood of the man in the street appears to be one of passive, though cynical, acceptance of the Regime's decision and plans to remain in power" (Despatch from the Ambassador, 1955–1957).

In spite of the prevailing feeling of resignation, the plebiscite angered Venezuelans. In addition, it was becoming increasingly apparent that the vast majority of the country was not benefiting from the massive economic boom, and they were not likely to see any benefits so long as things stayed the same. Anger among Venezuelans began to grow and, fortunately for the Venezuelan people, elements of the armed forces were beginning to lose patience as well.

A generation of young officers was growing in the Venezuelan armed forces. These junior officers were frustrated, because although the Pérez Jiménez regime was a boom time for the military, the benefits were concentrated at the highest ranks. Even more important was the legacy of those three years of democracy, 1945–1948, Venezuela's first experience with democratic civilian government. This combination of material and ideological motivations finally stirred some to action.

On January 2, 1958, elements of the Air Force revolted. Though the revolt was quickly put down, it represented the strongest challenge to Pérez Jiménez's rule yet. After this, things began to happen very quickly. Pérez Jiménez received increasing pressure from the Armed Forces, while civilian opposition grew bolder and bolder. Pérez Jiménez frantically scrambled to maintain power, proposing and granting numerous concessions to both civilian and military opponents. When that failed, he resorted to force, and by mid-January over 250 officers were under arrest. Students were in massed protest, and intellectuals circulated an anti-government manifesto that received hundreds of signatures (Szulc, January 17, 1958). "It was noted . . . that this was the first time since the inception of dictatorial rule here that such leaders, including influential business men, had been willing to identify themselves with the opposition movement" (Szulc, January 19, 1958).

Things came to a head on January 21, 1958. "It was a true popular revolution of Venezuelan citizens of all ages and social classes" (Kolb, 1974, p. 175). Venezuelans organized a general strike for January 21st. "Precisely at 12 o'clock noon on that day all editorial offices closed without having printed a single newspaper, church bells rang, factory sirens screamed, thousands of automobiles sounded their horns and, by common consent, shop owners locked their doors and walked into the streets, to be joined by great masses of *caraceños* [residents of Caracas] who converged toward the center of the city to protest the rule of Pérez Jiménez" (Kolb, 1974, p. 175). The *Seguridad Nacional* responded with force, opening fire on the protesters, who returned the violence: "Students and workers threw Molotov cocktails into police jeeps, incinerating the occupants, while women and children poured boiling water upon the uniformed men from windows and balconies" (Kolb, 1974, p. 176). The few shops that did open, mostly owned by foreigners, were vandalized. As the strife continued into a second day, several more shops and few factories dared open for business; the mobs broke the shops' windows, and set the factories ablaze.

The protests mobilized nearly the entire population, with all ages and occupations represented, but even such widespread and committed opposition could not oust the dictator. Regardless of the ferocity of this storm, Pérez Jiménez thought he could weather this one too. Thus, it came as a surprise to him when word came that all branches of the armed forces had risen up against him as well. In the end, a truly united Venezuela overthrew their dictator and finally began the process of a return to democratic civilian rule.

In February, 1958, the Eisenhower administration offered a cautious statement of approval of the popular overthrow of Pérez Jiménez: "while we are not in a position to intervene in the internal developments of the countries of Latin America, we are in a position to feel, and we do feel, satisfaction and pleasure when the people of any country determinedly choose the road to democracy and freedom" (U.S. Department of State Bulletin, March 31, 1958, p. 520; quoted in Rabe, 1982, p. 134). This is a remarkably reluctant response to such a landmark event in another nation. This is understandable, considering the close relationship between the Eisenhower administrator and the Venezuelan dictator. This close relationship would soon lead to some serious consequences.

IV

Vice President Nixon went on a tour of Central America in 1955, which went very well. Thus, when President Eisenhower began to believe that a high-level delegation to South America was needed, he unsurprisingly turned to his Vice President. "Nixon undertook the trip to strengthen United States relations with the region, and to congratulate the Latin Americans on their social and political achievements" (Cox, 2012).

The first stop on the trip was in Montevideo, Uruguay, where Nixon was able to overcome a disorganized attempt by Communists to mar his visit. The tour continued without incident until he reached Peru. While the Vice President was assured that he would find a warm reception, "Peru in fact echoed with angry complaints against the United States" (Zahniser & Weis, 1989, p. 175). Peruvians were upset over U.S. policies that adversely affected Peru's economy, as well as the Legion of Merit that United States awarded former dictator Manuel Odria. Nixon took advantage of the situation to seek another confrontation with Communists at San Marcos University, though the demonstrations he encountered were not Communist-inspired. This time, demonstrators began throwing stones, forcing Nixon to retreat. One of his companions was struck in the mouth, though Nixon himself was unharmed. As he retreated, one of the individuals confronting Nixon spit directly in his face. The vice president responded in a fashion appropriate for a high-ranking diplomat abroad: he kicked the man in the shin. After his escape, and a better visit at Catholic University, Nixon returned to his hotel, only to discover the San Marcos crowd waiting for him, forcing him and his retinue to enter the hotel through a shower of spit (Cox, 2012).

After relatively uneventful visits in Ecuador and Colombia, the final scheduled stop was Venezuela. This was just three months after the Venezuelans overthrew their brutally repressive, U.S.-supported dictator. Pérez Jiménez eagerly embraced all three of the Eisenhower administration's foreign policy goals for Latin America: he was fiercely anticommunist, though in practice much of this was simply labeling his opposition as Communists, then hunting them down in the name of anticommunism; he, with few exceptions, followed the U.S. line in all hemispheric affairs; and he made Venezuela, especially its oil industry, a haven for U.S. investors. In light of these traits, in March 1955, U.S. Ambassador to Venezuela Fletcher Warren declared that Venezuela under Pérez Jiménez was the best example in the world of the U.S. method of "doing business" and was a "showroom" for the success of the U.S. system (Telegram, 1955–1957). Warren made this claim in spite of the brutal political and social repression, the systematic theft of Venezuela's revenues through graft and corruption, and the electoral frauds that maintained the regime. The Eisenhower administration even awarded Pérez Jiménez a Legion of Merit, the highest award given to foreign persons, "for his exceptionally meritorious conduct in the discharge of high duties." It was to recognize "his spirit of collaboration and friendship toward the United States," going on to cite his "constant concern for the problem of Communist infiltration" (*El Universal*, October 22, 1954, quoted in Kolb, 1974, p. 142). The Eisenhower administration, in spite of their knowledge of the repression and abuses that took place under Pérez Jiménez, nevertheless worked hard to achieve and maintain not just a working relationship, but a friendly one. To this end, he and his military were pampered; Pérez Jiménez was also named an "honorary submariner" by the Navy Department in 1957 (Rabe, 1982, p. 127).

In March 1958, the Communist weekly *Tribuna Popular* of Caracas published a letter from U.S. Ambassador Warren, dated January 10, in the midst of the rising tide against Pérez Jiménez, in which Warren congratulated the Pérez Jiménez government on weathering the New Year's Day rebellion and offered well wishes for 1958. The Eisenhower administration chose to offer no response to the publication of this letter. In fact, they chose the very next week to announce that they had offered Pérez Jiménez, and the even more hated Pedro Estrada, asylum in the United States (Kolb, 1974, p. 181).

The governments of both Venezuela and the United States had received threats of violence. In spite of this warning, Venezuelan security forces were totally unprepared for what Vice President Nixon encountered. Nixon, his wife and the rest of the U.S. delegation, and several Venezuelan officials endured long minutes of shouting and a deluge of spit as the two countries' national anthems were played. As they stood at attention, spit and garbage rained down on them from crowds in an overhanging airport terminal observation deck. Nixon's wife's "new red suit quickly turned a dirty brown with tobacco juice stains" (Zahniser & Weis, 1989, p. 181). Ceremonies were cut short as they moved straight to the cars to escape the continued rain of saliva and vitriol (Cox, 2012).

Unfortunately, though the cars offered some shelter, the ordeal was far from over. The route the motorcade was to take was public knowledge, and cars containing demonstrators wove in and out of the motorcade as it made the 12 mile journey from the airport to Caracas. Even worse, demonstrators made use of this knowledge to organize a blockade. The cars were stopped and attackers came pouring out of side streets. The crowds were primarily youthful, almost certainly made up of some of the same individuals who took to the streets to oust Pérez Jiménez just three months before. According to U.S. officials, "the mob was made up of ruffians and riffraff and it was in an ugly mood" (Memorandum, 1958/1991). One historian described "a howling mob of Venezuelans who gave every indication of wishing to tear him to bits, wreaking vengeance on the person of the Vice-President for all of the indignities and deprivations endured in a decade of tyranny" (Kolb, 1974, p. 182).

For 12 minutes, the crowd assailed the cars with rocks, pipes, sticks, and still more spit. Nixon later reported that the attackers were rocking his vehicle, in an attempt to overturn it. "Rocks, dirt and dung flew everywhere"

(Zahniser & Weis, 1989, p. 181). A few Secret Service men jumped out to try to protect the occupants, fortunately maintaining the presence of mind to avoid resorting to deadly force, which would only have made the situation even more dangerous. Meanwhile, Venezuelan security forces stood by while the mob attacked. Just three months earlier, a mob very like this one hunted down *Seguridad Nacional* officers in the streets. Their successors were not eager to resist another such popular uprising. In a display of hemispheric solidarity, though not the type sought by the Eisenhower administration, Venezuelans were heard to shout "We won't forget Guatemala" as they attacked the vice president (Brands, 2010, p. 17). The rioters also screamed the names of Pérez Jiménez and Pedro Estrada, demanding to know why they were being sheltered in the United States.

The cars took a beating; windows were shattered, and a Venezuelan official received a face full of broken glass. Fortunately, no one in the U.S. delegation was seriously injured. They were able to negotiate the roadblock and drive the battered, spit-covered cars to the U.S. ambassador's residence. Following the attacks on the road, riots erupted throughout the city.

The protesters represented a new social mixture. "They were mostly young and literate, often led by adult university students or Communist Party cadres" (McPherson, 2003, p. 10). The violence Nixon encountered demonstrated "the readiness of mass-based groups to express hostility directly at the U.S. government" (McPherson, 2003, p. 9). A State Department officer declared of the demonstrations in Caracas, "This is something new in Latin America" (quoted in McPherson, 2003, p. 26).

After completing an abbreviated and modified schedule of appointments, the Nixon retinue was ready to travel the same road back to the airport to return to the United States. No chances were taken this time: "they were accompanied by the junta in automobiles well-stocked with small arms, tear gas canisters, and submachine guns, and were escorted by a riot-ready army filling nine buses and three trucks" (Zahniser & Weis, 1989, p. 183). Once the vice president returned to the United States, the Eisenhower administration began the process of understanding what had just happened, and responding.

V

Much of the Eisenhower administration's rhetoric about the Nixon trip initially focused on Communism, suggesting they had completely misunderstood the nature of the protests and the sources of the anger displayed. However, the administration's firm commitment to anticommunism necessitated a discussion of the role of Communism in the violence. Beginning immediately after the violence in Caracas, and continuing throughout the discussion of the Nixon mission, Nixon and other officials in the Eisenhower administration began discussing the actual sources of grievances. Ultimately, the violence led to serious discussions, effectively raising awareness and leading to substantial changes in policy.

The first official reaction to the Nixon tour came in a May 16, 1958, cabinet meeting. While much of the meeting was consumed with Nixon's discussion of the role of Communists, they quickly realized that even if the crowds were organized by Communists, the vast majority of protestors were not themselves Communist. The discussion quickly turned to an effort to identify who they were, and why they were protesting so violently (Cabinet meeting, 1958).

Costa Rican president José Figueres said, "People cannot spit on a foreign policy which is what they meant to do" (quoted in McPherson, 2003, p. 9). The Nixon trip led to a period of "creative tension," leading the United States "to reshape long-standing policies toward Latin America and recast them in major ways" (Zahniser & Weis, 1989, p. 163). Nixon believed "his mission had alerted his own nation that its relations with Latin America needed attention on a wide variety of fronts," forcing "a reassessment of the administration's policy toward Latin America" (Zahniser & Weis, 1989, pp. 184–185). He suggested the Eisenhower administration make Latin America a higher priority, and also suggested that they more clearly embrace and support democracies while distancing the United States from repressive dictatorships (Cox, 2012).

Seven months after the trip, a national intelligence estimate entitled "Latin American Attitudes toward the US" described what the Eisenhower administration had learned from the experience. "It pointed out the growing power of the middle and lower classes," including "the differences in culture and living standards" between them and the United States (National intelligence estimate, 1991). "It also stressed this group's feelings about the US interventions which contradicted stated policy and signed agreements, the role of US companies in the Latin American economies, and the relations between the United States and Latin American dictators" (Cox, 2012).

Congress also responded to the violence in Caracas. Senator Wayne Morse almost immediately began conducting hearings, featuring "the grilling of several State Department officers" (Zahniser & Weis, 1989, p. 185). About a year after Nixon's trip, a report was submitted to the House Committee on Foreign Affairs by the Subcommittee on Inter-American Affairs. "The report was dedicated to understanding the problems that led to the demonstrations of the year before, and how to fix them" (Cox, 2012).

It was not only the U.S. government whose opinions began to change. Immediately after the Nixon trip, and sporadically over the next few months, newspaper articles began detailing the problems in the U.S. relationship with Latin America. Tad Szulc wrote, "Nixon Tour Highlights a Continent's Crisis: South Americans Voice their Loud Complaints against the U.S.," in which he concisely outlined for the U.S. public the various political and economic sources of friction in the relationship (Szulc, May 11, 1958). Armed with a changed perception gained from articles such as this, the U.S. public added its voice to calls for change in United States–Latin America policies.

Ultimately, the violence Nixon experienced in Caracas led not just to a reassessment of policy, but to a complete reevaluation of Latin American society and the relationship between Latin Americans and the United States. "While Latin American governments continued a longstanding tradition of peaceful cooperation with the United States, US policy-makers began to understand that the real power in Latin America was shifting to the people, and it was the masses, not the ruling elite, that they had to court" (Cox, 2012). Caracas "revitalized the public relations approach to Latin America" (McPherson, 2003, p. 26). After the incident, United States Information Agency director began conducting presentations titled "The Image of America" (McPherson, 2003, p. 35).

Eisenhower finally began to publicly express his preference for democracy and respect for human rights. Upon receiving the Venezuelan ambassador three months after Caracas, Eisenhower became the first U.S. president to ever publicly, unequivocally announce his preference for representative governments in Latin America (Rabe, 1988, p. 105).

The mob violence Vice President Nixon encountered in Caracas represents a remarkable example of an angry political group, and the capacity of such expressions of anger to raise awareness and create policy changes. Though the violence itself shocked the Eisenhower administration, the sentiments behind it should not have. The history of United States–Latin American relations is full of examples of policies that have created hard feelings. In the wake of World War II, after participating in the global struggle of democracy against authoritarianism, Latin Americans became less willing to accept authoritarianism in their own lives. A surge of popular democracies followed the war, with dictators and military governments falling across the region. Shortly thereafter, though, authoritarian forces made a comeback, with U.S. backing. This betrayal of democratic forces in Latin America, paired with U.S. policies that exacerbated economic troubles, created the intense anti-United States feelings that Nixon encountered on his tour.

Although the anger had a long legacy, much of the way it was expressed was new. Mass-based politics in Latin America was quickly replacing traditional rule by elites. The social make-up of the crowds, and their willingness to commit violence against the vice president of the United States, were new developments. This novelty shocked many in the United States, ultimately leading to a broad reassessment of U.S. policy, and of the entire relationship with the region. Though this rethinking did not fix all of the problems, it forced the United States to confront the new situation in Latin America.

References

Bracker, M. (1958, December 2). Censor cloaks Venezuelan vote; Junta was losing in first returns. *New York Times*, p. 1.

Brands, H. (2010). *Latin America's cold war*. Cambridge, MA: Harvard University Press.

Cabinet meeting. (1958, May 16). C-45 folder, box 5, Cabinet Series (Minnich notes), OSS.

Coerver, D. M., & Hall, L. B. (1999). *Tangled destinies: Latin America and the United States*. Albuquerque, NM: University of New Mexico Press.

Confidential Memorandum on Latin America, Truman Library.

Cox, J. (2012). "They aren't friendly, Mr. Vice President." The Eisenhower Administration's response to Communist-inspired attacks during Vice President Nixon's 1958 tour of Latin America, *American Diplomacy*. Retrieved from http://www.unc.edu/depts/diplomat/item/2012/0712/comm/cox_nixon.html

Despatch from the Ambassador in Venezuela (McIntosh) to the Department of State. *Foreign Relations of the United States*, 1955–1957, Vol. 7, 1167.

Kolb, G. L. (1974). *Democracy and dictatorship in Venezuela, 1945–1958*. Hamden, CT: Connecticut College.

Mayhall, M. (2005). Modernist but not exceptional: The debate over modern art and national identity in 1950s Venezuela. *Latin American Perspectives*, 32(2), 124–146.

McMaughan, M. (2011). *The battle of Venezuela*. New York, NY: Seven Stories Press.

McPherson, A. (2003). *Yankee No! Anti-Americanism in U.S.–Latin American relations*. Cambridge, MA: Harvard University Press.

Memorandum of a telephone conversation among the Minister-Counselor of the Embassy in Venezuela (Burrows), the Assistant Secretary of State for Inter-American Affairs (Rubottom) in Caracas, and the Deputy Director of the Office of South American Affairs (Sanders) in Washington, May 13, 1958, 2 p.m. (1991). *Foreign Relations of the United States, 1958–1960: Volume V, American Republics*. Washington: United States Government Printing Office.

National intelligence estimate. (1991). *Foreign Relations of the United States, 1958–1960: Volume V, American Republics*. Washington, DC: United States Government Printing Office.

Progress report on NSC 5432/1. (1955, February 3).

Rabe, S. G. (1982). *The road to OPEC: United States relations with Venezuela, 1919–1976.* Austin, TX: The University of Texas Press.

Rabe, S. G. (1988), *Eisenhower and Latin America: The foreign policy of anticommunism.* Chapel Hill, NC: The University of North Carolina Press.

Szulc, T. (1956, March 17). Venezuela takes technocratic path. *New York Times,* p. 6.

Szulc, T. (1956, April 13). Latin American nationalism challenges policy of U.S., survey indicates. *New York Times,* p. 6.

Szulc, T. (1958, January 17). Caracas students stage 5 more riots. *New York Times* p. 1.

Szulc, T. (1958, January 19). New demands put to Caracas chief. *New York Times* p. 1.

Szulc, T. (1958, May 11). Nixon tour highlights a continent's crisis: South Americans voice their loud complaints against the U.S. *New York Times* p. E3.

Telegram from the ambassador in Venezuela (Warren) to the Department of State. (1955, March 30). *Foreign Relations, 1955–57,* Vol. VII, 1120.

Venezuela vote lead is taken by leftists. (1952, December 1). *New York Times* p. 1.

Zahniser, M. R., & Weis, W. M. (1989). A diplomatic Pearl Harbor? Richard Nixon's goodwill mission to Latin America in 1958, *Diplomatic History, 13*(2), 163–190.

CHAPTER FIFTEEN

The Greeks Know Anger: The Causes and Consequences of the Continuing Crisis of Capitalism in the Eurozone South

David L. Elliott

They did not invent it, but the Greeks have known anger for over three millennia, since the collapse of Bronze Age Hellenic Civilization, through the Peloponnesian wars, and down to four centuries of Ottoman rule that ended in the 19th century with its overthrow by the Greeks. In the 20th century, Greece was occupied by the Axis powers during World War II, which devolved into a civil war, and at the present time, Greece's economy is held hostage to the Eurozone powers led by Germany. Greeks have a right to be angry (you should be, too) and here is why.

Historically, and today as well, Greek anger was often rooted in the political: power plays among the ancient gods and the Greek city-states, loss of national self-determination in the Ottoman years, Nazi occupation, British meddling in Greek affairs as World War II ended, and now enormous pressure from the troika—European Central Bank (ECB), the International Monetary Fund (IMF), and the European Commission—to effect internal political and other changes. Germany wields enormous de facto power that is often realized through the ECB and especially the European Commission of the European Union. Today, Greeks are offended and angered by what they see as external meddling in their own internal political and socioeconomic affairs, by Germany, in particular.

Greece now finds itself in a severe financial bind, partly of its own doing. Due to the power wielded through the European Union (EU) and the Eurozone,[1] Greeks are angry because the effect of austerity measures forced by the troika and Germany include massive unemployment, reductions in pensions, undermining of the health care system, business losses and failures, near collapse of the banking system and loss of access to international markets, and numerous other economic issues. As a result, Greek fury sometimes erupts into violence and destruction of property that rivals what we have seen in American inner cities during the same period. While the causes of African American anger in the inner cities and of Greek anger in Athens are not exactly the same, they are both palpable and are both rooted in a sense of economic, social, and political injustice.

Finally, overlaying the anger Greeks feel for the troika and Germany are serious ideological, intergenerational, and cross-cultural misunderstandings that have initiated episodes of interpersonal anger on the part of both Greeks and key players in Germany and the European Commission. This, alone, has made resolution of this crisis nearly intractable. The resolution is likely to require, first, interpersonal reconciliation to reduce the anger on all sides and begin to establish a degree of trust. Second, political action needs take place to correct some significant inconsistencies and inequalities across the governments of the EU. Once a foundation of trust and social justice has been laid, the economic solution will be so obvious as to almost resolve itself. At the present time, hammering away at the economics with heightened calls for austerity in Greece simply fuels the existing flames of anger and a profound sense of injustice.

Background: Before the *Metapolitefsi,* 1974

Let us examine the larger historical context to understand today's anger-causing difficulties and challenges. Following six years of war for independence from four centuries of Ottoman Turkish rule, in 1827 the Treaty of London ended Turkish rule and established an independent Greece. The war-torn Greece that emerged was still locked into a premodern and violent political environment characterized by a still largely agrarian and seafaring economy. The process of recovery from Ottoman rule and metamorphosis of both polity and economy would occupy the next century and half of Greek history. During this period, and even into the 21st century, lands and islands neighboring Greece, most notably Cyprus, all with ethnic Greek communities, were the sources of regular international conflict, with Greece and Turkey often at the center.

The development process from 1827 through the 1970s was characterized by struggles of four major Greek forces: the military, a constitutional monarchy, advocates for a rightist republic, and socialists/communists. Each had its own successes and Greek self-rule vacillated among the monarchy, Hellenic Republics of right and left, military dictatorship, and various combinations. The one major interregnum from Greek self-rule was the devastating occupation by Germany (1940–1944) that saw fierce resistance by the Greek Communist Party–supported ELAS-EAM (National Liberation Front–National Popular Liberation Army) and the smaller British-supported, rightist EDES (Greek Democratic National Army).

The Nazi occupation was marked by mass executions and massacres of Greek partisans and civilians by the Germans, famine, heavy taxation by Germany, and massive murder and deportation of Greek Jews to Auschwitz. Moreover, the Nazi occupiers left the Greek economy in a shambles: The Germans "borrowed" money from the Greek government that was never repaid; the currency became worthless and the Greeks resorted to using gold coins from another age to conduct any transactions of consequence (Delivanis, 1950). The fury the Greeks felt toward Nazi Germany played into existing political divisions within the Greek opposition and as World War II approached its conclusion with the defeat of the Nazis, ideological anger erupted as ELAS and EDES turned on each other and in December 1944, communist-backed ELAS defeated the EDES in battle.

From independence onward, and even into World War II, if Greece had a "friend" in the world of global politics, it was Britain. World War II ended with Britain occupying Athens and returning Georgios Papandreou from exile in Egypt to Athens as Prime Minister. This British action, including support for the Greek right while firing on and killing members of ELAS, as well as the re-installation of King George II, set into motion an angry civil war between ELAS and the British-installed puppet government. This was a serious violation of Greece's right to national self-determination and the political dynamic established by the British has reverberated through the last 70 years of Greek history, until 2015.

As the British began rebuilding their own island and backed away from the right-wing monarchist regime they had installed in Greece, the United States, in the angry, anticommunist hysteria of the day, moved to take Britain's place in opposition to the ELAS. The deadly and devastating civil war continued until 1949, when the communists conceded defeat by signing a ceasefire that finally ended a decade of modern Greek trag-edy largely imposed upon Greece by Nazi Germany, Britain, and finally the United States.

Post–civil war rebuilding of the shattered Greek economy was spon-sored by the United States effectively by default. All the while in the 1950s, Greece struggled to re-establish a viable economy, with significant financial aid from Britain and the United States. Germany also began to rebuild and it did so much more successfully for two important reasons. First, even after the war, Germany was and remained a major industrial nation. German engineering and production are well-noted for their quality and German goods were in high demand across Europe as it rebuilt. Indeed, West Germany began to run surpluses in its balance of trade with other countries in Western Europe (Dernburg, 1954). Second, the United States pumped billions of dollars into Western Europe—including Germany—as the Cold War heightened and the US increasingly feared the Soviet Union's emergence as a nuclear power to match the US nuclear might. Also in this period, the early 1950s, an accounting of debts began to take place and this accounting made clear that Germany's unpaid debts from World War I and World War II, including reparations to peoples and nations that were destroyed by German military power, were unlikely to be repaid, notwithstanding Germany's robust economic growth. In 1951, Germany began discussions in London with its major creditors—Britain, France, and the United States—to find a way to resolve its own debt crisis. There were many other creditor nations with claims on Ger-many; Greece was one of the smaller ones. In 1952, the Tripartite Com-mission on German Debts ("Tripartite commission on German debts," 1952) met and worked out arrangements that varied across creditor coun-tries but that constituted a massive reduction in German debt—a "haircut" in today's terms.

Despite long-standing cultural affinities with some members of the Soviet bloc, and a lingering, though severely weakened leftist sentiment, Greece aligned itself on the global political scene with the United States. Greece's vote in the United Nations, and after 1952 its membership in NATO, made Greece a strategic geopolitical ally of the United States and it was rewarded with military and financial support over the subsequent two decades as part of the U.S. strategy to support European countries bor-dering on the Soviet bloc.[2] Despite its emergence on the international scene as a dependable U.S. ally, and the continuation of the monarchy installed by the British, Greek politics remained still sharply, often angrily, divided, though the anger manifested itself increasingly between the mon-archy and the military.

In 1967, the Greek military launched a successful coup, initiating violent suppression of dissidents and sending the king and many politicians into exile, which angered much of the Greek population. The military was probably more unloved than the monarchy it had exiled. In 1973, the military brutally suppressed student pro-democracy protests. Subsequently, in 1974, the military regime collapsed in the face of its support of a coup by angry Greek Cypriots in that nation (shared with a Turkish-Cypriot minority) that had led to the invasion of Cyprus by Turkey. The fall of the military and the reinstallation of civilian rule in that year is known as the *metapolitefsi*. With the return from exile of Konstantinos Karamanlis, who became Prime Minister following elections that brought to power his center-right New Democracy Party, and support from a national referendum, the exiled monarchy was abolished for the last time and the Third Hellenic Republic was established. In the same year, as a result of fellow NATO member Turkey's invasion of Cyprus, Greece withdrew from the military arm of NATO. The *metapolitefsi* was a dangerous and challenging period but Karamanlis was able to avoid war with Turkey and move the nation away from military dictatorship and more into alignment with other European democracies ("Metapolitefsi," n.d.).

According to Nikos Konstandaras, managing editor and a columnist of the Greek daily newspaper *Kathimerini* and long-time contributor to the *New York Times* newspaper, the events of 1974:

> set Greece on course for the greatest uninterrupted period of stability and prosperity in our history, but it also consolidated many problems that still plague us: deep mistrust of authority, resistance to reform, unbridled populism in politics and the media, a state-dominated economy that favors specific groups, and a political system that values expedience over efficiency and puts self-interest above the common good. (Konstandaras, July 27, 2014)

The following year, 1975, saw a further move away from military influence, legalization of the Communist Party, and the establishment of a republican government with a new constitution. Though not without the intrigue that has characterized Greek politics in the modern era, the second half of the 1970s set the political stage for the subsequent prosperity that Konstandaras cites. Cyprus, however, remained a key element in Greek politics, reflecting both an international dimension and a nationalist affinity for the Greek Cypriots who share that island with Turkish Cypriots. The Greeks had not forgotten the Ottomans and maintained the sense, *xeniteia* (Angelos, 2015), that Greek nationality transcends actual citizenship.

Perhaps the best analogy is between Greek and Jewish or Irish diasporas: three ancient civilizations whose peoples over the centuries have migrated across the globe but who still feel a strong affinity to the "home" country (Greece, Israel, or Ireland) irrespective an individual's actual birthplace or residence.

Meanwhile, in Europe, the U.S.–USSR Cold War was far from the only concern as Europe continued a lengthy recovery from the devastation of World War II. The original European Economic Community (EEC) was established in 1957 by France, West Germany, Italy, Belgium, the Netherlands, and Luxemburg. The EEC found itself facing both internal political issues, as France maneuvered to dominate the Community, and external western European economic competition with the European Free Trade Association consisting of Austria, Denmark, Norway, Sweden, Switzerland, and the UK. By 1973, the UK, Ireland, and Denmark had joined the original six-member EEC; in 1979 the European Monetary System was established to stabilize exchange rates. In 1981, Greece was admitted to (by then) the European Community (EC).

In that same year, 1981, the political locus of power in Greece shifted toward the left-center as the people voted in the Panhellenic Socialist Movement to assume state power. A series of important and long-delayed reforms then began to take place in Greece. For the next decade, Greek economic development remained a struggle and Greek politics were relatively stable compared with the past, though scandals and near-war with Turkey were ever-present. Greece became an increasingly active member of the EC, which itself had grown over the decade of the 1980s. But the growth of the EC in those years has never been fully integrated—neither politically nor economically.

While the Soviet Union did not collapse until 1991, for the EC the 1980s era effectively ended in 1989 when the Berlin Wall fell. This event, and the reintegration of Germany, set into motion massive changes within the EC as Germany was suddenly a much larger political-economic force. Nonetheless, by 1993, the EC had established an economic plan to aid the still struggling Greece and by the end of that year, as the Maastricht Treaty went into effect, the EC became the European Union (EU), and the Eurozone was established. The Maastricht Treaty and its subsequent amendments guiding EU economic policy stipulated that government debt in the EU should never exceed 60% of a nation's gross domestic product (GDP). Between 2001 and 2012, France, Germany, the UK, Ireland, Spain, Cyprus, Greece, Italy, and Portugal each exceeded this limit on at least one occasion, usually for years at a time.[3]

By the time the EU was formed and made operative, and the Eurozone was in place, the reunification of Germany had set into motion massive economic and political shifts that reverberated through the EU and the Eurozone, ultimately setting the stage for the current round of Greek economic austerity and resultant anger. The political-economic foundation upon which the Eurozone was built as of 1993 was unstable—perhaps terminally so. The key factor undermining the Eurozone is that euro policy is governed by the European Central Bank (ECB) that reports to the European Commission, a weak international political apparatus that is made up of all the sovereign states belonging to the EU. Some of these states, such as Britain, do not even use the euro as their currency. Under these circumstances, the ECB can operate relatively autonomously vis-à-vis smaller, less powerful members of the Eurozone (like Greece) locating its source of power in the larger political context of the most powerful members of the European Commission (primarily Germany, Britain, and France) each operating in its own national interests. Coupled with the International Monetary Fund (IMF), the troika of ECB, IMF, and European Commission wields enormous economic power over Greece. The Eurozone remains unstable today with the effects of its instability reverberating from the troika to some of the more peripheral nations that faced the harshest consequences of the 2008 crisis originating in the United States (Birnbaum, 2010a, 2010b; Broome, 2010, 2011; Brown, 2009; Erlanger, Audi, & Calin, 2009; Goldstein & Hillard, 2009; Harvey, 2010; Kaminski, 2010; Krugman, 2009; McDonough, Riech, & Kotz, 2010; Orenstein, 2009; Perry & Hertzberg, 2009; Popov, 2010; Rapley, 2004; Stiglitz, 2010a, 2010b). These peripheral nations included Greece, Cyprus, Italy, Spain, Portugal, and Ireland.

The economic sources of the instability also included vast macroeconomic imbalances with a united Germany, the UK, and France at the power center of the EU where they exercised neoliberal (right-wing, monetarist) economic policies over the Eurozone (Goolsbee, 2012; Habermas, 2012; Harvey, 2011; Laskos & Tsakalotos, 2013; Lazzaro, 2011; McBride & Teeple, 2011; Müller, 2012; Orwall, Enrich, Sonne, & Kowsmann, 2012; Palley, 2011; Peck & Brenner, 2012; Reddy, 2011; Reddy & Granitsas, 2012; Rose, 2011; Thomas, 2012; Weisbrot, 2011; Wolf, 2012). At the periphery we find countries that had been subject to the lingering effects of post-World War II rightist rule or quasi-post-colonial domination by Germany, Britain, or France: most particularly Ireland, Greece, and Cyprus, but also Spain and Portugal. Political forces of instability rest in the fact that each member of the EC has retained its own sovereignty but authority over a number of matters, related especially to trade and travel or population movement, has been increasingly ceded to the European Parliament largely dominated by the UK, Germany, France, and the Benelux countries (Belgium, Netherlands, and Luxembourg). Ironically—especially for Greece—the international political ideology of realism, that advocates for the supremacy of national interest in foreign policy matters, remains in force throughout the European Community; the foundation of realism dates to Thucydides's history of the Peloponnesian War, centered in what is today's Greece (Thucydides, 432 BCE). With realism as a crucial element of nationalism of the more powerful members such that they can influence EC policy for their own ends, Greece and other less powerful members have effectively become pawns in this continuing power play.

The Global Crisis Strikes Iceland and Far Beyond, 2008: From Fear to Anger to Resolve

On October 9, 2008, bank failures and nationalizations in far-away Iceland signaled the first in a series of crisis events that reverberated throughout North America, the European Union, the Eurozone, and with continuing shockwaves, especially in Greece, even as these words are written. The Great Recession, as the crisis came to be known, had its epicenter in the United States, where deregulation had allowed major corporations, such as banks and insurance companies, to operate largely without oversight and with no regard to risk of failure. In this neoliberal environment that led up the crisis, many such companies offered increasingly tenuous financial products. This financialization (McDonough, Reich, & Kotz, 2010) of the global economy saw profits realized through rent-seeking financial manipulation as opposed to productive operation in the unevenly deregulated, but neoliberal global economy. Small countries such as Iceland could and did purchase financial products from the United States with the expectation of high profits, using money invested by both its own trade unions and their retirement funds, as well as investors (large and small, public and private) from England and the Eurozone, seeking high returns. In fact, the international financial networks were so intertwined that one of Iceland's three large banks, Kaupthing, actually owned a British-registered bank, Kaupthing Singer & Friedlander. This environment allowed for quick profits—and quick losses, as well—as both capitalists and fearful, angry middle-class home-owners would learn as the crisis spread throughout the United States and much of Europe, including Greece.

For Iceland, this is where it got sticky: Although, ultimately, the Bank of England backed up the assets of British-owned banks and the Icelandic Central Bank backed up Iceland's three banks (bloated with toxic U.S. assets), the Bank of England refused to support British-registered

Kaupthing Singer & Friedlander (owned by Iceland's Kaupthing bank) as it struggled desperately with angry British depositors, private and municipalities, that were trying to withdraw their funds while the toxic American assets that Kaupthing Singer & Friedlander had invested in were increasingly worthless. Given the politics of realism, the British government, and the Germans as well, placed intense pressure on Iceland to honor the deposits made by British and German nationals and presaged the current pressures on Greece. The demand took place despite the fact that the root problems that caused the crisis were to be found in the United States and other advanced capitalist countries that followed the neoliberal economic ideology of deregulation and financialization. Deregulation and financialization opened the capitalist economy for fraudulent and other corrupt practices that precipitated the crisis. With crisis bearing down on Iceland (Broome, 2011; Capell, 2008; Loftsdóttir, 2010; Thorhallsson, 2010; Villa, 2010), its entire economy was on the brink of collapse. Iceland, small and effectively peripheral to the global economy, was unable to resist Britain's and Germany's demands to make good on their subjects' investments but equally unable to force Americans to make good on their nation's toxic assets.

Icelanders were crushed. From a strongly independent-minded country that had survived 11 centuries with its national self-identity intact (though with some long periods of Danish rule) as well as a strong, active labor movement that had benefitted significantly from Iceland's overindulgence in global financialization, Icelanders were suddenly rendered fearful and angry, but resolved to rebuild a devastated economy. Ultimately, Icelanders paid the unhappy price with loss of values in pensions and unemployment peaking at more than 13% in 2010 (Elliot, 2014), while the Icelandic Consumer Price Index soared from 88.75 in October 2008 to 117.40 as of March 2015 (Federal Reserve Bank of St. Louis, 2015).

Greece and other members of the Eurozone—especially Ireland, Italy, Spain, Portugal, and Cyprus—have also experienced severe consequences of the crisis (Blackstone, Karnitschnig, & Thomson, 2012; Bofinger, Habermas, & Nida-Rümelin, 2012; Bragues, 2012; de Graaf-Zijl & Nolan, 2011; Higgens, & Alderman, 2013; Hill, 2012; Jones, Clark, & Cameron, 2010; Roy, Denzau, & Willett, 2007; Shonfield, 1975; Smith, Fairless, & Perez, 2012; Weisbrot, 2011). Although the causes, especially for Greece, were different from those of Iceland, the effects were much the same. Iceland initiated its entrance into neoliberalism after its banks were privatized in 2000; Greece was initiated into neoliberalism by its membership in the Eurozone. Iceland, despite advice to the contrary from a Nobel Laureate in economics (Stiglitz, 2001), bought hook, line, and sinker into the corrupt neoliberal world of American financialization; Greece (and Cyprus) went along for the Eurozone ride—a rollercoaster ride into a tunnel of greed, with many Greeks still seeing only dark at the end that tunnel.

Before the current economic crisis troubles appeared, Greece saw important economic improvement and a renaissance of sorts in the second half of the 1990s and early 2000s. The new millennium dawned with Greece preparing to host the 2004 Olympics. Although the build-up to the Olympics provided a boost for the Greek economy and reinforced its national self-image, the robustness of the Olympic-charged economic advance was short-lived. Nonetheless, the overall economic impact of the *metapolitefsi* should be acknowledged.

Greece had long been a country more dependent upon agriculture than most other members of the EU and despite American-supplied mechanical equipment from the Cold War period, Greece agriculture remained more characterized by small holders in contrast to other EU nations of the north, especially Germany. By 2008, self-employment in Greek agriculture was 84.6% compared with less than 50% in Germany, Italy, and the UK. Moreover, Greek self-employment, 34.8% overall, was three times that of Germany (Laskos & Tsakalotos, 2013, Table 2.3). Although Greece's GDP is relatively low compared with other members of the EU, GDP per capita has grown markedly since the end of the Civil War: standardized on the 15 member states of the EU, Greece's GDP per capital has grown from just over 40 in 1950 to about 75 in 2007 (Laskos & Tsakalotos, 2013, Figure 2.2). Almost all of this growth took place from 1950–1971 and from 1994–2007. Real GDP growth in Greece outpaced the EU 15 for all periods since 1950 to 2008 except for the 1981–1995 time period (Laskos & Tsakalotos, 2013, Figure 2.1). Finally, with respect to the security of the Greek people, public sector employment was comparable to many EU members, but by 2008, income inequality was among the highest in the EU (Laskos & Tsakalotos, 2013).

Greece's unique political environment since the end of the Civil War, coupled with some problematical economic issues, including a neoliberal environment driving Eurozone monetary policy, has led to practices on the part of the troika that have effectively hamstrung the Greek economy since 2008. First, and Konstandaras alluded to this in his remark quoted previously, Greece never developed a legal-economic apparatus that would foster the kind of social democratic capitalism as realized in most members of the EU. As Laskos and Tsakalotos put it:

> Greece has been overburdened by laws since the nineteenth century, which simply add to the existing legislation without any attempt to simplify the

legal minefield thus created. In this light, most modernizing administrations tried to bypass the public administration altogether, creating a parallel system of political advisors, policy experts and consultants. But instead of providing a breeding ground for new values and more transparent bureaucratic practices, the parallel system was all too easily incorporated into the standard practices of clientelistic politics. (Laskos & Tsakalotos, 2013, p. 53)

Greek clientism, therefore, perpetuated oligarchic political rule; the politicians' names changed but regardless of the regime (the military excepted)—left, right, or center—the dynamic of power rested upon having sufficient clients to support one's political aspirations. But there was a price to be paid for this support and that price was often paid through public sector employment. The world today sees this as corruption and it is easy enough for an outsider to identify it as such. No nation is without its own flavor of corruption; 2008 proved that. But nations, and certainly the troika and its national clients, view corruption each from their own perspective. The corrupt practices of Wall Street that precipitated the crisis could go by with scarcely a word, and certainly no penalties levied by the ECB or the IMF. In the 1990s, Germany went through its own corruption scandal with arms trader Karlheinz Schreiber sentenced to jail for his role in the illegal campaign donations to the Christian Democratic Union (CDU), headed by Chancellor Helmut Kohl, who lost his position as a result. Angela Merkel was to succeed Kohl as party chief, and is at this writing Germany's Chancellor, edging out Kohl's heir apparent Wolfgang Schäuble, who later is reported to have admitted conveying DM 100,000 of Schreiber's corrupt donations to the CDU ("Germany: The scandal that rocked the government of Helmut Kohl," 2010, January 18; Paterson, 1999). Schäuble is at this writing Chancellor Merkel's Finance Minister.

But Greece: The shrill, scolding rhetoric coming from Germany and Britain with ever increasing demands for crippling austerity to address its debt and scandal past, six decades after Germany had destroyed Greece's economy and Britain had re-imposed a dysfunctional and unwanted political apparatus, the demands by the troika placed upon Greece for austerity finally pushed the Greek people to their limits of tolerance. Austerity is a contemporary neoliberal economic approach toward correcting debt and other economic issues in a country. This is associated with the monetarist approach advocated by Milton Friedman, who advised the Pinochet regime in Chile. Monetarists believe that market forces self-correct when the economy bears down on consumers and workers to allow the capitalist class to accumulate capital, reinvest, and begin to rebuild the economy. The other conventional approach derives from the classic liberal theory advocated

by John Maynard Keynes. Keynes argued just the opposite: deficit spending stimulates consumption, which in turn stimulates production and
employment sufficient to then (theoretically) repay the original debt and
that caused by the deficit spending. How do these alternate economic theories relate to anger? When a population is forced into austerity—high
unemployment, diminished services, high taxes, and lower wages—they
get angry. And it is not just the Greeks.

Armin Schfäer and Wolfgang Streeck of Germany's famed Max Planck
Institute for the Study of Societies examined the impact of austerity and
reached some insights that apply beyond Grecian anger. They argue that
"new tensions between the social rights associated with citizenship and
the commercial rights deriving from private ownership of financial assets
evolve not just within national polities but also and increasingly at the
international level" (Streeck & Schäfer, 2013, p. 20). This is certainly one
of the factors that exacerbates the situation facing Greece, as well as other
countries in the south of Europe, such as Spain, that has remained out of
the shadow of negative publicity but remains impecunious by the crisis
(Schäuble, 2015).

Wolfgang Schäuble would likely disagree. His advocacy for the benefits
of austerity in a *New York Times* opinion piece (Schäuble, 2015) cites the
post–World War II German experience of rebuilding an industrial economy. German economic recovery was unprecedented. And it could not
have taken place without severe austerity in a country thoroughly defeated
militarily, economically, politically, emotionally, and demographically.
Today, Germany has the largest economy in the EU and this was no small
feat. But there is more to the story of German austerity than Schäuble tells.
An opinion article is necessarily short, and *it is an opinion* on matters beyond
German austerity, so perhaps Schäuble can be forgiven for a less-than-
nuanced account of German austerity. But when austerity is being forced
upon the Greeks and Germany is being set as an example, we need to set
the record straight. Cruel measures of austerity appeared across industrial
Europe in its recovery from the devastations of World War II, not just Germany. Moreover, austerity did not appear evenly. Immigrant workers, often
Muslims from former European colonies in Central and East Asia, Africa,
and the Caribbean, as well as Turkey, suffered oppressive working conditions, low wages, often squalid living conditions, persecution and discrimination, and diminished civil rights. In all fairness, we need to acknowledge
that some native-born, ethnic Europeans of working-class origins also
suffered from the cruelties of austerity. In Germany, the Turkish and other
gastarbeiters contributed to the German economy from the 1960s onward
and when reunification took place, East German workers traded their Stazi

oppressors for West German capitalists. Ironically, today, the working-class Greek diaspora now reaches into Germany (Angelos, 2015), where austerity lingers on for the non-German population, in particular.

The Crisis Inflamed: Greek Anger Grows

Why is Greece being punished? Among the charges levied against Greece, especially in the aftermath of the onset of the crisis, were budget deficits, corruption (in many forms), and the provision of too much economic security for its population—security that the troika argued Greece could not afford. Greece or Germany; Iceland, Ireland, England, or the United States—oligarchs in each country played the rules for their own personal benefit in a deregulated neoliberal economic environment. With respect to economic security for the population, Greece followed in its own clientist version of the social democratic path established by the former West Germany, The Netherlands, Sweden, and other advanced states in the European north.

When economic crisis materializes, turmoil is set into motion. Typically, we see a cycle of reduced demand for goods coupled with a reduced demand for labor. As this cycle continues, the reduced demand for labor means layoffs and a consequent further reduced demand for goods until such time as the existing stock is exhausted and production begins to return along with employment. Governments usually play some role and, depending upon the prevailing ideology, this role may include significant support for the unemployed. In this crisis, many governments, particularly the United States, ran budget deficits. Deficits are not intended to be handouts to the poor though some unemployment benefits did improve the situation of the workers. Budget deficits have demonstrated a theoretical foundation in Keynesian economics: They constitute counter-cyclical pressure in a crisis period intended to reduce the macroeconomic severity and return the economy to a growth mode sooner. Neoliberal, monetarist policy assumes that market forces will self-adjust and there should be little reason for governmental involvement. For example, the libertarian Cato Institute argues that Greece lacked the competitive structure and open markets needed to realize lasting economic growth (Mitsopoulos & Pelagidis, 2009). As part of the Eurozone, Greece's (and Spain's and Portugal's) competitiveness was eroded by the larger, more industrial economies of the north—Britain, France, Belgium, The Netherlands, and especially a reunited Germany. In fact, Costas Lapavitas and colleagues demonstrate the deleterious economic effects upon Greece in the run-up to, and in the aftermath of, the huge crisis that visited the global capitalist system (Lapavitsas & Kouvélakis,

2012). Eight years after the height of the crisis, Greece is still waiting for the market forces to arrive.

A Crippling Blow: The Troika Strikes Greece, 2010

The market forces have not taken effect in no small part because the medicine prescribed by the troika through the ECB and at the constant urging of German Chancellor Angela Merkel and her Finance Minister Wolfgang Schäuble, in particular, sees the continuing crisis in Greece not as systemic in origin within the global capitalist economy, but as a fault of the Greeks, themselves. The medicine is austerity: Reduce government spending by whatever means necessary without regard to the human consequences for the Greek people.

By 2010, the austerity demanded by the troika was being felt all across an ever-angrier Greece. The *Greek Reporter* announced that medical supplies had become unavailable at the affordable prices found in other Eurozone countries, causing surgery postponements (Theophanides, June 14, 2010). The medical crisis continued into 2011 with doctors attempting to occupy the Ministry of Health (Kourti, 2011) as they were unable to provide suitable care for their patients. Also in 2010, as economic troubles continued to impact the population, in a theme that the neo-Nazi Golden Dawn Party would advocate five years later, the center-right New Democracy challenged the ruling center-left, socialist PASOK party on its plans to make Greek citizenship available to immigrants (Makris, June 30, 2010) following the drowning deaths of 11 men and women believed to be illegal immigrants (Theophanides, June 30, 2010). Six months later, Human Rights Watch urged Greece to provide better conditions for detained illegal immigrants, especially children (Makris, December 6, 2010). Two months later, detained immigrants initiated a hunger strike (Brousou, 2011) thus fueling Golden Dawn political activists. As the ultra-right gained more followers, nominal though some may have been (Theodossopoulos, 2013b), the progressive leftist party, Syriza, also grew from the depleting support for the two left- and right-centrist parties.

At this point, it bears noting that contemporary media reporting on Greek politics rarely mentions the Golden Dawn Party, and for good reason: It is a marginal, ultra-right organization that gains what little publicity it has from disruptive behavior and outlandish claims. Like such far-right organizations, it does gain some following when conditions are at the worst. It is no more a viable political force in Greece today than is the Nazi Party in Germany. On the other hand, international media repeatedly refer to

Syriza as a "far left" party. It is not. It represents the progressive left—not the center-left, a legacy of British meddling in Greek politics six decades ago; it is a coalition that does include some "far left" elements but as the deadline for this chapter rapidly approaches, under the leadership of Alexis Tsipres, Syriza is revealing itself as a much more pragmatic organization than is usually acknowledged.

The Crisis Unfolds: Greece Strikes Back, 2015

The austerity measures demanded by the troika resulted in massive unemployment, cuts in pensions, higher and higher taxes, and cuts in services, and they continued year after year without regard to the devastating impact upon the Greek people. Unemployed residents of Athens returned to their families in the hinterland. Each round of further austerity actions resulted in some incremental partial "bail-out" money to assist the Greek government in meeting its debts that sometimes came due on a weekly basis. Governments fell. In anger and desperation, Greeks protested repeatedly, sometimes with violent outbursts. Finally, in January 2015, the political landscape of Greece shifted in a direction that had not been seen since the Nazi occupiers were driven out in 1944.

The January 2015 election transcended the legacy of Greek clientism and resulted in a political widening of the electorate: the middle-ground center-right, center-left dynamic that had characterized Greek politics in the post-*metapolitefsi* period gave way to the extreme right and progressive left of, respectively the Golden Dawn and Syriza parties. Syriza was able to form a progressive leftist government committed to both ending austerity but remaining in the Eurozone. But this was not the image of Syriza as seen by Germany and the troika, nor the media. The following month a leftist newspaper published satire picturing Schäuble as a Nazi. This banal attempt at humor fed into Greek anger about long-standing grievances against the Third Reich and the claims that Germany still owes Greece significant sums of money. Moreover, Greece's flamboyant new Finance Minister, economist Yanis Varoufakis, by his own account (Lambert, 2015), was unable to successfully negotiate with Schäuble and other finance ministers largely, I would argue, due to the ideological, cross-cultural, and intergenerational misunderstandings that have continued to fuel interpersonal anger and its counter-productive effects.

In July 2015, Greek Prime Minister Alexis Tsipres called for a referendum by the Greek people on austerity measures demanded by the troika. The Greek people voted overwhelming against more austerity and with this mandate Tsipres returned to the negotiation EU table facing even tougher terms of austerity but agreeing to them, shedding some of the leftist elements in the party as well as his Finance Minister. In so doing, Tsipres demonstrated two things: He remains in control and he is a pragmatist. Few expect the Greeks to succeed under the conditions of austerity they face at this writing. But Tsipres may have opened the door to ultimate success.

The long Cold War has left its imprint upon the minds and hearts of many people. For those on the right who advocate for neoliberal solutions to the continuing crisis of capitalism, the "left" is always "far left," the bugaboo and cause of the problems faced in the economy. Having "won" the Cold War, the right feels pride at its accomplishment and vindicated with respect to any responsibility for the crisis. But the Cold War was more than an economic struggle; more deeply, it was a fear-laden emotional experience for several generations of people who were raised in the shadow of the mushroom cloud of possible nuclear annihilation. We understand that and we also understand how some folks may have trouble distancing themselves from that fear, having replaced it with anger and accusations of culpability against the "far left." But the world needs to move beyond this.

The Angry Crisis in Greece: Toward a Resolution

To analyze the "anger" that seems to have characterized the Greek populace since 2008, we ask: Is this anger embedded in Greek culture following five centuries of foreign domination and interference? Or is there another explanation for a Greek reaction to the crisis that makes the responses by Iceland, Ireland, Italy, Spain, Portugal, and Cyprus seem tame by comparison?

The easy answer, the answer that seems to resonate with many Greeks as well as the power structure of the European Union, is that the Greeks are corrupt and too lazy to work—they want handouts from the EU. Konstandaras said it more nicely (above) but this is a blame game that cuts in more ways than one. The Greeks, and others, would argue further that the real problem is the troika, Wolfgang Schäuble, and Angela Merkel. Good arguments could be made in both directions and this is what fuels that anger.

One answer captures some sentiments of each. Theodossopoulos argues that we must look into anger at the community level. Here, anger may have a useful purpose in directing attention away from the peripheral trajectory toward "a sense of discursive empowerment against their perceived peripheralization" (2013a, p. 200). In an entirely different context but one that may have important implications for this case, T. H. Hall argues that diplomacy anger (that we interpret here as the Schäuble/Merkel/troika tirades against Greece) "combines a punitive response with demands against further provocations" (Hall, 2011, p. 554). Perhaps the Greeks and the troika should set aside the sense of past wrongs and get on with the business of building an economy that meets the needs of all parties.

Perhaps it is time for the pragmatists in Germany to reach out to Greece, as Tsipres has done. Varoufakis is gone; maybe Schäuble's time has come, as well. A Merkel-Tsipres dialogue that begins to build trust and break down the tall barriers of ideology, anger, and out-sized personalities could lead to an economic solution to the Greek debt crisis. It would not solve the structural political issues that plague the EU and Eurozone. And it certainly will not resolve the contradictions of capitalism.[4] But Nicos Christodoulakis (2014) argues that the Nazi "loans" forced upon the Bank of Greece during World War II can, and should be, repaid. The current value of that debt, Christodoulakis claims, is approximately what Greece now owes Germany for bailout loans—about €15 billion. It will not fully meet any party's expectations, but it is a compromise; it would help settle Germany's burden from its hideous Nazi history, and it may position Greece with some breathing space to build an economy for the 21st century.

Afterword

Since this chapter was first written, a sea change has overtaken Europe (and the United States) driving the Greek crisis from the limelight of public attention into the shadows. The monetarist Euro economy remains stagnant and a fearful and angry Britain has voted to leave the EU. The refugees from fighting in Syria and Africa that Greece once faced seemingly alone—Turkey and Italy also faced them—have swept across Europe from south and east to north and west to an increasingly unsettled and angry Europe. Coupled with repeated Islamist-inspired terrorist attacks, the latest European crisis has fueled the appeal of rightist, angry xenophobic parties in Britain, Europe, and the United States. Compounding this situation is now the exit from the EU of Britain and the pending decision on the admission of Turkey to the EC. Turkey's President Recep Tayyip Erdogan has become more autocratic, navigating the troubled waters of fighting in neighboring Syria, a flood of refugees making its way through Turkey to Europe, angry internal dissent, and finally, in a distraction from the memory of the Third Reich's more recent and more enormous atrocities, Angela Merkel feeds into Europe's growing Islamophobia with a reminder of the Armenian Genocide carried out by the Ottoman Turks one hundred years ago.

But for Greece, little has changed.

Notes

1. The Eurozone that emerged in 1993 is composed of countries that use the euro as their common national currency. Greece gave up the drachma to become a member of the Eurozone.

2. This writer vividly recalls observing in 1971 the striking difference between the rural economies of southern Yugoslavia, where peasants still cleared rocks from the land by hand, and northern Greece, where farmers were equipped with new Ford tractors.

3. See Figure 6.3. Select European and Icelandic government debt as a percent of GDP, 2001–2102 (Elliott, 2014).

4. I have argued elsewhere that capitalism represents the root cause of this and many other crises (Elliott, 2014).

References

Angelos, J. (2015, July 28). Greece's relentless exodus. *The New York Times.* Retrieved from http://www.nytimes.com

Birnbaum, N. (2010a). The economic crisis, U.S. progressivism, and West European socialism and social democracy. *Social Europe: The Journal of the European Left, 5*(1), 5–10.

Birnbaum, N. (2010b). Is social democracy dead? The crisis of capitalism in Europe. *New Labor Forum (Murphy Institute), 19*(1), 24–31.

Blackstone, B., Karnitschnig, M., & Thomson, R. (2012, June 27). Optimism on Europe doesn't add up. *Wall Street Journal—Eastern Edition*, p. C1.

Bofinger, P., Habermas, J., & Nida-Rümelin, J. (2012). The case for a change of course in European policy. *Social Europe: The Journal of the European Left, 7*(1), 5–8.

Bragues, G. (2012). Portugal's plight: The role of social democracy. *Independent Review, 16*(3), 325–349.

Broome, A. (2010). The International Monetary Fund, crisis management and the credit crunch. *Australian Journal of International Affairs, 64*(1), 37–54.

Broome, A. (2011). Negotiating crisis: The IMF and disaster capitalism in small states. *Round Table, 100*(413), 155–167.

Brousou, A. (2011, March 8). Officials ask sick strikers to accept medical aid. *Greek Reporter.* Retrieved from http://greece.greekreporter.com

Brown, B. E. (2009). The fiscal crisis: Transatlantic misunderstandings. *American Foreign Policy Interests, 31*(5), 313–324.

Capell, K. (2008, October 9). The stunning collapse of Iceland. *Bloomberg Business Week*. Retrieved from http://www.nbcnews.com/id/27104617/ns/business -us_business/t/stunning-collapse-iceland/#.V2AXmfkguCg

Christodoulakis, N. (2014). *Germany's war debt to Greece: A burden unsettled*. London, UK: Palgrave Macmillan.

de Graaf-Zijl, M., & Nolan, B. (2011). Household joblessness and its impact on poverty and deprivation in Europe. *Journal of European Social Policy, 21*(5), 413–431.

Delivanis, D. (1950). Greek attempts of postwar monetary rehabilitation. *Ekonomisk Tidskrift, 52*(2), 84–97.

Dernburg, H. J. (1954). Germany's external economic position. *The American Economic Review, 44*(4), 530–558.

Elliott, D. L. (2014). The impact of the global capitalist crisis on the Eurozone. In B. Berberoglu (Ed.), *The global capitalist crisis and its aftermath* (Chapter 6, pp. 139–158). London, UK: Ashgate Publishing.

Erlanger, S., Audi, N., & Calin, G. (2009, June 8). Economic crisis pits the European Union against its members. *New York Times*, p. A1.

Federal Reserve Bank of St. Louis. (2015). Consumer Price Index: Total all items for Iceland©. Retrieved from https://research.stlouisfed.org/fred2/series /CPALTT01ISQ659N

A fifth bitter lemon. *Economist, 403*(8791), 74.

Germany: The scandal that rocked the government of Helmut Kohl. (2010, January 18). *Deutsche Welle (DW)*. Retrieved from http://dw.com/p/LYcA

Goldstein, J. P., & Hillard. M. G. (Eds.). (2009). *Heterodox macroeconomics: Keynes, Marx and globalization*. London, UK and New York, NY: Routledge.

Goolsbee, A. (May 30, 2012). A fiscal union won't fix the Euro crisis. *Wall Street Journal—Eastern Edition, 259*(125), p. A13.

Habermas, J. (2012). *The crisis of the European Union: A response* [in English]. (C. Ciaran, Trans.) Cambridge, UK: Polity.

Hall, T. H. (2011). We will not swallow this bitter fruit: Theorizing a diplomacy of anger. *Security Studies, 20*(4), 521–555.

Harvey, D. (2010). *The enigma of capital: And the crises of capitalism*. Oxford, UK and New York, NY: Oxford University Press.

Harvey, D. (2011). Roepke lecture in economic geography: Crises, geographic disruptions and the uneven development of political responses. *Economic Geography, 87*(1), 1–22.

Higgens, A., & Alderman, L. (2013, March 26). Europeans planted seeds of crisis in Cyprus. *The New York Times*. Retrieved from http://www.nytimes .com (A version of this article appears in print on March 27, 2013, on page A4.)

Hill, D. (2012). Immiseration capitalism, activism and education: Resistance, revolt and revenge. *Journal for Critical Education Policy Studies, 10*(2), 1–53.

Jones, A., Clark, J., & Cameron, A. (2010). The global economic crisis and the cohesion of Europe. *Eurasian Geography and Economics, 51*(1), 35–51.

Kaminski, M. (2010). Europe's other crisis. *Wall Street Journal—Eastern Edition, 255*(100), A15.

Konstandaras, N. (2014, July 27). Greece's watershed year. *The New York Times.* Retrieved from http://www.nytimes.com

Kourti, M. (2011, May 7). Demonstrating doctors prevented from entering Ministry of Health by riot police. *Greek Reporter.* Retrieved from http://greece.greekreporter.com

Krugman, P. R. (2009). *The return of depression economics and the crisis of 2008.* New York, NY: W.W. Norton & Company.

Lambert, H. (2015, July 13). Yanis Varoufakis full transcript: Our battle to save Greece. *The New Statesman* [Podcast transcript]. Retrieved from http://www.newstatesman.com

Lapavitsas, C., & Kouvélakis, E. (2012). *Crisis in the Eurozone.* London, UK and New York, NY: Verso.

Laskos, C., & Tsakalotos, E. (2013). *Crucible of resistance: Greece, the Eurozone and the world economic crisis.* London, UK: Pluto Press.

Lazzaro, J. (2011, October 18). Nouriel "Dr. Doom" Rabini: Karl Marx was right—unregulated capitalism leads to crises. *International Business Times.* Retrieved from http://www.ibtimes.com/nouriel-dr-doom-roubini-karl-marx-was-right-unregulated-capitalism-leads-crises-212340

Loftsdóttir, K. (2010). The loss of innocence: The Icelandic financial crisis and colonial past. *Anthropology Today, 26*(6), 9–13.

Makris, A. (2010, June 30). ND leader Samaras on migration issues. *Greek Reporter.* Retrieved from http://greece.greekreporter.com

Makris, A. (2010, December 6). Human rights watch calls on Greece to improve migrant conditions. *Greek Reporter.* Retrieved from http://greece.greekreporter.com

McBride, S., & Teeple, G. (2011). *Relations of global power: Neoliberal order and disorder.* Toronto, CA: University of Toronto Press.

McDonough, T., Reich, M., & Kotz, D. M. (2010). *Contemporary capitalism and its crises: Social structure of accumulation theory for the 21st century.* Cambridge, UK and New York, NY: Cambridge University Press.

Metapolitefsi. (n.d.) *HellenicaWorld.com* [Web site]. Retrieved from http://www.hellenicaworld.com/Greece/History/en/Metapolitefsi.html

Mitsopoulos, M., & Pelagidis, T. (2009). Vikings in Greece: Kleptocratic interest groups in a closed, rent-seeking economy. *CATO Journal, 29*(3), 399–416.

Müller, J. (2012). Europe's perfect storm. *Dissent, 59*(4), 47–53.

Orenstein, M. A. (2009).What happened in East European (political) economies? A balance sheet for neoliberal reform. *East European Politics and Societies, 23*(4), 479–490.

Orwall, B., Enrich, D., Sonne, P., & Kowsmann, P. (2012, August 11). Economic crisis now an Olympic one. *Wall Street Journal—Eastern Edition, 259*(35), p. A13.

Palley, T. I. (2011). *From financial crisis to stagnation: The great recession, the destruction of shared prosperity, and the role of economics.* Cambridge, UK and New York, NY: Cambridge University Press.

Paterson, T. (1999, November 27). Kohl accused of corruption. *The Guardian.* Retrieved from http://www.theguardian.com

Peck, J., Theodore, N., & Brenner, N. (2012). Neoliberalism resurgent? Market rule after the great recession. *South Atlantic Quarterly, 111*(2), 265–288.

Perry, J., & Hertzberg, D. (2009, January 30). Europe basks as U.S.-style capitalism draws fire. *Wall Street Journal—Eastern Edition, 253*(24), p. A6.

Popov, Đ. (2010). European Union and world economic crisis. (English). *Proceedings of Novi Sad Faculty of Law, 44*(2), 7–22.

Rapley, J. (2004). *Globalization and inequality: Neoliberalism's downward spiral.* Boulder, CO.: Lynne Rienner.

Reddy, S. (2011, July 20). IMF warns Euro-zone crisis risks global spillover. *Wall Street Journal—Eastern Edition, 258*(16), p. A12.

Reddy, S., & Granitsas. A. (2012, May 29). U.S. seeks action on Europe crisis. *Wall Street Journal—Eastern Edition, 259*(125), p. A9.

Rose, R. (2011). Micro-economic responses to a macro-economic crisis: A pan-European perspective. *Journal of Communist Studies and Transition Politics, 27*(3–4), 364–384.

Roy, R. K., Denzau, A., & Willett, T. D. (2007). *Neoliberalism: National and regional experiments with global ideas.* London, UK and New York, NY: Routledge.

Schäuble, W. (2015, April 15). Wolfgang Schäuble on German priorities and Euro-zone myths. *The New York Times.* Retrieved from http://www.nytimes.com/

Shonfield, A. (1975). Italy and its partners: A case study in international crisis management. *International Affairs, 51*(1), 1–2.

Smith, G. T., Fairless, T., & Perez, S. (2012, July 24). Spanish economy slides as Germany's sputters. *Wall Street Journal—Eastern Edition, 259*(19), p. A10.

Stiglitz, J. E. (2001). Monetary and exchange rate policies in small open economies: The case of Iceland. *Working Papers No. 15, Central Bank of Iceland.* Retrieved from www.cb.is/uploads/files/WP-15.pdf

Stiglitz, J. E. (2010a). *Freefall: America, free markets, and the sinking of the world economy.* New York, NY: W. W. Norton.

Stiglitz, J. (2010b). *The Stiglitz report: Reforming the international monetary and financial systems in the wake of the global crisis.* New York, NY: The New Press.

Streeck, W., & Schäfer, A. (2013). *Politics in the age of austerity.* Cambridge, UK: Polity.

Theodossopoulos, D. (2013a). Infuriated with the infuriated? Blaming tactics and discontent about the Greek financial crisis. *Current Anthropology, 54*(2), 200–221.

Theodossopoulos, D. (2013b). Supporting a party that you don't entirely support. *Suomen Antropologi: Journal of the Finnish Anthropological Society, 38*(1), 109–111.

Theophanides, I. (2010, June 14). Medical surgeries are postponed. *Greek Reporter.* Retrieved from http://greece.greekreporter.com

Theophanides, I. (2010, June 30). 11 bodies, believed illegal migrants, wash up on Evros river banks. *Greek Reporter.* Retrieved from http://greece.greek reporter.com

Thomas, L., Jr. (2012). Economic thinkers try to solve the euro puzzle. *The New York Times.* Retrieved from http://nyti.ms/1Uf2d7b (A version of this article appears in print on August 1, 2012, on page B1 of the New York edition with the headline: Pondering the Euro Puzzle.)

Thorhallsson, B. (2010). The corporatist model and its value in understanding small European states in the neo-liberal world of the twenty-first century: The case of Iceland. *European Political Science, 9*(3), 375–386.

Tripartite commission on German debts. (1952). *International Organization, 6*(2), 341–342.

Villa, E. (2010). The cold shoulder. *Harvard International Review, 31*(4), 9–10.

Weisbrot, M. (2011). Solving the Euro crisis. *Nation, 292*(23), 6.

Wolf, M. (2012). Confronting the Eurozone crisis. *Brown Journal of World Affairs, 18*(2), 11–16.

Zarrilli, L. (2011). Iceland and the crisis: Territory, Europe, identity. *Romanian Review on Political Geography / Revista Română Geografie Politica, 13*(1), 5–15.

CHAPTER SIXTEEN

Environmental Conflict, Collective Anger, and Resolution: Strategies in the Niger Delta Conflict

Olakunle M. Folami and Taiwo A. Olaiya

Anger is a psycho-social activity affecting human behavior (Diamond, 2014). Anger produces a negative outcome of human action, which in the first place, expresses the person's soul and, secondly, expresses in a destructive manner. Anger could be expressed at either the individual or collective level. Individual anger could lead to self-destruction, or destruction of others; it could, as well, result in mutual destruction. Anger has led individuals to commit crime, suicide, terrorism, arson, murder, and other unwholesome behaviors. As a result of anger, many individuals have been jailed, sentenced to death, banished, or put in a gulag. Collective anger could be expressed by members of a community, group, family, or country.

Collective anger has led to inter-family feuds, intra/inter-community/ group crises, and international conflict. The sources of anger are multifarious. Anger could be a result of intolerance, frustration, hatred, discrimination, inequality, domination, imposition, or segregation. Angry feelings may lead to explosion when things get too much. For example, anger led

Adolf Hitler to declare war against the Jews, which eventually led to World War II (Diamond, 2014). The terrorists' attack on the West and targeting American interests such as foreign embassies, nationalities, and establishments can be described as an outcome of a sectarian anger against the free society and individual freedom that the American nation represents (Diamond, 2014). The same anger stimulates Boko Haram to declare war on northeastern Nigeria (Marquand, 2014), and the Niger Delta militants' conflict in southern Nigeria (Afotan & Ojakorotu, 2009). It is natural for anger to occur both at an individual and a collective level, but the inability to resolve anger is undesirable. Anger could be curtailed by expressing oneself, finding ways of calming down or by dealing with the roots of the anger.

The focus of this chapter, however, is on collective anger among the Niger Delta inhabitants and methods used to address the anger. The chapter examines the sources of anger in the Niger Delta and how anger led to the Niger Delta conflict. It also examines how Niger Delta anger was resolved. We will discuss the origin of the Niger Delta conflict before situating it within the general theory of anger, and conclusions will be drawn as to appropriate ways of dealing with anger.

Roots of Niger Delta Anger

The Niger Delta is located in the southern part of Nigeria. The region is homogeneous in socio-cultural and religious terms. The Niger Delta is composed of nine states out of the 36 states that form the Federal Republic of Nigeria. The nine states are Abia, AkwaIbom, Bayelsa, Cross River, Delta, Edo, Ondo, Imo, and River State. Numerous ethnic groups live in the region, such as Ijaw, Urhobo, Ilaje, Itsekiri, Edo, Isoko, Ibibio, Ikwere, Ogoni, and other minority groups (Niger Delta Professionals for Development, 2011). The nine states are rich in oil and mineral deposits and produce two-thirds of the nation's gross national income. Despite abundant human and natural resources in the region, the majority of its inhabitants live with attendant poverty (Ikejiaku, 2009; Nisirimovu, 2000).

Anger in the Niger Delta conflict dates back to 1957 and primarily concerns the exploration and exploitation of oil in the region by multinational oil companies such as Shell, Chevron, Total Fina Elf, Mobil and a host of others (Tamuno & Edoumiekumo, 2012). Today, inhabitants of the region have been left with damaged farmlands and polluted rivers with no electricity, potable drinking water, or other basic social amenities. People in many of the oil-bearing communities live in desperate conditions, often alongside the high-tech and modern facilities of the multinational companies (Oviasuyi & Uwadiae, 2010). Oil-watch (2002) reports that anger led to conflict in the Niger Delta as a result of environmental degradation by the multinational oil companies and, also, human rights abuses and apathy by both multinational oil and gas companies and the federal government. The roots of the Niger Delta conflict can be understood from three different but interwoven and interrelated perspectives: (1) environmental degradation; (2) marginalization; and, (3) socio-economic rights abuses.

Environmental Degradation and Anger

The highly technological oil processing activities of oil and gas companies have untold effects on the inhabitants and on the environment. Understanding of the socio-technological nature of these activities is necessary to fully grasp their impact on the Niger Delta environment and how this related to anger. Oil exploration and exploitation in the Niger Delta led to environmental abuses, which take the forms of oil spillage, land degradation, gas flaring, loss of bio-diversity, and air and water pollution (Torulagha, 2003). Oil exploration can destroy farmlands, kill aquatic animals and fish, destroy farm products, cause disease, and contribute to climate change (Ite, Ibok, Ite, & Petters, 2013). These side effects of oil production anger Niger Delta inhabitants because they destroy their environment. The unwillingness of the oil companies to follow regulations that attempt to manage the impact of oil production on the environment also contributes to environmental degradation in the Niger Delta. Offu (2013) notes, for example, that the Shell Oil Company failed to carry out an Environmental Impact Assessment (EIA) and did not seek the opinion of members of the community before proceeding on environmentally hostile construction of oil pipelines in Opolo and other areas in the Gbaran clan area. In a study carried out by Dadiowei, the inhabitants of the region expressed their anger on the operation of multinational oil companies in the region this way:

> If Shell had consulted us, we would have educated them on the nature of our land. They call us illiterate even on matters over our environment. We would have told them where and how to put bridges or culverts and thus avoid this catastrophe . . . they have destroyed the habitat of our land, water and air. Our fish, our animals, our forests and our farmlands have all been destroyed. Does it mean that oil and gas companies do not know what is right or wrong? (Dadiowei, 2003, p. 11)

Dadiowei (2003) claims that misplacement of culverts on rivers in Gbaran resulted in flooding that washed away 10 communities in the area. According to Okoro and Nnaji (2012) multinational oil companies awarded construction to amateur contractors who lacked the local knowledge. They said that most of the bridges constructed by these contractors in the Warri west local government area have led to degradation and flooding of farmlands. The impact of oil exploration by the multinational oil companies on the Niger Delta environment can be further understood by looking at specific activities such as oil spillage, gas flaring, and land degradation and how these contribute to anger in the region.

Oil Spillage

Oil spillage is a major environmental problem affecting people of the Niger Delta. The inhabitants of the Niger Delta have become frustrated because oil spills have destroyed their environment. Frustration sets in when the inhabitants of the region found it almost impossible to challenge the oil spills in the local courts because of the existing law that provides a "proximate clause" on issues related to oil spills; for example, under Nigerian law, an oil company in principle is not liable for oil pollution damage caused by third-party sabotage. Most times, the frustration led to aggression (Prelogar & Bekker, 2013). According to Porter and Fittipaldi (1998), oil spillage results from a variety of factors, such as blow-outs, equipment failure, burst or rupture of flow-lines and pipelines, corrosion of flow-lines and pipelines, overpressure, over-flow (tanks), valve failure, operator and maintenance errors, engineering errors, sand cut (erosion), avoidable accidents, and sabotage. Nwilo and Badejo (2005) claim that in the Niger Delta between 1976 and 1998, a total of 5,724 oil spillage incidences were recorded, which included approximately 2,571,133 barrels of oil. Kashi and Watts (2008) say that oil spillages due to oil tanker accidents in Nigeria stand at 50%; 28% of oil spills are due to corrosion, 11% to sabotage, and 11% due to oil production operations. Some spillage is due to accidents as noted, but others occur as a result of carelessness during oil production operations and movement of crude oil from the rigs to the discharging ports. Only 1% of oil spills are due to engineering drills, inability to effectively control oil wells, failure of machines, and inadequate care in loading and unloading oil vessels. The quantity of oil spills always led to anger among the inhabitants of the Niger Delta region (Torulagha, 2003). Miriki (2003) highlighted the consequences of oil spills from pipelines belonging to the Shell Petroleum Development Company (SPDC) in the Karama community, Okordia/Zarama Local Government Area, Bayelsa State on the environment. This major oil spill heavily contaminated marine shorelines, causing severe ecological damage to the near-shore communities such as diseases, infertile soil, and water and air pollution.

The ecological effects of oil spills on the environment are numerous. Oil spills destroy plants and animals; if settled on the beaches, oil destroys soil organisms and marine animals such as fish and crustaceans (Aworawo, 2000). Oil spills endanger fish hatcheries in coastal waters and contaminate edible fish, and are capable of poisoning algae, disrupting major food chains, and decreasing seafood availability (Jereoma, 2001). They can also coat birds, damaging feathers and leading to the extinction of some species. Oil spillage on water surfaces also interferes with gaseous interchanges at the sea surface and diminishes the oxygen level (Porter & Fittipaldi, 1998). According to Ozoigbo and Chukuezi (2011), attempts to clean oil spills with the use of oil dispersants, which have serious toxic effects, could affect plankton, thereby poisoning marine animals. This could also lead to food poisoning and loss of lives (Barikor-Wiwa, 1997). Another factor that makes the inhabitants of the Niger Delta angry is fire outbreak from oil spills. Okoro and Nnaji (2012) also note that sudden fires from an oil spill are a common occurrence in the Niger Delta. It has led to the destruction of many villages. Loss of lives due to oil spillage occurred in Jesse in October 1998. This was caused by an outbreak of fire that was sparked off from an oil pipeline that was leaking fuel. This resulted in the death of over 1,000 people; a further 1,000 people were terribly burned and many were left homeless. According to Ihonvbare (2000) oil spillage can also lead to loss of income for the government. The oil spill must be followed by clean-up of the environment. The government spends massively to clean oil spills because when spilled, oil usually disperses by the combined action of tides, wind, and currents. The oil, therefore, spreads into a thin film, dissipates in water, and undergoes photochemical oxidation. Most often, the cleaning of oil spills was not done at all, neither by the government nor oil companies. The inhabitants of the Niger Delta were often frustrated by the inaction of the government to protect the environment. As noted above, the frustration has led to various court actions against the multinational oil companies (Prelogar & Bekker, 2013). The inability to get a conviction for the multinational oil companies' oil spills also led to frustration and this was mostly expressed in collective anger through destruction of oil installations, and kidnapping and killing of oil workers. Another factor is continuous gas flaring in the region. Afotan and Ojakorotu (2009) say that unceasing gas flaring by the multinational oil companies in the Niger Delta has frustrated the inhabitants to the extent of waging war against government and multinational interests, including attacks on oil wells and oil workers.

Gas Flaring

Gas flaring generally is the cheapest way by which oil companies can separate unwanted gas substances mixed with the crude oil, but it also the most environmentally destructive method (Egwurugwu & Nwafor, 2013). Gas flaring pollutes the air and suppresses plant growth close to the flaring points. It has potentially hazardous environmental effects on people, animals, and plants. In cassava cultivation, for example, there is a decrease in length, weight, starch, protein, and ascorbic acid (Vitamin C) content of this major staple food (Odjugo, 2007). Orogun (2009) notes that gas flares also contain widely recognized toxins, such as benzene, which pollutes the air. Local people complain of respiratory problems such as asthma and bronchitis. According to the U.S. Environmental Protection Agency (EPA), gas flares in Nigeria contribute to acid rain and villagers complain that the rain corrodes buildings. Ajugwo (2013) highlights how the particles from the flares fill the air, covering everything with soot. The inhabitants of the region live and work alongside gas flares without protection. The roaring noise and intense heat from the gas flare usually angers the people. In addition, it is ironic to note that people in this region rely on wood and candles for energy, in spite of abundant availability of gas (Action, 2002).

A United Nations Development Programme report (2013) noted that by 2020, flaring in Nigeria will have contributed more greenhouse gases to the earth's atmosphere than all other sources in sub-Saharan Africa combined. According to Onwumere (2013), the impact of gas flaring on climate change is a serious one. The region has already begun to feel its impact on food security, high temperatures, and increasing risk of diseases, as well as the rising costs of extreme weather (Ologunorisa, 2001). Over 3.5 billion standard cubic feet (scf) of associated gas was produced in 2010, of which more than 70% was burned off, that is, flared (Das, 2014). Proportionately, around 2 billion scf of gas is flared daily in Nigeria. This is equal to about 25% of the UK's total gas consumption in a year. Gas flaring represents an annual economic loss to the country of about U.S. $2.5 billion (Human Rights Watch, 1999; Leahey, Preston, & Strosher, 2001). The higher the demand for global oil production, the higher the propensity of oil companies in Nigeria to become the world's biggest gas flamers. In contrast to this approach, in Western Europe, 99% of associated gas is used or re-injected into the ground; but in Nigeria, despite regulations introduced more than 20 years ago to outlaw the practice, most associated gas is flared (Environmental Rights Action/Friends of the Earth Nigeria, 2005). President Olusegun Obasanjo promised that gas flare agreements with multinational oil companies would come into effect by 2008. This has still not occurred (Obi, 2011). Like oil spills, the consequences of oil flare on the inhabitants of the Niger Delta, on the health environment and economic activities, were the sources of anger. Also, the inability to ensure that oil companies follow rules and regulations on oil production frustrated most inhabitants of the region. Emotional reactions were often expressed in terms of conflict. The frustration experienced by the inhabitants of the Niger Delta was always expressed in anger because they are emotionally attached the environment. The environment provides them their daily needs. They realized the impact of continuous environmental abuses by the multinational oil companies on collective consciousness and worked together to destroy the oil companies' oil wells and installations before they destroyed them (Odjugo, 2007).

Land Degradation

Land degradation and soil fertility loss compounded the Niger Delta inhabitants' access to only a limited portion of land for agriculture in the area. The activities of oil and gas companies have led to severe and excessive flooding of forest and farmlands, destroying crops and trees. The continuous impact on farmlands by oil and gas companies reduces soil fertility and nutrients, the consequence of which is famine, a dearth of food crops and other forest products, as well as the reduction in game and wildlife. Deforestation poses additional problems. Most of the Niger Delta swamp and mangrove forest have been destroyed. A weak and polluted land cannot sustain deep-rooted trees and other commercial trees. Communities that depend on the forest for sustenance complain of deforestation and climate change (Jereoma, 2001). Land degradation by the activities of the multinational oil companies has also led to the blockade of access routes to other neighboring clans. Dadiowei (2003) highlights that before the Shell Oil Company discovered oil at Gbaran, traveling from Gbaran to the Ekpetiame, Epie, and Atissa clans was easy, as there were shortcuts by land, lakes, creeks, and swamp pools. Now the construction of the access roads to Shell facilities has blocked these access routes and balkanized clans of the same ancestral lineage. Limited access to land as a result of land appropriation by the multinational oil companies, coupled with flooding and destruction of the inhabitants' means of livelihood, resulted in frustration. The frustration is compounded by emotional neglect by the government and multinational oil companies. The frustration led to destruction, killing, kidnapping, and war with the government's military joint task force (JTF) (Jereoma, 2001).

Marginalization and Anger

Niger Delta inhabitants are short-changed in the nation's political-economic arrangements. Marginalization of Niger Delta inhabitants in the political and economic arrangements in the region has affected the region's development. Enemugwem (2009) notes that in 1957, the issue of marginalization and underdevelopment of the Niger Delta was discussed toward the end of colonial rule in Nigeria before oil became a factor in national politics. The underdevelopment of the region led to the establishment of the Henry Willink Commission by the colonial government. In 1957, the commission inquired as to the minority groups' concerns and attempted to allay their fears. The commission recommended, among other things, that the Niger Delta region be treated as a special area for development. In the 1960s, the commission's recommendations led to the creation of the Niger Delta Development Board (NDDB) to address the development issues in the region. Lack of funds and political turmoil marked its operations (Enemugwem, 2009). The same fate befell the development of the Niger Delta in 1976 when 11 river basin authorities were created in the country, and the Niger Delta River Basin Authority (NDRBA) was deliberately starved of funds because of the fear that such funds may be diverted to sponsor unrest in the region (Nnoli, 1980). In 1992, the Oil Mineral Producing Area Development Commission was also created (OMPADEC), and in 2000, the Niger Delta Development Commission (NDDC). They were all created for the socio-economic development of the Niger Delta region. Okpongkpong (2003) notes that the initiatives generally failed due to ethnic politics in the country, and the Niger Delta indigenes were not favored in occupying sensitive positions in most of these organizations. It should be noted that ethnic politics is associated with oil exploration and exploitation. Pavšič (2012) says many Niger Delta indigenes lack education; they could not occupy positions in the multinational oil companies and in government.

However, the oil revenue sharing formula was a subject of anger even before Nigerian independence. According to Olukoshi and Agbu (1996), the Mineral Ordinance of 1914 (section 1) stated that the entire property and control of all minerals on the land, and under the rivers, streams, and water courses in Nigeria, is and shall be vested in the colonial power. This language was replicated in the Nigerian Independence Constitution of 1960. The ordinance provides that every piece of land within the geographical entity called Nigeria belongs to the federal government of Nigeria and must be made available for use whenever a need arises. The law removes control over the land and its resources from the Niger Delta inhabitants. Integrated Regional Information Network (2005) notes that the oil revenue sharing formula in the pre-independence era, when the price of oil was low, was far better than the modern era, when the price was highly appreciated. In 1958, 50% of oil derivation was allotted to each state in the region; in 1968 it was reduced to 10%. The status quo was maintained until 1999, when it was increased to 13%. Attempts to increase it beyond 13% were rebuffed by the legislators from the northern part of Nigeria. The argument was that the oil belongs to the entire country but the land belongs to the indigenes of the Niger Delta (Iyobhebhe, 2005). This position is buttressed by the existing Land Use Act, which was inherited from the colonial masters (Mbanefo & Egwaikhide, 1998). To compound the problems of the Niger Delta inhabitants, many leaders have also called for an end to the derivation formula. The Governor of the Central Bank of Nigeria, Sanusi Lamido Sanusi, in an interview with the *Financial Times* in 2012, noted that Boko Haram, poverty, and the general unrest in the northern part of the country are a result of the lower sums they get from the federation account compared with the oil producing states, which get 13% derivation every month. The same position was echoed by the Niger State Governor Babangida Aliyu (Wallis, 2012). He called for a review of the revenue sharing formula to "reflect current realities." He went further to say that the North, apparently, is beginning to see the extra funds allocated to oil producing states under the 13% derivation allocation as an injustice that ought to be redressed, and a direct cause of the Boko Haram onslaught.

The governors from the Niger Delta states saw these provocative statements from two leading northern elites as political manipulation and calculated attempts to put the Niger Delta in perpetual poverty. This reflects the political tension between the North and the Niger Delta. According to Makinde and Adeyoke (2007) the colonial ordinances became the offshoots of subsequent legal statements on oil production in Nigeria. These include the Petroleum Decree of 1969, the Land Use Decree of 1978, the Exclusive Economic Zone Act of 1979, the Oil Mineral Pipeline Decree of 1990, the Petroleum Decree of 1991, the Land (title vesting) Decree of 1993, the Oil Pipelines Act of 1996, the National Inland Waterways Decree of 1997, and other relevant legislation, including those dealing with revenue allocation. These laws taken together vest all the land where oil is extracted, produced, transported, stored, and the proceeds thereof, in the State and are therefore sources of conflict in contemporary times (Omorogbe, 2003). Douglas (1999) opines that the ethnic nationalities in the Niger Delta have become observant of the marginalization tactics of the major ethnic nationalities in Nigeria. These major ethnic nationalities control political power and resources at the federal level to their advantage.

The ethnic minorities in the Niger Delta lack political power to make meaningful socio-economic policies in their favor. The balance of power in Nigeria is based on the supremacy of "sectional" or "national" interests over local rights. Bassey (2002) notes that Nigeria is a country where a powerful group of individuals, with the aid of state apparatuses, are able to influence national decisions in their favor to create an ethnic agenda, distort history, and ensure inequality in the allocation and distribution of resources. According to Idoko (2013) the "black gold" has become a "cabal gold" in the hands of few who hold political power. The entire nation, not just the Niger Delta region, is affected by the lack of security of life and property, as well as a lack of infrastructure, wanton ecological damage, theft, and unjust distribution of revenue from the sale of oil.

There is a shared belief among Niger Delta inhabitants that both the federal government of Nigeria and multinational oil companies have systematically marginalized the region from getting access to the proceeds of oil exploration. The Niger Delta inhabitants allege that the proceeds from exploited oil are used for the growth and development of other regions in the country, leaving the Niger Delta impoverished (Ikein, 1990). Moreover, Niger Delta inhabitants also believe the government has enslaved them to the multinational oil companies (O'Sullivan, 1995). The Niger Delta inhabitants feel that the government is interested only in oil and gas revenue coming from the region. As mentioned above, various reasons have been given for the resurgence among different groups in the Niger Delta. One is that the Niger Delta indigenes have been systematically excluded from power sharing. Under the 1999 constitution, the federal government holds mineral rights in Nigeria. Legislation was passed by the National Assembly to confer ownership of natural resources of Nigerian land to the government. This has aggravated the inhabitants' grievances in the region (Akinjide-Balogun, 2001).

Socio-Economic Rights Abuses and Anger

The federal government of Nigeria is primarily responsible for decaying or lack of infrastructural facilities in the Niger Delta. Provision of socio-economic facilities is described by the UN General Assembly (1966, p. 3) as a socio-economic right and that it is the duty of government to make it available. Odey, Eteng, and Odike (2013) say that the unconcerned attitude of the multinational oil companies and uncompromising and irresponsive attitude of the Nigerian National Petroleum Corporation (NNPC) to improve the well-being of the oil-bearing communities through corporate social responsibility contribute to anger in the Niger Delta. The inhabitants of the Niger Delta region lack electricity, potable drinking water, and health centers. Schools were closed down and many indigenous people were jobless as a result of the conflict. A report of the United Nations

Development Programme (2006) on the human development situation in the Niger Delta states that "poverty has become a way of life due to economic stagnation, unemployment, poor quality of life due to shortages of essential goods and facilities, an unhealthy environment and government insensitivity" (pp. 36–37).

The Geneva Declaration on Armed Violence and Development (Global Burden of Armed Violence and Development, 2015) provides a link between absence of socio-economic facilities and conflict. Ebegbulem, Ekpe, and Adejumo (2013) claim that in the Niger Delta, underdevelopment has largely been understood in the context of lack of social amenities such as indoor plumbing water, good roads, hospitals, schools, and employment opportunities. Omitola (2012) claims that the inability of the federal government to provide the basic needs of its citizenry, such as food, water, employment, hospitals, and good roads, among others, are contributing factors to the root cause of the Niger Delta crisis (Omitola, 2012, p. 262). Coble (2007) opines that "conflict in the Niger Delta region is caused by poverty, historical neglect, and aspirations by politicians." Ekine (2010) says that "the situation should be handled through dialogue along with providing infrastructure and employment" (p. 3).

The roots of the Niger Delta conflict, as identified above, demonstrated the emotional attachment of the people to the environment. This was reflected in the reactions of the inhabitants of the region to the oil spillage and gas flaring that destroyed the environment and consequently affect means of livelihood. The neglect of the region in terms of provision of basic socio-economic amenities compounded the frustration of the inhabitants. Their frustration led to aggression. The frustration-aggression hypothesis was formulated by Dollard, Doob, Miller, Mowrer, and Sears (1939), who argued that:

> the occurrence of aggression presupposes frustration . . . Frustration produces instigations to a number of different types of responses, one of which is an instigation to some form of aggression. (p. 2)

The frustration-aggression hypothesis is linked to a goal or ambition (Miller, 1941). The goal or ambition exists before frustration. According to Klandermans (2013), the inability to achieve one's goal often leads to frustration. Limited access to opportunity breeds aggression. For example, in the case of the Niger Delta, the inhabitants' goals are environmental protection, recognition, sharing of oil royalties, resource control, and improvement in socio-economic provisions. Their goals were not met because government and multinational oil companies are not interested in the welfare and development of the inhabitants of the region. The Niger Delta inhabitants construed this as hatred and they became emotionally disturbed. The inhabitants expressed the frustrations in collective anger at the government and multinational oil companies. Their aggression has consequences for disruption of peace and stability in the region (Afotan & Ojakorotu, 2009).

Consequences of Anger in the Niger Delta Region

Anger over destruction of the Niger Delta environment by the multinational oil companies and lack of socio-economic infrastructures led to the destruction of the oil installations and attacks on oil workers, foreigners, and government officials. The government responded by creating a military JTF to protect life and property in the region. The activities of this JTF led to confrontation with the militant groups formed by the inhabitants of the region. Frustration over environmental degradation resulted in anger, and anger led to the destruction of life and property. All parties in the conflict have lost human lives to military bombardment, kidnapping, and militant attacks. However, it is important to note that the Niger Delta inhabitants have lost more lives than the oil companies and the federal government of Nigeria's military (United Nations Development Programme, 2006). According to Courson (2009), the recurring incidents of human rights abuses started with the destruction of the Umuechem, Ogoni community in 1990. Since then, it has continued with the killing of Ken Saro-Wiwa and eight other Ogoni activists in 1995, and the razing of Odi, Opia, and Ikenyan in 1999, Odioma in 2005, Agge in 2008, and Gbaramatu in 2009. Human Rights Watch (2000) records that two local oil workers, Danjuma Basir and Malabu Ahmed of the National Petroleum Development Company (NPDC), Benin City, Edo State, were abducted by the militants in 2006. They were found dead near the Mosogar area of Delta State. In October 2005, Asari-Dokubo, the leader of Movement for the Emancipation of the Niger Delta, was charged with treason by the federal government of Nigeria. It was probably a response to the blowing up of a pipeline and killing of eight people in the area (Onwuka, 2013).

The inhabitants of the Niger Delta region are farmers, fishers, and traders. The means of livelihood of the Niger Delta inhabitants are largely agriculture. Anger in the region has led to the destruction of farmland, canoes, fishing nets, and markets. Gighi, Tanee, and Albert (2012) note that the Ogonis' population is about 500,000. They make a living from farming and fishing. Oil exploration by the Shell, Chevron, and other multinational oil companies has pushed the inhabitants of the region farther into the groves and swamps. Those who remain in the townships and villages are subjected to environment hazards and other health risks (Tanee & Albert, 2011). The Niger Delta conflict also affected the royalties paid by the multinational oil companies to the indigenous people. As noted by Okumagba (2009), nothing was coming to people directly from the sales of crude oil. Orubu (1999) highlights that most of the Niger Delta indigenous peoples live on less than $1 a day. The people lack electricity and potable drinking water. Schools were closed down and many indigenous people were jobless as a result of the conflict. Vrey (2012) states that payment of patronage and other royalties, which were stopped by the multinational oil companies, led to the involvement of the inhabitants of the Niger Delta region in oil theft. Similarly, according to Okumagba (2009), the cancellation of payment of royalties to the indigenous people of the Niger Delta region has resulted in anger and dissatisfaction in the region to the extent that local people are now involved in bunkering and oil spillage. It is worrisome to note that the inhabitants of the region believe that oil theft is a way of taking shares of the oil exploration and exploitation. The millions of barrels of oil stolen from the leaked oil facilities provide a source of funds to the militant groups to finance the escalation of the conflict (Human Rights Watch, 2003).

The formation of ethnic militia groups in the region was in response to insensitivity of government and the multinational oil companies to various demands and agitations of the Niger Delta people. The ethnic militia groups at various points in the history of the Niger Delta conflict issued threats and ultimatums, ran campaigns, and lobbied to press home their demands. The determination of the militant groups in the Niger Delta to engage the federal government of Nigeria military in armed struggle endangers the security of life and property in the region. With the proliferation of arms and ammunition in the region, oil installations were frequently destroyed, oil workers, foreigners, government officials, and wealthy individuals and their relatives were kidnapped and killed. Preboye (2005) gives an account of how oil workers, including foreigners and Nigerians, were kidnapped by a militant group named Iduwini. According to him, on December 25, 2004, a Croatian contractor for Shell Oil and 15 Nigerians were kidnapped by Iduwini militants. The kidnapped were released after the payment of ransom to the militant group. Also, on June 19, 2005, apparently with the same motives, the Iduwini Youths kidnapped and released two German and four Nigerian Shell subcontractors.

These are not the only kidnapping cases in the area. In December 2004, inhabitants of Gbaramatu Kingdom in the Niger Delta region temporarily occupied three foreign-owned oil installations, two run by Shell and one by Chevron-Texaco. Tony Gouldbourne, a Liverpool man, was seized during the hijack of an oil platform off the West African coast; he was later released after payment of ransom to the armed group (BBC News Channel, 2005). Also, according to a BBC (2005) report, three British oil workers and a Colombian were abducted by gunmen in Nigeria; they were also later released after negotiation. To combat the trend in kidnapping and killing of oil workers in the Niger Delta region, the Nigerian armed forces arrested Obese, a militant gang leader, and more than 60 of his followers believed to be behind the kidnapping of 19 oil and construction workers in Rivers State in the Niger Delta in 2010 (Omoweh, 2004). The hostages include two Americans, two Frenchmen, two Indonesians, one Canadian, and 12 Nigerians. Mr. Alan Preston, a Scotsman who was working for a Nigerian engineering firm, Adamac Industries, was also freed. He was the seventh of his countrymen to be taken hostage in Niger's volatile, oil-rich region (Lawrie, 2015). Many oil workers were withdrawn as a result of kidnapping and killing by the militant groups. The withdrawal of oil workers led to the inability of Nigeria to meet oil production quotas (Akpan, 2006; Omoweh, 2004). The oil production dropped by 10%, and it had a significant impact on the world demand for oil (Awolusi, 2009). Hundreds of foreign and local oil workers have been kidnapped in the Niger Delta since 2006; many were released unharmed, others after the collection of ransoms.

Dealing with the Roots of the Niger Delta Anger

Various attempts have been made to resolve the roots of the Niger Delta anger, though none have included reparations. Attempts at resolution by the federal government of Nigeria and multinational oil companies include accountability, memorialization, amnesty, and disarmament, demobilization, and reintegration (DDR) (Ifeka, 2000). The latest in the efforts of government toward redress of the Niger Delta conflict is the DDR given to the militants (Ojeleye, 2011). The different attempts at resolving the Niger Delta conflict by the Nigerian government specifically have included establishment of the Willink Commission of Inquiry (in 1958), the Popoola Commission (in 1999), and the Ogomudia Commission (in 2001).

Commissions and Panels of Inquiry

To have a clear understanding of the efforts of the Nigerian government toward resolving the Niger Delta conflict, it is important to examine the various commissions and panels of inquiry established to look into the Niger Delta conflict. A good starting point is the Henry Willink Minority

Commission of 1958, which recognized the need to develop the Niger Delta region (Dafinone, 2007). According to Rhodes (2012), the Willink Commission report revealed that the Niger Delta issue was a matter that went beyond the Eastern Region; it required a special effort and cooperation of the federal, eastern, and western Nigerian governments. This was not only because the area involves two regions, but also because it was poor, backward, and neglected (Collier & Venables, 2011). The Willink Commission, therefore, concluded that the whole of Nigeria is affected by the Niger Delta conflict. It suggested that there should be a federal board appointed to consider the problems of the region. The commission also recommended that some areas, such as the Western Ijaw Division, and the Rivers Province with Ahoada and Port Harcourt, should be included as parts of the Niger Delta region.

The Niger Delta hostilities stopped immediately after the independence in 1960 and later resurfaced in the 1990s. The conflict was protracted and it led to the establishment of the 1999 Popoola Commission (Adaka Boro Centre, 2008). The Popoola Commission, officially titled the Presidential Committee on Development Options for the Niger Delta, was composed of military administrators from the South-South zone and representatives from Oil Minerals Producing Area Development, Petroleum Trust Fund (PTF), and other government agencies to consider the needs of the Niger Delta. The committee stated that all the three tiers of government, government agencies, oil companies, and non-governmental organizations should be actively involved in the provision of infrastructure and support services for the Niger Delta inhabitants. The committee discovered that, contrary to widely held views, a substantial amount of resources have been invested in the Niger Delta and recommended the immediate expenditure of an additional ₦ 15.7 billion on development projects (Ikelegbe, 2013).

The intensity of the protracted conflict led to the commission of the Ogomudia Panel of Inquiry in 2001 (Adaka Boro Centre, 2008). The Ogomudia commission was set up by the federal government of Nigeria to address the prevailing conflict situation in the oil-producing area of the Niger Delta. Obi (2001) feels that the government's genuine desire to get to the roots of resistance in the region and the impact of the conflict on the image of Nigeria necessitated the formation of the Ogomudia Panel of Inquiry. We can see from the foregoing that government has made some effort to deal with and understand the situation, but failed to implement most of the committee's recommendations. Between 1958 and 2008, there were 25 commissions and reports, decrees designed to address the Niger Delta problems (Niger Delta Human Development, 2006). Taken together, it should be noted that the documents have no semblance of a purposeful peace agreement. The documents do not address issues that affect the Niger Delta region directly, such as the environment, resource control, women's rights, and socio-economic transformation (Akinwale, 2010). According to Bell and O'Rourke (2010), peace agreements have a distinctive quasi-constitutional quality, and sometimes even constitute or contain constitutions. Comprehensive peace agreements typically set out complex arrangements for new democratic institutions, human rights and minority protections, and reform, or the entire overhaul of the security justice sector (Bell & O'Rourke, 2010).

Human Rights Violations Investigation Committee

The dawn of democracy in Nigeria in 1999 ushered in the establishment of the Human Rights Violations Investigation Committee on June 14, 1999, by former Nigerian president Olusegun Obasanjo (Onyegbula, 2001). The seven-person commission was headed by Justice Chukwudifu Oputa and sought to investigate human rights abuses back to the military coup of January 15, 1966, until May 28, 1999, the day before the last military handover to civilians in Nigeria (Lamb, 1999). Cases of human rights abuses by the Niger Delta inhabitants were presented before the panel. A critical look at the administrative law that established the commission suggests that the Human Rights Violation Investigation Commission was not put in place specifically for the purpose of addressing cases of human rights abuses in the Niger Delta region, but it was designed to address past human rights abuse in Nigeria between 1966 and 1999 more broadly (Yusuf, 2013). The report of the commission has been submitted to the federal government of Nigeria but its findings were not made public (Nigerian Democratic Movement, 2005). It took the combined efforts of human rights groups and civil society groups to publish the document in the United States of America (Nigerian Democratic Movement, 2005). The commissions and panels of inquiry set up by the government have tended to come up with recommendations without significant participation and contribution by the Niger Delta inhabitants. Bekoe (2005) adds that most of the recommendations of the panels and commissions lack effectiveness because the process of their creation lacks legislative power.

Creation of the Amnesty Committee

As part of efforts of government to redress historical conflict in the Niger Delta, an amnesty committee was created. The amnesty proclamation (2009) states inter alia:

> Whereas certain elements of the Niger Delta populace have resorted to unlawful means of agitation for the development of the region including militancy thereby threatening peace, security order and good governance and jeopardizing the economy of the nation; whereas the Government desires that all persons who have directly or indirectly participated in militancy in the Niger Delta should return to respect constituted authority; and whereas many persons who had so engaged in militancy now desire to apply for and obtain amnesty and pardon. (Idonor, 2009, p. 7)

The creation of the amnesty committee was marked with submission of weapons, rehabilitation, and socio-economic transformation. This method of peacebuilding is referred to, as previously mentioned, as disarmament, demobilization, and reintegration (DDR) by scholars (Solomon & Ginifer, 2008; Tonwe & Aghedo, 2013). The various attempts at redress seem to have not satisfied many inhabitants of the region because many victims, most especially women, were excluded. No reparations have been paid in the region. Women in the Niger Delta want their roles and experiences to be recognized and compensated. The agreements in the Niger Delta do not, in their essence, contain this. Attempts at redress by the Human Rights Violations Investigation Committee mentioned above, though, make provision for compensation and reparations for victims, including women. The problem is the recommendations of the committee have not been made public, as noted above. Attempts at redress have included DDR but this has a limited impact on women and other victims.

Conclusion

This chapter has been able to link the Niger Delta conflict to collective anger over environmental degradation. The conflict resulted from frustration experienced in the hands of multinational oil companies, as related to the oil exploration and exploitation in the Niger Delta. The inhabitants were frustrated by the activities of multinational oil companies, which include oil spills, gas flaring, and land degradation. The activities of the multinational oil companies are concluded in this chapter to be major contributors to environmental degradation. Frustration in the Niger Delta led to anger. The inhabitants of the region expressed their anger by destroying oil installations, kidnapping oil workers and foreigners, and forming militant groups, to engage in conflict with the federal government of Nigeria military joint task force. The consequences of anger led to destruction of life and property and economic loss to the government.

The chapter concluded that frustration is a forerunner of aggression. People expressed their aggression as a form of conflict, which usually resulted in huge consequences. The Niger Delta anger over environmental degradation was doused by establishing panels of inquiry, human rights violations investigation commission, amnesty, and post-amnesty reintegration. The post-amnesty period has brought peace and security to the Niger Delta. The inhabitants of the region demand justice and guarantee of non-repetition of the conflict, which DDR alone cannot provide. Anger in the region could be totally diffused by combining security with justice. Collective anger such as the Niger Delta conflict requires collective resolutions such as DDR and reparation.

References

Action, E. R. (2002). A blanket of silence: Images of the Odi genocide. Special report published by Environmental Rights Action/Friends of the Earth, Nigeria. Amsterdam. Netherlands. Retrieved from http://www.ejolt.org/2011/09/era/

Adaka Boro Centre. (2008). Popoola report: Report of the presidential committee on development options for the Niger Delta. Retrieved from http://www.adakaboro.org

Afotan, L. A., & Ojakorotu. V. (2009). The Niger Delta crisis: Issues, challenges and prospects. *African Journal of Political Science and International Relations, 3*(5), 191–198.

Ajugwo, A. O. (2013). Negative effects of gas flaring: The Nigerian experience. *Journal of Environment Pollution and Human Health, 1*(1), 6–8.

Akinjide-Balogun, O. (2001). Nigeria: Legal framework of the Nigerian petroleum industry. *Mondaq: Connecting Knowledge and People*. Retrieved from http://www.mondaq.com

Akinwale, A. A. (2010). Amnesty and human capital development agenda for the Niger Delta. *African Studies and Development, 2*(8), 201–207.

Akpan, F. (2006). Ethnic militancy and the Nigerian State. *Journal of International Politics and Development Studies, 2*(1), 71–79.

Awolusi, B. (2009). *Amnesty to cost 10 billion*. Retrieved from http://nigerianbulletin.com/summary-plus-news/amnesty-to-costn10b-thenation/09102009/10344

Aworawo, D. (2000). *The impact of environmental degradation of the rural economy of the Niger Delta*. Lagos, NG: Friedrich Ebert Foundation.

Barikor-Wiwa, D. (1997). The role of women in the struggle for environmental justice in Ogoni. *CSQ, 21*(3).

Bassey, C. O. (2002). *Framework for the conflict transformation project in Warri*. Ibadan, NG: Spectrum Books.

BBC News Channel. (2005, June 15). Oil workers kidnapped in Nigeria. *BBC News*. Retrieved from http://news.bbc.co.uk/1/hi/business/4097410.stm

Bekoe, D. (2005). Strategies for peace in the Niger Delta. *United States Institute of Peace*. Retrieved from http://www.usip.org

Bell, C., & O'Rourke, C. (2010). Peace agreements or pieces of paper? The impact of UNSC resolution 1325 on peace processes and their agreements. *International and Comparative Law Quarterly, 59,* 941–980.

Coble, B. (2007). Shell's corporate social responsibility in the Niger Delta. *INASP.* Retrieved from http://www.inasp.info/uploads/filer_public/2013/04/03/3 _handout_4.pdf

Collier, P., &. Venables, T. (Eds.). (2011). *Plundered nations: Successes and failures in natural resource extraction.* London, UK: Palgrave Macmillan.

Courson, E., (2009). Movement for the emancipation of the Niger Delta (MEND): Political marginalization, repression and petro-insurgency in the Niger Delta. Discussion Paper 47. Nordiska Afrikainstitute/The Nordic Africa Institute, Uppsala. Retrieved from http://www.diva-portal.org/smash/get /diva2:280470/FULLTEXT01.pdf

Dadiowei, T. E. (2003). *Environmental impact assessment (EIA) and conflict issues in the Niger Delta: A case study of Gbaran oil field communities in Bayelsa State* (Working Paper No. 24 on the Niger Delta). Boston: Berkeley University.

Dafinone, D. (2007). *The Niger Delta crisis: Genesis, the exodus and the solution* [Chairman address in Niger Delta Peace Conference]. Retrieved from http://www.waado.org/nigerdelta/nigerdelta_federalgovt/dafinone _nigerdelta_peace_conference.pdf

Das, S. (2014, May 23). Shell could be held liable for Niger Delta oil spills, says London court. *DownToEarth.org.* Retrieved from http://www.downtoearth .org.

Diamond, S. A. (2014, December 20). How mad was Hitler? What motivated Adolf Hitler's destructive behavior? *Psychology Today.* Retrieved from https:// www.psychologytoday.com

Dollard, J., Doob, L. W., Miller, N. E., Mowrer, O. H., & Sears, R. R. (1939). *Frustration and aggression.* New Haven, CT: Yale University Press.

Douglas, O. (Ed.). (1999). *The Niger Delta question.* Port Harcourt, NG: Riverside Communications.

Ebegbulem, J., Ekpe, D., & Adejumo, T. (2013). Oil exploration and poverty in the Niger Delta region of Nigeria: A critical analysis. *International Journal of Business and Social Science, 4*(3), 279–287.

Egwurugwu, J. N., & Nwafor, A. (2013). Prolonged exposure to oil and gas flares ups the risks for hypertension. *American Journal of Health Research, 1*(3), 65–72.

Ekine, S. (2010). Women's responses to state violence in the Niger Delta. In J. Browdy de Hernandez, P. Dongala, O. Jolaosho, & A. Serafin (Eds.), *African women writing resistance: An anthology of contemporary voices.* Madison, WI: The University of Wisconsin Press.

Enemugwem, J. H. (2009). The development of the Niger Delta of Nigeria, 1900– 1966. *Sustainable Development in Africa, 10*(4), 162–178.

Environmental Rights Action/Friends of the Earth Nigeria. (2005). *Gas flaring in Nigeria: A human rights, environmental and economic monstrosity.* Retrieved

from http://www.foe.co.uk/sites/default/files/downloads/gas_flaring_nigeria
.pdf

Gighi, J. G., Tanee, F. B. G., & Albert, E. (2012). Post-impact soil assessments of crude oil spill site in Kpean Community in Khana LGA (Ogoni) of Rivers State, Nigeria. *Journal of Science, 2*(2), 109–120.

Global Burden of Armed Violence and Development. (2015). Geneva Declaration on Armed Violence and Development. Retrieved from http://www.gene vadeclaration.org/

Human Rights Watch. (1999). The price of oil: Corporate responsibility and human rights violations in Nigeria's oil producing communities. Retrieved from http://www.hrw.org/reports/1999/nigeria

Human Rights Watch. (2000). Update on human rights violation in the Niger Delta. Retrieved from http:hrw.org/news/2000/12/14/update-human-rights -violations-Niger-Delta

Human Rights Watch. (2003). The Warri crisis: Fueling violence. Retrieved from https://www.hrw.org/report/2003/12/17/warri-crisis-fueling-violence /fueling-violence

Idoko, I. F. (2013). The paradox of youth's unemployment in an oil producing country: The lesson from the Nigerian experience. *International Journal of Business and Management Invention, 2*(4), 74–79.

Idonor, D. (2009). Yar'Adua grants militants unconditional amnesty . . . frees Henry Okah. *Vanguard*. Retrieved from http://www.vanguardngr.com /2009/06/yaradua-grants-militants-unconditional-amnestyfrees-henry -okah

Ifeka, C. (2000). Conflict, complicity and confusion: Unravelling empowerment struggles in Nigeria after the return to democracy. *Review of African Political Economy, 83*, 115–124.

Ihonvbare, J. (2000). *A recipe for perpetual crisis: The Nigerian State and the Niger Delta question*. Lagos, NG: Committee for Defence of Human Rights.

Ikein, A. A. (1990). *The impact of oil on a developing country: The case of Nigeria*. New York, NY: Praeger.

Ikejiaku, B. V. (2009). The relationship between poverty, conflict and development. *Journal of Sustainable Development, 2*(1), p. 15–31.

Ikelegbe, A. O. (Ed.) (2013). Oil, environment and resource conflict in Nigeria. In the series *Politics and Economics in Africa*. Zürich, Switzerland: Lit.

Integrated Regional Information Network. (2005). Constitutional change conference deadlocks over oil dispute. Retrieved from http://www.irinnews.org

Ite, A. E., Ibok, U. J., Ite, M. U., & Petters, S. W. (2013). Petroleum exploration and production: Past and present environmental issues in the Nigeria's Niger Delta. *American Journal of Environmental Protection, 1*(4), 78–90.

Iyobhebhe, J. (2005). The resource control movement in Nigeria. *Gamji.com*. Retrieved from http://www.gamji.com/article4000/NEWS4767.htm

Jereoma, T. (Ed.). (2001). *Women and the challenges of the Niger Delta*. Port Harcourt, NG: Centre for Advanced Social Sciences.

Kashi, E., & Watts, M. (2008). *Curse of the black gold.* Brooklyn, NY: PowerHouse Books.

Klandermans, B. (2013). Frustration-aggression. In D. A. Snow (Ed.), *The Wiley-Blackwell encyclopedia of social and political movements.* West Sussex, UK: Wiley-Blackwell.

Lamb, C. (1999). Truth panel will call Nigeria's strongmen to account. *Probe International.* Retrieved from http://journal.probeinternational.org/1999/08/22/truth-panel-will-call-nigerias-strongmen-to-account/

Lawrie, A. (2015, April 30). Freed Scot oil worker Alan Preston home after abduction. *Deadline News,* p. 1.

Leahey, D., Preston, K., & Strosher, M. (2001). Theoretical and observational assessments of flare efficiencies. *Journal of the Air and Waste Management Association, 51*(12), 1610–1616. doi:10.1080/10473289.2001.10464390

Makinde, O., & Adeyoke, T. (2007). Nigeria: Environment law in Nigeria. *The International Comparative Guide to PFI /PPP Projects 2007* (4th ed.). London, UK: Global Legal Group Ltd. Retrieved from http://www.mondaq.com/x/53804/Energy+Law/Environment+Law+In+Nigeria

Marquand, R. (May 17, 2014). Boko Haram: An angry Nigerian youth revolt in the language of jihad (+video). *The Christian Science Monitor.* Retrieved from http://www.csmonitor.com/World/Africa/2014/0517/Boko-Haram-An-angry-Nigerian-youth-revolt-in-the-language-of-jihad-video

Mbanefo, G., & Egwaikhide, F. (Eds.). (1998). *Revenue allocation in Nigeria: Derivation principle revisited.* Lagos, NG: Spectrum.

Miller, N. E. (1941). The frustration-aggression hypothesis. *Psychological Review, 48*(4), 337–342.

Miriki, T. (2003). Ijaw National Congress (INC). Retrieved from http://ijawnationalcongress.com

Niger Delta Human Development. (2006). Niger Delta human development report. Retrieved from http://hdr.undp.org/en/content/human-development-report

Niger Delta Professionals for Development. (2011). Citizen report card on public services, good governance and development from 120 Niger Delta communities in three geopolitical zones. Warri: Niger Delta Professionals for Development. Retrieved from http://nidprodev.org/files/Summary%20Version%20of%20Citizen%20Report%20Card.pdf

Nigerian Democratic Movement. (2005). Human rights violations investigation commission report (a.k.a. Oputa Panel report). *Dawodu.com.* Retrieved from http://dawodu.com/oputa1.htm

Nisirimovu, A. (2000). *Poverty in wealth: Report on the people of the Niger Delta and the display of poverty in wealth.* Port Harcourt, NG: University of Port Harcourt Institute of Human Rights and Humanitarian Law (IHRHL).

Nnoli, O. (1980). *Ethnic politics in Nigeria.* Enugu, NG: Fourth Dimension Publishers.

Nwilo, P. C., & Badejo, O. T. (2005). Oil spill problems and management in the Niger Delta. *International Oil Spill Conference Proceedings,* Vol. 2005(1),

pp. 567–570. Retrieved from http://ioscproceedings.org/doi/pdf/10.7901
/2169-3358-2005-1-567

Obi, C. (2011). Democratising the petro-state in West Africa: Understanding the challenges. In M. Roll & S. Sperling (Eds.), *Fuelling the world: Failing the region? Oil governance and development in Africa's Gulf of Guinea* (pp. 102–120). Abuja, NG: Friedrich-Ebert-Stiftung.

Obi, C. (2001). The changing forms of identity politics in Nigeria under economic adjustment: The case of the oil minorities' movement of the Niger Delta. Retrieved from http://www.diva-portal.org/smash/get/diva2:246011 /fulltext01.pdf

Odey, E. S., Eteng, G. B., & Odike, E. L. (2013). The Niger Delta crisis in Nigeria: Pre and post amnesty situation. *Mediterranean Journal of Social Sciences, 4*(6), 421–427.

Odjugo, P.A.O. (2007). Some effects of gas flaring on the microclimate of yam and cassava production in Erhorike and environs, Delta State, Nigeria. *Nigerian Geographical, 5,* 43–54.

Offu, A. C. (2013). *The Nigeria dependent management and leadership development in the post-World War II colonial Nigeria.* Bloomington, IN: Author House.

Oil-watch. (2002). Protest against use of violence against unarmed women in peaceful protest [Special report]. Environmental Rights Action. Retrieved from http://www.waado.org/environment/OilCompanies/Women/Women 2002Rebellion/ERAReports/ERaProtestsViolenceAgainstWomen.html

Ojeleye, O. (2011). The application of demobilisation, disarmament and reintegration (DDR) at the sub-national level in the Niger Delta. *Civil Wars, 13*(2), 141–156.

Okoro, D., & Nnaji, G. O. (2012). Press coverage of environmental pollution in the Niger Delta region of Nigeria. A content analysis of the Guardian, Vanguard, Daily Sun and Thisday newspapers. *Journal of Humanities and Social Science, 3*(2), 34–46.

Okpongkpong, O. D. (2003). Industrialization as key to national development. Port Harcourt, NG: MSS. Cited by J. H. Enemugwem (2009). The development of the Niger Delta of Nigeria, 1900–1966. *Journal of Sustainable Development in Africa, 10*(4), 162–178.

Okumagba, P. (2009). Ethnic militias and criminality in the Niger-Delta. *African Research Review, 3*(3), 315–330.

Ologunorisa, T. E. (2001). A review of the effects of gas flaring on the Niger Delta environment. *International Journal of Sustainable Development and World Ecology, 8*(3), 249–255.

Olukoshi, A., & Agbu, O. (Eds.). (1996). *The deepening crisis of Nigerian federalism and the future of the nation-state.* Uppsala, SE: Nordiska Africainstitutet.

Omitola, B. (2012). The struggle for the Nigerian soul: Niger Delta debacle. *Journal of Alternative Perspectives in the Social Sciences, 5*(1), 252–270.

Omorogbe, Y. (2003). *Oil and gas law in Nigeria.* Lagos, NG: Malthouse Press.

Omoweh, D. A. (2004). Is it the Warri crisis or the crisis of the Nigerian state? *ACAS Bulletin, 68,* pp. 10–15.

Onwuka, A. (2013, May 14). Should Asari-Dokubo be arrested? *The Punch*, p. 16.

Onwumere, O. (2013, April 8). Evils of gas flaring and oil companies' contempt for Nigeria laws. *Niger Delta Standard*, p. 9.

Onyegbula, S. (2001). The human rights situation in Nigeria since the democratic dispensation. *Development Policy Management Network*. Retrieved from http://unpan1.un.org/intradoc/groups/public/documents/cafrad /unpan009247.pdf

Orogun, P. S. (2009). Resource control, revenue allocation and petroleum politics in Nigeria: the Niger Delta question. *GeoJournal, 75*(5), 459–507.

Orubu, C. O. (1999). Oil wealth and the derivation principle: The need for a new fiscal imperative towards oil-producing states. *Politics and Administration, 1*(1), 182–211.

O'Sullivan, T. (1995, November 16). Shell needs more than slick solution. *Marketing Week, 24*, 22–23.

Oviasuyi, P. O., & Uwadiae, J. (2010). The dilemma of Niger-Delta region as oil producing states of Nigeria. *Journal of Peace, Conflict and Development, 16*(1), 10–126.

Ozoigbo, B. I., & Chukuezi, C. O. (2011). The impact of multinational corporations on the Nigerian economy. *European Journal of Social Sciences, 19*(3), 380.

Pavšič, P. (2012). Niger Delta region: What is behind the oil conflict? Consultancy Africa Intelligence. Retrieved from http://www.consultancyafrica.com /index.php?option=comcontent&view=article &id=1152:niger-delta-regi on-what-is-behind-the-oil-conflict-&catid=60:conflict-terrorism-disc ussion-papers&Itemid=265

Porter, A. L., & Fittipaldi, J. J. (Eds.) (1998). *Environmental methods review: Retooling impact assessment for the new century.* Fargo, ND: The Press Club.

Preboye I. C. (2005). *The core Delta Iduwini clan: Otounkuku "the lost tribe."* Warri, NG: Rural Development Nig. Limited.

Prelogar, B., & Bekker, P. (2013, January 30). Dutch court orders shell Nigeria to compensate Nigerians for oil pollution damage caused by third-party sabotage in Nigeria. *Steptoe.* [Newsletter]. Retrieved from http://www.steptoe .com/publications-newsletter-714.html

Rhodes, T. (2012). Oil, money, and secrecy in East Africa. Committee to Protect Journalists. Retrieved 25 June 2016, from https://www.cpj.org/2013/02 /attacks-on-the-press-oil-money-and-the-press.php

Solomon, C., & Ginifer, J. (2008). Disarmament, demobilisation and reintegration in Sierra Leone: Case study. *Centre for International Cooperation and Security, University of Bradford.* Retrieved from http://www.operationspaix .net/DATA/DOCUMENT/4024~v~Disarmament_Demobilisation_and _Reintegration_in_Sierra_Leone.pdf

Tamuno, O. S., & Edoumiekumo, S. G. (2012). Nigeria in the Niger Delta: An allegory of the "legs tying the hands." *International Review of Social Sciences and Humanities, 4*(1), 113–120.

Tanee, F. B. G., & Albert, E. (2011). Post-remediation assessment of crude oil polluted site at Kegbara-Dere Community, Gokana L.G.A. of Rivers State,

Nigeria. *Journal of Bioremediation and Biodegradation, 2*(3). Retrieved from http://www.omicsonline.org

Tonwe, D., & Aghedo, I. (2013). Amnesty for sustainable peace and development in Nigeria's Niger Delta Region: Panacea or palliative. *Journal of Sustainable Development in Africa, 15*(5–6).

Torulagha, P. S. (2003). The Niger Delta, oil, and Western strategic interests: The need for an understanding. UnitedIjaw States. Retrieved from http://www.unitedijaw.com/torulagha0000121.htm

United Nations Development Programme. (2006). Niger Delta Human Development Report. Retrieved from http://hdr.undp.org/en/content/human-development-report

United Nations Development Programme. (2013). Niger Delta Politics: Dispatches on security in Nigeria's oil region. Retrieved from https://nigerdeltapolitics.wordpress.com/2013/04/11/reports-national-reports-africa-nigeria-human-development-reports-hdr-united-nations-development-programme-undp/

UN General Assembly. (1966, December 16). *International Covenant on Economic, Social and Cultural Rights, Treaty Series*, Vol. 993, p. 3.

Vrey, F. (2012). Maritime aspect of illegal oil-bunkering in the Niger Delta. *Australian Journal of Maritime and Ocean Affairs, 4*(4), 109–115.

Wallis, W. (2012, January 26). Nigerian central banker calls for end to imbalances. *Financial Times*, 26, p. 15. Retrieved from http://www.ft.com/intl/cms/s/0/02ce9e7e-4837-11e1-b1b4-00144feabdc0.html#axzz4BD9JTvN4

Yusuf, H. O. (Ed.). (2013). Human rights violations investigation commission, the Oputa panel (Nigeria). In L. Stan & N. Nedelsky (Eds.), *Encyclopedia of transitional justice* (Vol. 1, pp. 161–165). Cambridge, UK: Cambridge University Press.

CHAPTER SEVENTEEN

Anger and Politics in Iran

Mohammad Amjad

Anger is a natural human emotion that plays an important role in human interactions, including social conflicts. Anger as a motivating force for human action, has been reflected in holy texts such as the Koran and Bible, as well as in mythology texts and literature. The scientific study of this phenomenon, however, took place shortly before the breakout of World War II. The seminal work of John Dollard, Neal Miller, Leonard Doob, Oliver Mowrer, and Robert Sears (famously known as the Yale Group) on the frustration-aggression hypothesis in 1939, paved the way for understanding the causes of anger as a component of social conflict. Despite the sweeping generalization of the group that "Aggression is always a consequence of frustration" (Dollard et al., 1939, p. 1), the study of psychological factors in human interactions left a great impact on social scientists. Leonard Berkowitz modified the hypothesis to read that frustration results in a multitude of responses, including aggression and violence (Berkowitz, 1989, pp. 60–62). Political scientist Ted Robert Gurr, also argued that deprivation is the major cause of political violence. In *Why Men Rebel*, Gurr (1970) contends: "the greater the frustration, the greater the quantity of aggression and the magnitude of violence against the source of frustration" (p. 9). Gurr (1972) equates relative deprivation and frustration, and defines them as a perceived discrepancy between a person's value expectations and their value capability. He simplifies the process as follows: Relative deprivation results in discontent, and discontented people become angry and resort to violence against the source of deprivation.

James Davies (1962) looks at the frustration of the rising expectations and the role of popular anger in the political process. Borrowing from de Tocqueville, he argues: "Revolutions ordinarily do not occur when a society is generally impoverished, . . . [E]vils that seem inevitable are patiently endured, because the physical and mental energies of the people are totally employed in the process of staying alive" (p. 7). He also adds that political violence is more likely to occur if a long period of economic development is followed by a sharp reversal. He calls this process the J-curve of rising expectations and their eventual frustration (pp. 8–12).

The aim of this chapter is not to prove or disprove the validity of the deprivation/aggression hypothesis. Yet, something is clear. There is a direct relation between frustration, deprivation, and anger in the political process. Frustration and deprivation have various psychological ramifications, of which anger is one. Anger, however, is not necessarily destructive, and might play quite a constructive role in society. I define anger as the motivating force, reflecting the reaction of political actors to a situation in which they feel they have been deprived of what was rightly theirs. Severity of the situation has a great impact on the actor. The reaction might be rational or irrational, depending on the actor and the situation. We can observe manifestations of anger in political processes in different political systems, whether they are democratic, semi-democratic, or authoritarian. The presidential election of 2008 in the United States reflects the anger of a majority of Americans at the domestic and foreign policies of President George W. Bush, which led them to vote for candidate Barack Obama, since he was totally against those policies. The rise of the Tea Party as a populist political phenomenon also reflected the political anger of a large segment of the American population at policies they felt were elitist and harmful to the United States. In this chapter, I shall discuss three forms of political anger: democratic, radical, and theological.

Democratic Anger

By democratic anger, I mean using peaceful means for addressing social as well as economic and political issues. The philosophy of *Satyagraha* (passive resistance) which was put in practice by Mahatma Gandhi in India, the civil rights movement in the United States, and the May 1968 Movement in France, are clear examples of democratic anger. Going on strikes and staging peaceful demonstrations anywhere in the world are also examples of democratic anger, where demonstrators use non-violent means to achieve their goals. Whereas the aim of the *Satyagraha* movement was to achieve India's independence from Britain, the Civil Rights Movement in the United States targeted mainly racial discrimination. In the case of France, demonstrators were seeking social reforms, protesting consumerism, and demanding change of traditional values in their country.

Democratic anger rarely has the sympathy and cooperation of the government in power right from the beginning. It is usually after the protest movement, as the manifestation of democratic anger reaches a critical mass, that the government realizes the need for a new paradigm, and either reluctantly or willingly starts cooperating with the public. (In the case of the United States, Eisenhower, Kennedy, and Johnson came to the conclusion that they had no other choice but to work with the Civil Rights Movement.) In other situations, democratic anger might result in the fall of the government and the establishment of a new government that can address the issues that had resulted in the democratic anger in the first place. Rigidity of the political system and its failure to realize the need for a new paradigm might result in the overthrow of the regime (e.g., the Solidarity Movement in Poland).

Democratic Anger and the Military Coup of 1953

Democratic anger in Iran was ignited by a multitude of issues. In 1950, Iran was an underdeveloped country with a corrupt, yet semi-democratic, political system. The power bloc of Iran, composed of landlords, religious hierarchy, and the Shah, had control of the Iranian Parliament. The Anglo-Iranian Oil Company (AIOC), which was run by British managers exclusively, dominated the Iranian political system and society. To understand how badly Iranians were exploited by Britain, it is worth noting that the revenue the Iranian government received in royalties and taxes for the years 1945 to 1947 was £19.89 million (British sterling pounds). The British government, however, received £48.04 million from the AIOC during the same period in taxes alone (Mina, 2004). The revenues generated by the AIOC allowed Britain to establish a pro-Britain network among politicians, landlords, and journalists. Domination of Iran by Britain resulted in indignation of millions of Iranians who had come to believe that Britain was behind all the evils of the country. This condition gave the National Front, which was created by veteran politician Mohammad Mossadegh in 1949, an opportunity to champion grievances of people against the corrupt political system, poverty, dictatorship, and foreign domination. Major aims of the National Front were democratization of the political system, non-interference of foreign powers in Iran, and nationalization of the oil industry, which was the domain of Britain.

Angry demonstrations against the AIOC, and in support of Nationalization of the oil industry, in 1950 and early 1951, forced the Iranian lower

House of the Parliament (Majlis) to reluctantly pass the Oil Nationalization Bill on March 20, 1951. The Oil Nationalization Bill became the law
of the land when the Iranian Senate ratified it, and the Shah found no
choice but to sign it. Immediately after this process, Mossadegh was elected
Prime Minister by the Majlis, with the mission to carry out the nationalization of the oil industry. The AIOC was renamed the National Iranian Oil
Company, and its management was transferred to Iranian managers, engineers, and technicians. Britain did not recognize nationalization of the Iranian oil industry and announced it would take punitive measures against
Iran. British managers and technical staff also refused to serve under the
Iranian managers and left the country.

Mossadegh's plan for the democratization of Iran had three major parts:
containing the Shah to his constitutional power, freedom of press, and
reinvigoration of the electoral process by allowing all political parties to
participate in elections freely. For this reason, he lifted the restrictions that
had been imposed on the Tudeh Party (Iran's communist Party) following
an unsuccessful attempt on the Shah's life in 1948. This Mossadegh policy agitated the power bloc, which was afraid this initiative might gradually pave the way for the victory of Tudeh Party in future elections.

Despite some skirmishes between the supporters of the Tudeh Party
and the National Front, these two political organizations started working
together in the streets of Tehran for mass rallies aimed at ending political
corruption, eliminating foreign domination, and fighting poverty. The Shah
and his conservative pro-British allies, who were opposed to Mossadegh's
domestic and foreign policies, enlisted two groups to force Mossadegh out:
Fadayan-e Eslam or Self-Sacrificers of Islam (a small terrorist group whose
aim was to establish an Islamic government in Iran), as well as gang leaders
and villains (*Laatha*) to render the Mossadegh government powerless and
erode its social base. Later on, a faction of theologians, such as Ayatollah
Abolghasem Kashani, who had initially cooperated with Mossadegh on
nationalization of the oil industry, was enlisted by the court. This latter
development resulted in a split within the national movement for democracy and social reform, with devastating consequences for the country.

The boycott of the Iranian oil industry by Britain and its Western allies
angered millions of Iranians, who felt they were forced to either surrender
to British domination or face starvation. The Majlis deputies, who had
wrongly stipulated that Mossadegh would not accept the Premiership, were
now hoping he would fail to manage the oil industry and were elated to
see the impact of the boycott on the Iranian economy. They were conspiring with the Shah and Britain against the Mossadegh government, in the
hope that he would resign and would be replaced by a politician who would
be acceptable to Britain. Because the efforts of this group to force Mossadegh

out failed, they decided to overthrow him through a military coup, and while keeping the façade of oil nationalization, entered into negotiations with Britain for a new contract that would be acceptable to that country.

The CIA/MI6 engineered coup of August 19, 1953, was the last stage of this drama. After the coup, the Shah, who had fled the country after his failed first coup three days earlier, returned and established a bloody dictatorship. All of the opposition political parties were suppressed and their leaders and many of their members and supporters were imprisoned and tortured, and hundreds of them were executed. Immediately after the coup, the Shah decided to destroy all independent political organizations and impose a tight censorship on media, in order to protect his throne. The Tudeh Party, as a Marxist organization, was specifically targeted and its members and supporters who were imprisoned would have to condemn the party in order to be released. The Syndicate of Iranian Workers (*Sandicay-e Kargary-e Iran*), which had close ties with the Tudeh Party, was also dissolved and the workers were prevented from unionization. Mossadegh was tried for "treason" and sentenced to three years in jail; he was later put under house arrest, where he remained until his death in 1965.

The coup and its aftermath left a huge impact on the psyche of the masses and intellectuals. Political apathy replaced the enthusiasm for political participation, which manifested itself in low turnout throughout the Shah's regime. The poetry of this time, reflected in works of major poets such as Ahmad Shamloo, Mehdy Akhavan Sales, and Hooshang Ebtehadj, demonstrates the bitterness, pessimism, and agony of the society.

Within a year after the coup, Iran signed a contract with a consortium of Western oil companies (U.S., British, French, and Dutch) for the exploration, production, and sale of its oil in a 50–50% profit sharing. The consortium, however, was in charge of decision making, which was contrary to the principles of the oil nationalization movement (Engler, 1961, pp. 207–210). The United States, which before the coup had a marginal role in Iran, became very influential in the country, and its financial and military advisers played a crucial role in Iran's economic and security policies. The Eisenhower administration granted Iran a $40 million emergency loan shortly after the coup and continued providing loans and grants for at least a decade. Between 1954 and 1962, Iran received $861 million in economic aid and another $500 in military aid.

Economic Development and Democratic Anger

Rapid economic growth of Iran following the coup of 1953 made the pre-capitalist social formation of Iran untenable. In 1962, the Shah promulgated a series of reforms including a land reform, which paved the way for capitalist development in Iran. The rapid industrialization, which was funded by increasing oil revenues since 1968, convinced the Shah that he did not need the support of the middle class as the support base of his regime. This development further alienated the middle class and resulted in its unofficial boycott of the electoral process. Low voter turnout (usually under 35 percent) became a major challenge to the legitimacy of the regime and eventually worried the Shah about the future of his throne. The solution the Shah found for mobilizing people around his plans for the future of Iran, was to create a one party system, based on royal ideology. Interestingly enough, the Shah had previously boasted that as a constitutional monarch, he was against a one party system (Pahlavi, 1961, pp. 172–173).

It seems that some of the Shah's advisors, who were fascinated by modernization theorists such as David Apter and Samuel Huntington, had convinced him that in developing countries, a disciplined single party system was the best mechanism for mobilizing people as the support base of the regime (Apter, 1965, pp. 12–16; Huntington, 1970, pp. 395–404; Stemple, 1981, pp. 30–35). On March 2, 1975, the Shah announced the establishment of the Rastakhiz (Resurgent) Party and the dissolution of the multi-party system in Iran. To make the situation worse, he threatened that those who were opposed to the new development would have to leave the country (Abrahamian, 1982, p. 440). This development angered millions of previously apolitical Iranians, who found no choice but to join the anti-Shah opposition later on.

Worse yet, the economic boom of 1973–1976 was followed by the bust of 1977. The ambitious industrialization plans to turn Iran into the world's fifth economic power, without taking into consideration the many shortcomings of the country, including insufficient infrastructure and a shortage of skilled labor and experienced managers, turned out to be catastrophic. Moreover, the importation of capital-intensive factories and wasting billions of dollars on sophisticated weapons and an ambitious nuclear program, had depleted the Iranian treasury. To remedy the serious economic problem Iran was facing, the Shah forced Prime Minister Amir Abbas Hoveyda to resign, and replaced him with the veteran technocrat, Jamshid Amouzgar on August 7, 1977.

Amouzgar's main goal was to resolve the financial problems of the country and to energize the economy by cutting wasteful spending. His first step was to slash the budget of religious institutions, which infuriated the religious hierarchy. He also put several major construction projects on hold to prevent financial collapse. As a result, tens of thousands of construction workers, most of whom were rural migrants, lost their jobs. To make the situation worse, he decided to level the shantytowns which had sprung up outside of Tehran as the result of rural exodus to major cities including Tehran. The shantytown inhabitants, who were mostly rural migrants (many of whom had lost their jobs as the result of new economic policies of the regime), found no alternative but to resist the government representatives who had arrived with bulldozers to level their houses. A fight broke out between them and the military personnel who had been sent to carry out the mission. Fear of the spread of violence to the rest of the shantytowns around Tehran forced the government to shelve the plan. Amouzgar's miscalculation had politicized this otherwise apolitical sector of the Iranian population. Rural migrants became the most active participants in the anti-Shah movement from early 1978, when religious symbolism played a crucial role in the movement.

Before the beginning of 1977, with the exception of university students, a handful of pro-Khomeini theologians, and underground political organizations, no other group dared to openly challenge the regime. Despite this, a volcano of anger was simmering beneath and was waiting for the right condition to erupt. This opportunity was provided when Jimmy Carter became President in 1976. The announcement of Human Rights Policy as a foreign policy objective by President Jimmy Carter had a great impact on Iran. Both the Shah and the opposition took the Human Rights policy of Jimmy Carter seriously. The Shah felt obliged to somehow relax repression in order to buy the support of the new president and to appease the people who were enraged by the economic downturn. Although the Shah was looking at this new development as a breathing space to overcome economic setbacks, the opposition found a window of opportunity to demand an end to political repression and revival of the Constitution of 1906, according to which the monarch was solely head of the state and was prevented from meddling in policy-making.

Iranian students, who have historically played an important role in political process, were the first group to challenge the Shah's dictatorship and put his liberalization policy to the test in early 1977 by going on strike and staging demonstrations. The reaction of security forces was, amazingly enough, not harsh, and usually ended with no casualties. This development inspired other social groups to join the struggle for democratization of the political system. Modern middle class, social democratic opposition such as the National Front, and various civil society institutions also resumed the political activities that had been previously suppressed. Between the months of May and June 1977, 53 lawyers and 45 members of the Iranian Writers Association separately wrote open letters to the Shah, expressing their grievances against the interference of the executive branch in the judicial process and violation of human rights in Iran. The latter group's activities had been suspended upon its inception in 1965, and it was not recognized as a legitimate entity by the regime. Shortly afterwards, three prominent leaders of the National Front, Karim Sanjabi, Dariush Foruhar, and Shapur Bakhtiar, wrote an open letter to the Shah and demanded dissolution of the Rastakhiz Party, freedom of speech, assembly, and press, and the freedom of all political prisoners. To the astonishment of many, none of these people were arrested, which energized other civil society actors to express their anger toward the regime for political repression, and demand return to the rule of law and revival of the 1905 Constitution, which had been gravely violated by the Shah.

In early summer of 1977, several political organizations such as the Freedom Movement of Iran (founded by Mehdi Bazargan and Ayatollah Taleghani in 1961) and the Radical Movement of Iran, created by Rahmatollah Moghaddam Mareghehi (a Majlis Deputy from Miandoab, Azerbaijan), started their activities. Several human rights organizations were also created in early 1977, demanding an end to repression and recognition of the Universal Declaration of Human Rights by the regime. The democratic anger expressed by civil society and the modern middle class put the Shah (who at the same time was trying to find a way to resolve the economic woes of the country and keep President Carter happy) in a very difficult situation.

From Protest Movement to Revolution

The mass mobilization against the Shah, which gradually started in 1977 and ended in the overthrow of monarchy in 1979, suggests the validity of James Davies's J-curve theory. The economic boom of the 1960s through mid-1970s, which was followed by the bust of 1976, accompanied by political liberalization of 1977, after a long period of dictatorship, provided the condition for a huge eruption in Iran. The real or perceived support by President Carter for human rights was also a contributing factor in this process. It seems very likely that the Shah and his associates, who had studied David Apter and Samuel Huntingon's work so avidly, either did not have a chance to follow the works of Davies and his predecessors such as Alexis de Tocqueville and Crane Brinton, or did not take them seriously. The Shah, who had painted himself against the wall by establishing a one party system, was now on collision course with history, by his liberalization policies following a quarter of a century of repression, while trying to deal with an economic bust following a long period of economic growth. Worse yet, as the protest movement was developing into a full-fledged revolution, the Shah was constantly vacillating between refraining from the use of violence and using brute force against the opposition. The latter was probably due to the fact that he had not designed a clear-cut plan to deal with the complicated events that were occurring almost daily, and hoping everything would go back to normal miraculously.

By late 1977, various social groups had something to protest about: The salaried middle class was angry because of political repression, workers were enraged because their salary had not kept pace with inflation, peasants were disenchanted with the regime for failing to pursue a coherent policy in rural areas following the land reform, and rural migrants either could not find suitable jobs or had lost their jobs, all as the result of austerity measures pursued by the Amouzgar government. University students and human rights organizations were furious over the treatment of political prisoners, the intellectuals were resentful because of the severe restrictions imposed on freedom of the press and expression, and finally, the religious hierarchy was against secularization of the country.

During the months of August and September of 1978, two incidents occurred that radicalized the movement and made any compromise with the Shah impossible. First, while anti-Shah demonstrations and strikes had become daily events in Iran, on August 19, 1978, the Rex movie theater was set on fire in the oil city of Abadan, resulting in the deaths of over 400 people. Despite the mishandling of the incident by the government, especially the fire department, there is some evidence that a small group of agitators close to top religious authority in Iran had instigated it, in order to discredit the Shah further and intensify popular anger against him. The opposition, however, unanimously blamed the Shah for the incident.

The next event is the so-called Black Friday. On Friday, September 8, 1978, several thousand people who were participating in a quiet sit-in in Jaleh Square in Tehran were surrounded by military units, who opened fire at them after they refused to disperse. According to government sources, 88 died as the result, although clerics claimed several thousand had been killed. Regardless of the real number of the victims of this dreadful incident, it was the beginning of the end for the Shah (Abrahamian, 1982, pp. 516–517). Prime Minister Sharif Emami, who had replaced Jamshid Amouzgar, resigned and General Gholam Reza Azhari, a moderate and incompetent general, replaced him. In protest against the Jaleh Square massacre, the oil workers went on strike, depriving the government of revenues, which made the fall of the Shah inevitable.

Democratic Anger since the Revolution

With the overthrow of the monarchy, political parties, various interest groups, and newspapers sprang up. Underground political organizations as well as social democratic and liberal political parties and organizations started their activities openly and freely. Marxist organizations such as the Fadayan Khalq Guerrilla Organization, the Tudeh Party, Ranjbaran, Peykar, and Komeleh as well as the Mojahedin Khalq Organization, which had surfaced, became very popular with the new generation, especially among university students. The National Front and the Freedom Movement were popular with the older generation and were put in charge of the provisional government, with Mehdi Bazargan as its prime minister. The expectation of the democratic opposition was that dictatorship, censorship, and restriction on civil society would never return. But within a few weeks after the overthrow of the monarchy, things turned sour. Ayatollah Khomeini, who in Paris had promised a democratic political system with no restrictions for any political party, turned his back against all of those promises and expressed his decision for the creation of an Islamic order (Ashkevari, 2015). Gradually, the secular politicians were either purged, became discouraged and left, or were forced to resign, and were eventually replaced either by theologians or staunch pro-Khomeini non-clerics.

The dictatorship returned, but this time in the guise of "revolutionary Islamic" principles. Khomeini started criticizing intellectuals, independent newspapers, feminists, secular political parties, and universities for the problems of the country. Middle-class women, who were enraged by the regime's pressure to force women to wear veils, organized a huge demonstration on March 8, 1979 (International Women's Day), to show their opposition to this policy and demand equal rights with men. This event was, however, broken violently by Khomeini's supporters, who threw rocks at them and beat a large number of demonstrators. Sadly enough, the leftist forces did not support the women's show of force and dismissed it as a bourgeois attempt to divert the attention of people from the class struggle. This short-sidedness of leftist forces eventually cost the left and the entire civil society dearly.

The only chance that remained for the civil society activists to prevent the total control of the state by the proponent of a theocracy was the upcoming election for president and the parliament (Majlis). Abolhasan Bani-Sadr, who despite his liberal views was allowed to run for president, was able to win the presidential election with 75% of the popular vote. Happiness over this victory did not last long, because pro-Khomeini theologians, who had created the Islamic Republic Party (IRP), won the majority of seats in the parliament. By controlling the Majlis, the IRP leaders were in a position to oust Bani-Sadr, who had become the major obstacle to the total control of the state by pro-Khomeini theologians. Disagreements between Bani-Sadr and leaders of the IRP-dominated Majlis created a crisis in the country. With the blessing of Khomeini, Akbar Hashemi Rafsanjani, the Majlis speaker, mobilized the parliament members to impeach Bani-Sadr on June 21, 1981, and put an end to the possibility of democratic process in Iran. This development allowed the IRP, which already had the control of judiciary and the Majlis, to gain the control of the executive branch as well. Within a few months, the regime was in a position to ban all non-conformist political parties, shut down independent newspapers, and purge the universities (which were already closed down) of dissident professors and students in order to "Islamize" them. With the total domination of the state by the staunch proponents of theocracy, the civil society became dormant and listless. The result was bitterness, bewilderment, and passive anger of millions of Iranians who found no other choice but to wait for the disintegration of unity in the power bloc.

Despite the totalitarian understanding of Khomeini about the nature of the state, it soon became clear that various groups within the power bloc had different, divergent, and even contradictory interests. Despite the façade of unity within the Islamic Republic Party as the party of Khomeini and his instrument of Islamization of the country, three different factions within the party emerged: right wing, left wing, and centrist. Ali Khamenei, with strong roots in the bazaar, was the leader of the right wing, while his prime minister Moosavi, who was also deputy leader of the party, represented the left wing of the party. Hashemi Rafsanjani, as a centrist, was more of a pragmatist. He mostly sided with the right wing, but kept his close contacts with the leftists in the party. While the right wing of the party supported a free market and was in favor of less government intervention in economic activities, Moosavi was a staunch supporter of state control of the economy and a welfare state. Although Khomeini was trying to stay above these differences, he mostly sided with the left wing of the party. Ideological differences between Khamenei as the president and Moosavi as prime minister created a division in the Islamic Republic Party. Khamenei's aim was to dismiss Moosavi and execute his own policies, but Khomeini's support for Moosavi prevented the Iranian president from achieving his goal. Clashes between Moosavi and Khamenei over domestic and foreign policy issues eventually resulted in the dissolution of the Islamic Republic Party in May 1987. This new development was instrumental in restructuring of civil society in the 1990s.

Khomeini's death in June 3, 1989, left the Iranian theocracy without a suitable successor. According to Article 109 of the original Iranian constitution, *Valy-e Faghih* (the Supreme Leader) should have the qualification of *Marja' Taghlid* (highest Shi'a religious authority). In the emergency meeting of the Assembly of Experts, held immediately after Khomeini's death,

Hojjatol Islam Ali Khamenei, a junior theologian, who was serving as the president, was selected as the new *Valy-e Faghih*. As Khamenei did not have the qualification to succeed Khomeini as the *Valy-e Faghih*, the Assembly of Experts elevated him to the rank of Ayatollah to make his appointment look less conspicuous (Kadivar, 2015, pp. 95–120).

Post-Revolutionary Democratic Anger

It took the democratic anger more than a decade to come to the surface as the result of the restructuring of civil society in Iran. The civil society, which was besieged by the state, was able to break its encirclement when the contradiction within the power bloc surfaced in the mid-1990s. The democratic anger eventually erupted in the 1997 presidential election, when Hojjatol Islam Mohammad Khatami, the reformist candidate, announced that his main objective upon winning the election would be to strengthen the civil society in Iran. Khamenei had strongly supported the Majlis Speaker, Hojjatol Islam Ali Akbar Nateq Nuri, a conservative cleric who had promised to Islamize the country further. Contrary to the conservative circle's expectation that Khamenei's support would guarantee Nuri's victory, Khatami won the 1997 presidential election by landslide. Victory of Khatami was the result of the mobilization of millions of young people who, as the infantry of civil society, enthusiastically worked in his headquarters and prevented further Islamization of the country. Khatami received 70% of the vote, which gave him the mandate for change.

Khatami, who owed his presidency to pro-democracy groups and individuals, did good on his promise and lifted most of the restrictions that had been imposed on civil society. Despite the opposition of conservatives, reformist newspapers sprang up, the dress code (especially for women) became less restrictive, the tight control on employment of non-conformists was lifted, and political openness (relatively speaking) became the norm. Newspapers started writing freely about people's grievances and shortcomings of the theocratic system of the country, and publicized the abuse of power by conservatives. The conservative theologians who were concerned that the freedom of expression, assembly, and speech might weaken their position, started an all-out war against the reformists and did all they could to derail Khatami's government. Despite the fact that Khamenei and his conservative camp were able to weaken the reformers, the civil society remained vibrant and did not surrender to the conservative camp's attempts for the creation of a monolithic political system.

The democratic anger erupted one more time during the presidential campaign of 2009, when Mahmoud Ahmadinejad, the super conservative and populist president of Iran, started campaigning for re-election. The Reformist camp had two candidates who reinforced one another: Mir Hossien Moosavi (former prime minister), and Mehdi Karrubi (former Majlis speaker). Moosavi's presidential campaign was colorful and attracted millions of young people, especially university students and women. Moosavi, who had selected the "color green" as the symbol of his campaign, was genuinely in favor of democratization of the political system, reviving democratic values which had been severely restricted during four years of the Ahamdinejad presidency, and putting an end to discriminations against women, ethnic and religious minorities, and ending confrontational policies of Ahmadinejad toward the West. What separated Moosavi from all other candidates in 2009, was his wife and his unofficial running mate, Zahra Rahnavard. Rahnavard, a painter, sculptor, writer, university professor, and the first female university president, had great appeal among millions of women. As an Islamic feminist, she had played an important role in publicizing discriminations that existed against women. She campaigned tirelessly by Moosavi's side, which endeared both of them to millions of young people who, for the first time since 1979, saw a candidate holding hands with his wife in public. This simple and meaningful gesture electrified Moosavi's campaign and encouraged millions of young women to join his campaign enthusiastically.

The results of the election angered pro-reform supporters when Ahmadinejad was announced winner of the presidential election held on June 12, 2009. Millions of people throughout the country poured to the streets to protest the outcome of the election and demanded its annulment. These protesters believed the election had been rigged, and the loser had been announced the winner. The main slogan of the protesters was "Where is my vote?", indicating their votes had been stolen by the candidate who had lost the election. The widespread protests, known as the Green Movement due to protesters wearing green bracelets, head scarfs, scarfs, or shirts, shook the regime. The security forces and plainclothesmen (an unofficial pressure group that has been set up by the regime since 1979 to attack anti-government rallies) physically attacked the demonstrators, after Ali Khamenei, the Iranian Supreme Leader, openly expressed his support for Ahmadinejad, and threatened that if demonstrations and rallies continued, the demonstrators would be responsible for the outcome of their actions.

To the surprise of many, Khamenei's threat did not scare demonstrators, and they continued expressing their disappointment and anger toward what had happened by continuing their protest. Dozens of demonstrators were killed by security forces and pro-Khamenei supporters. Several hundred people were arrested and were imprisoned following mass trials, reformist political parties were disbanded, and many political activists, university professors, and journalists were forced to leave the country to escape persecution. The leaders of the Green Movement: Mir Hossien Moosavi, Zahra Rahnavard, and Mehdi Karrubi, were also put under house arrest without due process of law.

Radical Anger

The frustration-aggression hypothesis, which indicates that frustration or relative deprivation will result in some form of violence against the source of deprivation, is manifested in the use of violence by underground political organizations against the state. This kind of political activism, which mostly (but not exclusively), takes place in non-democratic countries, views violence as the only possible means to impact the political process. Proponents of the use of violence as a political action usually justify their use of violence as the counter-violence or revolutionary violence, and deny the fact that what they are engaged in, is terrorism. These groups usually rob banks to finance their activities, and assassinate government officials to terrify and weaken the regime. The same trend was followed in Iran in the 1960s, when a new generation of political activists who were greatly influenced by the Cuban, Algerian, Palestinian, and Vietnamese experience, came to the conclusion that the use of violence was a legitimate means for the achievement of political ends. The underground political organizations of Iran that used violence as the manifestation of political activism fall into three categories: Islamic, Left-wing Islamic, and Marxist.

The main aim of Islamic groups that emerged between the 1940s and 1970s was the creation of an Islamic state by assassinating those who were considered to be the enemy of Islam. Fadayan Islam (Islam's self-sacrificers) was the first group in this category. Fadayan Islam was founded by a young *Tollab* (singular; *Talabeh*, students of religious seminaries) in Qom by the name of Navvab Safavi in the early 1940s. Navvab Safavi was greatly influenced by Egypt's Muslim Brotherhood. This group assassinated the prominent Iranian historian Ahmad Kasravi and Prime Minister General Haji Ali Razm Ara in the 1940s. They were later enlisted by the court to harass Mossadegh and his associates. They also had an unsuccessful attempt on Mossadegh's right-hand man and his Minister of Foreign Affairs, Hossein Fatemi. The group was rounded up after the coup of 1953. Hayathay-e Mo'talefeh Eslami (the Association of Islamic Coalitions) is yet another pure Islamic group whose main base of support was in the bazaars (Iranian traditional market place). This organization managed to assassinate the

Iranian Prime Minister, Hasan Ali Mansur, in 1964. The group was discovered and destroyed in 1965, and it remained dormant until 1977.

Contrary to the pure Islamic group, the Mojahedin Khalq Organization (MKO), which was founded in 1965, was a modern Islamic group that had both Islamic and Marxist tendencies. Founders of the group and most cadres were college graduates, and they recruited their members from university students as well. This organization split into a Marxist faction and the original Islamic group in 1974. The Marxist group was later renamed Sazman-e Peykar dar Rah-e Azadi Tabagheh Kargar or simply Peykar (The Organization for the Liberation of the Working Class), but the Islamic Mojahedin retained the original name. Lastly, several Marxist activists created the Fadayan-e Khalq Organization (FKO) to violently overthrow the Shah's regime and establish a socialist state in its place. In contrast to the strictly Islamic group, which had a limited following, both MKO and FKO were very popular among the youth and university students.

The violent campaign these organizations either carried out or planned, resulted in swift and harsh reaction by the regime. Members and supporters of the underground political organization were imprisoned, tortured, and some of them were executed. Despite this, in contrast to the apathy and fear of 1950s, the repressive measures of 1960s and 1970s convinced the new generation that the only way to overthrow the Shah's regime was direct and violent confrontation. In contrast to the lamentation of 1950s, the poetry of the 1960s and 1970s is full of praise for counter-violence, revenge, underground mobilization, and armed struggle. The most prominent poets of this period who used revolutionary terminologies and supported confronting the regime violently are Ahmad Shamloo, Khosrow Golsorkhi, and Saeed Soltanpoor. The execution of Khsorow Golesorkhi, who was falsely accused of trying to organize a group to kidnap royal family members in 1973, made the young generation angrier with the regime and resulted in its further isolation from the people. The Iranian secret police, SAVAK, forbade the use of terminologies such as revolution, red, forest, and rose (the latter because its Persian translation is Golesorkh and therefore reminded people of the executed poet Golesorkhi).

Although the regime was able to weaken both MKO and FKO, these two organizations played a crucial role in mobilizing people for disarming military garrisons and forcing the military to surrender on February 11, 1979. Shortly after the overthrow of the Shah, both FKO and MKO, along with other leftist political organizations, found themselves at odds with the new regime and gradually went underground again. The new regime's determination to eliminate all non-conformist political organizations convinced FKO and MKO and several underground Marxist political organizations, such as Sarbedaran, Komeleh, and the Democratic Party of Kurdistan, that they had no choice but to resort to violence as a means to survive. The result was, however, disastrous; all of leftist political organizations were uprooted and forced to migrate abroad, and since then have not been able to play an important role in political life of Iran.

Theological Anger

By theological anger, I refer to the reaction of the hierarchy of Shi'a theologians (*Foghaha*) to the secularization of Iran since 1963, their activism for the creation of a theocracy, and their determination to eliminate anyone who dares to challenge the Islamic regime. Theological anger in Iran was triggered by the promulgation of land reform and other reform measures popularly known as the Shah's "six point reform measures," the "White Revolution," and "the Revolution of the Shah and the People." While the Shah allayed the fear of landlords by selling them shares of state-owned factories in exchange for their lands to be owned by landless peasants, he did not have anything to offer to the hierarchy of theologians. Theologians were angry at the Shah for granting equal rights to women as part of his reform measures. The religious hierarchy of Shi'a *Ulama* in Qom considered these measures anti-Islamic and the sign of surrendering to pressure from the United States. Ayatollah Ruhollah Khomeini, who in the early 1960s was not well known, played a crucial role in the fear and concern of Shi'a theologians in Iran. He vehemently attacked these new policies as anti-Islamic and contrary to the 1906 Constitution (Khomeini, 1981, pp. 168–178). He was arrested and later exiled to Iraq, where he remained until his triumphant return to Iran in 1979.

While in exile, Khomeini kept close contacts with both senior and junior theologians, as well as *Tollab* (singular; *Talabeh*, students of religious seminaries). Khomeini and his associates later changed their tactics and started voicing their opposition to corruption, poverty, political repression, shortages, social inequality, and finally to the foreign policy of the Shah. Although opposition political parties were banned, the religious hierarchy was able to use the network of 80,000 mosques to masterfully reach out to the people and voice their grievances against the injustices in society in religious terms, without directly criticizing the Shah's regime.

Khomeini, who was initially only critical of the Shah's regime for not abiding by Koranic principles, gradually became the major proponent of theocracy. While in exile in Iraq (1964–1979), Khomeini came to the conclusion that in order to roll back secularization of society in Iran, it is absolutely necessary to establish an Islamic state and revive Islamic laws (Shari'a). Khomeini's views in regard to an Islamic state are reflected in his *Velayat-e Faghih* (*Governance of Jurisprudence*) book, in which he argues that theologians inherit the mantle of the prophet and as a result are his trustees. He further concludes, because of their position in Muslim countries, theologians have the duty to establish an Islamic order, revive and apply Shari'a, rescind all secular laws, and create a society based on Koranic principles. "The Just Foghaha must be leaders and rulers, implementing divine ordinance and establishing the institutions of Islam" (Khomeini, 1981, p. 75).

The secular opposition did not take Khomeini seriously, but felt he could contribute to the mobilization of people against the regime. From the mid-1960s through 1977, it was the leftist forces with Marxist ideology and socialist tendencies that had the backing of the people in Iran. Even activist theologians such as Ayatollah Mahmoud Taleghani, Ayatollah Hossein-Ali Montazeri, Ayatollah Mohammad Beheshti, Hojjatol Islam Akbar Hashemi Rafsanjani, and Hojjatol Islam Ali Khamenei, believed that the only political force capable of overthrowing the Shah was underground leftist organizations, especially FKO and MKO. When the mobilization against the Shah started in early 1977, supporters of Khomeini were few, absent, and insignificant. From early to late 1977, the modern middle class, composed of students, lawyers, and writers, was in the forefront of the movement. The major aim of the democratic anger was revival of the 1905 Constitution, respect for human rights, an end to dictatorship, and freedom of the press. During this time, the National Front and the Freedom Movement led the movement. Despite clashes between the security forces and demonstrators, there was no call for the violent overthrow of the regime. The main slogan of demonstrators was revival of the constitution and an end to dictatorship.

An incident on October 23, 1977, changed the fate of the movement and its direction drastically. On that day, Khomeini's elder son, Mostafa, died suddenly. Khomeini's associates accused the regime of murdering him, although Khomeini personally did not make a comment about the cause of the death. Yet he became more vociferous in his anti-regime messages. Commemoration of Mostafa Khomeini's death in Iran, which was accompanied by clashes between the mourners and police, brought the name of Khomeini to the fore. Terrified by the popularity of Khomeini, the Shah made the deadliest mistake of his life, which cost him his throne. To discredit Khomeini, the Shah ordered the publication of a degrading and inflammatory article against Khomeini. This article, which was published in the semi-official *Ettela'at Newspaper* under a pseudonym, changed the fate of the Iranian revolution. American journalist Joseph Kraft, who was covering Iran during the tumultuous last few months of the Shah's regime, as well as Iran's former minister of information, Dariush Homayoun, suspect that this letter was written either by the Shah or by somebody in the court (Homayoun, 1984; Kraft, 1978). Publication of this article deeply angered Khomeini's staunch supporters. Several thousand Talabeh (seminary students), marched in the holy city of Qom to protest this event on January 9, 1978. Police opened fire at the protestors and killed 12 of them. Ayatollah Kazem Shariatmadari, a top Grand Ayatollah in Qom, issued a *Fatwa* (religious declaration), in which he announced that participation in the commemoration of the dead Talabeh was an Islamic duty. The Islamic public mournings, which are held on the third, seventh, and fortieth day of the passing of a person, gave a great opportunity to the religious hierarchy to put an Islamic stamp on the anti-Shah movement. On February 9, the fortieth-day commemoration of Qom incident was held in several major cities. The commemoration in Tabriz took the form of a popular uprising when police shot and killed a young worker. Angry demonstrators attacked banks, movie theaters, and government headquarters, and clashed with police who killed dozens of them. The people, however, managed to take the control of the city and pushed the security forces back. The Shah, who was frightened by this incident, tried to mend fences with the opposition and publically criticized security chiefs for mishandling the situation. In another gesture to make peace with the opposition, he removed the powerful head of SAVAK, General Nematollah Nasiri, and replaced him with moderate General Naser Moghaddam.

In mid-October 1978, Khomeini went to France to mobilize people against the Shah. While in France, he presented himself as the voice of democratic opposition and refrained from calling for the creation of a theocracy in Iran. Witnessing the ever-increasing popular unity, the Shah decide to compromise with the moderate opposition in order to keep his throne. The middle class was ready to strike a deal with him, but Khomeini refused to do so and called instead for the overthrow of monarchy and the establishment of a democratic order in its place. The Shah, who had totally lost self-confidence and was worried about his life, made the fateful decision to leave the country, hoping that this move might sooth the popular anger. Before leaving the country, he appointed Shapour Bakhtiar, one of the National Front leaders, as prime minister. Both men erroneously believed that the Shah's departure would end the crisis and that everything would go back to normal within couple of months. Bakhtirar's premiership, however, only lasted five weeks (January 4 to February 11, 1979), and ended when the military surrendered to angry demonstrators and armed opposition.

The Establishment of Theocracy in Iran

The overthrow of the monarchy on February 11, 1979, gave Khomeini absolute control over the machinery of the state and enabled him to push for the establishment of theocracy based on his *Velayat-e Faghih* (the Guardianship of Theologian). The concept of *Velayat-e Faghih* is included in the Iranian constitution of 1979 (Articles 5, 57, and 107–111) and constitutes the backbone of the Iranian political system. The Iranian Constitution of 1979 subordinates three branches of government (judiciary, executive, and legislative) to Velayat-e Faghih, who has the final word on all important issues.

Khomeini's insistence on the establishment of an Islamic state ended the coalition that had been established in the months leading to the overthrow of the Shah. This new development antagonized not only secular forces, but some of the top theologians who found Velayat-e Faghih harmful to Islam. While the former were disappointed and angry with the breach of Khomeini's promises in France about the establishment of a democratic order in Iran, the latter were concerned about the ramification of the establishment of an Islamic state. The latter group argued that theologians should only advise the government to act according to Islamic principles, since the enforcement of Islamic laws by theologians would turn those negatively affected by Shari'a, against Islam. Ayatollah Khomeini, however, was determined to go ahead with the establishment of a theocracy based on Velayat-e Faghih theory without any compromise.

On the occasion of the anniversary of anti-reform riots of 1963 that Khomeini had incited, he criticized all of the groups, personalities, and political organizations that did not share his views about the establishment of a theocracy in Iran. Khomeini had this to say to theologians who were warning him about the danger of the creation of a theocracy: "If you do not implement the laws of Islam now, in full detail, you must give up all hope of ever being able to do so. Those who believe in Islam and whose hearts beat for the Qur'an must act decisively today" (Khomeini, 1981, p. 271).

He also threatened secular forces with severe punishment if they did not stop criticizing his attempt to create a theocracy. "As for those who oppose us because of their opposition to Islam, we must cure them by means of guidance, if it is at all possible; otherwise, we will destroy these agents of foreign powers with the same fist that destroyed the Shah's regime" (Khomeini, 1981, p. 269). And for the final word, he said: "We do not want anything other than Islam; Islam can be implemented at all times, and particularly at the present time" (Khomeini, 1981, p. 271).

In order to create a theocracy based on the Velayat-e Faghih, the following steps were taken by Khomeini and his close associates:

First, by establishing Islamic Revolutionary courts, top generals and politicians of the Shah's regime were summarily executed to prevent the possibility of a military coup against the new regime.

Second, instead of total destruction of the military and police force of the ancient regime, Khomeini opted for gradual replacement of these institutions with the new yet highly ideological ones. The Islamic Revolutionary Committee (Komiteh Enghelab-e Eslami) and Islamic Revolutionary Guards (Sepah-e Pasaran-e Enghelab-e Elami) were parallel police and military institutions whose original cadre came from the most dedicated followers of Khomeini. The Islamic Revolutionary Committee, which served as the police force, was in charge of arresting the suspected pro-shah officials and "counterrevolutionaries," as well as providing internal security. The Islamic Revolutionary Guard (Sepah-e Pasadran-e Enghelab-e Eslami, or Sepah) was to protect the "Islamic Revolution" and defend the country against violent opposition to the regime. The backbone of the Sepah came from several small underground Islamic guerrilla organizations such as Hizbollah and Mansouroun, which were created in the 1970s. In November 1979, Sazman-e Basij-e Mostasz'afin (the Organization for the Mobilization of Poor) was created as the paramilitary unit of Pasdaran. This highly ideological paramilitary organization had branches throughout the country, and its members were mainly recruited from rural migrants, the urban poor, and peasant families in rural areas. There was no age limit for joining Basij, and most of its members were volunteers between the ages of 15 and 17. (Some had even joined at a much younger age.) Basij played a very important role during the Iran–Iraq war. By the end of the war in 1988, both Basij and Pasdaran had developed into formidable military-political institutions and paved the way for militarization of the country. These two groups play a significant role in the Iranian economy now.

Third, in regard to writing a new constitution, instead of the Constituent Assembly that Khomeini had promised in France, the Assembly of Experts (Majlis Khobregan), composed of top theologians and some Islamic intellectuals, was put in charge of this task. Despite the dismay of Islamic intellectuals such as Prime Minister Mehdi Bazargan and Abolhasan Bani-Sadr (the man who had a crucial role in Khomeini's public relation success in France, and Iran's first president), the Assembly of Experts wrote a theocratic constitution, with central role for Valy-e Faghih.

Fourth, Khomeini's most dedicated junior Mojtaheds, composed of Akbar Hashemi Rafsanjani, Hossein Beheshti, Ali Khamenei, Abdel Karim Ardebili, and Mohammad Javad Bahonar, created the Islamic Republic Party (IRP). The major aim of this political organization was to mobilize followers of Ayatollah Khomeini for the establishment of a theocracy and crush secular opposition as well as Khomeini's competitors in the religious hierarchy. Leaders and associates of the IRP monopolized political power and marginalized other groups and factions, both secular and religious. Domination of the first Majlis by the IRP allowed it to oust the first Iranian president, Abol Hasan Bani-Sadr, who was against the Islamization of the country.

Fifth, all of the secular laws were replaced by Islamic laws, and the judiciary became the domain of Shi'a Foghaha. According to the Article 157 of Iranian Constitution, the Head of Judiciary, who is appointed by Valy-e Faghih, must be a Mojtahed who is dedicated to the implementation of Islamic laws. To ensure the application of Islamic laws in society, the Prosecutor General and the Supreme Court Chief must also be theologians.

Sixth, Khomeini's preoccupation with eliminating those who might pose a threat to the regime was not limited to secular politicians. Even top theologians and long-time associates of Khomeini who did not share his views about the future of the country were sidelined, harassed, or killed. The most prominent theologians who were punished for their disagreement with Khomeini included Grand Ayatollah Shariatmdari, Grand Ayatollah Hasan Qomi, and Ayatollah Hossein Ali Montazeri. In order to oust Sahriatmadari, he was falsely accused of plotting against Khomeini's life (Menasheri, 2001, p. 22). For this accusation against which he was not allowed to defend himself, his title as Marja' Taghlid was taken away (something which was unheard of in Shi'a history until then), and he was denied access to medical treatment for his prostate cancer. Ayatollah Hasan Qomi was put under house arrest in 1984, where he remained until his death in 2004. Lastly, Ayatollah Montazeri was forced by Khomeini to resign his position as the acting *Valy-e Faghih* in 1989. The harsh treatment of these prominent theologians demonstrated to all top religious leaders that Khomeini's anger could destroy them, and therefore they kept quiet, despite their disagreement with him.

Khomeini's Anger

Khomeini's anger was directed toward individuals, ideologies, political organizations, and governments he suspected might pose a threat to theocracy in Iran. The long list included symbols of the ancient regime (including universities), secular political organizations and institutions, his competitors, non-conformists, freedom of press, democracy, nationalism, Western countries (especially the United States), Israel, conservative and pro-Western governments in the Middle East, as well as theologians who did not share his view about the *Velayat-e Faghih*.

The immediate problem after the revolution was how to resolve the dichotomy between Khomeini's promises in France for a democratic political order and his theory of Velayat-e Faghih. While a democratic order would require free and fair elections, strengthening the civil society through promoting political parties and enhancing independent media, guaranteeing gender equality, and empowering religious and ethnic minorities in Iran, the theory of *Velayat-e Faghih* was totally opposed to all of these principles. Despite this, as a shrewd strategist, he moved against all of these groups, cautiously, and with each step carefully calculated. The brilliant tactic of Khomeini to marginalize all non-conformists and pave the way for the Islamization of country was the adoption of "Neither East, Nor West" slogan. This simple slogan provided a great opportunity to Islamize the country within the constraints of Velayat-e Faghih. Invoking Neither East, nor West, all political parties, institutions, and entities that contradicted *Velayat-e Faghih* were considered allies of either the Soviet Union (East) or the United States (West) and were destroyed with absolute cruelty. Within just a year, freedom of the press was non-existent, political parties (with the exception of those supporting the regime) were either closed down or severely restricted, universities were shut down for three years (1980–1983) and were reopened only after they were "Islamized," women were forced to wear veils, and the stage was set for the establishment of a theocracy.

Khomeini's anger toward the United States played a crucial role in the American hostage crisis in Iran, ending diplomatic relations between the two countries, and eventually contributed to the Iran–Iraq War of 1980–1988. Although there is no evidence that Khomeini had previous knowledge about this incident, his support for the American Embassy takeover, after it took place, was instrumental in its continuation, with catastrophic consequences. The crisis provided the best opportunity to Saudi Arabia, which was terrified by the Iranian Revolution to encourage Saddam Hussein to invade Iran. American investigative journalist Robert Parry reports that Saudi Arabia had convinced Saddam Hussein that the United States would support the invasion (Parry, 2015). Whether the United States had given Saddam Hussein the green light to invade Iran or not, Khomeini's preoccupation with war efforts played a crucial role in the release of American hostages who had been held in Iran for 444 days.

The war enabled Khomeini to stabilize the regime, Islamize the country, and destroy all non-conformist political parties and organizations. During the war with Iraq, the military, which was reorganized by the first Iranian president, Abolhasan Bani-Sadr, played a crucial role in preventing Saddam Hussein from achieving a quick victory. The IRP leaders, especially Beheshti, Rafsanjani, and Khamenei, were afraid that the victory in war would boost Bani-Sadr's popularity and he could pose a serious threat to the stability of regime. They convinced Khomeini to oust Bani-Sadr and put the newly established Pasdaran in charge of handling the war. They had correctly calculated that continuation of the war with massive casualties, accompanied by injecting the Shi'a ideology among the Basij volunteers, would stabilize the regime further and pave the way for institutionalization of an Islamic regime.

The war continued for eight years and ended when Hashemi Rafsanjani, who was the acting commander-in-chief, in July of 1988 came to the realization that the war could not be won, and that it was in the best interest of the regime to accept the United Nations Security Council Resolution 598 to end the war. Khomeini bitterly accepted this advice, that he referred to as "drinking the cup of poison" (*Jam-e Zahr*), and ordered all of his supporters to abide by it. Many die-hard followers of Khomeini felt betrayed and were angry at those who had played a role in convincing him to end the war. While unhappy about accepting the Security Council Resolution, Khomeini was convinced that the regime could not afford to continue the war. Therefore, he felt it was necessary to find scapegoats to calm the anger of his supporters. Two incidents took place around the same time that allowed Khomeini to show his supporters that he had not given up shedding blood for the preservation of the Islamic regime.

Embarrassed by accepting to end the war that he had promised not to end before toppling Saddam Hussein, Khomeini targeted political prisoners and British-Indian novelist Salman Rushdie, whose *Satanic Verses* novel was considered blasphemy in the Muslim World. Immediately after both Iraq and Iran accepted the United Nations Security Council Resolution 598, MKO forces that were stationed in Iraq invaded Iran in the hope of toppling the regime. The invasion failed to achieve its objective, but made Khomeini angry enough to put an end to the existence of leftist forces who had been imprisoned since 1979. In July of 1988, he ordered the summary execution of political prisoners affiliated with the MKO and various Marxist organizations who were not willing to "repent" or condemn their respective political organizations (without warning them that failing to do so would result in their execution). This order was put immediately into effect during the summer of 1988. The exact number of victims of this crime is still unknown, but it seems to be between 5,000 and 6,000. Ayatollah Montazeri, who had protested this mindless killing, was forced to resign in early March 1989. Khomeini also issued a *fatwa* (a religious declaration) for the assassination of the British-Indian novelist Salman Rushdie, as well as all those who had participated in the publication of his *Satanic Verses* book.

Khamenei's Anger

Khamenei inherited both Khomeini's title as the Valy-e Faghih and his anger. As a result, like Khomeini he considers civil society, democracy, freedom of press, as well as the West, Israel, and conservative Middle Eastern leaders as a threat to the security of the regime. Khamenei's anger is directed against his opponents among theologians, former associates, and reformers. During his reign as the Valy-e Faghih, he has masterfully bought the support of top theologians such as Ayatollah Naser Makarem Shirazi, Ayatollah Javadi Amoli, and Ayatollah Mesbah Yazdi. He also tightly controls junior theologians who as Friday Prayer leaders have great influence on more traditional and conservative groups in Iran. The common theme of these theologians is that reform movement in Iran will result in secularization of society, and that political power will slip into the hands of liberals and seculars.

But unlike Khomeini, who had earned the religious and political leadership, he was granted the title of *Valy-e Faghih* as a matter of convenience. In order to make up for his shortcomings, he mobilized Basij, Ministry of Intelligence, and plainclothesmen against top ranking *Shi'a* theologians, who had reminded him that despite his appointment as the *Valy-e Faghih*, he did not have the qualification to issue a fatwa. Two top Marja' Taghlid, Ayatollah Ahmad Azari Qomi and Ayatollah Hossein Ali Motazeri, were put under house arrest because they had criticized him openly for overstepping religious boundaries. The former died in 1999 while under house arrest, but the restrictions were lifted on the latter, when news about his depression broke out. Ayatollah Montazeri remained critical of Khamenei, and he supported the Green Movement and was considered its spiritual leader. He died in 2009. Several other former associates at the rank of Grand Ayatollah have either been marginalized (Grand Ayatollah Abdolkarim Ardebili), or have been harassed and their houses ransacked by Basij and plainclothesmen (Grand Aytaollah Ali Mohammad Dastghaeyb and Grand Ayatollah Yusef Sane'i).

After the humiliating defeat of his favorite candidate, Nateq Noori, Khamenei became more determined to isolate and eventually defeat reformers. He personally led the opposition to the reform movement by mobilizing Friday prayer leaders, the judiciary, the Guardian Council, the Ministry of Intelligence, Pasdaran Corps, Basij, religious institutions, populist and semi-fascist pressure groups such as Ansar-e Hizbollah (Supporters of the Party of God), and anti-reform clerics to start a war of attrition on Khatami's government. In Khatami's words, during his first four years as Iran's president (1997–2001), the conservatives on the average created one crisis every nine days (Taghibeigi, 2001). Khatami's reelection in 2001, with 80% of the votes, made the matter even worse for him, and the conservatives were creating more crises in order to force him to resign.

In line with this tactic, the Ministry of Intelligence mobilized its special unit to assassinate a large group of intellectuals and secular politicians to render Khatami powerless and force him to resign. The victims of this campaign, known as the Murder Chain (Ghatlhay-e Zangirehi), included members of Iran's Writer's Association, including Mohammad Ja'far Pooyandeh and Mohamad Mokhtari, as well as the Leader of the National Front, Daroiush Forouhar and his wife Parvaneh Eskandari.

Khatami's courage in publicizing murder chains and his promise to bring perpetrators to justice, made the conservatives angrier. All the fingers in civil society were pointed at Khamenei and his close associates. Khamenei eventually felt it was necessary to discuss the matter, but instead of accepting responsibility for what had happened in the Ministry of Intelligence (as it is directly responsible to Khamenei, and its minister is appointed with his blessing), he blamed the incidents on the "enemy," Israel, and the United States, which he claimed had infiltrated this intelligence organization. Two prominent reformist journalists Saeed Hajjarian and Akbar Ganji, who had tirelessly worked on the subject, suffered the consequence. Saeed Hajjarian, the renowned journalist and the strategist of reform, became the victim of an assassination attempt that kept him paralyzed for life. His assailant, Saeed Askar, was a Basij member. Akbar Ganji, as an investigative journalist, played a crucial role in revealing the murder chains and the hands behind them. His articles about the people behind the scene of these political murders and his human rights activities resulted in his arrest several times (Ganji, 2000). He was sentenced to six years imprisonment in 2000.

To tame the reform movement, the judiciary chief, Ayatollah Mahmoud Hashemi Sharoodi appointed a young, ambitious and ruthless judge by the name of Saeed Mortazavi, as the Prosecutor of Islamic Revolutionary Courts, with a clear mission to close down reformist newspapers and imprison reformist journalists. Mortazavi, nicknamed "butcher of the press" in Iran, managed to closed down 120 pro-reform newspapers and websites and imprison several journalists including Abbas Abdi, Omid Me'marian, and Reza Alijani. His harsh treatment of political prisoners and journalists got the attention of the international media for his role in the death of Iranian-Canadian photographer, Zahra Kazemi on July 11, 2003, and the death of at least four political prisoners during the Green Movement of 2009. He was relieved from his duties as the Prosecutor of Islamic Revolutionary Court, but later was promoted to the position of Deputy Prosecutor General and even later as the Head of Iran's Social Security Administration.

Khamenei's anger against reformers and secular opposition has not intimidated them. After the 2009 election, pressure against reformist and secular opposition of Iran has intensified. Some reform leaders are under house arrest, some are imprisoned (Mostafa Tajzadeh and Mohsen Mirdamadi), some are excommunicated (Khatami), and many have found no choice but to leave the country, yet the reform movement is alive and strong. The presidential election of 2013 in which Khamenei's candidate Saeed Jalili, who was a younger version of Mahmoud Ahmadinejad, was badly defeated by Hasan Rouhani, shows one more time that Khamenei cannot dictate the result of a relatively fair election. Jalili, who was Iran's nuclear negotiator (2007–2013) with 5+1 (five permanent members of the United Nations Security Council plus Germany), received only 11.31% of the vote despite the official and unofficial support of Khamenei, Sepah, Basij, and conservative clerics. Rouhani, a former nuclear negotiator and proponent of moderation in both domestic and foreign policy, received 50.88% of the vote; 34.39% of the vote was divided among other candidates, and 3.42% of the votes were announced to be invalid or blank. Although Rouhani, like Khatami, has to deal with the crises the conservative circles create for his government, his survival is evidence that Khamenei's anger is not the determining factor in Iranian political process any more.

Conclusion

Anger, or more precisely political anger, plays a very important role in the political process. Success or failure of political movements to a great extent depends on how this anger is directed, the nature and reaction of the political system to which this anger is directed, as well as the social milieu in which this process takes place. The success of Satiagraha in India, the PNC in South Africa, and the Civil Rights Movement, in bringing long lasting change, is the result of their leaders' commitment to the stated goals. Mahatma Gandhi, Nelson Mandela, and Martin Luther King, Jr., who led the democratic anger in their country, did not have a plan to eliminate their opponents. Their aim was to institutionalize tolerance, understanding, and mutual respect in their respective societies. The problem in Iran was that Khomeini, like many revolutionary leaders of the 20th century, wanted to create a society based on authoritarian or totalitarian models of government. Worse than that, Khomeini was not honest about his plans for the future. Although he had the plan for the creation of theocracy in Iran, while in France he presented himself as representing all groups and as a disinterested individual whose only aim was to liberate his people and play the spiritual leader of the movement. The grand design that Khomeini had for Iran (the creation of a pure Islamic state) has prevented Iran from achieving political and economic development. Khamenei as the successor of Khomeini is following the same policies with devastating consequences for Iran.

References

Abrahamian, E. (1982). *Iran between two revolutions.* Princeton, NJ: Princeton University Press.

Apter, D. (1965). *The politics of modernization.* Chicago, IL and London, UK: Chicago University Press.

Ashkevari, H. Y. (2015). *Mo'zal-e janeshini dar nezam-e faghih shahi-khelafati.* Retrieved from mihan.net/1394/03/23/288

Berkowitz, L. (1989). Frustration-aggression hypothesis Examination and reformulation. *Psychological Bulletin, 106*(1), 59–73.

Davies, J. (1962). Toward a theory of revolution. *American Sociological Review, 27*(1), 5–19.

Dollard, J., Miller, N., Doob, L., Mowrer, O., & Sears, R. (1939). *Frustration and aggression.* New Haven, CT: Yale University Press.

Engler, R. (1961). *Politics of oil: A study of private power and democratic direction.* New York, NY: Macmillan.

Ganji, A. (2000). *Alijenab sorkhpoosh va alijenaban khakestari.* Tehran, IR: Tarh-e Now Publisher.

Gurr, T. (1970). *Why men rebel.* Princeton, NJ: Princeton University Press.

Gurr, T. R. (1972). A causal model of civil strife: A comparative analysis using new indices. In I. K. Feierabend, R. L. Fierabend, & T. R. Gurr (Eds.), *Anger, violence, and politics: Theories and research.* Englewood Cliffs, NJ: Prentice Hall.

Homayoun, D. (June 1984). "Causes of the Iranian revolution." The author's interview with Former Iranian Minister of Information Dariush Homayoun, Washington, DC.

Huntington, S. (1970). *Political order in changing societies.* New Haven, CT: Yale University Press.

Kadivar, M. (2015). *Ebtezal-e Marja'iyyat-e Shi'a: The trivialization of Shi'i authority: Impeaching Iran's Supreme Leader's claim to religious authority.* http://dukespace .lib.duke.edu/dspace/handle/10161/11131

Khomeini, R. (1981). *Islam and revolution: Writings and declarations of Imam Khomeini.* (Hamid Algar, Ed. & Trans.). Berkeley, CA: Mizan Press.

Kraft, J. (1978, December 18). A letter from Iran. *The New Yorker.* Retrieved from http://www.newyorker.com/magazine/1978/12/18/letter-from-iran

Menasheri, D. (2001). *Post-revolutionary politics in Iran: Religion, society and power.* London, UK and New York, NY: Routledge.

Mina, P. (2004). Oil agreements in Iran. *Encyclopaedia Iranica.* Retrieved from http://www.iranicaonline.org

Pahlavi, M. R. (1961). *Mission for my country.* New York, NY: McGraw Hill.

Parry, R. (2015, May 11). Saddam's green light. *ConsortiumNews.com.* Retrieved from http://consortiumnews.com/2015/05/11/saddams-green-light

Stemple, J. (1981). *Inside the Iranian revolution.* Bloomington, IN: Indiana University Press.

Taghibeighi, Y. (2001, June 13). Iran: Despite Khatami's win, road to reforms remains rocky. *IPS: Inter Press Service.* Retrieved from http://www.ipsnews .net/2001/06/iran-despite-khatamis-win-road-to-reforms-remains-rocky/

Burning for Independence: Anger, Violence, and the Evolution of the Tibetan Independence Movement

Jeannine Chandler

Getting what I do not want
And that which hinders my desire—
There my mind finds fuel for misery,
Anger springs from it and beats me down.
            —Shantideva, *A Guide to the Bodhisattva's Way of Life*[1]

In Tibetan Buddhist doctrine, anger is a manifestation of suffering and weakness, born of ignorance regarding the state of reality. Rage poisons perceptions, creates unhappiness, and enables the abandonment of reason. The Fourteenth (and current) Dalai Lama notes that "as a destructive force there is nothing as strong as anger" (Gyatso, 1994, p. 52). Yet he also acknowledges that some anger can be positive, if one is motivated by compassion or the desire to enact positive change. Anger may thus serve as an impetus for unity or collective action, or may even be used as a demonstration of solidarity or an expression of identity, as on the political stage (Gyatso &

Cutler, 1998, pp. 248–249; Tolchin & Tolchin, 2006, pp. xv, 94). Contagion, as a property of anger, has facilitated the spread of conflict and sparked change; this is particularly accurate in today's world, in which emotion and opinion are consistently shaped and driven by the internet and social media (Tolchin & Tolchin, 2006, p. 94). Without a doubt, in the modern era, anger (positive and negative) has altered national boundaries and global politics (Tolchin & Tolchin, 2006, p. xv).

Anger propels the debate regarding the status of Tibet and the genesis of the Tibetan independence movement. Since 1950, Tibet has been occupied by the People's Republic of China; in 1959, the Dalai Lama fled to India (where he has since lived in exile in the hill town of Dharamsala), and was eventually followed by more than 100,000 of his fellow countrymen. Led by the Dalai Lama, Tibetans in exile have sought international recognition of their plight and pushed for global intervention (especially by the West) on their behalf, guided by the Dalai Lama's calls for nonviolence. However, although Western citizens have demonstrated their support for the Tibetan cause, Western governments have yet to take up the mantle of Tibetan independence, unwilling to risk the ire of the Chinese government. More than 55 years later, many Tibetans (both in Tibet and in exile) are exasperated, frustrated by the Dalai Lama's seemingly failed approach with regard to the issue of Tibet's status and the increasing repression of Tibetans inside China. Over the past few decades, Tibetan youth (both in Tibet and in exile) have become radicalized, and although they express a deep respect and reverence for the Dalai Lama, they believe that time is running out for Tibet, and they must act. Tibetan anger can thus be viewed as a consequence of fear and humiliation, a sign of despair, and, to some, an acknowledgment of defeat. Martin and Susan Tolchin maintain that a sense of defeat is a fundamental element of political anger; defeat becomes anger, anger begets violence (Gyatso, 1994, p. 54). The most recent explosion of this anger is the rash of self-immolations that have plagued Tibetans since 2009. The act of self-immolation for Tibetans is simultaneously an expression of anger and a gesture of defeat, with the primary goal being the continued radicalization and unification of Tibetans in a quest to win back their homeland. A Tibetan writer named Gudup posted the following message on his page on a Chinese social networking site prior to his self-immolation on October 4, 2012. He noted that "in order to let the world know about the real situation in Tibet, we have to radicalize our peaceful action, voice out Tibetan independence by lighting up our bodies" (Lam, 2012). In this plea, the imagery of bodies on fire demonstrates the dramatic evolution of Tibetan anger regarding the occupation of their native land.

The historical relationship between Tibet and China is complex, spanning several hundred years.[2] In the 600s, as China experienced its Golden Age of Buddhism and cosmopolitanism during the Tang Dynasty (618–907), Tibet became unified and emerged as a strong kingdom along China's western boundary. The two powers formalized their relationship through the signing of treaties and engaging in diplomatic marriages, and in this way interacted as equals. The introduction of Buddhism into Tibet from India during this period was perceived as a threat to the indigenous Tibetan folk religion of Bön, and subsequent political intrigues and assassinations resulted in the repression of Buddhism and the disintegration of the Tibetan kingdom, lasting for two centuries. The 11th century witnessed a revival of Buddhism in Tibet and the creation of strong, politically influential religious sects that would ultimately solidify into the four principal schools of Tibetan Buddhism (Nyingma, Kagyu, Sakya, and Gelug) (Goldstein, 1997, pp. 1–2).

After the fall of the Tang Dynasty, Sino-Tibetan relations would be nearly nonexistent until the 13th century, when the rise of the Mongols drastically changed the landscape of much of Asia and Europe. The Mongols did not invade Tibet, as the Tibetans submitted to the conquerors and began to pay tribute to the Mongol leader, Genghis Khan. The Chinese resisted the Mongols' attempts at subjugation until the late 1200s, when they were ultimately forced to capitulate, and Khubilai Khan (Genghis Khan's grandson) founded the Yuan Dynasty (1279–1368), coopting the structure and components of previous Chinese dynasties and ruling as Great Khan over the immense Mongol empire from his seat in China. Melvyn Goldstein notes that "contemporary Chinese scholars and officials consider this the period when Tibet first became part of China," although pro-independence Tibetans argue in contrast that Tibet and China were both conquered by the Mongols, and "incorporated into a Mongol empire centered in China" (Goldstein, 1997, p. 4). The Tibetans and Mongols ultimately entered into a "priest-patron" relationship in which the Tibetan *lama*, or teacher, would provide religious instruction, and the khan, or ruler, would afford political support to the lama and his religious sect. In this way, the Mongols would play a crucial role in Tibetan history, as the Mongols bestowed the title of Dalai Lama[3] on the leader of the Gelug school in the late 1600s; successive Dalai Lamas would be recognized in their youth as reincarnations of Chenrezig, a *bodhisattva* (a deity who delays his/her own enlightenment in order to help all beings end the suffering of the cycle of life, death, and rebirth) who embodies compassion. With Mongol backing, the Gelug sect would reach political prominence in Tibet, and the institution of the Dalai Lama would provide spiritual and temporal leadership for millions of

Tibetan and Mongolian Buddhists. Most importantly, Buddhism would comprise the core of the Tibetan identity (Goldstein, 1997, pp. 2–10).

In the early 1600s, Chinese sovereignty, which had been restored after the fall of the Mongol Yuan Dynasty with the success of the ethnically Chinese Ming Dynasty (1368–1644), was threatened once again by the ascendancy of an emerging semi-nomadic, non-Chinese group known as the Manchus. The Manchus, who conquered the Ming and founded the Qing Dynasty (1644–1911), initially entered into a cordial relationship with the Dalai Lama; however, in the Qing quest to subdue the remaining Mongol tribes, the Manchus began to perceive the Tibetans, whose religious sects were aligned with different Mongol tribes, as potentially dangerous. A combination of Buddhist sectarianism, weak Dalai Lamas, competing Mongol tribes, and Manchu political calculations resulted in the subjugation of Tibet to the Qing Empire in the early 1700s. The Qing would not rule Tibet directly, however; instead, they stationed two Manchu imperial officials (known as *ambans*) in the Tibetan capital of Lhasa. For the most part, the *ambans* exerted little direct control over Tibet, which was ruled by powerful regents in the absence of strong Dalai Lamas, in a period stretching from the mid-1700s through the late 1800s (Goldstein, 1997, pp. 10–21).

The mid-1800s witnessed the beginnings of China's declining power during its "century of humiliation," as the modern age of imperialism brought the Qing Dynasty into conflict with the West. As a result, the Qing's grasp on its border lands faded. In Tibet in the late 1800s, the Thirteenth Dalai Lama was enthroned. Strong and progressive, he increasingly made decisions regarding Tibet's affairs without consulting the *ambans*, and thus Qing control continued to wane. This status quo was disrupted in the early 20th century as Tibet's strategic value as a buffer area in Central Asia made it a pawn in the Great Game among imperialist Western nations. The Thirteenth Dalai Lama's independence, in combination with the Qing Dynasty's incapacity to save itself from inevitable collapse, resulted in Tibet's ability to negotiate its own treaties with outside powers (actions that pro-independence Tibetans and scholars interpret as indications of Tibetan sovereignty). As the last dynasty of China ended in 1911, nationalistic Chinese emphasized the need to reunify the motherland and counter foreign threats (tasks at which the Qing Manchus had failed) (Goldstein, 1997, pp. 21–29).

As both China and Tibet entered the 20th century, each country was wary of the other, and looking to protect itself from outside threats through modernization.[4] The Thirteenth Dalai Lama attempted to institute social reforms and create a strong military; however, he faced resistance from the feudal aristocracy and monastic elites, and ultimately was forced to rescind his policies. In China, the Nationalist Party (under Chiang Kaishek) and the Communist Party (under Mao Zedong) emerged as China's strongest candidates for leadership of the country. As China was entrenched in civil war (1928–1949), as well as the Second Sino-Japanese War (1937–1945), Tibet fostered its de facto independence without Chinese interference. However, as China reached a peak of nationalism, Tibet continued to adhere to feudal policies, and was further weakened by the death of the Thirteenth Dalai Lama in 1933. The Fourteenth Dalai Lama was not officially recognized and enthroned until 1939, at the age of four. Tibet was thus shocked and unprepared when Mao's army invaded Tibet in 1950, with the intent of "liberating" Tibetans from their feudal oppression under the Dalai Lama's theocracy. Tibetans were unable to counter the large modern Chinese army and, in 1951, Tibetan government delegates were forced to sign the Seventeen Point Agreement, which (to the Chinese) solidified Tibet's status as part of China. During the 1950s, as the Dalai Lama reached the age of majority, China pushed for socialist reforms in Tibet, which exacerbated conflict between the Chinese and Tibetans. In 1959, rebellion erupted, and the young Dalai Lama fled to India and founded his government-in-exile. China cracked down on Tibetan resistance to its policies, continued to reform Tibetan society and politics, and tightened its control over all Tibetan regions (Goldstein, 1997, pp. 30–60). In 1965, the Chinese government created the Tibet Autonomous Region (TAR), a designation similar to a Chinese province.

The Chinese government's insistence that Tibet has always been a part of China, in comparison with the exile government's argument that Tibet has historically been independent, demonstrates that the two groups have fundamentally divergent understandings of history, and have been unable to reach an agreement on the most basic elements of this issue. For example, since the late 1980s, the Dalai Lama and the Tibetan government-in-exile have urged the Chinese government to consider granting Tibetans political "autonomy," potentially similar in status to the special administrative regions of Hong Kong and Macau. However, the two sides have been unable to reach a decision on a definition of "autonomy." The two governments cannot even reach an agreement on the definition of "Tibet." For the Chinese, it is solely the TAR; for the Tibetan exile community, it is the region commonly referred to as Greater Tibet, a designation that includes not only the TAR, but also the traditional Tibetan regions of Kham and Amdo (parts of which are currently located in the Chinese provinces of Qinghai, Gansu, Sichuan, and Yunnan) (Johnson, 2011, p. 89).

Contemporary Tibetan anger is primarily fueled by the continued occupation of Tibet and the treatment of ethnic Tibetans within China's borders. Tibetans in exile argue that Tibetans in China lack rights and freedoms and, like other minorities in China's frontier areas, they are condemned by Han (ethnic) Chinese (who comprise more than 90% of China's population) and repressed by Chinese authorities. Human rights organizations report that Tibetans are frequently abused, arrested, and imprisoned for alleged political crimes. According to Amalendu Misra, ". . . with less than 1 per cent of the total population, Tibet contributes more political prisoners than the rest of China's provinces combined" (Misra, 2000, p. 82). Many of those abused and imprisoned are monks and nuns, leaders of the Tibetan Buddhist monastic establishment. Tibetans (in exile and in Tibet) have frequently noted that the communist government has placed restrictions on Tibetan religious practices, as well as drastically reduced the admissible number of ordained monastics. During the Cultural Revolution (1966–1976), when the "Four Olds" campaign targeted for destruction "old customs, old culture, old habits, and old ideas," minority ethnic groups and religions endured the brunt of the Red Guard attacks. Monasteries were torn down, religious relics were damaged, and monks and nuns were beaten, tortured, and killed (Ardley, 2002, p. 9). Furthermore, the Dalai Lama, who, for most Tibetans, is revered and adored as an enlightened being, has long been demonized and attacked in official Chinese propaganda. These denunciation drives spiked in the early 1990s, as the Chinese government attempted to counter his rising popularity and visibility in the Western media (Barnett, 2014, p. xxxii). This new campaign attacked him personally (casting doubt on his religious credentials) and accused him, in Chinese communist parlance, of leading the "Dalai clique," being a "splittist" (attempting to split Tibet from the Chinese motherland), and inciting unrest among Tibetans. Tibetan monks, nuns, and laypeople, especially those subject to political reeducation, are told they must denounce the Dalai Lama, they are forbidden from displaying his image, and they must endure his continued absence from their homeland (Human Rights Watch: China, 1997, pp. xx–xxi). Liu Xiaobo, Chinese political prisoner and recipient of the Nobel Peace Prize, wrote that "denying a devout citizen the right to meet his spiritual leader for more than 40 years is like depriving Tibet of its core values. To accuse and defame the Dalai Lama is like taking a knife and cutting out the Tibetan people's heart" (Woeser, 2010).

In addition to religious persecution, Tibetans (in exile and in Tibet) maintain that Tibetan culture (closely intertwined with Tibetan Buddhism) has been targeted for elimination. Chinese language is the primary language of instruction in Tibetan schools; Tibetan children are forced to celebrate traditional Chinese holidays and are restricted in their celebrations of Tibetan culture (many of which are religious in context). According to some Tibetans, these shackles on their cultural expression have negatively impacted the lives of the families, and they see the Chinese government as responsible for their disappearing way of life. A 53-year-old nomadic herder fumed, "After I die, my sons and grandsons will remember. They will hate the government" (Johnson, 2011, p. 29). Aiding in this cultural destruction, Tibetan exiles argue, is the government's "Developing West" campaign that encourages Han Chinese migration to Tibet via economic incentives. Tibetan architecture, art, and culture are being eclipsed by the Chinese cultural influences that have been brought in by an overwhelming influx of Han workers. The Dalai Lama has referred to the government's actions as "cultural genocide" ("Dalai Lama accuses China," 2008). Scholars have also noted that Chinese racism toward minority groups (referred to more specifically as "Han Chauvinism") has resulted in the stereotyping, mythmaking, and denigration of Tibetans and their culture. Tibetans are perceived by ethnic Chinese as lazy, incompetent, and superstitious, as well as dangerous (Tuttle, 2015). One report notes that the 2008 protests (during which Tibetans attacked Han businesses) "intensified the views among many Han Chinese that minority groups in the nation's west, including the Tibetans, are 'remote and backward barbarians'" (Johnson, 2011, p. 96).

An additional impact of the Chinese government's policies in Tibet (along with the more recent unchecked Han migration) has been the uneven economic development between the TAR and the rest of China, as well as within Tibet between the Han Chinese and Tibetans. Tsering Woeser sardonically refers to this phenomenon as "economic imperialism with Chinese characteristics." State money has done little to benefit the Tibetans in the TAR. Han Chinese, accustomed to a capitalist system, are able to outperform Tibetans in the marketplace; even many of the traditional "Tibetan handicrafts" are now made by ethnic Chinese (Woeser & Wang, 2014, pp. 19–20). Relatedly, this unrestrained economic development has had a detrimental impact on the delicate environment of the Tibetan plateau, sometimes referred to as "the world's most fragile ecosystem." In 2006, the Qinghai-Tibet railway was completed, facilitating the Chinese government's ability to exploit Tibet's natural resources, including wildlife, forests, minerals, lakes, and rivers. Tibetans lament also the unrestrained tourism (from Han and foreigners) that has not only damaged the environment, but has also polluted sacred spaces. In 2012, the local government and media announced that Yamdrok Lake, where high lamas traditionally retreat to pray, chant, and receive signs regarding the locations of potential holy reincarnations, would be the site of boat tours and pleasure cruises, which sparked outrage and protests from pious locals and environmental activists (Liu, 2012).

It is important to distinguish among the many entities that impact this discussion of Tibet's status and have therefore played a role in scaffolding, challenging, directing, and mollifying Tibetan anger. Since the 1950s, the Chinese government has not wavered in its rhetoric to unite the races of China under the leadership of the Chinese Communist Party and in this way, views Tibetan actions against the state as treasonous. The state further resents the interference of the Dalai Lama, the Tibetan exile community, and the sympathetic West in what they see as a domestic affair, pertinent to the integrity of the Chinese polity. The state has focused on blaming the Dalai Lama and the exile community for the unrest, and counters any protests with severe punishments and repression. Using official pronouncements and propaganda, the Party casts aspersions on the Dalai Lama, accusing him and outside elements of provoking the turmoil in order to re-establish his Buddhist theocracy. By painting the Dalai Lama as a splittist, the government is able to stoke the fires of Han nationalism, in support of the state's actions, while at the same time avoiding any discussion of the root of Tibetan anger (Johnson, 2011, p. 18). The Chinese state is thus perceived by Tibetans (and the sympathetic international community) as the epitome of the traditionally oppressive Communist power and as such, is ultimately the source of and target for Tibetan rage over the occupation of Tibet. As for Chinese citizens, in country and overseas, regardless of their perceptions of the Chinese government, most will find common ground on the issues of Tibet and Taiwan, especially in this era of heightened Chinese nationalism. After the unrest in minority areas in 2008–2009, many Chinese "otherwise critical of the government, underwent unprecedented mobilization around Chinese national identity" (Anand, 2009, p. 30).

Contrary to popular opinion in the West, the Tibetans, as an ethnic minority, are fragmented. Although Tibetans are often portrayed in Western literature and media as peaceful refugees of Shangri-la, this myth conceals the very real divisions between Tibetans in Tibet and the diaspora. Heather Stoddard argues that in pre-1959 Tibet, "the Tibetan people at large were aware essentially of two types of identity: religious and regional affiliation" (Stoddard, 1994, p. 125). Within these two categories, individuals identified themselves by a variety of associations: mountains, valleys, local lamas, monasteries, chieftains, tribes, dialects and deities. People of different Buddhist schools, regions, languages, and customs generally treated one another with suspicion and aggression (Goldstein, 1968, p. 134). In light of this historical friction, Ronald Schwartz contends that "Tibetan nationalism is very much a modern phenomenon" (Schwartz, 1994, p. 92). Beginning in the 1960s, the Dalai Lama worked from exile to unite Tibetans in order to clearly demonstrate to the international community that there was in fact a unified, independent Tibetan nation. Even in the exile community, Tibetans themselves make distinctions between those who have been in exile for a long time (including those born in India and those who have spent time in the West), versus those who have recently crossed the Himalayas (who are often perceived by the former as being uncultivated, vulgar, or even, Chinese). Each group claims to be the source of authentic Tibetan identity (Hess, 2009, pp. 65–66, 146–147). Thus, current notions of Tibetan unity and identity stem from the Dalai Lama's efforts to mask the religious and regional distinctions among Tibetans. His success in this endeavor is a testament to his status and role in the eyes of Tibetans, regardless of their birthplace or residence.

It is difficult to overstate the significance of the Dalai Lama to contemporary Tibetans, as the perception of him as sacred, symbolic, and divine is embedded and internalized in the Tibetan mindset. In the West, the Dalai Lama is often incorrectly referred to as a "god," "priest," or "Pope" of Tibetan Buddhism. However, whereas the Pope is a *representative* of the deity (God), the Dalai Lama is rather regarded as a *manifestation* of the deity (Chenrezig) (Goldstein, 1968, p. 161). Tibetans have traditionally perceived him as being not only a *bodhisattva*, but also a protector of (Tibetan) Buddhism, Tibetan people, and Tibet itself. In discourse, the Tibetan cause, Tibetan Buddhism, the Dalai Lama, *and* Tibet are often explicitly or implicitly equated with one another. The idea of the Dalai Lama as Tibet has been a prevalent idea since he entered exile in 1959. Scholar Robert Barnett argues that within the exile government, the Tibetan community, and the international media, "the representation of Tibet" has been the Dalai Lama (Barnett, 2001, p. 299). As this involves seeing the exile community in India and abroad as "Tibet," this theory implies that where the Dalai Lama is, so is Tibet. The Dalai Lama himself has said that "Tibet is not just about being an independent country. It is about a valuable belief system that is being destroyed by China. So when you support what I have to say you also support the belief system and therefore Tibet" (the Dalai Lama, quoted in Chhaya, 2007, p. 243).

Winner of the 1989 Nobel Peace Prize and the 2007 Congressional Gold Medal, the Dalai Lama has become an international spokesperson for Buddhism, ethics, and human rights. He has consistently adhered to a "peace philosophy," informed by his Buddhist belief, Gandhian non-violence, a sense of realpolitik, and an abiding concern for the welfare of Tibetans (Puri, 2002, p. 3501). He cautions fellow Tibetans to cultivate patience in order to counteract any anger they feel toward the Chinese:

> To be patient means not to get angry with those who harm us and instead to have compassion for them. That is not to say we should let them do what they like. We Tibetans, for example, have undergone great difficulties at the

hands of others. But if we get angry with them, we can only be the losers. This is why we are practicing patience. But we are not going to let injustice and oppression go unnoticed. (Gyatso, 1994, p. 74)

In facing injustice and oppression, the Dalai Lama contends that one should not allow anger to grow into violence, as violence only begets more violence. Regarding the plight of Tibetans vis-à-vis China, he claims that "in our case, violence is more or less suicidal. It is not at all practical" (Shiromany, 1998, p. 251). In light of that realization, the Dalai Lama's recommendation is to engage in nonviolent forms of protest in order to continually publicize the Tibet issue to the world. "Therefore, I feel that the Tibetan people should show their resentment to the Chinese because the Chinese never seem to accept the problem that exists in Tibet. Expressions such as prayers, hunger-strikes, demonstrations without violence are all meaningful" (Shiromany, 1998, p. 252). Despite his advice to Tibetans, many of them view his nonviolent approach as having failed, and their anger has prompted some to conclude that "his message of peace has divided the exiled Tibetan community" (Puri, 2002, p. 3500).

In contrast to the successful non-violent strategies of Gandhi and Martin Luther King, Jr., the Dalai Lama's policies have not resulted in a victory for Tibetans. Perhaps his lack of success is due to the nature of his opponent; whereas Gandhi and King were up against democratic regimes with a certain regard for international opinion, the Dalai Lama has been forced to engage an aloof, often despotic, Chinese communist regime. On the other hand, the Dalai Lama's critics, such as Jamyang Norbu, have contended that the success of Gandhi's non-violence was found in its aggressive and confrontational approach. Norbu has provocatively argued that the Dalai Lama's non-violent strategy has failed because he does not "comprehend the nature of modern politics" and he lacks "an understanding of totalitarian regimes." He criticizes the Dalai Lama's non-violent policy as inaction, claiming that non-violence "cannot be an excuse for not doing anything" (Norbu, 2008).

However, despite the criticisms, what the Dalai Lama has accomplished with his "message of peace" is the acquisition of enough "soft power" in the global forum to challenge China's overwhelming military might. John Whalen-Bridge claims that the Dalai Lama is able to simultaneously play both victor and victim on the world stage, a dual role that "multiplies the dramatic effect" of his propagation of the Tibetan cause and, in so doing, he has been able to wield "power-in-defeat" (Whalen-Bridge, 2013, p. 181). His inability to achieve autonomy or independence for Tibetans can be perceived as a "performance of failure," an act in which "a successful performance" is determined not by his ability to gain concessions from the Chinese at the negotiating table, but rather by his effectiveness in retaining international sympathy (Whalen-Bridge, 2013, p. 181).

The Western world thus comprises the audience for the theater of political protest showcasing Tibetan anger. In theory, the West functions as "hypothetical fair arbitrator," passing judgment on the Tibet issue (Schwartz, 1994, p. 21). Ronald Schwartz, a visitor to Tibet during the 1989 protests, observed that "Tibetans were grateful for the presence of Western witnesses. Their presence brought international attention to the situation in Tibet" (Schwartz, 1994, p. 38). It is noteworthy, however, that the West seems far from unbiased on this issue, given its rocky relationship with China, and the tendency for Westerners (particularly Americans) to see themselves as global arbiters of democracy and justice. Furthermore, since the late 1980s, Tibetans have been able to appeal to the West on these principled grounds, highlighting transgressions of human rights (thereby attracting Western liberals) ("Studying Tibet Today," 2014). Western political ideals, such as democracy and freedom, are portrayed in Tibetan exile discourse as compatible with Tibetan nationalism and the independence movement, and Westerners are regarded as allies in a quest for independence (Schwartz, 1994, p. 92). The Chinese, in contrast, base their argument on Chinese nationalism and historical absolutes, a position supported by the Chinese public yet seen as provocative by Tibetans and their allies in the West ("Studying Tibet Today," 2014). In recent years, as the West's relationship with China becomes closer and more economically complex, the Tibet issue has become an increasingly awkward situation: the proverbial elephant in the room. The Chinese government harangues the West (in particular the United States) for feting the Dalai Lama and seemingly condoning what the Chinese perceive to be seditious activities. The Tibetan cause continues to compete for the support of Western governments and media, and meanwhile faces threats from heightened Chinese nationalism and economic dominance, which has been shown to be the West's primary concern (Anand, 2009, p. 30). As one journalist noted, "it is clear that there is no appetite in the West to risk relations with China because of Tibet" (Abraham, 2008, p. 9).

Various communities in Tibet, in exile, and in the West, have made concerted efforts to bring attention to the Tibetan independence issue, gain international support for the cause, and apply pressure to the Chinese government in order to effect change. At the beginning of the occupation, during the 1950s, many Tibetans, particularly those in the regions of Kham and Amdo, engaged in active resistance against the Chinese. In this early Cold War era, as part of the American attempts to thwart the spread of

Communism around the world, the Central Intelligence Agency (CIA) began to nurture and train Tibetan freedom fighters in order to counter the Chinese occupation. In 1958, the volunteer military force known as Chushi Gangdruk ("Four Rivers, Six Ranges," the traditional name for the eastern Tibetan regions of Amdo and Kham) was formed, comprising Amdowa and Khampa resistance leaders. Over the next few years, the CIA trained nearly 300 Tibetan guerrillas at Camp Hale in Colorado, later reintroducing them into Tibet to fight against the Chinese; the freedom fighters, however, had little success in halting the occupation (Knaus, 1999, pp. 142–146). Lhasa-area Tibetans rose up against Chinese troops in Lhasa in March 1959, sparked by the rumor that the Chinese planned to kidnap the Dalai Lama. In the chaos, the 24-year-old Dalai Lama fled through the snow and mountains, protected by Khampa guerrilla fighters, ultimately arriving in India. The CIA program in Tibet was ultimately phased out in the 1960s, and discontinued all together by the time of President Nixon's rapprochement with China in the early 1970s. It was during this time that Tibet's status ceased to be of concern to the American government (Goldstein, 1997, pp. 49–58).

In the late 1960s, throughout China, people endured the chaos and violence of the Cultural Revolution (1966–1976). Mao began this movement in order to eliminate his opposition in the Communist Party and to galvanize the populace through revolutionary fervor. As a result, authority, tradition, religion, and history were attacked in regions across China, especially in Tibet, where these aspects seemingly coalesced in the age-old feudal theocracy of Tibetan Buddhism. As noted above, monasteries were destroyed, monks and nuns were beaten and humiliated, and religious relics were damaged or disappeared completely. China attempted to heal itself in the late 1970s and early 1980s through the policies of Deng Xiaoping, who initiated the Reform Era responsible for China's spectacular economic growth. Initially, these reforms also included a more relaxed atmosphere for cultural and intellectual expression. In Tibet, this involved fewer restrictions on cultural and religious behaviors, as well as the spontaneous rebuilding of monasteries destroyed by the Cultural Revolution (Schwartz, 1994, p. 59). An unintended consequence of this period of tolerance was the growth of Tibetan nationalism as Tibetans participated in the revival of their culture and religion. While the Chinese government seemingly had planned to co-opt the performance and symbols of this revitalization of Tibetan religion in order to exert more control over the region, for the Tibetans, the mere assertion and practice of their religion and culture (as different from the Han) became their means of protesting China's actions in Tibet (Schwartz, 1994, p. 1). This has led to the blurring of the line between religious actions and political actions; as Ronald Schwartz states, "political protest has come to be framed in religious idioms" (Schwartz, 1994, p. 22). The ethnic repression and political repression combined has resulted in a dramatic level of resistance to the Chinese state's attempts to stabilize and extend their authority over the Tibetan regions (Whalen-Bridge, 2013, pp. 169–170). Tibetan identity is dictated and reaffirmed by the performance of cultural and religious behaviors, such as the celebratory throwing of *tsampa* flour, engaging in monastic debates, displaying the picture of the Dalai Lama, and flying the Tibetan national flag. These activities have been variously politicized and criminalized by the Chinese government, which sees these actions as conspicuous and threatening attempts to assert an identity separate from the Chinese state (Schwartz, 1994, pp. 111–112). "Tibetanness" is thus defined by the performance of these cultural and religious rituals, which thereby unify (to borrow from Benedict Anderson) an "imagined community" of Tibetans, including those in the diaspora and in China (Anderson, 1991). Tibetan activist Tsering Woeser wryly notes the connection between identity creation and political protest: "Perhaps we should thank our authoritarian government for its devious ways to publicize Tibetan tradition and history. Thanks to Beijing's efforts to snuff out our cultural practices, even more Tibetans, especially the younger generation, are taking them to heart" (Woeser & Wang, 2014, p. 66).

The pro-independence demonstrations and riots of the late 1980s in Tibetan areas were in reaction to the continued repression from the Chinese government. At this time, the Chinese state was dealing with political unrest in its Han areas as well, as pro-democracy activists in Beijing and other major cities engaged in widespread protests, demanding intellectual freedoms and an end to government corruption (the demonstrations were ultimately ended when the Chinese military crushed the movement, culminating in the Tiananmen Square Massacre of June 1989). In Tibetan areas, the protests grew in intensity and violence between 1987 and 1989, leading up to the 30th anniversary of the Tibetan Uprising of March 1959. From 1987 to 1993, there were nearly 200 protests by Tibetans against Chinese rule (Barnett, 2014, p. xxxii). Schwartz (1994) claims that, between 1987 and 1992, there were 140 demonstrations by Tibetans against the Chinese government. Almost all of the demonstrations occurred in Lhasa and were carried out by young monks and nuns. Interestingly, these young Tibetans had grown up in Tibet under a more liberal Chinese regime; however, as Schwartz states, they "still found reasons to challenge Chinese rule in Tibet" (Schwartz, 1994, p. 3). Many were frustrated with government interference in monasteries; others demanded the release of political prisoners or called for independence. Hundreds were arrested and unknown numbers were killed (Schwartz, 1994, pp. 1, 87). In January 1989, a letter from independence activist Lobsang Tenzin to fellow university students was smuggled out of prison. In the letter, he explained why he took part in the protests in March 1988: "I have tried to contain the fire of anger burning freely inside my body. But this time, though I knew the Chinese would arrest me, I needed to express the strong feelings I have had for many years" (Schwartz, 1994, p. 147). Indeed, the frustration that prompted the Tibetan protests of the late 1980s can be perceived as the merger of despair and anger.

The role of Buddhist monastics in these demonstrations piques the curiosity of Westerners, who have been saddled with the Orientalist trope of the Asian religious man as reasonable, calm, and profound. The Dalai Lama is certainly the personification of this trope; since he also represents Tibet and Tibetans, the land and its people have been stereotyped as peace-loving and content, thus the myth of Shangri-la. Contrary to Western perceptions, the Tibetan monastic community has long been associated with activism and unrest, even violence. Tibetan monasteries are traditionally known as hubs of dissent and conflict, particularly in consideration of the history of sectarianism and even warfare between (and within) the schools of Tibetan Buddhism (Chandler, 2009, pp. 40–57). In pre-occupation Tibet, the *dob-dobs*, or "fighting monks," were known for their aggressive behavior; they wielded weapons, engaged in combat, and served as bodyguards for the monasteries (Goldstein, 1989, pp. 25–26). Tsering Woeser claims that Tibetan monks, free of the worldly constraints of modern society, are commonly characterized as fearless resistors, and have historically provided leadership for uprisings (Woeser & Wang, 2014, p. 34). Schwartz (1994) contends that "it has been the best scholars among the young monks who have been the most active in politics" (p. 71). As Tibetans continue to fear the loss of their religious and cultural heritage, "the monasteries have come to signify Tibetan nationhood and survival, and thus have become the principal background for Tibetan resistance to the Chinese state" (Schwartz, 1994, p. 17).

In a recent analysis, John Whalen-Bridge refers to the phenomenon of monastic resistance as "Angry Monk Syndrome" (AMS). He argues that the monks' effectiveness is derived from their performance of anger in a context of political protest. Since (Buddhist) monastics are perceived as being beyond worldly emotions such as attachment and anger, an image of a monk seemingly unable to control his emotions is a paradox for the audience (in this case, the international media). Whalen-Bridge (2013) contends that the imagined weakness of the monks is the source of their "soft power" (pp. 164–165). Just as the Dalai Lama finds success in defeat with his "performance of failure" (see above), the monks' "honorable powerlessness" manifests in their angry protests, which are effective as long as they continue to appear as victims (Whalen-Bridge, 2013, pp. 169–170).

In the run-up to the Beijing Olympics in 2008, Tibetan monastics again seized the opportunity to draw attention to the Tibetan cause. For the Han Chinese, hosting the Olympics was a badge of honor, celebrating their arrival on the world stage. Increasing Han nationalism brought with it more unrest and anti-Chinese sentiments in ethnic areas like Tibet (Barnett, 2014, p. xxxiii). As a consequence, and in order to create stability, the Chinese government increased their repressive actions across the Tibetan areas, amplifying patriotic education in monasteries and forcing monastics to denounce the Dalai Lama in writing (Demick, 2011). Coinciding with the observation of Tibetan Uprising Day (commemorating the anniversary of the uprising of March 10, 1959), several monks (in particular, those from the three main Gelug monasteries of Drepung, Sera, and Ganden), staged protests against the government in early March. Their grievances included socio-economic inequalities, the Dalai Lama's continued exile, increased political repression, and the detainment of political prisoners (Johnson, 2011, p. 92). The protests became violent as demonstrators destroyed Han Chinese businesses and attacked Han residents. The riots spread outside of the TAR into Tibetan areas of Chinese provinces, and, along with the police response, resulted in dozens of deaths, hundreds of wounded, and potentially thousands of arrests. The Chinese blamed the "Dalai clique" for the unrest, yet still suffered a black eye from the negative publicity just months before the Olympics. Tim Johnson maintains that the 2008 unrest in Tibet "marked the biggest and most widespread ethnic upheaval to challenge the ruling party since it came to power, surpassed only by the Uighur riots more than a year later." Between mid-March and early June, there were 125 documented protest incidents (Johnson, 2011, p. 93). From his seat in exile, the Dalai Lama cautioned against the escalating violence. However, as discussed below, the increasing repression by the Chinese government in combination with the radicalization of young Tibetans demonstrates that the Dalai Lama's exhortations to adhere to a path of nonviolence are falling on deaf ears.

Since arriving in India in 1959, the Dalai Lama, along with the Tibetan government-in-exile, has worked tirelessly to keep the Tibetan issue in the international press. He has received a great deal of sympathy and assistance from individuals and organizations in the West. The spread of the Tibetan diaspora, including the exodus of high lamas, resulted in Tibetan Buddhism's diffusion around the world. The combination of an exotic religion with the appeal of a human rights issue attracted many Americans to both Buddhism and the Tibetan cause, which were often conflated. Many individuals in Hollywood (including Richard Gere, Sharon Stone, Goldie Hawn, and the late Adam Yauch of the Beastie Boys) have used their fame to publicize the Tibet issue and garner support for their cause. In the late 1980s, Gere, along with composer Philip Glass and Robert Thurman (former ordained Buddhist monk, personal friend of the Dalai Lama, professor of Indo-Tibetan Studies at Columbia University, and perhaps most famously, father of actress Uma Thurman) founded the Tibet House at the request of the Dalai Lama to help protect Tibet's endangered cultural and religious heritage ("Tibet House," n.d.). The late 1990s witnessed a flurry of books and films that furthered the discussion in the West about the Dalai Lama, Tibetan Buddhism, and the occupation of Tibet. Organizations such as Students for a Free Tibet (based in New York City) attracted Western youth with Tibetan Freedom Concerts and held protests in front of U.S. governmental agencies and Chinese embassies; their efforts to agitate for Tibetan independence have included disrupting the 2008 Olympic torch relay (Students for a Free Tibet, n.d.). Despite condemnation from Beijing, the Dalai Lama has been able to meet with the most recent four American presidents (George H. W. Bush, Bill Clinton, George W. Bush, and Barack Obama); over the course of several years, his visits with the U.S. presidents have become less covert ("U.S. Presidential Statements on meetings with the Dalai Lama, 1991–2014," n.d.). However, in spite of this outpouring of support from individuals and organizations in the West for the Dalai Lama and his cause, Western governments have for the most part been unwilling to firmly and publicly stand with the Dalai Lama out of fear of provoking China (Wong, 2008).

The lack of strong public endorsement from Western nations and prospects of continued violence in Tibet have prompted the Dalai Lama to change tactics over the course of his tenure in exile. Although the Dalai Lama and his administration initially advocated for Tibetan independence, he changed his approach in the late 1970s. Beginning in 1979, in response to seemingly encouraging words regarding Tibet's status from China's new reform leader Deng Xiaoping, the exile leader began to endorse what he described as the Middle Way approach (*Ume Lam*, or MWA). This policy was so named in reference to the historical Buddha's epiphany concerning the path to enlightenment (sometimes referred to as the Middle Way). The Buddha's view was that in order to achieve Nirvana, one must lead a life of moderation, avoiding the two extremes of indulgence and self-denial. With regard to the Tibet situation, the new strategy of the Dalai Lama involved promoting a solution of autonomy as the "middle way" between complete independence (favored by most Tibetans) and incorporation into the People's Republic of China. In the 1980s, China hosted several Tibetan delegations and engaged in negotiations with the Chinese government, although little was accomplished and relations between the two entities continued to deteriorate. In 1987, in a speech to the U.S. Congress, the Dalai Lama elucidated a Five Point Peace Plan, which included the "transformation of the whole of Tibet into a zone of peace" and recognition of Tibetan human rights within China (Gyatso, 1987). He reiterated these remarks in 1988 during an address to the European Parliament, which became known as the Strasbourg Proposal. In this speech, which occurred in the midst of the late 1980s unrest in Tibet, the Dalai Lama elaborated on the Five Points and urged acceptance of the Middle Way approach in order to obtain authentic autonomy for Tibetans in China. He admitted that, for those Tibetans who still backed the goal of independence (*Rangzen*), many would be disappointed by his conciliatory and moderate position (Gyatso, 1988). Indeed, the absence of a resolution for the Tibet question has fueled Tibetan anger regarding what some perceive as the "utter failure" of the Dalai Lama's Middle Way approach (Chhaya, 2007).

Supporters of *Rangzen* are most often young Tibetans. The Tibetan Youth Congress (TYC) has been vocal in criticizing the Middle Way approach and the political policies of the Dalai Lama. Founded in 1970 with the blessings of the Dalai Lama, the group currently claims 30,000 members around the world. Called the "largest pro-independence group in exile," the TYC contends that its members are "united in our common struggle for the restoration of complete independence for the whole of Tibet" ("Largest Tibetan pro-independence group," 2012). Jamyang Norbu (1990) (TYC co-founder, former guerrilla fighter, and prolific activist/ blogger) refers to the organization as the "loyal opposition to the government." And while they do not support the Middle Way, they still respect the Dalai Lama as a leader (Chhaya, 2007, p. 277). TYC followers pledge to "to struggle for the total independence of Tibet even at the cost of one's life" ("Tibetan Youth Congress," n.d.). According to Schwartz, the TYC "sometimes advocates violence and sabotage directed at the Chinese. . . ." (Schwartz, 1994, p. 7). Kalsang Godrupka Phuntsok, former TYC president, has promoted "targeted victimless violence," which includes blowing up bridges and railroads in order to wound China economically (Pocha, 2003). Needless to say, the TYC is hated and feared by the Chinese government. Beijing has accused the TYC of openly advocating terrorism against Chinese inside Tibet and has claimed that the TYC "does not have much difference with Al Qaeda and Chechen terrorists" (Puri, 2008). Although the radicalism and violent tendencies of Tibetan youth are generally condemned by the government-in-exile and proponents of the Middle Way, the Dalai Lama states that he empathizes with them and can appreciate their frustration. "The younger Tibetans in and outside Tibet are less patient and some of the younger Tibetans outside Tibet criticize me for being too mild. Of course that is understandable. They are very patriotic and have little patience. They want things immediately" (Shiromany, 1998, p. 251).

This quotation highlights the sentiments behind the recent self-immolations by Tibetans protesting China's actions in Tibet. Some of the victims were seemingly driven to set themselves on fire by feelings of disappointment with the ineffectiveness of the Middle Way approach. One young man related prior to his suicide that "he saw no option but to inflict violence on himself to make a point about how frustrated young Tibetans were becoming that the Tibet question was not getting resolved fast enough" (Chhaya, 2007, pp. 276–277). It is therefore important to note that these events were not necessarily carried out to effect change. Rather, they should be perceived as performances of anger and defeat.

Videos of their immolations and letters they left behind have illuminated the reasons why some people resorted to such extreme measures. Some victims renewed the call for independence; others expressed fears for the future of Tibetan culture, religion, and language (Barnett, 2014, p. xxxv). Some expressed a desire for the Dalai Lama to return to Tibet. Still others wanted to demonstrate ethnic and political solidarity, and some sought solely to translate into action the regret and sadness they felt on behalf of Tibetan people (Butler, 2014, p. 10). Thus, the impact of the series of immolations has been amplified with the use of modern technology. Several of the immolations have been filmed, photographed, and posted on the Internet; Tibetans have showed their support by sharing pictures and sentiments on blogs, Facebook, and Twitter. Again, contagion plays a role as new links, re-tweets, and re-posts provide tangible evidence of the spread of frustration, indignation, and empathy (Butler, 2014). As Jamyang Norbu (2015) imparts: ". . . we've all seen the blurry cellphone videos of the self-immolations in Tibet, that have filled us with concern, sadness, but most of all, admiration for the courage and resolve of those giving up their lives for our freedom."

Between 1998 and 2010, self-immolations were rare among Tibetans (Demick, 2011). Self-immolation as a Tibetan protest movement emerged in 2011 when, according to John Whalen-Bridge, Tibetans lost their temporary soft power they had collected in the run-up to the Olympics (Whalen-Bridge, 2013, pp. 186–187). As of June 1, 2015, 147 Tibetans have lit themselves on fire in protest, and most have died (Tibetan National Congress, 2015). Most of these immolations have occurred not in the TAR, but in Greater Tibet, primarily in Sichuan. At first confined to monks and nuns (indeed, many of those who self-immolated had been kicked out of monasteries for protesting), the epidemic gradually spread to young lay-people (Barnett, 2014, pp. xxxiv–xxxv; Demick, 2011). Epidemic appears to be the right word; contagion is not only a property of anger but also of suicide, both of which form the basis for the recent immolations. Woeser claims that "after every immolation, emotions stir and arguments rage to no avail" (Woeser & Wang, 2014, p. 17). People are then galvanized to act, and to show solidarity. Dibyesh Anand also contends that there is a "copy-cat dimension" to these suicides, in the form of competition. "If I immo-late myself, my friends are under pressure to do the same to show they are just as patriotic" (Demick, 2011).

The Chinese response has been to accelerate the crackdown by placing further restrictions on Tibetan monastics, with more arrests and increased violence. Predictably, the government has blamed the Dalai Lama for the recent immolations, referring to the Dalai Lama's alleged "support" for immolators as "terrorism in disguise" (Branigan, 2011). The Chinese government's fear may be appropriate; some analysts have compared the Tibetan suicides with that of Tunisian fruit-seller Mohamed Bouazizi, whose immolation sparked the Arab Spring (Demick, 2011). A "Beijing Spring" could potentially bring down the Chinese communist regime.

In the press, the Dalai Lama has acknowledged that he is in a difficult position in relation to the self-immolations, as he has neither definitely con-doned them nor condemned them. Calling the immolations a "very, very delicate political issue," he admitted that "now, the reality is that if I say something positive, then the Chinese immediately blame me. If I say some-thing negative, then the family members of those people feel very sad. They sacrificed their own life. It is not easy. So I do not want to create some kind of impression that this is wrong" (Branigan, 2012). Ultimately, the dramatic deaths confirm increasing Tibetan desperation and discontent. In December of 2012, Dr. Lobsang Sangay, leader of the Tibetan government-in-exile, declared that the spate of self-immolations constituted "a new threshold of Tibetan despair and resentment" ("Statement of Sikyong Dr. Lobsang Sangay," 2012). Ultimately, contemporary Tibetan anger has assimilated earlier waves of frustration and has catalyzed the radicaliza-tion of the independence movement, taking it from its roots in hope to its current state of disillusionment. In the diaspora, anger has manifested in more vocal support for political leaders whose opinions on Tibetan-Chinese relations are in opposition to those of the Dalai Lama and his exile gov-ernment, a trend that was not visible decades ago. Tracing this historical evolution of Tibetan anger illustrates the increasing desperation and extremism among Tibetan activists and offers a means of predicting the course of the Tibetan issue.

As the immolations continue, however, it is difficult to calculate the future for Tibetans. Two major factors will ultimately change the trajectory of the issue. The first is that of increasing youth radicalization, in exile and in Tibet. Young Tibetans are exasperated; many claim they don't want to engage in violence but they feel they are out of options (Chhaya, 2007, p. 281). Exile youth are in a particularly frustrating situation. They lack citizenship and stability; they are rootless and stateless. Facing restrictions on work and travel, they are enflamed by events happening in Tibet, "a land that most of them have never known" (Johnson, 2011, pp. 104–105). As noted above, and as evidenced by the spike in violence since the late 1980s, the youth in Tibet, especially the monastics, have been galvanized to oppose China's continued attempts to tighten its control over the Tibetan regions. Of the 147 immolations, 24 of the victims were under the age of 18. Kirti Monastery in Sichuan has been a center for the monastic unrest; 41 of the 147 immolations have occurred in the Ngaba region, home to Kirti Monastery. Of the Ngaba deaths, 24 were monks or former monks from the monastery (International Campaign for Tibet, 2015). Regarding the discontent among young Tibetans, one young Tibetan explained that "they are very angry at the Chinese government and the Chinese people. But they have no idea what to do" (Johnson, 2011, p. 29). Although they may not know what to do, most feel that the time to act is now. According to Lhasa Tsering, the former head of the TYC, "we are going to be wiped out in another thirty years. It is now or never, do or die" (Johnson, 2011, pp. 112–113). In their anger, some have not ruled out guerrilla warfare or terrorist activities (Burke, 2008, p. 83). A young doctor named Tashi Dorje clearly stated: "If you can blow up a railroad track, it means more than a protest" (Johnson, 2011, p. 105). A controversial independent film titled "We're No Monks" tells the story of four disaffected young Tibetan exiles who are engaged in a violent crusade for Tibet's freedom. Fulbright scholar Pema Dhondup, who directed the film, claims his work plays a role in dissolving the myth of Shangri-la. He maintains that "there are very ordinary Tibetans who get angry, have ordinary vices. If tomorrow they take to violence as a means to express themselves, please do not be surprised" (Biswas, 2004).

The second factor that will change the course of the Tibet issue is the inevitable death of the Fourteenth Dalai Lama (on July 6, 2015, he celebrated his 80th birthday). His death will not only impact the future of Tibetans inside and outside of Tibet, but will also dramatically alter the

Chinese government's Tibet policy. The current strategy of the Chinese leadership appears to be to bide their time in consideration of the Dalai Lama's advancing age (Wong, 2008). Upon his death, the Chinese government will control the search for the highest incarnation in Tibetan Buddhism. Once they have found a suitable candidate, he will be raised under strict government tutelage. From the government's perspective, their control over the Fifteenth Dalai Lama will, by extension, afford them greater control over the Tibetan populace, both in the TAR and in outlying Chinese provinces.

However, the likely scenario is that China's involvement in the search and recognition of the next Dalai Lama will be viewed as intrusive and manipulative by most Tibetans around the world. The Tibetan government-in-exile, along with the Tibetan Buddhist religious leadership, will conduct their own quest to find the Dalai Lama's reincarnation. Once dueling lamas have been enthroned, the Chinese government's candidate will be perceived as illegitimate, this perception fueled by the current Dalai Lama's insistence that his successor will not reincarnate in occupied Tibet. Following custom, the Fifteenth Dalai Lama will be guided by a regent in his minority until he is able to assume his spiritual responsibilities. During this time, Tibetans will lack a strong Dalai Lama to serve as a rallying point and unifying force. Divisions and tensions among Tibetans will be exacerbated in the absence of the current Dalai Lama's abilities to mollify and pacify the Tibetan diaspora and devoted Tibetans in the TAR.

While the Chinese government has worked tirelessly over several decades to undermine and delegitimize the efforts of the Dalai Lama to bring attention to the issue of Tibet's status and to the plight of the Tibetans, the Dalai Lama's exhortations to adhere to a path of non-violence have mitigated the anger of Tibetans in Tibet and in exile. Ironically, the Dalai Lama may be China's best chance of maintaining order in the Tibetan region. Tenzin Choden, Tibetan activist and member of the Tibetan parliament-in-exile, contends that "if the Dalai Lama is not there, that moral authority is not there to guide Tibetan people; then you can certainly predict that people will do desperate things" (Johnson, 2011, p. 147). Tempa Tsering, the Dalai Lama's brother-in-law and former official in the exile government, asserts that the Dalai Lama is the solution, not the problem, in China's Tibet crisis. "It is His Holiness's uncompromising insistence on nonviolence and pacifism and his stature to ensure that it remains so that has stopped Tibet from going out of control. I don't think the Chinese recognize that fact at all and they should" (Chhaya, 2007, p. 299).

As a symbol of hope and unity, he is perhaps uniquely qualified to quell the tide of frustration and discontent among Tibetans around the world, as numerous scholars have pointed out. Orville Schell (as quoted in Strober & Strober, 2005, p. 271) states:

> Nobody will ever be able to replace him because he represents continuity with that past—the last time when Tibet was separated, isolated, and culturally and religiously whole. . . . I don't really know what the alternative to him is; I don't think there is one. It could be very bad for Tibet because if something happens there, there would be no one to calm it down.

Tsering Woeser similarly notes that the Dalai Lama's death may also serve as a spark to the flames of violent protest. She maintains that Tibetan grief over his passing will manifest in an outpouring of anger and sorrow, a volatile situation in which "hope becomes despair, hatred overcomes fear, and bereavement fans fanaticism." According to Woeser, at that time, "Tibetans will not need to coordinate or be organized; they will all rise up spontaneously" (Woeser & Wang, 2014, p. 10). His death "will send out the call to arms for Tibetans," presenting the Chinese government with a situation for which they will be ill-prepared (Johnson, 2011, p. 97). Radicalized Tibetans will not be afraid to die for the Tibetan cause. After all, she reflects, "If you are not afraid of setting yourself on fire, what else can scare you?" (Woeser & Wang, 2014, p. 18).

Notes

1. As quoted in Gyatso (1994, p. 54).

2. The best introduction to the complex historical background of this dispute over Tibet's status is Goldstein (1997).

3. *Dalai* means "ocean" in Mongolian. Combined with the Tibetan term, *lama*, the title can be variously translated as "ocean of wisdom" or "oceanic teacher," a spiritual teacher whose wisdom and compassion is as vast as the ocean.

4. An excellent resource for early 20th century Tibetan history, including the vagaries of Sino-Tibetan relations, is Goldstein (1989).

References

Abraham, T. (2008). Little can be achieved through negotiations on Tibet. *Economic and Political Weekly, 43*(14), 8–11.

Anand, D. (2009). China and Tibet: Tibet matters. *World Today, 65*(4), 30–31.

Anderson, B. (1991). *Imagined communities: Reflections on the origin and spread of nationalism.* New York, NY: Verso.

Ardley, J. (2002) *The Tibetan independence movement: Political, religious, and Gandhian perspectives.* New York, NY: Routledge Curzon.

Barnett, R. (Ed.). (1994). *Resistance and reform in Tibet.* Bloomington, IN: Indiana University Press.

Barnett, R. (2001). 'Violated specialness': Western political representations of Tibet. In T. Dodin & H. Räther (Eds.), *Imagining Tibet: Perceptions, projections and fantasies* (pp. 269–316). Boston, MA: Wisdom Publications.

Barnett, R. (2014). Introduction. In T. Woeser & L. Wang (Trans. & Eds.), *Voices from Tibet: Selected essays and reportage.* Honolulu, HI: University of Hawai'i Press.

Biswas, S. (2004, January 8). Tibet film blasts 'Shangri-la image.' *BBC News.* Retrieved from http://news.bbc.co.uk

Branigan, T. (2011, October 19). Dalai Lama's prayers for Tibetans 'terrorism in disguise', China says. *The Guardian.* Retrieved from https://www.theguardian.com

Branigan, T. (2012, July 9). Dalai Lama says he must remain neutral on self-immolations. *The Guardian.* Retrieved from https://www.theguardian.com

Burke, D. J. (2008). Tibetans in exile in a changing global political climate. *Economic and Political Weekly, 43*(15), 79–85.

Butler, C. D. (2015). Tibetan protest self-immolation: Ecology, health and politics. Retrieved from http://www.tibetanreview.net/tibetan-protest-self-immolation-ecology-health-and-politics

Chandler, J. (2009). *Hunting the guru: Lineage, culture and conflict in the development of Tibetan Buddhism in America* (Doctoral dissertation) University at Albany, State University of New York.

Chhaya, M. (2007). *Dalai Lama: Man, monk, mystic.* New York, NY: Doubleday.

Dalai Lama accuses China of 'cultural genocide.' (2008, March 16). *USA Today.* Retrieved from http://usatoday30.usatoday.com/news/world/2008-03-16-china-tibet_N.htm

Demick, B. (2011, October 23). In China, self-immolations add radical bent to Tibetan protests. *LA Times.* Retrieved from http://articles.latimes.com/2011/oct/23/world/la-fg-china-tibet-20111023

Goldstein, M. C. (1968). *An anthropological study of the Tibetan political system* (Doctoral dissertation). University of Washington.

Goldstein, M. C. (1989). *A history of modern Tibet, 1913–1951: The demise of the Lamaist state.* Berkeley, CA: University of California Press.

Goldstein, M. C. (1997). *The snow lion and the dragon: China, Tibet and the Dalai Lama.* Berkeley, CA: University of California Press.

Gyatso, Tenzin (The Fourteenth Dalai Lama). (1987, September 21). Five point peace plan: Address to US Congressional Human Rights Caucus. Retrieved from http://www.dalailama.com/messages/tibet/five-point-peace-plan

Gyatso, Tenzin (The Fourteenth Dalai Lama). (1988, June 15). Strasbourg Proposal 1988: Address to the members of the European Parliament, Strasbourg, France. Retrieved from http://www.dalailama.com/messages/tibet/strasbourg-proposal-1988

Gyatso, Tenzin (the Fourteenth Dalai Lama). (1994). *A flash of lightning in the dark of night: A guide to the Bodhisattva's way of life.* Boston, MA: Shambhala.

Gyatso, Tenzin (The Fourteenth Dalai Lama) & Cutler, H. (1998). *The art of happiness: A handbook for living.* New York, NY: Penguin Putnam.

Hess, J. (2009). *Immigrant ambassadors: Citizenship and belonging in the Tibetan Diaspora.* Redwood City, CA: Stanford University Press.

Human Rights Watch. (1997). China: State control of religion. Retrieved from https://www.hrw.org/report/1997/10/01/china-state-control-religion

International Campaign for Tibet. (2015). Map: Tibetan self-immolations from 2009–2015. Retrieved from https://www.savetibet.org/resources/fact-sheets/self-immolations-by-tibetans/map-tibetan-self-immolations-from-2009-2013

Johnson, T. (2011). *Tragedy in crimson: How the Dalai Lama conquered the world but lost the battle with China.* New York, NY: Nation Books.

Knaus, J. K. (1999). *Orphans of the cold war: America and the Tibetan struggle for survival.* New York, NY: PublicAffairs.

Lam, O. (2012, November 23). China: Last words of 19 Tibetans who committed self-immolation. *Global Voices.* Retrieved from https://globalvoices.org

Largest Tibetan pro-independence group to launch indefinite hunger strike in solidarity with self-immolations. (2012, August 12). *Phayul.com.* Retrieved from http://www.phayul.com/news/article.aspx?id=31892

Liu, J. (2012, August 20). Tibetans fight tourism on holy lakes. Retrieved from https://www.chinadialogue.net/article/show/single/en/5114-Tibetans-fight-tourism-on-holy-lakes

Misra, A. (2000). Tibet: In search of a resolution. *Central Asian Survey, 19*(1), 79–93.

Norbu, J. (1990, November 30). Opening of the political eye. Retrieved from http://www.rangzen.net/1990/11/30/opening-of-the-political-eye

Norbu, J. (2008, May 6). The Dalai Lama's 'middle way' has failed [Web log post]. *Shadow Tibet.* Retrieved from http://www.jamyangnorbu.com/blog/2008/05/06/dalai-lamas-middle-way-has-failed

Norbu, J. (2015, April 27). The subliminal clarity of blurry cell phone videos [Web log post]. *Shadow Tibet.* Retrieved from http://www.jamyangnorbu.com/blog/2015/04/27/the-subliminal-clarity-of-blurry-cellphone-videos

Pocha, J. (2003, December 1). Tibet's gamble: Can the Dalai Lama's China talks succeed? *InTheseTimes.com.* Retrieved from http://inthesetimes.com/article/656/tibets_gamble

Puri, B. (2002). Deconstructing the Dalai Lama on Tibet. *Economic and Political Weekly, 37*(4), 3500–3503.

Schwartz, R. D. (1994). *Circle of protest: Political ritual in the Tibetan uprising.* New York, NY: Columbia University Press.

Shiromany, A. A. (Ed.). (1998). *The political philosophy of His Holiness the XIV Dalai Lama: Selected speeches and writings.* New Delhi, IN: Tibetan Parliamentary and Policy Research Centre.

Statement of Sikyong Dr. Lobsang Sangay on 23rd Anniversary of Conferment of Nobel Peace Prize to His Holiness the Dalai Lama. (2012, December 10). *Central Tibetan Administration.* Retrieved from http://tibet.net

Stoddard, H. (1994). Tibetan publications and national identity. In R. Barnett (Ed.). *Resistance and reform in Tibet* (pp. 121–157). Bloomington: IN: University Press.

Strober, D. H., & Strober, G. S. (2005). *His Holiness the Dalai Lama: The oral biography*. Hoboken, NJ: John Wiley and Sons.

Students for a Free Tibet. (n.d.). [Web site]. https://www.studentsforafreetibet.org

Studying Tibet today: A discussion with Robbie Barnett. (2014). *The China Story*. Retrieved from https://www.thechinastory.org

Tibet House US–Cultural Center of H.H. the Dalai Lama: Mission and history. (n.d.). [Web site]. Retrieved from http://tibethouse.us/about/overview

Tibetan Youth Congress: About us. (2015). Retrieved from http://www.tibetanyouthcongress.org/about-tyc

Tibetan National Congress. (2015). Facebook page. Retrieved from https://www.facebook.com/tibetnc

Tolchin, M., & Tolchin, S. J. (2006). *A world ignited: How apostles of ethnic, religious and racial hatred torch the globe*. Lanham, MD: Rowman & Littlefield.

Tuttle, G. (2015). China's race problem: How Beijing represses minorities. *Foreign Affairs, 94*(3). Retrieved from https://www.foreignaffairs.com/articles/china/2015-04-20/china-s-race-problem

"U.S. Presidential Statements on meetings with the Dalai Lama, 1991–2014." (n.d.). *International Campaign for Tibet*. Retrieved from http://www.savetibet.org/policy-center/us-government-and-legislative-advocacy/u-s-presidential-statements-on-meetings-with-the-dalai-lama

Whalen-Bridge, J. (2013). Angry monk syndrome on the world stage: Tibet, engaged Buddhism and the weapons of the weak. In J. Whalen-Bridge & P. Kitiarsa (Eds.), *Buddhism, modernity and the state in Asia: Forms of engagement* (pp. 163–207). New York, NY: Palgrave Macmillan.

Woeser, T. (2010, October 28). Liu Xiaobo: 'Han Chinese have no freedom, Tibetans have no autonomy.' Retrieved from http://highpeakspureearth.com/2010/liu-xiaobo-han-chinese-have-no-freedom-tibetans-have-no-autonomy-by-woeser

Woeser, T., & Wang, L. (2014). *Voices from Tibet: Selected essays and reportage*. (V. S. Law, Trans. & Ed.). Honolulu, HI: University of Hawai'i Press.

Wong, E. (2008, November 22). At exile meeting, Tibetans debate independence. *The New York Times*. Retrieved from http://www.nytimes.com

CHAPTER NINETEEN

The Role of Anger in the Radicalization of Terrorists

Cory Davenport

The Problem of Terrorism

In just the past few years, the world has experienced hundreds of terrorist attacks that, when combined, have resulted in the deaths of thousands of civilians (National Consortium for the Study of Terrorism and Responses to Terrorism, 2013). Along with this loss of life, these attacks have also resulted in the destruction of priceless cultural artifacts; the disruption or elimination of any number of social institutions, including hospitals, businesses, and schools; and tremendous economic harm. Obviously, terrorism also terrorizes. People become angry and afraid in response to terrorist attacks, even if they were not a direct victim of the violence. Governments often respond by passing new laws, some of which limit the freedom of ordinary citizens, and by expanding law enforcement, intelligence, and military capabilities. So, what is the cause of terrorism and is there anything we can do to prevent it from occurring?

Radicalization

Radicalization is the process that leads to an individual espousing radical beliefs or engaging in radical behavior. It is also a primary cause of terrorism. Something is considered radical if it deviates from accepted norms. Radicalization, then, is both subjective and existing on a continuum ranging from not radicalized at all to fully radicalized in thought and behavior. A radicalized individual is not automatically, or even objectively, "bad." As an example, an individual might have beliefs that lie beyond accepted norms but that lead them to engage in very pro-social behaviors.

Most people who have radical beliefs do not end up engaging in violent behavior. In line with this, a number of researchers distinguish between radical beliefs (supporting violent ideals without directly engaging in or supporting violent acts) and radical behavior. One of the primary proponents of this dual theory of radicalization is Clark McCauley (Leuprecht, Hataley, Moskalenko, & McCauley, 2010). In McCauley's Dual Pyramid Model of Radicalization (a model specific to radicalization by Islamist extremists), one pyramid represents four progressive levels of *opinion* radicalization and the other pyramid represents four different progressive levels of *action*, leading to the actual use of violence. The antecedents of opinion radicalization are distinct from those of a willingness to engage in violent action. Importantly, anger very likely contributes both to the development of radical beliefs and the decision to engage in violent behavior.

Anger

Anger is a powerful motivation. As with radicalization, anger can motivate us to pursue either pro-social or anti-social goals. For example, someone who gets angry as a result of being criticized for not working hard enough can choose to let the anger motivate them to set the goal of working harder or they can let the anger motivate them to set the goal of retaliating against the person who criticized them. This chapter will focus only on the anti-social effects of anger. More specifically, it will focus on the ways in which anger facilitates the radicalization of beliefs and behaviors to the point of willingness to support or join a terrorist group and engage in terrorism.

At an individual level, anger affects how we think. If we believe we have been harmed or unjustly treated, we are likely to get angry. We might become angry even if we are not directly harmed or mistreated. For example, if a close other (e.g., friend, family member), group we identify with highly (e.g., political party, religious denomination), or an idea we support is attacked, anger is a commonly experienced emotion. Often, the anger then shapes our subsequent thoughts. For example, it might facilitate our developing antipathy toward the individual or group we believe brought about the harm or mistreatment. Once we have a target for our antipathy, anger might lead us to derogate or act in a prejudiced manner toward the target individual or group. Anger might lead us to rationalize immoral or illegal behavior, including violence, in response to the perceived harm or mistreatment. Finally, anger might reduce our ability or willingness to inhibit our support for this behavior. In other words, if we experience little or no anger, we might automatically dismiss the use of violence, whereas if we experience a great deal of anger, we might actively avoid the inhibition of these thoughts or avoid strongly considering the possible consequences of our violent behavior.

The effects of anger are not confined to the individual level, however. As humans are social creatures who interact with one another, our thoughts can affect these interactions. Anger, then, affects things such as the content and manner of our communications with others; our willingness to violate rules, laws, and social norms; and our decision to associate with certain people and groups. When the right cognitive, ideological, and social factors are combined, anger can greatly facilitate the process of radicalization to violence.

Just as it is important to think about the role of anger in the radicalization of individuals, it is equally important to think about the role that anger plays at the group level. There are two reasons in particular as to why this is so. First, group dynamics are distinct from the dynamics of individuals in a social environment. In other words, it is important to consider the behavior of groups (e.g., al Qaeda) separately from the behavior of individual members of a group. A terrorist group is not likely to become more violent just because an individual member believes they have been harmed by an outside individual or group. The factors that lead to group anger and radicalization are potentially very different from those that lead to individual anger and radicalization. Second, groups are more likely to be influenced by macro factors that have an impact on a large number of people (e.g., civil war; discussed more at length in the section that follows) versus individuals, who are largely influenced by factors that directly affect them personally (e.g., mistreatment by an outgroup). As I describe the role of anger in the radicalization of terrorists, I will begin at the individual level, and will then move to the group level, providing historical examples throughout for reference.

Specific Effects of Anger on Radicalization and the Likelihood of Terrorism

An examination of the research literature on the topic of radicalization reveals that anger is very rarely listed as a cause of radicalization. On one hand, this is surprising given the numerous ways that anger can contribute to the advancement of radical beliefs and behaviors. On the other hand, however, much of this literature is focused on examining radicalization's "root" causes. Root causes are both necessary (i.e., they must be present) and sufficient (i.e., enough to meet a need by itself) for radicalization to occur. These root factors, or primary causes, are differentiated from factors that merely contribute to radicalization. When anger is mentioned in relation to radicalization, it is as a contributing factor or something that moderates a shift from being non-radicalized to being more highly radicalized. Given the many ways that anger can facilitate the process of radicalization, this is perhaps not very surprising. What has received no attention, to my knowledge, however, is the possibility that anger mediates the process of radicalization. In other words, perhaps anger is necessary (but not necessarily sufficient) for radicalization to occur.

Causes of Radicalization

So, if anger is generally not listed as a primary or root cause of radicalization, then what is? Dozens of these potential causes of radicalization (i.e., root causes and contributing factors) have been identified in the literature. While a thorough discussion of each is beyond the scope of this chapter, it is useful to have an idea of the variety of variables identified as being causes. A sample of these include a number of personal factors consisting of individual differences and psychological factors (e.g., relative deprivation, thrill), micro social factors consisting of more localized social factors (e.g., social networks, social isolation), and macro social factors at the societal level (e.g., globalization, civil war). There is quite a bit of debate over both what constitutes a cause of radicalization as well as over the extent to which different causes are responsible for the radicalization we see across the globe. Sometimes, what we think we know regarding the causes of radicalization changes over time. For example, it used to be widely accepted that lack of education was a major cause of radicalization, whereas today, as evidenced by the large number of terrorists who have levels of education beyond that of the general population, lack of education does not appear to contribute significantly to radicalization (Gambetta & Hertog, 2009). In an attempt to try to make better sense of the large number of potential causes, researchers have taken steps to organize categories of causes and develop models of the process of radicalization.

There are several useful ways to conceptualize different types of causes besides the root causes versus contributing factors dichotomy. Causes can be divided up based upon whether they are at the organizational, group, and individual level or at the macro, meso, and micro level. They can also be put into external, social, and individual causal categories or divided up based upon whether they are ideological or personal or whether they push or pull an individual toward radicalization. Along with categorization of causes, another useful endeavor is proposing models of radicalization that identify the basic ingredients of radicalization and explain how the process of radicalization unfolds. Most of these models describe the process of radicalization as a set of specific stages of increasing radicalization. A different approach is to identify the psychological and socio-cultural factors that determine the degree of radicalization.

There are two approaches to identifying determinants of degree of radicalization. One approach consists of compiling lists of motives apparently involved in radicalization. The other approach focuses on an overarching motive assumed to underlie a large number of radicalization cases. The listing approach assumes that radicalization can be prompted by different and unrelated motives. The single motive approach assumes that though the various motives in the list are valid descriptions of specific cases, underlying them all is a higher order motivation that ultimately drives all instances of radicalization. Kruglanski, Chen, Dechesne, Fishman, and Orehek (2009) suggest that the *quest for personal significance* lies at the heart of almost all cases of radicalization.

Quest for Significance Theory

The quest for significance is the desire to matter and have a purpose in accordance with the norms and values of one's society. The quest may be initiated by a significance loss (humiliation, dishonor), a threat of such loss (if one should decline to engage in a required action), or the opportunity for significance gain (the possibility of becoming a hero or a martyr venerated by one's group). As with radicalization and anger, the behaviors that stem from a quest for significance can be either pro-social or anti-social. When it comes to a quest for significance leading to radicalization, three components are necessary: (1) An individual must have the *motivation* to pursue significance. This process begins with quest for significance being aroused or made salient. Then, a person forms goals that revolve around gaining significance. (Similar goals may be aroused concerning avoidance of significance loss.) Finally, these goals must predominate other goals that one might have. (2) There must be some *ideology* that an individual buys into that identifies violence and terrorism as the justifiable means to significance. Generally, this ideology is established by some group (e.g., terrorist group) that an individual identifies with. (3) There is a *social* process that links the goal of significance attainment to an ideological belief in the use of violence to achieve goals related to significance quest. The individual comes into contact with significant others (friends, relatives, charismatic leaders) whose views he or she comes to adopt in the process of forging a shared social reality with these persons. Thus, arousal of the significance quest as well as the adoption of violence as a means to significance occurs in the context of social interactions and the exposure to influential views of persons the individual trusts and is eager to satisfy. Very often this social process occurs because the individual is a member of or identifies highly with, some group. More often than not, when the group is accepting of violence as a means to achieve a goal, individual members share this belief.

What has largely been absent from the discussion of the causes of radicalization up to now is the role that anger plays in these processes. If anger is not a root cause of radicalization, what is its role? Does it play a role in our quest for significance? Is it always involved in the process of radicalization or are there times when radicalization occurs absent any anger?

How Anger Facilitates Radicalization and Terrorism

While anger is not necessarily an influencing factor in all cases of radicalization, it likely is an influencing factor in all cases of radicalization to violence. Thinking about the process whereby one decides that violence is an acceptable means of goal attainment, there must first be an assignment of blame for some wrong that was committed and a decision that violence is an appropriate (i.e., able to be carried out and likely to lead to goal attainment) means of goal attainment. It seems exceedingly unlikely that one would decide to support or engage in violence directed at a specific target if one were not driven, at least in part, by anger. As described previously, anger increases our antipathy toward targeted groups. Once we decide that someone or some group is responsible for some wrong, our thoughts immediately turn to how to right the wrong and/or exact some form of revenge. Anger makes it easier for us to derogate and discriminate against these identified individuals or groups. If we could assign blame but not feel any anger, we would likely not ultimately support or engage in violence. Anger appears to be a key component of radicalization at the stages following assignment of blame. Anger makes it easier for us to accept and rationalize the use of violence. Finally, anger inhibits our usual goal to not violate social norms. These last two are similar in that anger is disrupting our normal thought processes regarding conflict resolution. We become much more willing to set irrational and even unproductive goals and to ignore the consequences of adopting violent means to goal attainment when we are angry.

Turning our attention to identified causes of radicalization including the higher order motivation of quest for significance, it is easy to see a number of places where anger might facilitate the process of radicalization. Research has frequently identified relative deprivation, humiliation, and victimization as causes of radicalization (Gurr, 1970; Stern, 2004). Each of these causes lends evidence to quest for significance theory in that each one appears to be an example of a situation where an individual is, or members of a group are, trying to gain significance or trying not to lose significance. More importantly, perhaps, the role of anger in radicalization following these causes is pretty clear. When a person or group is experiencing relative deprivation, humiliation, or victimization, they are automatically going to assign blame to someone or some group that they see as being responsible for the harm to them. Once a target for blame has been established, anger can result in derogation of the target and greater acceptance of violence as a means of correcting the wrong that was done to them. Previous examples of these causes leading to anger and radicalization are ubiquitous. For example, a study of Muslim youth in the Netherlands found that "perceived injustice" was a primary cause of radicalization (Doosje, Loseman, & Bos, 2013). In a commentary based on the findings of three articles in a special edition of the *Asian Journal of Social Psychology*, the author comes to the conclusion that a crucial element in the radicalization of Indonesian terrorists is "the expression of a grievance based on perceived injustice, or unfairness . . ." (Kruglanski, 2013, p. 112). Whether the result of actual or perceived injustices and victimization, it is clear that many Islamist terrorists radicalized because they were angry at a group that they believed had caused and/or was planning on causing harm to them, their significant others, or to a group that they identified highly with. While this anger is often directed at Western governments or other religions, it can also be directed at certain segments of their own government or religion, which they perceive as corrupt, complicit with those doing the victimizing, or ineffectual at preventing their victimization.

Additional Roles for Anger in Radicalization and Terrorism

There are at least two additional areas where anger contributes to the process of radicalization and peoples' willingness to engage in terrorism that warrant mention. The first area is when anti- and counter-terrorism policies do not have their intended effect. This is essentially an offshoot of the larger notion of an outside group or country engaged in victimizing. While some nations engage in behavior that clearly may lead to perceptions of victimhood and anger in a target population (e.g., waging war on a nation, passing laws that discriminate or facilitate discrimination against a particular group), some actions with the specific intention of reducing radicalization or terrorism end up doing the exact opposite. Examples of this might include Western nations overtly partnering with a foreign nation's military or police force for anti- or counter-terrorism efforts, reinforcing the notion that an outside group is trying to exert control over their beliefs and behavior. A similar situation might arise if a Western nation provides instructors for classes focused on de-radicalization versus using instructors whom the radicalized individuals are more likely to respect (e.g., a religious figure from their own nation).

The second area where anger contributes to the process of radicalization and peoples' willingness to engage in terrorism is when there is competition within or between terrorist groups. Intra-group competition can be seen in some of the past activities of the East African terrorist group, al-Shabaab. Many experts believe that al-Shabaab's attack on the Westgate shopping mall in Nairobi, Kenya, was largely motivated by one faction's attempt to demonstrate superiority over another. Inter-group competition takes place as well. In 2008, Lashkar-e-Taiba launched a series of attacks throughout Mumbai, India, at least in part because they believed al-Qaeda was stealing their members and the attacks were a way to show prospective members that they were an effective group. More recently, al-Qaeda and ISIS have engaged in behaviors (e.g., new fundraising, recruitment drives) that are a direct result of wanting to be the top terrorist group in the world. These competitive behaviors are a direct result of membership anger. At both the individual and group level, there is anger directed at another individual or group because of an actual or perceived (potential) loss of status and power.

Different Actors in the Process of Radicalization

Up to now, I have described the process of radicalization and the role of anger in this process. It has been established that radicalization can be objectively bad if it leads to violence or support for violence against innocent people, and that anger is likely always involved in one way or another in the process of radicalization to violence. What has only been indirectly addressed is the role that various actors (individual and groups) play along the path to radicalization and terrorism. What follows is a description of the different categories of actor (individual actor, terrorist groups, governments) found along this path.

Individual Actors

Individuals sometimes support or commit acts of violence without being a member of an organization that endorses violence as a means of achieving their goals. These individuals are sometimes referred to as lone actors, lone wolves, or self-radicalized individuals. Even though, for a variety of reasons, it might be important to have the individuals who have no formal connection to a specific terrorist group in a category of their own, it is a mistake to believe that they radicalized outside the influence of other radical individuals or groups. Those who have already radicalized are the ones providing the ideology that the lone actor is to adopt and they are the ones engaging in the social influence that ultimately radicalizes the lone actor. They are the ones making the videos that the lone actor watches, running the social media that the lone actor engages with, and writing the pamphlets that the lone actor reads. They are often the ones telling the lone actor what they ought to be angry about and how they can remedy the situation. Because the activities of groups are generally easier to monitor, lone actors have become a point of concern for the U.S. government over the past few years. This concern is not entirely without merit as some of the most recent acts of terrorism within the United States have involved lone actors (or small unaffiliated cells). More recent examples include the attack on the U.S. Holocaust Memorial Museum by James Wenneker von Brunn, the attack by Maj. Nidal Hasan at Fort Hood, Texas, and the Boston Marathon bombing by Dzhokhar and Tamerlan Tsarnaev.

Looking at the example of Nidal Hasan as emblematic of other acts of lone actor terrorism (Cain, 2010), Hasan killed 13 people and injured over 30 others in an attack on the Fort Hood military installation in 2009. Though Hasan had no formal links to any terrorist group, he previously had e-mail contact with Anwar al-Awlaki, an American Imam who went on to join al-Qaeda. In addition, there were a number of signs that the process of radicalization was progressively increasing over time. In 2004, when he earned his medical degree, there were no outward signs that Hasan might have radical beliefs. From 2004 on, Hasan publicly stated his belief that the wars in Iraq and Afghanistan were unjust, that he had been discriminated against because of his religion, and that some soldiers had committed illegal acts while deployed. (Hasan might have learned about these acts in his role as an Army psychiatrist.) These beliefs, on their own, certainly do not signify radicalization, but Hasan seemed to get more and more angry about these events over time to the point where he was behaving in anti-social ways to express his anger (e.g., suggesting a belief that terrorist groups were justified in using suicide bombers, yelling at fellow soldiers). At the same time he was more frequently visiting extremist websites and growing in (his own version of) the Muslim faith. It appears that Hasan met all of the criteria for radicalization to occur. His actual or perceived personal victimization and actual or perceived victimization of close others (e.g., fellow Muslims) made him angry and gave him the motivation to assign blame and seek a remedy for the injustices. His own version of the Muslim faith and interaction with like-minded others provided him the ideological and social support necessary to develop more radical beliefs and accept the use of violence as a means to achieve his goals.

Terrorist Groups

Terrorist groups are interesting in that they, as entities, are already radical and accepting of violence as a means to achieve their goals. In some ways, terrorist groups are similar to individuals. For example, they can become more or less angry and more or less radical. These fluctuations, however, depend upon the collective sentiment of the group's members. Typically, if one member experiences something that causes them to become more radicalized, it will not affect the level of radicalization of the entire group. For the group to become more radicalized, a significant number of its members need to become more radicalized. This can happen through social interaction (e.g., some members convince others, group leadership steers the group in that direction), because some cause is large enough to affect many people (e.g., new laws are passed in which those with anti-government opinions can be imprisoned), or both. Religion may or may not be involved. Just as someone can radicalize without the influence of any religion, terrorist groups exist with ideologies that are expressly non-religious. So, while many of the more well-known terrorist groups of today do have a religious ideology (e.g., ISIS, al-Qaeda, Boko Haram), many others do not (e.g., PKK, ETA).

If religion is not a necessary precondition for radicalization, why do we so often hear that acts of terrorism are committed by Muslims? It is true that most acts of terrorism across the world today are committed by those with an Islamist ideology. This has not always been the case, however. Many scholars believe that there have been periods of time typified by one form of terrorism over others and that this form changes. According to this theory, modern terrorism began in the 1880s during which anarchists were the primary perpetrators. This was followed by the anti-colonialists beginning in the 1920s, the leftists in the 1960s, and the religious around 1980. In other words, religion, including Islam, is not a necessary condition for terrorism. What has likely been occurring over the past couple of decades is a significant increase in certain ideological beliefs (e.g., offensive jihad) and social conditions (e.g., broader acceptance of violence as a means to achieve ones goals) among some practitioners of Islam (e.g., some followers of Salafism and Wahhabism).

Terrorist groups play a very important role in the radicalization of individuals. For example, some people radicalize *after* joining a terrorist group. They may initially join for money, or adventure, or to have the social benefits of group membership, only to develop similar ideological beliefs over time. In addition, terrorist groups provide a goal and means for goal attainment to those who might be angry due to perceived victimhood. Finally, terrorist groups facilitate the radicalization of individuals through their direct and indirect communication with these individuals. These communications may take the form of propaganda videos, decrees of radicalized religious figures, or comments on social media.

Governments

The policy decisions that governments make can result in either a reduction or an increase in the number of radicalized individuals and terrorist groups. Governments that are weak or corrupt are unintentionally facilitating radicalization and terrorism. These governments are either directly causing an increase in anger felt by their citizens or they are demonstrating an inability to help citizens who have been victimized. In addition, these governments are attractive to terrorist groups because it is easier for them to operate in weak or corrupt states than states that have more of a will and ability to crack down on their activities. Sometimes, governments that are attempting to reduce radicalization and terrorism end up creating more of both through ill-conceived policies that do not appropriately address the primary causes of radicalization and terrorism. Finally, some governments succeed in their efforts to reduce radicalization and terrorism. Whereas these efforts are often the result of militaries, intelligence agencies, and police forces, new efforts are being developed, based upon the recommendations of researchers who study these issues, that reduce the likelihood of unintentional increases in radicalization and terrorism. Some of these efforts are described in what follows.

Reducing and Eliminating Radicalization

Steps have been taken, usually by governments, to both reduce the number of people who will eventually radicalize and to shape the beliefs and/or behavior of those who have already radicalized. Most of these programs were created in the wake of the terrorist attacks on September 11, 2001. Whether of their own accord or because they were pressured to by nations leading the "Global War on Terrorism," numerous nation-run de-radicalization and disengagement programs and a handful of counter-radicalization programs have been established.

De-Radicalization, Disengagement, and Counter-Radicalization

It is generally thought that de-radicalization and disengagement are two distinct constructs, where de-radicalization is focused on changing both radical behaviors and radical beliefs, and disengagement is focused just on the radical behavior component (e.g., reducing violent behavior without necessarily changing other related beliefs; Horgan, 2009). Counter-radicalization refers to the prevention of radicalization among individuals who have not yet radicalized. Most of these programs are implemented in regions typically associated with Islamic extremism (e.g., Middle East/North Africa, South Asia, Southeast Asia). Although more and more of all of these types of programs are being created every year, relatively few currently exist, and those that do exist may or may not be working as intended. Most of these programs are designed based upon the best guesses of the designers as to what should work. While some of the programs are at least based upon research that provides evidence in support of some policies over others, very few studies have ever been conducted to examine the effectiveness of existing de-radicalization, disengagement, and counter-radicalization programs. One of just a few exceptions to this is Horgan and Braddock (2010).

Most of the programs that exist are focused on disengagement. This is true because the ultimate goal of all of these programs is the cessation of violence, and disengagement is the easiest way to achieve this goal. To get someone to disengage from violence, a government need not necessarily change a majority of the radicalized individual's beliefs. The government just needs to convince the radicalized individual that violence will not help them achieve their goal, or that violence is counter-productive, or that other strategies for goal attainment are more likely to succeed. Although seemingly providing the greatest benefit from among the different programs in terms of return on costs, because the program essentially relies upon changing just one of the radicalized individual's beliefs, it is potentially the most unstable of all of the types of programs. In other words, it might be just as easy to convince a person once again that violence is the best way to achieve their goal as it was to convince them to abandon violence.

De-radicalization programs attempt to not just end radical behavior but also reverse radical beliefs. Changing an entire belief system is difficult to do, so to the extent these programs are successful at all, they are usually only partially so. This means that most de-radicalization programs are de facto disengagement programs. Along with scope, these programs also tend to be the most comprehensive in scale. As an example, the most famous of de-radicalization programs is that of Saudi Arabia (Wagner, 2010). A radicalized participant in this program can expect either to be imprisoned or at least isolated from anyone who might encourage the maintenance of radical beliefs and behaviors. Those who are not imprisoned will be monitored by the government and will have to regularly check in with what is essentially a parole officer. All participants will be a part of a re-education process, focused on shifting their belief system to one more amenable to the Saudi government. Religious leaders are often brought in to help change their religious beliefs. Participants who remain de-radicalized are often given material rewards such as money, housing, and employment (and occasionally even a wife).

Counter-radicalization efforts are currently uncommon but they are becoming more and more common. While preventing radicalization from occurring in the first place is the surest way to eliminate radical beliefs and behavior, it is not very easily carried out. Some tangible success might come from strategies that re-focus the goals and means to goal achievement of angry individuals who perceive some form of victimhood or injustice; however, many counter-radicalization efforts should be focused on eliminating the causes of radicalization. Here is the primary problem with counter-radicalization efforts. It is often not possible to eliminate the factors that lead to perception of victimhood and injustice. While manifestations of an issue may be experienced at an individual level (e.g., being taunted for being Muslim), the source of the problem exists at more of a societal level (e.g., marginalization of Muslims globally).

Research

Along with de-radicalization, disengagement, and counter-radicalization programs, research is being conducted on how best to reduce instances of radicalization and terrorism. Though certainly biased by my choice of profession, I am confident that these findings will ultimately lead to policies that both reduce the likelihood of radicalization and terrorism as well as address the causes that led to those beliefs and behaviors in the first place. Already, the findings of some empirical studies are considered as new policies and new laws are drafted. In addition, the social science being applied to the problems of radicalization and terrorism is finally mature enough to produce useful results at a more frequent rate year after year.

Conclusions

Radicalization is a problem in that it can lead people to engage in anti-social, including violent, behavior toward others. Occasionally, this behavior takes the form of terrorism. Although many factors have been identified that cause or contribute to radicalization, they all tend to fall under the higher order motive of a quest for significance. When someone has the goal of gaining significance or avoiding significance loss, they will engage in behaviors directed at fulfilling those goals. When goal attainment is threatened (e.g., they are prevented from gaining significance or avoiding significance loss), people become angry and look for new ways to achieve their goals. Sometimes, these new ways include supporting or carrying out violence against the individual or group that one deems responsible for preventing the fulfillment of their goals. Along with the motivation to gain and avoid losing significance, radicalization to violence is usually accompanied by an ideology that supports the use of violence to achieve its goals and social influences that facilitate each of the steps on the way to radicalization to violence.

In order for a reduction in radicalization and terrorism to take place, a number of things need to happen. We must identify the different ways in which the goals related to quest for significance might be threatened (i.e., the causes of radicalization) as well as the most effective strategies for their reduction or elimination. We must more carefully consider the laws and policies that are written to address radicalization and terrorism. For example, will a particular military intervention in a given specific circumstance actually lead to a net reduction in radicalization and terrorism? While we might not be able to answer question like this in a definitive way, a full consideration of all of the possible consequences of our actions should be taken with deference paid to research evidence in order to maximize the likelihood of success. We should increase the collection of data related to radicalization and terrorism as well as measurements of the effectiveness of laws and policies focused on reducing radicalization and terrorism. These efforts can be facilitated by the governments that are designing the laws and policies if they insist upon, and provide resources for, data collection and program analysis. Finally, researchers should continue to seek answers for all unanswered questions, employ novel techniques to help answer these questions, and advocate for or against policies based upon whether they are likely to succeed or fail given the evidence that exists.

References

Cain, A. C. (2010). *Protecting the force: Lessons from Fort Hood.* Department of Defense. Washington D.C. Retrieved from http://www.defense.gov/Portals /1/Documents/pubs/DOD-ProtectingTheForce-Web_Security_HR_13Jan10 .pdf

Doosje, B., Loseman, A., & Bos, K. (2013). Determinants of radicalization of Islamic youth in the Netherlands: Personal uncertainty, perceived injustice, and perceived group threat. *Journal of Social Issues, 69*(3), 586–604.

Gambetta, D., & Hertog, S. (2009). Why are there so many engineers among Islamic radicals? *European Journal of Sociology, 50*(2), 201–230.

Gurr, T. R. (1970). *Why men rebel.* Princeton, NJ: Princeton University Press, 1970.

Horgan, J. (2009). Deradicalization or disengagement? A process in need of clarity and a counterterrorism initiative in need of evaluation. *Revista de Psicología Social, 24*(2), 291–298.

Horgan, J., & Braddock. K. (2010). Rehabilitating the terrorists? Challenges in assessing the effectiveness of de-radicalization programs. *Terrorism and Political Violence, 22*(2), 267–291.

Kruglanski, A. W. (2013). Psychological insights into Indonesian Islamic terrorism: The what, the how and the why of violent extremism. *Asian Journal of Social Psychology, 16*(2), 112–116.

Kruglanski, A. W., Chen, X., Dechesne, M., Fishman, S., & Orehek, E. (2009). Fully committed: Suicide bombers' motivation and the quest for personal significance. *Political Psychology, 30*(3), 331–357.

Leuprecht, C., Hataley, T., Moskalenko, S. & McCauley, C. (2010). Containing the narrative: Strategy and tactics in countering the storyline of global jihad. *Journal of Policing, Intelligence and Counter Terrorism, (5)*1, 42–57.

National Consortium for the Study of Terrorism and Responses to Terrorism (START). (2013). *Global Terrorism Database.* Retrieved from http://www.start.umd.edu/gtd

Stern, J. (2004). *Terror in the name of God: Why religious militants kill.* New York, NY: Ecco.

Wagner, R. (2010, August 1). Rehabilitation and deradicalization: Saudi Arabia's counterterrorism successes and failures. *Peace and Conflict Monitor.* Retrieved from http://www.monitor.upeace.org/innerpg.cfm?id_article=735

Conclusion

Steven A. Leibo and Susan C. Cloninger

Neither anger nor angry groups are likely to disappear any time soon. Indeed, just as this volume was in its final stages of preparation, populations of angry groups not only began to assert themselves with significant levels of energy, but also with profound and perhaps long-term geo-political and social implications.

In the United States, an extraordinary level of anxiety and anger against what was often simply referred to as the "establishment" emerged, an anger that focused with some variation on an anger with government or, in some cases, to what was sometimes called the "main stream media," helped fuel the presidential campaigns of Donald Trump and Bernie Sanders, both of whom attracted an enormous number of angry followers in their respective campaigns. True, Donald Trump tended to focus on immigrants potential and real, from Hispanics to Muslims, while the Sanders campaign fixated on the "crimes" of Wall Street or simply Hillary Clinton, who was portrayed as the embodiment of the Democratic Establishment. Nevertheless, despite the differences, significant levels of anger drove both campaigns. Among conservatives, of course, the establishment, represented most probably by the campaign of Jeb Bush, son and brother to two previous presidents, went down in flames.

Meanwhile, across the Atlantic, angry groups of British voters were aroused by issues from the economic dislocations of a globalized world to feelings of having been made uncomfortable due to the recent transformative diversification of British society, and the more immediate fear of more refugee-driven immigration caused by warfare and economic dislocations in the Middle East and Africa. As a consequence, they voted to withdraw from the European Union, an action with as yet unimaginable short- and long-term complications. That decision itself has aroused new sets of angry groups from both within the United Kingdom and among the member states of the European Union.

Anger and angry groups are a common and perhaps growing phenomenon, as the 21st century introduces ever-new economic- and identity-based stresses that are likely to expand even further the growth of angry groups in the contemporary world. This is why the study of such phenomena at both a psychological and geo-political level is especially important. We have the example of the truth and reconciliation program in South Africa as evidence that intervention to mitigate group and individual anger-based prejudice and apartheid can succeed. In those efforts, which were established after the collapse of the racists' apartheid regime, formal court proceedings were established to allow victims of the previous government to openly present their narratives of suffering while others, perpetrators of the violence, were allowed to similarly testify under promises of amnesty, all in an effort at smoothing the way for the new multi-racial South Africa many were hoping to build.

In this volume, we have examined anger from many perspectives. **Donald Saucier, Russell Webster, Conor O'Dea, and Stuart Miller** note that attitudes related to anger and violent behavior may, hopefully, be changed by social communication to help prevent undesirable consequences of anger. The analysis by **Stuart Miller, Amanda Martens, and Donald Saucier** focuses on cognitions; because different attributions for the causes of prejudice may lead to either aggressive or non-aggressive behavior, we may infer that changing cognitions, through any of a variety of social influence methods, can circumvent the potentially destructive consequences of anger. The laboratory studies reported by **Jarryd Willis** demonstrate that while groups risk becoming polarized to extreme positions, which often lead to conflict, this outcome is not inevitable. Military action, especially during war, often mobilizes anger to motivate military force; **Kate Dahlstedt** and **Ed Tick**'s chapters suggest that the experience of some other cultures, reflected in their myths and narratives of returning warriors, could be used to help mitigate unnecessary suffering of our own returning veterans. **David Salomon**'s description of anger in the Bible suggests that even narratives of divine anger can be challenged. **Rob Edelman**'s overview of anger themes in film and **Sybillyn Jennings**'s analysis of developmental themes in the *Harry Potter* series show the wisdom to be learned from the diversity of anger themes portrayed in the humanities.

From history, we learn that anger has often fueled war, protest, and revolution, for example, in the French and Russian revolutions described by **Frank Jacob**, extremist groups, including the Neo-Nazis described by **Ryan Shaffer** and various American radical rightist groups inspired in recent decades by *The Turner Diaries* described by **Carmen Celestini**, might be less dangerous if we could implement, in the much more complicated real political environment, what we have learned in laboratory studies about avoiding polarization. We can see the influence of rhetoric and political persuasion in anger around the fictional *Turner Diaries* (described by Carmen Celestini) and the real-world Affordable Health Care Act described by **Terry Weiner**. History is still unfolding, and it is yet to be seen whether the decades-long conflicts around Cuban-American relationships described by **Trevor Rubenzer** can be amicably resolved. Perhaps enhanced communication and contact, now that the U.S. travel ban has eased, may lead to better relationships than that encountered by then Vice President Richard Nixon in Latin America over a half century ago, described by **Jeffry Cox**. In international relationships, economic issues can readily lead to anger and its adverse consequences, whether in Greece as described by **David Elliott**, or in Nigeria, with its environmental complications, described by **Olakunle Folami** and **Taiwo Olaiya**, or in the multifaceted conflict in Iran described by **Mohammad Amjad**. Even within the context of a tradition known for its peaceful values, Tibetan Buddhism is not immune to violence, as described by **Jeannine Chandler**, so we are reminded that multiple levels of understanding must be considered together if we are to resolve the problematic anger-aggression link that is so frequently exploited in the radicalization of terrorists described by **Cory Davenport** and that is all too frequently exemplified in history and in the current world.

Doubtless, anger and its sequelae will not end any time soon, though we may hope to learn how to avoid their worst outcomes. We can hope that history not only does not repeat—Mark Twain is reputed to have quipped that instead, it rhymes—but that it does so more as an ode than as a dirge.

About the Editors and Contributors

The Editors

Susan C. Cloninger, Ph.D., is a Professor Emerita from The Sage Colleges, Troy and Albany, New York, where she taught psychology for 36 years. She has authored *Theories of Personality: Understanding Persons,* now approaching its seventh edition, and a chapter in the *Cambridge Handbook of Personality Psychology.* In retirement, she is active as a volunteer in a supportive housing unit for persons with a history of homelessness and mental illness; in her Unitarian Universalist church; and as an amateur gardener and proud grandmother. Her professional curiosity is a quest for understanding that bridges issues from biological to social-political understanding.

Steven A. Leibo, Ph.D., of The Sage Colleges in New York, specializes in Modern International History and Politics. He teaches courses on a range of topics from modern China, the Middle East, modern world history to classes on big history, the history of medicine, and a course on climate change. A former Fulbright scholar and currently Associate in Research at Harvard, Professor Leibo specializes in the relationship between Asia and the West. He has authored numerous books from *East and Southeast Asia 2015–2016* to *Tienkuo: The Heavenly Kingdom,* a historical novel. Leibo is probably best known for his work as a frequent international political analyst for regional television, radio, and newspapers.

(The co-editor, Mohammad Amjad, is also a chapter author. His biographical description is located under *The Contributors.*)

The Contributors

Mohammad Amjad received his Ph.D. from the University of California, Riverside, and has done post-doctoral research at U.C. Berkeley and UCLA. He has taught extensively in the United States and in Iran. In Iran, he taught at Imam Sadegh University, Tarbyat Mdarres University, and Azad University of Iran. Broadly trained in political science, his areas of expertise include Iran, Middle East, international security, human rights, Islamic revivalism, radical Islam, and U.S.–Muslim world relations. He is currently an independent scholar and is working on a book about ISIS. Amjad has served on the editorial board of several academic journals including the *Journal of Law and Politics*, *Cultural Studies Journal*, and *Journal of Politics (Iran)* as well as *Digest of Middle East Studies (US)*.

Carmen Celestini is currently a Ph.D. candidate in religious studies at the University of Waterloo. Focusing on politics and religion, with a concentration on millennialism and on the role of religion in the public sphere, her research interests provide scholarship to contextualize the contemporary tension between religion and politics.

Jeannine Chandler, Ph.D., is Clinical Assistant Professor of Global Liberal Studies at New York University, where she teaches East Asian and modern world history. Her research focuses on the intersections of violence and sectarianism in global Tibetan Buddhism, as well as contemporary Western imaginings of Asian cultures and religions.

Jeffry M. Cox is a Ph.D. candidate in the history department at the University of Oklahoma. His research focuses on the role of the Latin American press in early Cold War political transitions. Other areas of interest include U.S.–Latin American relations and modern world history.

Kate Dahlstedt, M.A, is a psychotherapist who has worked with veterans and their families for over 30 years. She is the co-founder of Soldier's Heart, a veteran's community-based healing program. She currently directs the Soldier's Heart Military Families Project and the Athena's Shield for Women Veterans Project.

Cory Davenport is a Senior Researcher at the National Consortium for the Study of Terrorism and Responses to Terrorism (START), a Department of Homeland Security (DHS) Center of Excellence at the University of Maryland. Dr. Davenport has a Ph.D. in experimental psychology from Texas Tech University.

Rob Edelman's credits include film commentator, WAMC Northeast Public Radio; contributing editor, Leonard Maltin's *Movie Guide*; author, *Great Baseball Films, Baseball on the Web*; co-author, *Meet the Mertzes, Matthau: A Life*; lecturer, various universities; frequent contributor, *Base Ball: A Journal of the Early Game*; author, articles in many newspapers, magazines, and journals.

David L. Elliott has a Ph.D. in sociology from the University of Oregon. He published two books and his faculty/administrator career has taken him to Sage, SUNY-ESC, Regis, and Excelsior. Now retired, his current writing includes a book-length manuscript on the sociology of debt: "IOU: The Coming Bankruptcy of Human Civilization."

Olakunle M. Folami holds a Ph.D. in Transitional Justice from the Ulster University, Northern Ireland, United Kingdom. He teaches sociology, criminology and research methods at the Adekunle Ajasin University, Akungba Akoko, Nigeria. He is currently a research fellow at the International Nuremberg Principles Academy.

Frank Jacob received an M.A. from Würzburg University in 2010 and a Ph.D. from Erlangen University in 2012. He is Assistant Professor of World History at the City University of New York (QCC). In addition to several monographs and edited volumes, he is the editor of the interdisciplinary journal *Global Humanities*.

Sybillyn Jennings, Ph.D. and Professor Emerita, chaired the Psychology Department at Russell Sage College, Troy, NY. She coordinated a number of curricular programs including a seminar entitled Developmental Trajectories in Harry Potter. Her continuing projects at the Center for Pre-College Education, Rensselaer Polytechnic Institute in Troy, New York, explore adolescents' developing identities applied to STEM education.

Amanda L. Martens, M.S., is a doctoral student in the Department of Psychological Sciences at Kansas State University. Her research interests focus on the consequences of gender role expectations, specifically in manifestations of masculine and feminine honor.

Stuart S. Miller, M.S., is a doctoral student in the Department of Psychological Sciences at Kansas State University. His research interests focus on how individual differences in beliefs that prejudice is prevalent and problematic in society interact with features of social situations in predicting third party observers' attributions to prejudice.

Conor J. O'Dea, B.S., 2013, is a doctoral student in the Department of Psychological Sciences at Kansas State University. His research interests include how expressions of prejudice are justified by perceivers against targets, and in particular how these expressions manifest in the use and perceptions of racial slurs and humor.

Taiwo A. Olaiya is a multidisciplinary scholar and holds a unique mix of academic and professional skills in law, public policy, and administration, and a considerable field perception in comparative politics and governance of Africa. He is a faculty member and researcher at Nigeria's leading academic institution, the Obafemi Awolowo University.

Trevor Rubenzer, Ph.D., is an Associate Professor of Political Science at the University of South Carolina Upstate. His research specialties include the impact of ethnic identity groups on U.S. foreign policy and African politics. Dr. Rubenzer's research appears in the *American Journal of Political Science, International Studies Quarterly,* and *Foreign Policy Analysis.*

David A. Salomon, Ph.D., is Professor of English at Russell Sage College of The Sage Colleges in Troy, New York, where he also serves as Director of The Kathleen A. Donnelly Center for Undergraduate Research and General Education Program. Among his recent publications are *An Introduction to the Glossa Ordinaria as Medieval Hypertext* (University of Wales Press, 2012) and *Redefining the Paradigm: Faculty Models to Support Student Learning* (New American College and Universities, 2015). He holds the Ph.D. from the University of Connecticut and lives in Troy, New York, with his wife and 13-year-old daughter. He is currently at work on a history of sin in Western culture.

Donald A. Saucier, Ph.D., is an Associate Professor in the Department of Psychological Sciences at Kansas State University. His research focuses broadly on how individual differences (e.g., prejudice, social vigilantism, and masculine honor beliefs) interact with situational factors to produce expressions of prosocial and antisocial behavior (e.g., helping, aggression, discrimination).

Ryan Shaffer, Ph.D., is a post-doctoral fellow at the Institute for Global Studies at the State University of New York, Stony Brook. He has written many articles, book chapters, and review articles, including "The Soundtrack of Neo-Fascism: Youth and Music in the National Front" (2013) and "British, European and White: Cultural Constructions of Identity in Post-War British Fascist Music" (2015).

Edward Tick, Ph.D., is an internationally recognized transformational healer, psychotherapist, writer, educator, and poet, who co-founded and co-directs Soldier's Heart with Kate Dahlstedt. Ed is honored for his ground-breaking work in the psycho-spiritual, holistic, and community-based healing of war's invisible wounds. He is the author of five books, including the pioneering works *War and the Soul* and *Warriors' Return*.

Russell J. Webster, Ph.D., is an Assistant Professor in the Department of Psychological and Social Sciences at Pennsylvania State University–Abington College. His research examines how the person and situation contribute to intergroup prejudice, and in particular how beliefs in pure good and evil relate to aggression and pro-sociality.

Terry Weiner, Ph.D., is the Chauncey H. Winters Professor of Comparative and Social Analysis, Emeritus at Union College, Schenectady, NY. At Union, he served as the Chair of the Department of Political Science and as Associate Dean of Faculty. He also served as Provost of The Sage Colleges for five years.

Jarryd Willis, Ph.D., is Social and Political Psychologist at the University of California–San Diego. His lab at UCSD is focused on intergroup relations, close relationships, and bullying/victimization. He loves teaching more than anything and hopes to inspire the next generation of scientists.

Index